WAR BY OTHER MEANS

WAR BY OTHER MEANS

Aftermath in Post-Genocide Guatemala

EDITED BY

**Carlota McAllister and
Diane M. Nelson**

Duke University Press   Durham and London   2013

Designed by Heather Hensley

Typeset in Arno Pro by Tseng Information Systems, Inc.

Library of Congress Cataloging-in-Publication Data
War by other means : aftermath in post-genocide Guatemala /
edited by Carlota McAllister and Diane M. Nelson.
pages   cm
Includes index.
ISBN 978-0-8223-5493-2 (cloth : alk. paper)
ISBN 978-0-8223-5509-0 (pbk. : alk. paper)
1. Guatemala — History — 1985–   2. Violence — Guatemala.
I. McAllister, Carlota, 1969–   II. Nelson, Diane M., 1963–
F1466.7.W37 2013
972.8105′3 — dc23   2013012812

*To all those who, when the powerful insisted
"Death to intelligence," refused to the last.*

For all those who carry on.

CONTENTS

ACKNOWLEDGMENTS

We would like to thank our contributors for having faith, and all the Guatemalans and Guatemalanists who have supported us over the years, especially AVANCSO and Clara Arenas. Wenner-Gren generously supported the preliminary workshop that led to this volume. We also thank Carol Smith, Valerie Milholland (for also having faith), Miriam Angress, Netta van Vliet, Yasmine Cho, Brian Smithson, Elena Turevon, Michelle Switzer, Anabella Acevedo, and Valia Garzón for all their help. George Lovell, Ellen Moodie, and two other truly heroic anonymous reviewers have greatly improved this volume with their support and challenge, for which we are deeply grateful. And, of course, we thank our companions, families, and each other.

We go to press just as former General Efrain Rios Montt, head of the Guatemalan state and commander-in-chief of the Guatemalan Army from March 23, 1982, to August 8, 1983, has been declared guilty of the crime of genocide, in a historic verdict for Guatemala and the world. The contributors to this book would like to honor the enormous courage and decades-long efforts of the survivors of genocide, together with activists, lawyers, judges, forensic scientists, Guatemala's attorney general, and myriad other allies to make justice happen against enormous odds. The struggle to put the post- in post-genocide has a long way to go, but a critical milestone has been reached.

Revolution cannot take its poetry from
the past but only from the future.

—KARL MARX

MAP 1 Map of Guatemala.

AFTERMATH
Harvests of Violence and Histories of the Future

Where Were You?
1992

"Where were you in 1992?" On December 12, 2006, a group of Maya and ladino Guatemalans, with a sprinkling of outsiders, met to ponder this question. They were invited by the Mayan publishing house Cholsamaj and met in the offices of CODISRA, a new state agency dedicated to eradicating racism. The first person to answer was *en la montaña*, serving as a doctor in one of the guerrilla groups of the Guatemalan National Revolutionary Unity (URNG). A woman who identified herself as ladina remembered discussing Rigoberta Menchú Tum's Nobel Peace Prize in school and, for the first time, questioning her assumption that indigenous women should be servants, not international celebrities. A woman in handmade *corte* and *güipil*, the distinctive Mayan skirt and blouse, said she was a little girl in a Mexican refugee camp and remembered the effervescence and also the deep-seated terror as people began organizing to return home. A ladino man remembered the elation of being involved in early peace treaty negotiations: maybe the decades of war would finally end! Francisco Cali, formerly with the Campesino Unity Committee (CUC), now wearing the ponytail and colorful coat showing he identified as Mayan, was in Menchú's entourage when she received The Call from the Nobel Committee and remembered the delirious joy, the shock, and the dawning realization that something fundamental had changed. Rigoberta Menchú Tum was the first indigenous person to receive the Nobel Prize, and it was not lost on her detractors that in her famous *testimonio* (1983) she ac-

FIG INTRO 1 "Rigoberta Menchú Tum leads a march to celebrate her 1992 Nobel Peace Prize in Sololá." PHOTO BY DANIEL HERNÁNDEZ-SALAZAR, © 1992, WWW.DANIELHERNANDEZSALAZAR.BLOGSPOT.COM. USED WITH KIND PERMISSION.

knowledged participation in the guerrilla war. Cali concluded by saying, "I want to make something very clear. We were not *engañados* [fooled]. Then and now people will tell you we were. But when we rose up we were not mistaken. We were not wrong."

For many Guatemalans, 1992, the Columbus Quincentennial, was a generative moment for contemplating the aftermath of five hundred years of invasion and occupation, the sedimentation of structures of economic and political power, and the aspirations of people enmeshed in complex identity formations. Indigenous people, increasingly identifying with the new category "Maya," seemed impressively well organized, self-assured, and reveling in their millenarian identity. Their confidence troubled the long-standing assumptions that those with the lightest skin, greatest wealth, and most international connections were the natural rulers of Guatemala (despite the massive violence deployed to sustain that rule). As a prominent ladino journalist said at the time, "We are just like Columbus. We don't know where we're going. We don't know where we are when we get there. And we're doing it all on borrowed money." The Quincentennial also provoked a reevaluation of the ambivalent and slippery label *ladino*. Defined pejoratively in Spanish dictionaries as "crafty" or "cunning" and, in the context of Guatemalan nation-building discourses, as those who are neither Indians nor members of the elite, it is often used indiscriminately by foreigners to refer to all nonindigenous Guatemalans. In the early 1990s some self-identified ladinos affirmed the label to detach themselves from an elite that had always disdained them for their humble circumstances and darker skin. They insisted that, unlike the *canches* (whiteys), they were "100 percent *chapín*" (Guatemalans). Many began to explore forms of cultural expression that were derived neither from European high culture nor folklore but rather embedded in urban middle-class Guatemalan life. Others delved into the darker history of the category, rejecting the limited racial privilege it historically has offered and reclaiming their indigenous heritage by identifying as *mestizos*, people of mixed heritage.

1982

This generative rethinking was an unexpected turn of events, as the state was still wrapping up its extraordinarily brutal, and disturbingly effective, counterinsurgency efforts to extinguish all glimmers of resistance to Guatemala's race, class, and gender tyrannies. If the question had been "Where were you in 1982?," the answers would have been much bleaker. Some were fighting a guerrilla war in which they were logistically wildly overmatched; many more were suffering the onslaughts of the army's scorched earth counterinsurgency campaign or were already in exile, wondering whether they could ever return to Guatemala—and what they would return to. In the capital, radical university students and union activists were living in clandestinity, losing contact with the institutions and *compañeros* that had once sustained their work. In the rural area a million men and boys (out of a total population of about eight million) were *forcivoluntariamente* serving in the civil patrols (PAC),[1] a paramilitary force organized by the army in which local men carried out surveillance, capture, and massacres against their neighbors and sometimes even family members. Many women in the highlands were captives, cooking, cleaning, and enduring gang rape by soldiers and patrollers, who were also sometimes family members.

Learning where people were in 1982 (and why) is made more difficult by the fact that so many of them number among the lost. Our understanding of the aftermath of the war in Guatemala is ineluctably shaped by the enormous absence of all those who were killed, displaced, or irreparably damaged. But it is also shaped by their continuing *presence*, in part through ongoing struggles over what their loss means. For some, the dead were dangerous subversives, killed in the defense of society. For others, they were their own children, forcibly recruited into the army. For many, they were simply victims. Or they were fools caught up in forces they didn't understand. And for still others, like Cali, they were *not* engañados, they were not mistaken. They were murdered, and the perpetrators of this crime remain at large. Facing the future produced by this past begins with understanding the dialectical relation that violence has with the discourses that attempt to account for its reasons and with forms of memorialization (and temporal lag) that themselves do violence. This is war by other means.

For example, it was not until March 2008 that widows from Choatalúm, San Martín Jilotepeque were able to testify about the disappearances of their husbands and children in a case against the local civil patrol leader, first filed in 1983. The courtroom was both bureaucratically rational and intimately emotional. The women described the murders of family members in 1981 and 1982 and being forced to flee their homes and live in the mountains, where many children died of exposure and starvation. Upon return to the army-controlled village, they lived side by side with the men responsible for their suffering. One woman broke down: "Why did they kill him? Why? All he wanted was fair pay for his work. All he wanted was to feed his children." Her question—How could seeking access to the basic means of life generate such mortal destruction?—remains at the heart of efforts to understand war's aftermath. As is the fact that earning a fair wage and feeding one's children may be even more difficult now.

When Guatemalans "rose up" in different parts of the country at different times, it was to demand access to the basic necessities of life, but also to transform the relationship between people—particularly indigenous and poor people—and the state as both agent of coercion and guarantor of (as yet) unfulfilled promises of citizenship and development. These uprisings articulated new nodes in the global networks emerging out of cold war and postcolonial geopolitical shifts. Driven by what Tania Li (2007) calls "the will to improve," these struggles intensified linkages between small rural villages across the so-called Third World and with planetary power spots. Developmentalism and its armies of aid workers and experts, along with liberation theology, Evangelical Christianity, consumerism, and new media, collaborated in directing the hearts, minds, souls, and calculative agencies of the world's most marginalized peoples toward the betterment of their own condition, seeking to instill the art of governing by "arranging things so that people, following only their own self-interest, *will do as they ought*" (Foucault 1991, in Li 2007: 5). Meanwhile the circulation of new strategies for guerrilla warfare, promoted by left-wing intellectuals, activists, national liberation fighters, and artists through parallel socialist networks, also helped link many of the world's poor to alternative visions of improvement. The specter of a world governed by these alternatives stoked the fears of elites and militaries.

In Guatemala, as in other "developing" nations, security forces were important actors in these dynamics. Beholden to superpower directives and aid but enmeshed in national and local struggles that demanded autonomous action and strategizing, they helped reformulate counterinsurgency as a mix of repressive state apparatuses and "civil affairs," producing novel configurations of what military theorists call "low-intensity conflict" and Foucault (1980) calls biopolitics: the simultaneous "right of life and power over death." The military regimes ruling Guatemala almost continuously since 1954 responded to grassroots challenges by directing counterinsurgent violence not only against the bodies of those they perceived as enemies but at the integrity of subaltern forms of life and at the hearts and minds of the population as a whole. A central component of this psychological warfare (psyops) was the argument that people were fooled by hope: that improving oneself or one's community outside of the market is a dangerous illusion, that the possibility of another world is only communist propaganda. This argument was repeated over and over in newspapers, billboards, pamphlets, reeducation lectures in concentration camps, and training sessions for soldiers and civil patrollers. Repeated until the idea became so deeply embedded that when cadavers appeared on the streets or the families of the disappeared clamored for their loved ones, good-hearted people could turn away, saying, "They were involved in something, *los babosearon* [they were fooled]. It's their own fault."

1999

A central component of the war's aftermath has been to challenge this story. Where were you in 1999? On February 23 many of Guatemala's national and international human rights activists, along with politicians, military officers, and diplomats, were seated in the National Theater for the official presentation of *Memory of Silence*, the findings of the United Nations Commission for Historical Clarification (CEH), mandated by the peace accords.[2] The commission's purview, however, was gravely limited, particularly because it was not allowed to name those held responsible for human rights violations. Once the commission began its work, moreover, sharp divisions emerged over its use of legal and quantitative methods to represent the violence, when the dimensions of what had happened — and the question of who it happened to and why — demanded a more historical and culturally sensitive approach. Hopes for the final report were low.

To the surprise of even the CEH's harshest critics, that day in the theater felt like a triumph. Without naming names, the report firmly adjudicated responsibility for the war's crimes to state forces, which had committed 93 percent of the documented violations. The guerrillas were found responsible for 3 percent. Tallying the dead and disappeared at 200,000, the report also provided an unsparing account of Guatemalan history, arguing that the enduring structures undergirding Guatemalan society and its export-oriented plantation economy, particularly racism against the Mayan majority and deep economic inequality, had enabled the violence. To the visible rage of the political officer from the U.S. Embassy, it insisted that foreign interventions were an exacerbating factor in the war. But the presentation's most extraordinary moment came when the commissioner reading the report announced that the Guatemalan state had committed acts of genocide against certain Mayan communities. Naming these as crimes against humanity lifted them out of the reach of national immunity laws, raising hopes for their prosecution, perhaps even internationally, and giving Mayan claims of suffering and demands for restitution a powerful symbolic boost.

As the reading of the report's findings went on, the balcony where the representatives of Mayan and community organizations were gathered exploded in cheering and stomping, repeatedly drowning out the commissioner and forcing him to pause and call for silence. Afterward that euphoria was carried into the bars and public spaces where the Left gathers in downtown Guatemala City. Tables overflowed with people celebrating as they had not for years—laughing, catching up, and above all sharing their surprise and delight that the report had so publicly vindicated their understanding of Guatemala's war. Spirits were too high to focus on the day's dissonant moments, as when President Alvaro Arzú, a member of the landowning oligarchy, refused to receive the report, or when the only indigenous commissioner, Otilia Lux de Cotí, asked for pardon in the name of the Maya, explaining, "We became involved in an armed conflict that was imposed on us and that was not ours." Her remarks treated indigenous people once again as engañados, foreshadowing a postwar phenomenon that Oglesby and Ross describe as a "strong logic for indigenous communities to reposition themselves as victims . . . untethering the understanding of genocide from the concrete connections made in the report between territory, history, political practice, racism, and violence" (2009: 35).

Since 1999 the dissonance has increased and the euphoria has faded. The first signs that the triumph of the CEH would be short-lived came only two months later, when the Consulta Popular, a national referendum to ratify the

1996 peace accords, failed, leaving hard-won concessions from the state on issues like indigenous rights and reforms to the military in limbo. The following years have brought more bad news than good. Attempts to bring to justice the perpetrators of genocide and war crimes have been wearyingly slow and difficult, hampered by official obstructionism, fearmongering, and outright violence. As the tendrils of narcotraffic penetrate ever deeper into state structures and everyday life, the unresolved crimes of the past are compounded by the ever more frequent appearance of new cadavers, now reaching rates comparable to the worst years of the war. Violent evictions of peasants from the land to plant biofuel crops or build mines and dams are increasing, and an army general has returned to power, now through "democratic" elections.

Worse still, uncertainty about who is responsible for "peacetime" crimes heightens the sense of insecurity. Are violent deaths and events connected to each other or to the past, or are they senseless and random, perhaps the more unbearable possibility? Who are the criminals? Are they thieves, *maras* (gangs), police, the rich, narcotraffickers, angry neighbors, cuckolded spouses, or fed-up citizens taking the law into their own hands? People live with a constant, grinding anxiety that they may be victims of *delincuencia*, common crimes that can easily turn fatal. While there is no longer a state-mandated curfew, Guatemala City's streets empty out at dusk, leaving only sex workers, drug dealers, their clients, and taxi drivers scuttling frightened people home. New languages try to give shape to the violence. Perhaps *femicidio*—the war-enabled lethal expression of long-running patterns of hatred for and violence against women—is the key to identifying the demons still at large. Or maybe there are other hidden entities at work—cartels, or conspiracies, or corrupt officials, or simply evil itself. All these anxieties, in turn, can generate their own violence. In the absence of any trustworthy authority, *linchamientos* or mob violence sometimes seems like the best solution for meting out justice. And, as in the war years, good people again turn away from the bodies in the street, assuming they must have been involved in something, to mask their own vulnerability and terror.

Human rights activists also develop new analyses and tactics for untangling the rhizomatic tendrils that extend out from government offices, secret bases, and narcopalaces to find eager recruits among the vast armies of the un- and underemployed. One step is simply to identify them as illegal bodies and clandestine security apparatuses (CIACS). But maybe "involvement" in these networks runs even deeper. Maybe surviving in the neoliberal economy installed in the aftermath of the war requires entering into and wrestling with its shadows, making ends meet any way you can (Goldin 2011; Offit 2008;

FIG INTRO 2 Leslie Velásquez weeps for her cousin Eduardo, murdered in a robbery, 2008. PHOTO BY DORIAM MORALES. USED WITH KIND PERMISSION.

O'Neill and Thomas 2011). In Guatemala two-thirds of the employed work in the informal economy, living hand-to-mouth, hustling anything from blender parts, shoeshines, and stolen SUVs to under-the-table labor and semi- or illegal goods, services, and substances. Some levy "protection money," extort ransoms for kidnappings, and even sell babies or, it is rumored, their organs. The logic of taking from the rich(er) if you are desperately poor may justify the actions of thousands of unemployed decommissioned soldiers, guerrillas, and paramilitaries, armed with firepower and experience using it and networks and geographic reach acquired during the war years. In response, private security, which puts more firearms into men's hands, is one of Guatemala's few growth industries (Dickens de Girón 2011).

Meanwhile the poorest Guatemalans, already profoundly dispossessed by centuries of the plantation economy and the ravages of counterinsurgency, are now forced to defend what little is left of their agrarian livelihoods against renewed depredations of mining, oil, and hydroelectric companies, the introduction of ecologically devastating monocrops like African palm, and deepening indebtedness. These extractive technologies benefit some of the same old *finquero* families, now in league with new national financial elites and global capital brokers, even as poor people's capacities to struggle against dispossession are increasingly constrained. And the argument that people were fooled by hope is repeated over and over, gathering strength from the painful failure of so many valiant attempts to transform this unbearable situation.

How could the demons of 1982 remain so lively while the hopes of 1992 and 1999 seem so moribund? How could all the labor (and money) put into processing peace, creating a culture of dialogue rather than violence, empowering those most affected by the war—indigenous people, women, and the poor—have produced so little of value? Why does war persist in Guatemala's postwar? "Where does the future lie" (AVANCSO 1992)? And how can we get there?

Harvests and Aftermath

aftermath [OE *maeth*, cutting of grass < *mawan* to mow] 1. A result or consequence, esp. an unpleasant one 2. A second crop

harrow [ME *harwe*] 1. Break up and level plowed ground, root up weeds 2. Torment, vex 3. Rob, plunder, pillage 4. To enter hell and rescue the righteous

When farmers go to the field to begin the harvest they know that what they bring home will be intimately linked to the specific qualities of that piece of land, its soil, incline, sun and shade, irrigation, as well as to what they have put in to it: seeds, fertilizer, pesticides, and the energy and love of tending it. Since the land gives back what it receives, some Maya insist that the necessary rituals must be performed with a full heart and appropriate sacrifices to ensure a plentiful return (Cook 2000; ILEURL 2007; López García 2010; Wilson 1995). But even a farmer's most thoughtful preparation and planning cannot guarantee predictable results. The harvest will also depend on the *temporada*, the time itself. Was there a hurricane? Was it unseasonably hot? Was the *canícula* (break in the rains) later than usual? The land's history also shapes its qualities: Is it "burned" or chemically overfertilized? Has it been left fallow long enough? Was it tended correctly over the decades?

If aftermath is a second harvest, we might argue that, similarly, the effects of the violence of the civil war are both specific to the qualities and histories of specific places, as examined in the essays that follow, and generalized across wider landscapes and temporalities. The whole Central American region suffered the impact of the apocalyptic counterinsurgent violence some people in the highlands call *el ochenta* (the '80s), although only in Guatemala, with its indigenous majority, did it take the form of genocide. Recognizing the common Central American postwar aftermaths of widespread "criminal" violence, deepening immiseration and hunger, and forcible integration into neoliberal political and economic schemes should dispel any sense that

the storm that has shaped contemporary Guatemala was whipped up by exclusively Guatemalan pathologies (Moodie 2010; Binford 1996; Binford and
Lauria-Santiago 2004; Lancaster 1988, 1992).

Yet a storm will leave different marks as it passes across a varied landscape, some of which may be visible only years later. A recent crop of studies
of postwar Guatemala suggests that sufficient time has passed for the emerging features of its particular terrain to be perceived (e.g., Adams and Bastos
2003; Bastos and Cumes 2007; DeHart 2010; Garrard-Burnett 2010; Goldin
2009; Goldman 2007; Hale 2006; Hurtado Paz y Paz 2008a; Konefal 2010;
Little and Smith 2009; O'Neill 2010; O'Neill and Thomas 2011; Vela 2009,
Way 2012). This book is about that aftermath and about new means of wag-
ing a long-fought war. It is about the violence war both channels from earlier
times and generates anew, and the promise that an "after" to this war will
someday come. The "math" in *aftermath* is not the same as in *mathemat-
ics*, although counting the dead and accounting for these and other losses
has been extremely important in making that violence "count" as genocide
under international law. After's "math" instead comes from *mow*, as in cutting
grass, and can mean an unpleasant result or consequence. Etymologically it
is connected to *harrow*, meaning "to cut, lacerate, or torment," and it is certainly harrowing to contemplate Guatemala's civil war. But, more heartening,
"math" also refers to a second crop or harvest, like grass that grows after an
earlier mowing. This volume is just such an aftermath, building on accounts
published in the waning years of the genocide, like Robert Carmack's essential *Harvest of Violence: The Maya Indians and the Guatemalan Crisis* (1988)
and Carol Smith's pioneering volume *Guatemalan Indians and the State, 1540–
1988* (1990), which provided rich ethnographies, historical context, and analytical frameworks for understanding the repression of indigenous communities. They set a new standard for North Americans working in Guatemala,
demanding that they join their intellectual engagements to political ones.
Carmack, Smith, and their collaborators related their current moment to the
war and the war to its contexts, while attending to the ways that violence
and its effects resonate years after, a project that remains, we believe, terribly
timely.

This volume explores later periods, after a new constitution and the return to elections and civilian rule, after the signing of peace accords and
refugee returns, and after the work of truth commissions, UN peacekeepers,
and brave and persistent efforts to institutionalize indigenous, women's, and
sexual minority rights and to reform the justice, health, education, and production systems. We name these times *post-genocide* to insist that the bloody

events of the early 1980s have not yet been overcome, as in the notion of the postcolonial, where nominal independence can hide ongoing subordination. We also use this term to mark the shift in frameworks for acting on and against the war that the CEH's 1999 genocide ruling provided, and the effects on ethnic identifications and reelaborations of "peace" that it produced. *Post* here might also convey the sense of "a place for displaying notices" and "a strong timber set upright, a point of attachment."

In turn, these essays engage with a new generation of Guatemalans who have come of age in the aftermath of war and genocide, experiencing exile, refugee camps, Mayan revitalization, ladino self-questioning and pride, a diminished sense of the naturalness of overt machismo and racism, improved literacy, and Internet access — as well as missing relatives, the presence of gangs and drugs in their villages and neighborhoods, and increasing pressure to migrate to the United States. They also carry the weight of the past, in all its silenced genocidal horror, but also, sometimes, its reminder that even five hundred years (and counting) of repression have not been sufficient to extinguish all traces of hope. Like many of the subjects of our chapters, most authors collected here formed our intellectual and political projects in the wake of el ochenta, in a Guatemala immediately and indelibly marked by massive violence, and thus with the painful knowledge of how repression shapes action. Assembled from an array of professional backgrounds, including journalism, activism, NGO and UN work, and academics, with a range of formal training, including economics, geography, anthropology, and history, we share a commitment to merging scholarship and activism.

Unlike most collections on Guatemala published in North America, our numbers include a rich harvest of Guatemalan scholars, whose work represents a double confrontation with the aftermath of a repression that targeted not only Maya and the poor but also intellectuals who worked in solidarity with them. We are pleased to make their work available in English, often for the first time, and hope it will encourage our Euro-American colleagues to engage more systematically with the lively debates about Guatemala's past, present, and future taking place among and within different communities of Guatemalans. Readers will note the productive traces left by the authors' range of training and identifications on our writing styles and theoretical approaches. Our ongoing conversations across this range of backgrounds has pushed us to extend the long-standing North American anthropological tradition of providing accounts of life in Mayan communities to address broader scales of aftermath. These chapters refuse easy dichotomies between ladino and Maya, right and left, local and global, and instead explore the complex subjectivizations of and relationships among Guatemalans within the political economies of the post-genocidal state and transnational capital. Without losing touch with the post of genocide, the essays also carry narratives through longer and more complicated political histories. This is partly due to the length of time — in many cases, decades — we have spent thinking about and working on these issues, separately and together. We cannot afford the luxury of dismissing the social movements of the 1970s and 1980s as mere *engaño*, or duping, for to do so would mean denying many of our own most extraordinary and formative experiences.

Seeding the Terrain

While the thirty-six-year civil war lies at the center of our account of aftermath, we join the CEH in insisting that its violence was a long time in the making. Tracing this history brings us back to the 1520s, when the Spaniard Pedro de Alvarado perpetrated the first genocide in the Guatemalan highlands. The legal and social structures inaugurated by the cross and the sword delimited the place, obligations, and rights of the *pueblos de indios* with regard to other raced classes of people, including Spaniards, *criollos*, Africans, and their descendents — and eventually ladinos, a category of people who "mixed" all of the above over hundreds of years of colonial occupation. The seeds of the regime of racialized labor extraction that still shapes Guatemala's economy, however, were sown in the late nineteenth-century Liberal Reforms, which "liberated" the pueblos de indios from their colonial strictures and protections. The Reforma made indigenous land available for purchase (but almost never by indigenous people), opened indigenous communities to ladino residents — now as representatives of the still-forming independent Guatemalan state — and created a suddenly available and cheap (i.e., "ideal") workforce for plantations growing the new tropical commodities of coffee, bananas, cotton, and sugar. In just a few decades these policies concentrated 72 percent of Guatemala's arable land in the hands of 2 percent of landowners, many of European or North American origin.

This regime was naturalized in the political and social landscape as apparently "simple" contractual transactions between capitalist and laborer, but it was sustained by the consistently rapacious and brutal "accumulation by dispossession" via debt and the ongoing violence of non- or semicapitalist modes of production (Harvey 2003: 137). For example, through the *fincas de mozos* (worker plantations) indigenous people maintained subsistence agriculture on tiny landholdings (*minifundia*) in the highlands but were available for harvest labors on the large sugar or coffee plantations (*latifundias*), freeing finqueros from the obligation to maintain them the rest of the year. People did not easily acquiesce to dispossession. Throughout the colonial and early postcolonial periods people rose up in the hundreds, perhaps thousands, in what the Guatemalan historian Severo Martínez Pelaez (1991) calls *motines de indios*, refusing to accept the identity of *mozo*, or "those who will work for nothing" (González 2002; McCreery 1994; Lovell and Lutz 2009).

These processes also produced a large class of capital-poor ladinos, now defined by their distance from rather than connection to indigenous people, holding some claim on whiteness and its perks (such as exemption from vagrancy laws) in exchange for subordination to the landholding elite. The military was one of the few vehicles of social and economic advancement available to members of this intermediary class. Leveraging their authorization to deploy force into a claim to lead the Guatemalan nation, junior army officers staged the 1944 October Revolution, an uprising against landowning capital and its servants in government that brought a socialist intellectual, Juan José Arévalo, to power in free elections. Over the next decade Arévalo and his successor, Colonel Jacobo Arbenz, abolished forced labor and passed legislation protecting workers' rights, established a social security system, allowed unions to form, encouraged industrialization through import substitution, and finally and fatally redistributed land in an agrarian reform. No radical scheme, the reform gave the fallow lands of large landholders to landless peasants to stimulate a market for Guatemala's nascent industries. But Guatemalan elites and the United Fruit Company used the specter of communism to enlist the help of the United States, enmeshed in its cold war struggle with the USSR, in organizing a coup. Unable to foresee that his downfall would set the pattern for innumerable U.S. interventions and ensuing dirty wars, Arbenz resigned to prevent further bloodshed. Colonel Carlos Castillo Armas, the CIA mercenary selected to replace Arbenz, rounded up thousands of labor and peasant union leaders, sometimes for summary execution, while presiding over the replacement of the Revolution's developmental initiatives with others more friendly to global markets and capital (Gleijeses 1992; Handy 1994; Adams and Smith 2011).

Officially the civil war began in 1960, when junior army officers again rose up to protest Guatemala's support for the attempted Bay of Pigs invasion of Cuba. Two years later these same officers formed Guatemala's first major guerrilla group, the Rebel Armed Forces (FAR). At first the armed struggle was almost gentlemanly; urban legends tell of amicable soccer games between FAR and army commanders, who, after all, belonged to the same cohorts (*promoción*) from military school and were sometimes kin. But a 1963 coup led by army officers trained in cold war anticommunism at the U.S.-run School of the Americas severed the local ties that had mitigated counterinsurgency. The United States funded new technologies for surveillance and repression, producing Latin America's first case of mass "disappearance" with the March 1966 arrest of twenty-eight activists from the Guatemalan Workers Party (PGT), who were never seen again (Grandin 2004, Weld forthcoming). The multiplication of such incidents under the nominally civilian government of Julio César Méndez Montenegro confirmed the impossibility of a democratic removal of the pro-American Right and its military backers from power and pushed government opponents into the armed struggle. By the late 1960s the FAR had developed a significant base of popular support in the capital and eastern Guatemala and carried out several high-level kidnappings and executions — notoriously of the American ambassador, killed in 1968. To stop this surge, Colonel Carlos Arana Osorio led a counterinsurgent campaign that violently dismantled the FAR's civilian support, prefiguring the brutality of the 1980s.

That first wave of guerrilla warfare included Q'eqchi' and Achi' Maya in the Sierra de las Minas, but not indigenous communities in the populous western highlands or the new settlements of indigenous and ladino colonists forming in the Ixcán jungle near the Mexican border. These groups were engaged in a process of rapid social and economic transformation, in part enabled by anticommunist modernization programs, but exceeding their intended scope (Manz 2004; McAllister 2008). This process entailed its own violence; the patriarchal and gerontocratic structures of community governance that had developed along with the coffee economy were gravely undermined by the emergence of a class of young, bilingual, and sometimes literate young men who served as the interlocutors of religious authorities, development officials, and state representatives (Brintnall 1979; Colby and van den Berghe 1969; Warren 1978). As these "traditional" structures began to crumble, long-standing community tensions among generations were exposed and new ones came into play.

The Catholic Church, a historically important mediator between indigenous communities and the state, was simultaneously undergoing the upheaval of Vatican II, which transformed pastoral relations between clergy and parishioners by insisting that the Church serve the poor and dispossessed rather than the rich and powerful and emphasized internalized forms of worship over external ritual. These moves made the church a central arena for generational clashes within indigenous communities, leaving a legacy of religious and moral disputes that is still bitterly central to rural politics (Falla

1980; Le Bot 1995). Energized and empowered by these struggles but frustrated by their all too evident limits, the young (mostly) indigenous men who spent the 1960s and early 1970s forming agricultural cooperatives and teaching catechism eventually began to search for more transcendent projects.

New guerrilla organizations, regrouping after the FAR's disastrous defeat, offered what some of them were seeking. The Revolutionary Organization of the People in Arms (ORPA), created by former FAR members, made indigenous concerns the center of its revolutionary program and stayed small, recruiting indigenous combatants but eschewing mass organization. The Comité de Unidad Campesina (Campesina [peasant] Unity Committee or CUC) became the preeminent vehicle of a convergence between what its founder, Pablo Ceto, calls "two clandestine movements:" the millenarian resistance of indigenous communities to the Spanish invasion, and the armed struggle. It was also a vivid example of the frictions this convergence entailed (Arias 1990; Konefal 2010; Fernández Fernández 1988). The CUC's still unmatched 1980 mobilization of 100,000 plantation workers marked a critical shift in Guatemalan politics and class relations. At first allied with and then swallowed up by another FAR offshoot, the Guerrilla Army of the Poor (EGP), the CUC led an unprecedented number of indigenous people into frank rebellion against the Guatemalan state, making the EGP the largest and most ideologically unwieldy of Guatemala's guerrilla groups and perhaps the most threatening to the powerful. But neither the CUC nor the EGP had the force to protect their supporters from the state, whose apocalyptic violence from 1978 to 1983 targeted the hybrid of communists and Indians, who were not always but sometimes the same people. The army's drive to "remove the water from the fish," its powerful metaphor for disarticulating the guerrilla movement from its popular base, slowly defeated the Revolution.

"Never before did regimes visit such holocausts on their own populations," as Foucault (1980: 137) said of the twentieth century more generally. But after a series of military coups, intensifying outside pressure, and the rout of guerrilla forces, the state also began to "incite, reinforce, control, monitor, optimize, and organize . . . [becoming] a power bent on generating forces, making them grow" (136). General Efraín Ríos Montt, a Pentecostal pastor who took power in a coup in 1982, most explicitly joined these two faces of biopower and counterinsurgency in his "bullets and beans" campaign, conceived and overseen by General Héctor Gramajo, Guatemala's own Clausewitz. Inverting the Prussian strategist's maxim, Gramajo practiced politics as a "continuation of war," joining the outright massacre of entire communities to amnesties, model villages for captured refugees, public relations campaigns, increasing indigenous participation, and infrastructure projects (Gramajo 1995; Schirmer 1998). This book's title comes from this counterinsurgent project aimed at thwarting hopes for structural transformation, but we also use it to insist that struggles against this project are likewise ongoing, taking many guises of their own.

The project of "war by other means" was military, political, economic, and, like the wave of Catholic modernization that preceded it, also spiritual. In 1985 Maya-Ixil peasants told Diane Nelson that under Ríos Montt soldiers had come to their hamlet, separated the Catholics from the Protestants, and shot all the Catholics. Not surprisingly, many people quickly discovered Jesus as their personal savior. However, the spectacular rise in Protestant conversion among indigenous and poor Guatemalans that, by the late 1980s had made Guatemala the most Protestant country percentage-wise in Latin America, cannot be attributed only to expediency. Conflict within and repression of the Catholic Church contrasted with state support for Protestant missions, bringing massive inflows of (mostly U.S.) aid, particularly in the immediate aftermath of the worst violence of the war. Scholars of Pentecostalism also suggest that the resonance of its apocalyptic message with the violence of everyday reality in these years, along with the *alegría* and joyful expressiveness of "worship services defined by song, testimony, healings, and speaking in tongues," presented a compelling alternative to the structured services and hierarchies of Catholicism (O'Neill 2010: 10; see also Adams 2001; Garrard-Burnett 2010). Throughout the 1980s the "silence" commemorated in the CEH's title was a terrifying weight across the highlands, yet the daily, sometimes all-night Pentecostal services were one of the few places where people could make noise—lots of it—without risk.

It has been argued that Pentecostal Christianity's emphasis on the spiritual allows the faithful to withdraw from the public sphere and concentrate on remaking themselves through faith. There is a profoundly unsettling moment in Olivia Carrescia's film *Todos Santos: The Survivors* (1989) in which a Mayan man, his eyes darting about in fear, his face drawn taut with malnutrition, insists that he is not political, that he has no politics. He is Evangelical now. Certainly the otherworldliness of Pentecostalism fits well with the official message that hopes for transformation in *this* world are an engaño. Protestantism surely also offered relief to survivors burdened with the sense that they had brought violence down on their families. Likewise, through preaching and practicing abstinence, it has helped liberate many from the ravages of alcoholism—another form of seeking relief. Laying aside progressive repugnance at these churches' willfully antiliberal practices helps us see that converts, no more than leftists or anyone else, are not just engañados (Harding 2001). Indeed O'Neill argues that Pentecostals have not really withdrawn from the public sphere. Their "active demonological imagination that understands the world as constantly under attack" and the church's responsibility to "save nations from the power of Satan" (2010: 10) might graft rather generatively onto similar understandings that, at a different moment, had led people to "rise up," making religion yet another means of continuing war.

Ríos Montt was deposed in 1983, and gradually massacres gave way to the "peace of the graveyard," as a transitional military government sought to redeem Guatemala from its pariah status by holding elections. In 1984 a Constituent Assembly drafted a new constitution, and in 1985 the first civilian president in twenty years was elected, but on a short leash held by the military. Clashes continued between soldiers and guerrillas in the countryside, and thousands of activists, students, union members, and intellectuals were murdered, but stuttering negotiations with the URNG over the next four governments finally yielded a peace treaty, signed in December 1996. That same year, the Arzú government signed a series of resource-extraction concessions with transnational companies that charged only 1 percent royalties and no sales, income, or import taxes. Peace came to Guatemala hand in hand with open markets.

During the long and troubled "peace process," some brave women and men began organizing as "sectors arising from the violence" to demand justice for the crimes so recently committed. The Mutual Support Group for Families of the Disappeared (GAM) was the first of many organizations to challenge state impunity and the deadly silences it contained. Formed in 1984 primarily by widows, GAM publicly challenged the military government with the demand "Alive they were taken, alive we want them back!" Others followed: Families of the Disappeared of Guatemala (FAMDEGUA), National Coordination of Widows of Guatemala (CONAVIGUA), composed of rural indigenous women, and the Ethnic Council "Runujel Junam" (CERJ) which resisted the civil patrols and the militarization of indigenous communities. These groups, which had roots in the long history of "rising up," laid bare the gendering and racializing of the violence, and their political pressure helped end the armed conflict. They also paved the way for truth commissions and other projects for bringing justice to the war's victims, including forensic anthropological investigations of mass graves, legal proceedings against human rights violators, and, as of 2004, the National Reparations Program.

The insistence on remembering the dead and disappeared has in turn helped sow the seeds of renewed contestations over class, race, and sometimes gender inequalities in Guatemala. Land tenure and access are once again central issues in Guatemalan popular politics, thanks to the efforts of a revived CUC, its branch, the National Indigenous and Campesino Coordinator CONIC, and the Plataforma Agraria (Agrarian Platform), a multisectorial alliance working for structural agrarian change. The threats of ecologically and socially destructive mountaintop-removal mining and hydroelectric dams have galvanized Guatemalan communities and international solidarity, leading to a nationwide referendum movement in which almost a million people have so far registered their resistance to rampant resource extraction. Other fruits of popular mobilization include advancing the rights of returned refugees, indigenous people, women, queers, and various combinations of these identities, while the growing and diversifying Mayan movement unpredictably intersects with all of these struggles. Activists who have lived this history of political organizing before, during, and after the violence, moreover, find that the capacities of social movements have not only resisted extinction but improved: "Ya no necesitan intermediarios," said one; they have matured, they can speak for themselves. In turn, a resigned member of the sugar-producing elite admitted, "We are no longer dealing with fools" (Oglesby this volume).

To provide this timeline is not to suggest that the violence and its harvest can be fully explained as a series of causes and effects, nor that the troubles of aftermath can be laid to rest by narrating the truth about the past. The continual emergence of new seedlings with roots in different sediments of this past, and Guatemalans' ongoing emotional, political, and intellectual struggles to reckon responsibilities and remedies for its legacies, render such claims difficult to sustain. Instead we provide this background to make explicit our own contingent sense of the past. This is an interested account of the war because storytelling itself is one of the major sites of struggle over its consequences. Our brief history grounds the questions this volume raises: How do long-entrenched political and economic structures and contemporary aspirations, identity formations, and political projects shape one another? What range of futures can be imagined within this dynamic, and what paths are available or closed off to people seeking to realize these futures? Why do so many valiant efforts by the living to confront the nightmarish weight of the dead generations seem to come to naught? And finally, what do we need to know to persist in and strengthen these efforts?

Coyunturas

Understanding aftermath requires exploring the dialectical relation between the planned outcomes and the unintended consequences of war. To be clear: many of the effects of violence—terror, community disintegration, murders of elders and leaders, alienation—were products of counterinsurgency doctrine, detailed in handbooks and taught in special courses (Gill 2004; Huggins 1991). "Improving" on experiments conducted elsewhere (Algeria, Vietnam, Argentina, Palestine), they were planned and deliberately implemented to achieve particular goals—even if these were not always met. In turn, Guatemala, along with its neighbors El Salvador, Nicaragua, and Honduras, served as a staging ground, an intellectual system, and a condensation of counterinsurgency reaction time that has subsequently served as the basis for U.S. and NATO war-making in Afghanistan, Iraq, and elsewhere (Grandin 2006; Maass 2005; U.S. Army and U.S. Marine Corps 2007). But there are other aftereffects of violence that may equally serve counterinsurgent or capitalist purposes without being so masterminded. They often emerge, complexly, from the best intentions of people who may not identify themselves as engaged in counterinsurgency. To explore these we acknowledge politics as war by other means, but also temper that pessimistic functionalism with the knowledge that power is polyvalent, that alliances can be disrupted and turned to other agendas, that the political entails the possibility of reversals and changes of course and not simply the smooth execution of strategy. In short, we need both optics—ferreting out conspiracies and attending to contingencies—to remind ourselves that resistance is not futile. The next sections of this introduction present the book's chapters and critically evoke the moment (in Spanish, the *coyuntura*) of aftermath that surrounds, penetrates, circumscribes, and enlivens the conspiratorial and contingent stories we tell here.

This book is divided into four sections, each engaging a different configuration of the themes we have just laid out. We begin with three essays that explore the claims that are enabled by particular accounts of the war and postwar. Much of the peace process was devoted to addressing this question via the twinned projects of uncovering the truth about war crimes and overcoming the impunity enjoyed by their authors. *To harrow* means to enter Hell and rescue the righteous, and an immediate goal of the late 1990s was to rescue the victims of the violence of the early 1980s by bearing witness to their suffering and recovering the historical memory of genocide. Two major

FIG INTRO 3 A member of the Foundation for Forensic Anthropology in Guatemala shows CEH Commissioner Otilia Lux de Cotí what are believed to be the remains of the indigenous activist Mamá Maquín in a mass grave in Panzós, 1997.
PHOTO BY CARLOTA MCALLISTER.

nationwide initiatives, the Catholic Church's Interdiocesan Project to Recover Historical Memory (REMHI 1998), and the UN's CEH (1999), generated vast new stores of *testimonios* along with archival and statistical knowledge about the war. In their wake, the potential uses for testimonial evidence have proliferated as human rights documentation, evidence for court cases, reparations demands, and academic research; as tools for restoring mental health; and generally as touchstones for social justice activism. Yet despite these harrowing descents, the work of bearing witness in Guatemala remains incomplete.

In part this is because each new crop of testimonios reveals the magnitude of the violence to be greater than previously imagined: estimates of the number of civilian wartime deaths have risen from 150,000 (in the mid-1990s) to 200,000 (according to the CEH) to 250,000 (as programs to provide reparation have been implemented), demanding that ever more testimonios be collected. Likewise when the secret National Police Archives—a store of some 75 million moldy and decaying documents representing the police's internal workings since the nineteenth century—were discovered by accident in 2005, it opened vast new fields for memory work, which had been previously focused on the countryside (Doyle 2007; Weld forthcoming). But the labors of memory are also incomplete because of the resistance such massive and perverse violence presents to attempts at a final accounting.

Testifying can take many forms, some extraordinarily fruitful for those struggling with the legacy of the past. But it also can force identifications that sit poorly with experience or reinforce other forms of silence. Asked by friends in Chupol to help review a funding proposal for a project to foment nontraditional crops, Carlota McAllister was surprised to find that they nowhere mentioned their community's history of internal displacement, a hot subject among funders. Her suggestion that they invoke this past in their petition made them visibly nervous. Learning later that this group had led the community, sometimes coercively, during its period of displacement, helped her make sense of their refusal to present themselves as victims. The assumption that the past is simply awaiting narration can mean that tactically concealed histories are simply rendered inaudible, as McAllister shows in this volume. In their essay, Santiago Bastos and Manuela Camus help explain the back history of a surprising encounter Nelson had in 2001 at the Mayan Language Academy (ALMG). Giving a presentation, she quoted interviews she'd done with several of the Academy's founders in the early 1990s, saying they were revolutionaries but hid their radical projects in the guise of cultural rights and bilingual education. She was taken aback by the hostility of many in the younger generation who adamantly denied any links with the Left. Such reactions reveal emotion-laden political divisions as well as quite rational fears of reprisal, but they are also symptoms of the essentializing of identities that clandestinity once kept strategically flexible. And they serve to naturalize a depoliticization that mirrors counterinsurgent war by other means (see also Hale 2004, 2005; Montejo 2005).

The promised redemption of these harrowing returns can also feel indefinitely postponed. During her fieldwork in Chupol, McAllister lived with a family whose son, Domingo, was kidnapped by soldiers at the age of twelve, while his family and neighbors were hiding in the mountains in 1982. Mingo, as his family calls him, was among the young people keeping watch while their mothers cooked inside a makeshift kitchen, but they failed to notice the arrival of an army patrol in time to give warning. While their mothers hid, the children tried to escape, not all successfully. Some were shot; one toddler's

FIG INTRO 4 Efraín Ríos Montt during one of the hearings where he was accused of genocide and crimes against humanity. PHOTO BY DANIEL HERNÁNDEZ-SALAZAR, © 2012, WWW.DANIELHERNANDEZSALAZAR. BLOGSPOT.COM. USED WITH KIND PERMISSION.

head was split open by a machete. Mingo was handcuffed and led off, presumably for torture and interrogation, but the family has never learned anything further about what happened. This event has shaped the course of their lives, driving his parents, Tomás and Manuela, to join the GAM in 1985, making them among its first rural members. Tomás believed that the GAM provided him with a sense of strength and purpose: "I feel well-planted now. I can sway better with the winds."

The years of struggle, however, have also cost them dearly. One day the local GAM office gave Tomás a questionnaire, prepared by the Psychology Department at San Carlos University, to assess Chupol's need for a mental health project. Since he, like many older rural Maya, cannot read, McAllister was helping him through the survey's many questions about the war and its lingering consequences, when suddenly he became irritated. "That's why I drink," he said, "because I have a pain, a pain for my poor son. Who knows where he went, whether he is alive or dead? That's why I got into human rights, to find my son, but now I'm tired of that work. I'm angry. I've been working for fifteen years now, struggling with human rights, and still nothing happens. My son has never come back." The survey's rationalization of the painful labor of remembering made a mockery of Tomás's long-held hopes.

As the post-genocide stretches into more than thirty years since the original deeds, trials of some of those responsible for Guatemala's most horrible crimes are finally breaking down the wall of impunity. In 2012 the former president General Ríos Montt was brought to trial for genocide through the heroic persistence of families of the dead, forensic anthropologists, archivists, human rights activists, lawyers, and judges undaunted by the thousands of obstacles thrown up against them (including former rulers dying or losing their minds to Alzheimer's before they could be indicted). These trials have become a site of renewed hope for Guatemalans seeking to put an end to aftermath. But the tens of thousands of less highly placed but still deeply guilty perpetrators who remain at large, despite the superabundance of evidence for convicting them, beg the question of whether the law's individualizing of responsibilities — and heavy consumption of resources — are adequate to the task of doing justice. Maintaining the political will to pursue war criminals, moreover, is a heartbreakingly difficult and dangerous endeavor, especially under a government in which many officials are directly implicated in wartime crimes and use their power to insist "No hubo genocidio" (There was no genocide). At times, the demands of testimonio and the postwar organizing that takes place under its sign seem to exhaust the desires they once promised to fulfill.

The papers gathered in part I seek to push beyond the testimonial moment in accounting for Guatemala's violent past and its relation to the present. Greg Grandin's paper situates counterinsurgency structures, including the civil defense patrols, in the longue durée of five hundred years of relations between the state and indigenous communities and the "forcivoluntary" labor regimes that mediated them. Describing the vicissitudes of the Coordination of Maya People's Organizations of Guatemala (COPMAGUA), which brought over a hundred Mayan groups together to engage the proposals emerging from the government-guerrilla peace talks, Bastos and Camus illuminate five decades of indigenous organizing and the complex relationalities between struggles framed as serving class interests versus those framed as advancing ethnic rights. McAllister explores the responses of former CUC members to the humanitarian demand that they "tell their story" in the interests of overcoming the violent past. Deploying genres of speech that defer revelations of the truth, they gesture at a realm of clandestine significances, not least relating to their own revolutionary past, asking researchers to expand their repertoire of collaboration with those who bear complex political histories.

All three papers recover the relationship between genocidal violence and projects for "rising up" to explore how Guatemala's war has shaped not only the nation's present traumas but also its political possibilities for the future.

They suggest that the coincidence of the "transition to democracy" with the implementation of neoliberal policies is not in fact coincidental, and urge reflection on how the "end of war" has been inflected by a complex, subtle, and omnipresent violence that makes it impossible to simply lay the war to rest. The ongoing forcible incorporation of places and people into the so-called free market that has accompanied and indeed been quickened by the signing of the peace in Guatemala is a reiterative process working at ever more intimate levels of the body, mind, and soul. The freedoms of postwar democracy are secured by parties, elections, and more or less fair voting and audited by funding agencies and foreign governments concerned with "governance" and "citizenship." But not only do they bear little resemblance to an ideal of popular sovereignty based on participation, equality, and collective ownership of the state, they have also been directly contravened by centuries of racialized counterinsurgent labor discipline that systemically restricted citizenship rights (Taracena Arriola, Gordillo, and Sagastume 2004). Still more intractably, as Marx reminds us, in capitalist democracy the free will of the citizen is subverted by the *forcivoluntary* "freedom" of workers to sell their labor. We must alienate this critical means of life in order to go on living. In drawing attention to what he calls a loss of self, Marx was not affirming the counterinsurgent message that hope is an engaño, but rather, like the *motines de indios*, showing how this loss works in order to imagine how things can work otherwise. In this mutinous spirit, we now turn to considering the double faces of aftermath, beginning with the outline of an emerging political economy that is both a harvest and a reseeding of war.

MARKET FREEDOMS AND MARKET FORCES: THE NEW BIOPOLITICAL ECONOMY

In 1955, during the postcoup counterinsurgency cleanup, the Guatemalan government teamed with the World Health Organization to eradicate malaria. The land reform of the deposed president Arbenz was replaced by large-scale state investment in and control over infrastructure, part of the standard operating procedures of modernization theory and its very vigorous will to improve. In this spirit, the National Service for Malaria Eradication (SNEM) organized brigades that tested for malaria, destroyed mosquitoes, administered quinine, and organized volunteers to report suspicious fevers. People now remember the incredible spirit of the SNEM teams, their *mística*, organization, discipline, and sense of mission. And it succeeded. By the mid-1970s malaria cases had dropped precipitously. By the late 1980s, however, increased resistance in both the mosquito and the plasmodium, combined with the DDT ban, lowered human immunity, and lack of medicine, caused cases to rise again. Now they may be as high as ever. But no one really knows; the brigades and volunteer networks were mostly disbanded under health guidelines drawn up to implement International Monetary Fund (IMF) support for the new civilian government in 1986.

Current IMF and World Bank funding is predicated on theories rather different from those of the 1950s, when everyone pitched in to eliminate the scourge of malaria (while retaining the army's Civic Action foundations in opposing land reform except through free market purchase). Often lumped together as "neoliberalism" or "structural adjustment," these theories prescribe a one-size-fits-all set of policies that governments the world over have been *forcivoluntariamente* made to implement if they want foreign aid, investment, debt relief, or balance of payments support. Neoliberalism locates the cure for every ill in "the Market" and "Free Trade" and demands that governments privatize state enterprises, open domestic markets to foreign capital and goods, and eliminate any policies (or actors) that might hobble the market—like food subsidies, unions, or large public health initiatives. Even scorched-earth counterinsurgency might fit this bill, as the maximum expression of what Naomi Klein (2007) calls "shock doctrine," clearing the field for the market's new (mono)crops.

Capitalism has always produced uneven geographies of exploitation and (under)development (Harvey 2005). Neoliberalism represents a further recursive move in an ongoing process of differentiation among coeval formations of capitalism, none of which is itself fully complete (Brenner et al. 2010). In Guatemala, as Grandin argues and Luis Solano, Elizabeth Oglesby, and Irmalicia Velásquez Nimatuj show in part II, the long-term legacy of the enclosures begun in the colonial period and drastically intensified by the coffee economy was reconfigured between 1954 and 1975, when population growth and movements into previously uncharted regions of the country finally closed off the possibility of expanding subsistence production as a substitute for, or at least significant subsidy to, entering into wage labor. The ratcheting up of war thus coincided with the moment when local and national "traditions" of exploitation were definitively subordinated to the dictates of the global economy. The stakes of struggle of both the war and its aftermath are now squarely within the dynamics of capitalism as a global system (DeHart 2010; Way 2012). At the same time, neoliberal forms of subjectivization that locate responsibility for dealing with these realities within the self and the self's will to work toward its own improvement demand that individuals take ever more heroic or dastardly action to sustain life.

Guatemalans tell a harsh joke about how neoliberalism frustrates efforts at sustaining oneself and one's community outside of its dictates:

A young man spends his last money on bus fare. On the ride, masked men begin robbing everyone. Reaching the young man one thief can't believe he doesn't have a cent. The rider pulls out his wallet and shows it to be empty. "You don't have any money?" asks the robber. "Why not?!" "Well, I studied history at the National University," said the man. "'Mano!" (Brother!) exclaims the thief, pulling off his mask and smiling. "Qué promoción?!" (Which graduating class?!).

The civil war decimated San Carlos University—known as the voice of the national conscience—and intellectual life in general with the motto "Death to intelligence!" (Kobrak 1999). But the army's efforts to disarticulate capacities for critical thought are reinforced by the "adjustments" within the rational free market that now pit brothers against each other on the bus with an empty wallet between them. What options for making a living in the fuller sense are open to "rational" people as legal and ethical routes out of poverty are systematically shut down, dreams deferred, decisions forcivoluntariamente taken? What good is history if you can't eat it?

From some perspectives, this reduction of possibilities is all according to plan. One U.S. Embassy official enthused to Nelson about the peace process and free trade agreements: "Guatemala is our big success story!" Indeed the postwar period has produced a number of new fortunes among the usual small and pale elite in Guatemala. "Structural adjustments" in Guatemala, as elsewhere, have been stutteringly imposed, with governments mounting more or less resistance at different moments. For example, in late 2004 the Guatemalan Congress approved a progressive generic drugs law that led the United States to threaten to cut aid, refuse to renew the IMF stand-by agreement, and exclude Guatemala from the Central America Free Trade Agreement. U.S. Trade Representative Robert Zoellick (later president of the World Bank) made personal calls to a number of politicians using what was described as "not very diplomatic language" (Rodríguez 2004: 3). The government caved. While Guatemala is the largest *maquila* drug producer in Central America, medicine prices are among the highest, unlike Nicaragua and Honduras, where the governments legally limit price increases. The most industrially developed Central American country and the richest on a per capita basis, Guatemala also has the lowest rate of taxes paid in Latin America. For the U.S. Embassy official, perhaps Guatemala is a "success story" compared with transitional efforts in Africa and other places where armed confrontations continue despite peace treaties and UN missions, but perhaps it is also due to this successful implementation of neoliberal orthodoxy, with its accompanying investment (and profit extraction) opportunities.

"Surprisingly," according to the *Financial Times*, "Guatemalan debt is regarded as a relatively safe bet. Because it was shut out of the capital markets during its civil war, from 1960 to 1996, its debt load is among the lowest in Latin America" (Silver 2003). In 2007 the World Bank, after decades of inattention to agrarian issues, decided that agriculture would be its new focus and found in Guatemala an unexpectedly fit candidate for following what it calls an "evolutionary" path to development (World Bank 2007: 4). In its 2007 annual report, the Bank takes the success of some Guatemalans in growing broccoli and raspberries for export as a model for how countries still based in agrarian production, with its attendant poverty and inequalities, can nonetheless "sustain spectacular growth" (Fischer and Benson 2006: 238). Statistics showing a trend toward increasing diversification of rural employment are lauded as a measure of the shift of rural labor away from the "meager bounty of subsistence" toward higher-value forms of agrarian production (World Bank 2007: 1). When former U.S. president George W. Bush visited Guatemala in 2007, he emphasized free trade *as* development by helping load trucks with lettuce alongside members of one such enterprise while praising these "ethnic entrepreneurs" and their partnership with Walmart (DeHart 2010: 1).

Yet this growth looks less spectacular when other numbers, usually left conveniently off-book, are added to the account. In theory, stripping workers and the environment of protections attracts investment that grows the economy. Importing U.S. government–subsidized transgenic corn grown cheaply in Iowa will "free" Guatemalan peasant farmers to produce for export and raise their standard of living. Never mind that for most, the reality has been lower wages and higher prices, the accelerated fraying of what was already a precarious social net, the privatization of infrastructure, and increased exposure to food price shocks. Nor that many Mayan people consider themselves "people of corn," as expressed in the origin stories of the *Pop Wuj* (often called the Mayan "Bible"), making the grain more than a commodity and its production more than work. Inequalities in land distribution have sharply increased since 1979, when they were already among the highest on the continent. Currently the largest 2.5 percent of farms occupy nearly two-thirds of agricultural land, while 90 percent of farms share only one-sixth of the arable land (USAID 2010).

The essays in part II insistently ground our agrarian metaphors in fine-grained depictions of human relations with the land because agriculture continues to sustain the majority of Guatemalans and serves as the foundation of the Guatemalan economy as a whole. The essays follow ongoing struggles to further squeeze surplus out of peasants, many of them indigenous, who in turn seek to escape from such brutally exploitative relations with astounding tenacity. Through a detailed genealogy of connections among the notoriously secretive Guatemalan elite, national economic and agrarian policy, transnational capital, and resource extraction, Solano shows how the peripheral northern zone of the Franja Transversal del Norte (Northern Transversal Strip or FTN) is a central site for understanding the connections between war and a particularly rapacious form of accumulation by dispossession. Oglesby describes how sugar elites have attempted to mitigate their own fears of popular uprising by instituting new hyperrationalist and developmentalist labor governance regimes on their plantations on the South Coast in a long-term strategy to prevent any recurrence among their mozos of the kind of mobilization that led to the historic 1980 CUC strike. Velásquez Nimatuj shows us the other face of this coin by exploring the lengthy struggle of the people of Nueva Cajolá to win access to land and then survive on it. She shows their complex relations with fractious social movements, rural-urban solidarities, and state actors as they work—through legal and extralegal means and within and against deeply racist structures—to achieve goals first identified over a century ago.

Building on Grandin's history, Oglesby explores recent transformations in internal labor migration emerging from these structures and statistics, and the challenge transnational migration poses to the sugar elites. Guatemala's indices of inequality rise year after year; currently it ranks 116 out of 169 countries on the Human Development Index (measuring life expectancy, education, and standard of living), considerably below where it would be on a ranking of per capita income (UNDP 2010). On the ground, rural people try a bit of *milpa* (corn) farming here, paid work in a neighbor's fields there, plus some informal commerce or maquiladora employment to try to round it all off, in an increasingly desperate and exhausting piecing together of the inadequate offerings of the labor market for workers without the capital or community organization to move into horticulture or pay for migration to the United States. As Velásquez Nimatuj shows, also mostly off-book is the widespread destruction caused by recent hurricanes and the famine and mass unemployment unleashed by the 2001–3 "coffee crisis." After global overproduction sent prices of this key commodity down to 1950s levels, plantation owners left beans to rot in the trees since they couldn't make back the cost of harvesting. Tens of thousands of laborers were consigned to starvation with no work, often owed years of back pay and with only the most desultory state attention to their welfare—and that only because of intense pressure from popular organizations like CONIC and the Plataforma Agraria. The Central American Free Trade Agreement, which passed by only one vote in the U.S. Congress, went into effect in Guatemala in June 2006. This has flooded the Guatemalan market with subsidized (and often genetically modified) U.S. corn, seriously undermining local subsistence agriculture (DeHart 2010), just as a global financial crisis began to unfold, with the U.S. war economy faltering, and rising energy and food prices steadily undermining food independence (Bello 2008). It's been raining on wet ground.

Even in areas where workers depend less on the coffee economy, postwar political economies pressure families and communities to find escape routes that increasingly involve off-book "gray" or informal economies, such as emigration. So ensconced are these strategies in Guatemalan livelihoods that former president Oscar Berger (a finquero himself) said education policies were unnecessary in his government, as schools needed to train people only for manual labor in the United States. Ricardo Falla (2008), in his study of migration in Zacualpa, El Quiché (site of one of the four genocide cases in the CEH), poetically evokes the *Pop Wuj* to argue that Maya have always been on the move. But he also calculates that 20 percent of the town's population is now in the United States, which is certainly historically unique. The massive transformations in kinship relations, local politics, financial circuits, and the national economy occasioned by increasing migration cannot be overstated (Camus 2008; Foxen 2008). While there is no chapter dedicated solely to transnational migration, this book is, like Guatemala and the United States, permeated with migration's effects; almost every essay addresses it, and here we offer a general overview of its impacts on post-genocide Guatemala.

Migration is part of a larger "graying" of the economy in the sense that remittances flow through semi-shadow economies as no one declares wages and as money transfers operate on the edges of banking systems, through far-flung networks of human traffickers and informal exchanges of many kinds. Without remittances families and states would be mired in debt, so the risks and dangers confronted by the migrants and their families are actually what keep the nation in the black. *Graying* also refers to familial effects, as often elderly grandparents raise the children left behind, try to maintain community organizing, and pay off debts to coyotes (human traffickers) and everyone tries to muddle through without children, spouses, and parents. Widespread investment in cell phones means loved ones haven't (always)

FIG INTRO 5 Graves in the cemetery of Todos Santos Cuchumatán display the effects of the influx of remittances. PHOTO BY JAMES RODRIGUEZ / MIMUNDO.ORG. USED WITH KIND PERMISSION.

disappeared from everyday life, but their absence poignantly recalls wartime losses (Worby 2006).

The material effects of migration are visible in satellite dishes, SUVs, and spanking new multistory concrete buildings amid traditional adobe houses, but also in boarded-up homes and a marked lack of young men. Less visible are the credit and debt relations remaking landholding and family economics more generally. Some of these are based in prewar structures that positioned labor contractors as moneylenders, while some emerge from newer patterns of accumulation by dispossession, as when civil patrollers parlay their military status into improved class positions. Traditional inequalities are distorted and reworked by the war and its aftermath. People put up land and houses as collateral to get someone to the States, and they may be rewarded, able to build new brick houses, pay for other children's education, or even (as town dwellers now grumble) come down from the hamlets and snap up urban properties *in cash*! Or they may lose everything if the migrant is grabbed in transit, finds only occasional employment, gets too depressed to bear the hardships of life in the United States, or gets deported. In the worst cases migrants don't make it: a boat founders off the coast of Mexico with a dozen young men from one village, or the Arizona desert swallows people whole. With new financialization, insuring against this insecurity is now a profit-making venture. A poster outside a new bank in Joyabaj, El Quiché shows hands cradling a seedling and reads "¡NEW! INSURANCE for repatriation. Guatemala Your Land in Your Hands." Q350 a year ($45) will cover the costs of bringing a migrant's body home.

Other costs are rendered as gender relations and are both reinscribed and challenged by migration. Young, recently married, and often pregnant women are frequently left for years with their in-laws while their new husband goes to the States. Unsurprisingly, many seek more local companionship, resulting in transnational scandals. A migrant's parents may receive remittances in part because they house their son's wife and child, making them dependent on domesticating her sexuality. She may also decide to up and leave, with or without her children. This may empower her, as she too can earn 7.5 Guatemalan quetzals to each dollar. Yet it also entails facing the same risks that men take: of losing touch with her children and finding it hard to maintain a sense of ethnic identification away from family, village, time to weave, and ceremonial calendars, as well as the terrors of rape and assault on the road. (This is so widespread a fear that Nelson has heard women counsel each other to visit the doctor for contraception before they go, to ensure that if they're raped at least they won't get pregnant.)

The graying of the economy takes place at the highest levels as well. Even as U.S. financial foreign policy encourages the free play of market forces of supply and demand, its interdiction arm tries to keep the Latin America drug supply away from eager gringo consumers. This raises prices and increases incentives to take the risk of trafficking for both major operators and poor youth, who have few other opportunities for employment. The way narco-money, narconetworks, and gang organization have coiled through the politics, economics, banking systems, and everyday social worlds of a peripheral country like Guatemala is both a general phenomena—what Carolyn Nordstrom (2007) calls "extrastate globalization of the illicit"—and a shadow of the particular war fought there (mixed with the detritus of the "drug wars" in Mexico). Indeed Guatemala's experience with war constitutes a kind of competitive advantage for its participation in this extraordinarily profitable sector of the global economy. The jungles and mountains that provided refuge to guerrilla fronts, and were subsequently militarized through the counterinsurgency, are also congenial for airstrips and marijuana and poppy plantations. The "FARC-ization" of the Guatemalan military—its transformation, in many of its operations, from an institution with a national mission to one in business for itself—is the culmination of decades-long trajectories of mixing national security with profit making and of army members moving from protecting the interests of oligarchs to protecting their own. Skills in enacting the violence sustaining the shadow economy are also ones some Guate-malans have mastered to world-class standards. Los Zetas, the drug cartel notorious for escalating the violence in Mexico, has hired former Guatema-lan Special Forces members (*kaibiles*) to carry out its gruesome campaigns of mass beheadings and nightclub massacres. These same actors frequently force migrants to carry drugs across the border and/or extort extra money from their families, often leaving the bodies of those who refuse (or might identify them) strewn across the desert.

The patterns of wartime impunity are rewoven for these new worlds of lawlessness unleashed by the market, in which secrets both deeply distort on-book accountability and produce magical profitability, along with terrible local costs. In 2008 Nelson visited Livingston, the Caribbean outpost acces-sible only by water and the center of Afro-Caribbean Garífuna culture, where she heard the *avioneta* story. An avioneta is a small propeller plane; several years ago one full of cocaine fell out of the sky near town. One storyteller said that before the avioneta she couldn't give away a bag of coke left by a visitor because Rastafari influences made people understand it as poison. But then the plane crashed and everything changed. "Who knows?" she said. "Curi-osity, avarice, the devil? Who knows? But people went out there and took the stuff." Soon addictions took hold, accompanied by robberies, sex work, and nasty characters from the Oriente, Jalapa, Zacapa (reputedly the center of the drug trade). People began to die, some of overdoses, some of violence, sometimes leaving mangled corpses. Because this is all clandestine, Living-ston at first looks like a laid-back tourist mecca until someone points out the drug deals going on by the playground or tells you her mother was found dead in the cemetery, her breasts cut off and her body mutilated, raising fears of Satanism.

The informal economy "would be more appropriately called *the economy itself*, since it accounts for some three-quarters of all economic activity" (Way 2012: 7). The shadow worlds of traffickers and coyotes operate both against and through state and military networks, via above- and underground econo-mies. Where is one to turn for help in this gray zone? In areas like the Franja Transversal, returning refugees and those who remained through the war, along with the military, former revolutionaries, traditional and new elites, and transnational finance and narcocapital, are all engaged in struggles over control of territory, resources, profit, and hope. For many, migration to the United States is an escape valve, a solution, a salvation. But it is an individu-alist one that also destroys families, communities, and collective projects, as Velásquez Nimatuj movingly shows. Such biopolitical economies of war by other means seem to defy the kind of clear planning and strategizing that we imagine as necessary to bring another world into being. Understanding how Guatemalans act on their inhumanly limited possibilities is nonetheless an enterprise poorly served by the concept of victimhood. As Oglesby reminds us, "International migration is more than just an economic option. . . . It's the social project of a post-war generation, one that arguably demands as much ingenuity as joining a revolutionary movement must have required of their parents" (2003: 670). The next section explores how the social projects of new generations of Guatemalans take shape within and against these limits, as means to ends degenerate into ends in themselves and Guatemala's face of postwar transparency is repeatedly revealed to hide something else.

Means into Ends: Neoliberal Transparency and Its Shadows

With the end of armed conflict, a Mayan activist lamented to Nelson, "We are still at war, but now it is a war against violence and you never know where to fight or who to fight against. Against delinquency? It's very different. Who is the enemy?" This mimics "the oft-expressed sentiment that in Guatemala you can no longer do anything, *en Guatemala ya no se puede*" (Oglesby 2003: 670). Understanding this frustration requires returning to other histories of the future and how they twined through the peace process and its aftermath. In 1987 Nelson was offered a job in Mexico City to work with Guatemalan refugees. When she arrived the job had changed to a diagnostic study for development work with Mexican indigenous people. After laboring for months with limited funding and little criteria from the funders she finally realized (being a bit slow on the uptake) that it was a cover for sending money somewhere else, presumably to the guerrillas.

As cold warriors knew, transnational funding and alliances are also politics; anticommunist governments like the United States, Israel, Taiwan, and Argentina supported the Guatemalan military state, while socialist states like Cuba and the USSR funded the guerrillas.[3] But we know far less about what solidarity groups and international development, religious, and humanitarian NGOs transacted under the sign of clandestinity. Nor can we calculate the effects of these earlier relations on later development and political work, in part because they remain cloaked in secrecy, as McAllister's paper suggests. One way of thinking about these connections, however, is as harbingers of the postwar phenomena of international "cooperation" and nonprofit or nongovernmental organization (ONG in Spanish) funding, which have become a crucial actant in the war's aftermath. The ONG-*ización* of the peace process, with its accompanying training, lobbying, legitimizing, and simple human solidarity, as well as its paternalistic meddling, has recombinantly transformed many conditions of possibility in Guatemala. Providers come in many forms, from embassies and church organizations to classic NGOs like Oxfam and Doctors Without Borders, to volun-tourists, spring break mission trips, and human rights experts working (and receiving generous "combat pay") for the CEH or UN peacekeeping, with most aid coming from over-developed parts of the world like the United States, Western Europe, and Japan.

In the late 1980s and early 1990s, with the Guatemalan state bankrupt in every conceivable way, this support was a huge boon, founding research institutes and human rights, Mayan, and women's organizations. With the 1996 peace treaty the stream became a flood, energizing hopes, forming new leaders, and employing tens of thousands of people. Activists were returning from exile with powerful experiences of organizing and new gender and multiethnic dynamics, training, and education, to join those who had stayed to fight the long and grinding struggle from within. Perennially impoverished, they now, at long last, had access to the resources to put their imaginaries of change into practice. By the late 2000s over $2 billion had been spent on "peace."

The money has supported interventions into most aspects of national life, including health and education reform, sanitation infrastructure, improvement of ethnic relations, prison and police reform, decentralization, customary law, human rights, testimonio collection, indigenous cultural revitalization, women's rights, environmental activism, municipal government capacitation, tourism, mental health, exhumations, political parties, and all-around economic development. Sometimes it felt like a magical abundance: just hand in the correctly filled-in forms, and you too could start a Mayan women's organization or turn a struggling coffee plantation into an organic fair trade cooperative. Picturesque but devastated areas saw offices sprout up almost overnight as the white vehicles of *los derechos humanos* (human rights) began to clog the roads. The infrastructure to support foreign relief workers' needs (and, as a byproduct, local people's aspirations) was close behind, from paved roads to lattes, from hotels with hot water and cable TV to underground parking garages. One of the most popular forms of aid came in the form of workshops, or *talleres*, that trained people in hygiene, the Constitution, traditional law, spirituality, women's rights, safe sex, *poder local* (local power), taking testimony, and, of course, how to get funding for *proyectos*.

Proyectos have in turn reshaped the practice of politics, perhaps most of all among former revolutionaries. When the war ended, the URNG was "reincorporated" into Guatemalan society as two separate entities: a political party, which kept the name of the former guerrilla group, and the Fundación Guillermo Toriello (FGT), an NGO (leading to dismissive word-play on O[UR]NG, suggesting the revolutionaries had sold out their principles). Indeed becoming a "nongovernmental" agency implies renouncing any claim on state power and seems like a profound political transformation for those once bent on seizing the state. But the head of the FGT, the former EGP commander Enrique Corral, told McAllister the transition had been smooth. His formation as a Jesuit had taught him to plot his actions toward the goal of salvation. These skills were very useful for elaborating strategies for a complex military-political organization like the EGP and, perhaps less obviously, for the exigencies of NGO work, like managing the temporal complexities of constantly applying to donors. But if seeking funding is war by other means, is it revolutionary struggle or counterinsurgency?

Another way the magical money has reshaped politics comes, rather surprisingly, from the strong accompanying emphasis on transparency and accountability, meant to limit aid money lost to "corruption" (or, more innocently, *mal manejo de fondos*, or bad money management). This emphasis means that *auditoria*, or "audit culture" (Strathern 2000), has become the frame for postwar efforts at transforming Guatemala. San Bartolenses told Matilde González (2002) that the war had disrupted time itself, a central aspect of humanness: "se cambió el tiempo." More subtly, so have *la cooperación* and proyecto culture. The aid bonanza has led to new subjectivities as people, both locally and nationally, metamorphose into "Pedro Proyectos," a person adept at *gestionando*, or maneuvering through the complex paperwork, new languages, and bookkeeping requirements necessary to bring projects and money to their locales. Nelson's experience in Mexico suggests that in the 1980s demands for accountability were probably accompanied with a knowing wink as money for a study might actually have gone to plant corn for the Communities of the Population in Resistance. Popular organizations like GAM still heroically resist ongoing injustices, but nowadays it is considerably more likely that their members will be sitting in a workshop learning to do project profiles and *monitoreo* (audit), or filling in forms to justify past and future spending rather than planning a demonstration or lobbying Congress.

"Forma se convierte en fondo," one long-term organizer said, referring to the uncanny way aid seems to convert what were means to an end—like peace, democracy, justice, and equality—into ends in themselves. This is a more chilling kind of magic. Becoming dependent on jobs—on selling the means of life to go on living—means the survival of the organization can become paramount, regardless of its political goals or efficacy. In turn the very *form* of the work can delicately discipline people's priorities. For example, to receive aid requires *personalidad jurídica*, a time-consuming process that lays one bare to state surveillance and legally limits what one can say and do. Then there are the constraints imposed by the required proposal format, embodied in the dread *marcológico* (the one-page strictly parametered overview), even before one tries to align pressing needs at the local level with funders' priorities. With few jobs in either the public or private sector, intellectuals, including many Guatemalans with master's degrees or PhDs earned at great cost elsewhere and eager to give back, can find employment only with NGOs. There, instead of drawing on their training, they must conform to research rubrics handed down from outside: whatever the gringos are interested in this year. Because reports and "diagnostics" become the property of funders, their work also frequently disappears into archives rather than fertilizing Guatemala's parched informatic terrain. Likewise activists ensconced in NGO temporality spend weeks feverishly working on end-of-the-fiscal-year reports, often for a variety of funders with different criteria, rather than "doing" politics.

Another uncanny property of transparency is that it doesn't necessarily clarify. Scoring organizations on accountability and devoting reams of paper and countless hours to balancing the books and to the frequent audits of beneficiaries do not dispel the problems created when a donor needs to spend a certain amount of money in a set amount of time. "One group had a million dollars they had to spend on a deadline and it had to be on customary law. We were scouring the place looking for any one we could give the money to," said one friend. Nor do they necessarily catch how intentions can go very wrong, as when a project aimed at empowering women allowed the very PAC leaders who killed local men in San Bartolo to use their victims' widows as a front for enrichment, or when a former death squad member parlayed NGO interest in street children into a lucrative postwar career, as Matilde González-Izás and Deborah Levenson explore here.

Likewise it does little to insulate people with access to resources from the often desperate pleas of friends, family, fellow war sufferers, or church members to spread the wealth around or risk losing these precious human relations. Dishearteningly, disputes over the very money meant to encourage social organizing have instead ripped organizations apart, along with communities, long-term friendships, and even families. We do not want to romanticize. Markets have been features of highland community life since before the Conquest, and indigenous Guatemalans are the original "penny capitalists" (Tax 1963; also Goldin 2009), but the logic of the proyecto participates in centuries-long processes of enclosing those spaces of communal living that stand apart from the cold cash nexus. For organizing work, long reliant on solidarity and enlightened consciousness to compensate for an absence of funding, the exchange of money for political labor is particularly destabilizing. Human rights workers are disturbed to discover people want to be paid to help dig out mass graves containing their own relatives or attend marches to make what are supposed to be their own demands. But for rural communities, the requests for help in the form of labor, from activists whose own work seems well funded, can also feel like a revival of age-old expectations that Indians should work for free.

For many it has felt like a rude awakening to find themselves enmeshed in these unintended consequences without quite knowing how it happened, but canny activists had highlighted many of these dangers in the mid-1990s in this anonymously authored popular education pamphlet collected by Paula Worby in the Ixcán (and jokingly called a "Quick Impact Circular," playing on the name for the UN's "Quick Impact Projects" that were being implemented at the time).[4] Throughout the essays in this volume we see the same effects laid out here, the role of the ex-PAC in postwar "development" in M. González, the way money divides communities in Velásquez Nimatuj and Worby, the limited understandings of "modernization" in Grandin, Solano, and Jorge Ramón González Ponciano.

The areas hardest hit by the war's violence have been most heavily funded, even as attempts to "make perpetrators pay" through the court and justice system have foundered. At the same time, the state-funded reparations program for victims of the violence began to make cash payouts (about $3,200) for a death, but families can receive only two payments, regardless of how many members they lost. Perhaps no ledger can account for this monetarization of both everyday life and existential loss.

Nor can an economistic logic take the place of functioning justice systems in repairing injury or account for the new forms of violence that both enable and flow from the massive increase in proyectos, disciplines of accountability, and the licit and illicit monies these garner as they circulate through postwar Guatemala. The chapters in this section explore how the neoliberal logics of NGO-ization, postwar developmentalism, and auditing disarticulate and rearticulate desires for something other than stark market rationalities into shadowy forces. Children become *maras*, or youth gangs, neighbors turn into lynch mobs while mobs turn into liberators, and masked dancers are also war criminals. But other hybrids may also emerge from these articulations.

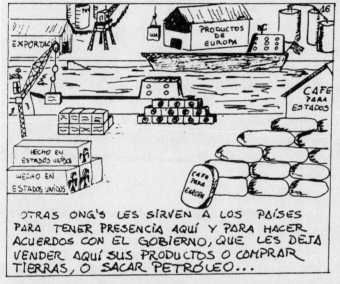

FIG INTRO 6 An anonymously authored pamphlet critiquing development NGOs that circulated in the Ixcán in the years after refugee return from Mexico.

Paul Kobrak illuminates the ongoing relevance of wartime actors in postwar attempts to bring the rule of law to the Guatemalan highlands, describing the machinations of the long war through which the people of Colotenango work out their relations to one another through participation in the PAC, the CUC, the state's legal system, and the guerrilla movement. In so doing they confront the limits of judicial attempts to account for violence that cannot be understood as confined to a single event, as well as the way "democracy" may reinscribe indigenous people as second-class citizens. Levenson's chapter traces the shifting effects of state counterinsurgency and neoliberalism on the youth gangs popularly known as maras. She argues that in the mid-1980s these groups offered their members an alternative and often warmer form of life than their birth families, along with certain political possibilities, even a working-class consciousness. She contrasts this with the present, in which they have become central actors in the post-1996 urban street ecology of violence, crime, and drugs, providing less community and meaning than articulation into a cheap and highly rationalized underground labor supply chain for transnational narcotrafficking. In turn, their tattooed, cold-eyed faces have supplied a new photographic fetish for representing Guatemala's pathologies. Jennifer Burrell situates the spectacularized lynching murders of a Japanese tourist and a Guatemalan guide in the Mayan town of Todos Santos in the context of debates about how to understand such events. The struggles of the state and Todosanteros themselves to adjudicate responsibility for this crime, made unusually public by the town's prominence as a tourist magnet, show how easily acts of violence in the postwar raise popular fears of the hidden intentions of the state and the state's fears of the hidden intentions of the people. Matilde González-Izás shows how a group of San Bartolense PAC leaders consolidated power during the war via their relations to the counterinsurgency state, and how their hold on the community persists. Through relations of gender, terror, and economic power, they affect women's freedom of movement, the development aid coming into the community, the town's traditional festival, and young people's very imaginaries.

After 2005, when UN peacekeepers declared "Mission accomplished," and still more after the global recession of 2008, the money geysers began to sputter out. As a Guatemalan activist said in 2006, "It's not an emergency anymore. Now we're just another Third World country." But the transformation of the desire for progress into the desire for projects, licit and otherwise, had already left many Guatemalans disillusioned with money's magic. The apparently healing powers of international financial support were beginning to look more like a pharmakon: both a medicine *and* a poison. As *Inforpress*

Centroamericana put it: Is aid "altruistic or does it respond to commercial interests? Does it strengthen or atrophy a country? Is it a medicine or a drug?" (García 2004). But aid's powerful effects, as we argue in the next section, should not be understood only as a necro- or de-politicization but rather as part of the reworking of the Guatemalan polis within the global rebalancing of forces since the end of the cold war.

WHITHER THE FUTURE? POSTWAR ASPIRATIONS
AND IDENTIFICATIONS

When someone else picks up the tab, there are always strings attached, and we would be naïve to think the revolution will be funded by the nonprofit industrial complex (INCITE! 2007). But before assuming that the formerly revolutionary and popular subjects who sought aid are *engañados*, we might remember the sustaining history of solidarity through the war years, the personal contacts and trust built over decades, and the fact that donors themselves are often caught by surprise by unintended consequences. Perhaps most important is the fact that in war (and war by other means) people are often well aware of the resources massed against them and know that they need to assemble their own supports and alliances, not just to go on living but also to attempt to recover the means of life in war's aftermath. To move beyond lamenting what was lost in the war, the essays collected in part IV engage with the messy terrain of everyday struggles to make politics effective post-genocide.

Nelson's chapter shows how Omnilife, a Mexican health care product distributed through direct sales, flowed into spaces circumscribed by the limits of state and NGO processes. Now the product links indigenous women and their aspirations, which were previously articulated through public service and revolutionary action, to entrepreneurial activities that also, a bit incongruously, allow them multiethnic spaces for contemplation of gender identities and of co-memoration. González Ponciano examines how historically and violently entrenched constraints on social mobility within Guatemala play out among high school students in the capital city. He shows how they situate themselves within, and simultaneously transform, the complex legacies of racial difference, class stratification, and interpersonal violence left to them by the war. They use the mobile category of the not-quite-not-white *shumo* to face the challenge posed to elite privilege by the "cosmopolitanism from below" made possible by labor migrants and returnees like those Worby discusses in her chapter. Worby likewise engages with the possibilities and limits of state and transstate projects as she details some of the contradictions within the cosmopolitan legacy brought home by returning refugees to the Ixcán and FTN. The optimism surrounding their carefully calibrated mass return to some of the areas hardest hit by the violence confronts the continuing realities of fractious community relations, divisions in their organizations, the reassertion of oppressive gender structures, and limited options for survival.

The neoliberal Right and the postrevolutionary Left share a certain contempt for the state. For the Right, the state is nothing but a beast to be starved; for the Left, working up the will to power required to ply its instruments of rule seems like succumbing to a tattered illusion, or perhaps as simply too dangerous to risk in the wake of significant defeats. Given the conditions we have been outlining, it is little wonder that Guatemalans often express similar sentiments. Chupolenses, disappointed with the state's repeated failures to provide the wise and responsible governance they believed was its proper task, let alone basic security or services, repeatedly described it to McAllister as "a thief," a category of person they consider akin to an animal, incapable of reason. Likewise an urban activist, describing a Ministry of Education program that actually worked but was cancelled after applications rose from single to triple digits after one year, saw it as prime evidence of the hopelessly treacherous nature of state power: "Every time they create any kind of social fabric they tear it apart." During the 2011 presidential run-off elections between General Otto Pérez Molina (the eventual winner, connected to the 1980s genocide) and a newcomer, Manuel Baldizón (widely suspected of links to drug trafficking), people likened voting to choosing between getting AIDS and cancer. The plaints of Guatemalans about their deeply circumscribed political possibilities echo the emerging transnational ethnographic record of neoliberalism creating "nongovernmental states" with "resource-extraction enclaves" (Ferguson 2006; Gupta 1998; Moodie 2010; Tsing 2004; Babb 2001).

But is the Guatemalan state only a criminal failure? We conclude this introduction by arguing for the importance of the post-genocide state precisely insofar as it has ceased to be a site for hopeful politics — and yet may still offer more than simply engaño. Seen ever more as a marketplace — a dirty, pragmatic space of negotiation and resource distribution that suffocates most aspirations — it also limits its own ability to exert its sovereignty over alternative terrains of struggle.

One evening in July 2008, bouncing over unpaved backcountry roads in her Jeep, a progressive Maya-K'iche' woman recounted how she was transformed from a neutral journalist covering the mayoral campaign in Zacualpa into an enthusiastic supporter of the Guatemalan Republican Front (FRG) candidate (who won). "It was these villages. Their passion, their emotion, their hope. Before I knew what was happening, I was yelling along. The people just love him. He built roads, the new municipal building, but also because he's Maya. He understands. When the ladinos in town got scared and rallied around their candidate, the villages all came out in force. I've never had so much fun. I'd be exhausted, but I couldn't stop." She had spent several years in exile and in the three elections since her return had vocally and financially supported the URNG candidate, but now she was serving as the FRG mayor's unpaid advisor.

It is hard for many observers to understand the popularity of political parties whose leaders are generals implicated in crimes against humanity, like the FRG and Pérez Molina's Patriotic Party (PP). The continuing appeal of *mano dura* (iron fist) politics, often among those who bore the brunt of counterinsurgency, is an enduring thorn in the side of almost anyone not among the FRG's or PP's supporters. Many people, from right-wing businessmen and urban progressives to foreign academics and journalists, have treated this support as evidence of the backwardness of rural (and, by extension, indigenous) Guatemalans, who were the FRG's base. They are, once again, engañados or duped. The fact that the PP's vote came primarily from Guatemala City should spread the blame around a little. But in fact these parties mobilize a wide range of tactics and symbolics that may, as Nick Copeland (2007) argues, draw on what remains of the revolutionary imagination. Both parties have allied with former leftists and astutely meld populist discourse with strongman promises of order and security, anticorruption campaigns, development projects, and direct cash payments to former civil patrollers. The army in Guatemala (as elsewhere in Latin America) has also historically been a vehicle for class and "race" advancement, and both parties appeal to strongly held anti-elite and anti-*canche* (white) sentiments.

Like any attempt to represent a nonexistent homogeneity, Guatemala's political parties have tended to either split (like Protestant sects) or become deeply, complexly hybrid (like the Catholic Church, which contains both right-wing Opus Dei and liberation theology, priests and nuns who joined the guerrillas and clergy who used confession to rat people out to the army). The military parties, however, have presented a populist authoritarian face with unusual consistency over the past fifteen years, while other parties win national elections only to disintegrate when dumped from power on a wave of popular discontent. Well aware of their sanguinary past, many people would no sooner vote for parties led by generals than stick pins in their own eyes. But others, even in sites of genocide like Zacualpa, are more sanguine, seeing their vote as a pragmatic move to hook into an effective clientelist distribution network. The Zacualpa mayor says he was formerly with the URNG, and after winning with the FRG switched in turn to the officialist UNE Party in 2011 (when he won again). Similarly McAllister, hearing an angry Chupolense announce "Here, we would never vote for the FRG!" and imagining it bespoke a triumph of *Nunca Más*–style historical memory (Never again!), was chastened when he went on to explain that this was because a previous FRG mayor had promised aid for building houses that had never arrived. As the state becomes a mediator for aid, political parties and projects (just like social movements) have begun to serve as investment opportunities and *gestionadores de fondos* (as with the ONG-ización of the URNG). The same journalist who came to support the Zacualpa mayor was later approached by a different party and offered a place on their candidate list for the Congress. She would just have to pay them Q10,000 plus her expenses — an investment, they assured her, she would make back many-fold once in office. She declined. Like all of the modalities of post-genocide Guatemala that we have examined, current state functioning carries along older ways of working (including violence) as well as complex reciprocities and long-standing networks of patronage. And perhaps, in Guatemala and elsewhere, only those with no experience in the rough-and-tumble worlds of sausage making and politics expect something more idealistic, more transparent, more "transitional government by the book."

The frustrations and compromises pragmatism imposes as the condition of political efficacy inspire other Guatemalans to imagine ways around it, including overt desires for more necropolitics. The fall before the 2003 elections, McAllister spent a pleasant hour lamenting Ríos Montt's candidacy for the presidency with a thoughtful and progressive-minded taxi driver. "How is all this going to get resolved?" she asked, rhetorically. "Yo creo que sólo matando a un montón de gente, usted" (I think only by killing a whole bunch of people), he replied, perhaps less rhetorically. Describing this conversation to a friend who is a former guerrilla, McAllister was surprised to find she supported the driver's plan: "Yes, I've often thought that the first step to fixing things around here would be to get rid of everyone who has ever been in the army — I calculate it at about 300,000 people. Borrón y cuenta nueva. [Erase the tab and begin again.]" Her figures included her own father, an army officer of the 1963 generation.

Yet progressives, former guerrillas, and renowned Mayan activists do sometimes find themselves working for former enemies in the complex site and stake of struggle that is the state. A seasoned organizer said, in disgust, "Did we spend our youth trying to destroy this unjust system, only to dedicate our adulthood to perfecting it?" But others have also sometimes accomplished long-term goals such as state apologies, reparations, increased Mayan representation, bringing the perpetrators of genocide to court, or novel transnational justice projects like the UN-backed Commission against Corruption (CICIG), which grew out of attempts to rein in the death squad–connected clandestine apparatuses. People do take office and do a few things besides stealing, and there are different people doing it than before. While far from a proportionate representation of their demographic weight, many more Maya, more women, and more Mayan women than before the war are serving in Congress, in ministries, in town halls, in the courts, and throughout the governmental bureaucracy, hooking in to new forms of networking, forming potential leaders, and disbursing funds. Sometimes these alliances close down political options, but like the connections of cooperación during and after the war years, and the emerging cosmopolitanisms from below of returning exiles, circulating migrants, Omnilife entrepreneurs, transnationalizing antimining activists, and urban artists, they also work in remaking a social fabric, in restocking seed piles, preparing terrain.

Much has been made recently, at least in New Age circles and Hollywood disaster films, of the Mayan "prophecy" that the world would end in 2012. Serious Mayan horologists dismiss the doomsday scenario, pointing out that the end of one b'aktun is just the beginning of another. Some activists, however, are lashing together the promise of a cosmic realignment with their everyday struggles for a more equitable distribution of power to glean hope in times of trouble. Powerful affect circulates around the threat and promise of an end time—whether it is the Mayan guerrilla leader Pablo Ceto's conjoining of two clandestine movements; or the state's scorched-earth erasure of hundreds of villages and sowing of new subjectivities through reeducation, civic action, and entrepreneurial self-fashioning; or Evangelical imaginings of apocalypse; or those who welcome a generative catastrophe in 2012. This is aftermath. Mostly, world historical change happens in slow motion as hegemonies are challenged and, little by little, sometimes without quite knowing how or why, people change their ways of living. But there are also coyunturas, moments when things move very fast, and forms of collective life hang in the balance. We hope the essays gathered here, which trace both slow accumulations and sudden transformations, help us understand the space and time of aftermath so that we can prepare for new and different sowings in the conviction that other harvests are still possible.

Notes

1. Guatemalans often use this ambivalent term, which means "forcible-voluntary," to describe the not-so-covert threat of coercion that has historically undergirded and subverted many of the ostensible forms of liberal citizenship (Schirmer 1998).

2. Over eighteen months the CEH opened fourteen offices throughout the country to collect testimonies. Over twenty thousand people gave them information, and the Commission documented 7,517 cases of human rights violations, which the authors admit constitute only a fraction of what actually occurred.

3. Reluctantly and stingily, in the case of the USSR, which disapproved of the armed struggle (Gleijeses 2002). In the case of Cuba, moreover, it should be noted that those responsible for fomenting revolution were quite transparent about which forms of revolutionary struggle they felt merited funding and which did not, and how groups had to transform themselves organizationally to receive funding. This had a significant impact on the viability of particular guerrilla groups. In Mexico, for example, the friendly relations of the Cuban and Mexican states meant Mexican guerrillas had almost no external support and fizzled out quickly. In Guatemala the EGP's mass organizational strategy was not one the Cubans supported, impoverishing it and disastrously diminishing its ability to purchase weapons.

4. Text for panel 15: A woman is explaining: "So, many NGOs let the government off the hook: They can get international funding for public works, education, highways and who knows what and that way the government doesn't have to worry about the people, which is its duty. Panel 16: "Other NGOs give their countries a presence here and they make treaties with the government to sell us their products or buy up land, or drill for oil. . . ." (the image shows imports from Europe and the United States and coffee being exported in return). Panel 17: A man says, "In other words, cooperation doesn't come free." "Well no, my friend, don't let them make a fool of you! Panel 18: "In addition, the NGOs need to do projects to get money for their cars, their houses, and their workers." "Oh, I see! That's why they show up in our communities to offer us their products, saying that they're the best." Panel 19: "Yes, just like the vendors in the market." "Well it seems to me that the NGOs are just like middlemen. They profit off us by bringing projects and they end up keeping a bunch of the money."

PART I

SURVEYING THE LANDSCAPE
Histories of the Present

FIVE HUNDRED YEARS

Guatemala has more than its share of martyrs but few, if any, national heroes. It is impossible to imagine a child of a Guatemalan president being named after an indigenous leader or a peasant revolutionary, as were Cuauhtémoc Cárdenas and Emiliano Zedillo, the sons of Mexican presidents from opposing ends of the political spectrum. Of Central America's three major New Left insurgencies — the Farabundo Martí National Liberation Front in El Salvador, the Sandinista National Liberation Front in Nicaragua, and the Guatemalan National Revolutionary Unity — only the last didn't take the name of an idealized leader whose death symbolized frustrated national aspirations.

One reason for this distinction is the persistence of the country's extreme racial divide, which has restricted the kind of multiclass politics that memorializes popular figures like Emiliano Zapata and Augusto Sandino. In Mexico by the late colonial period, an expanding economy had begun to break down indigenous ethnicity in the central valley into a homogeneous rural identity, which, though still ethnically marked, allowed for the emergence of fluid alliances (Knight 1994: 78). Peasants participated on all sides during Mexico's tumultuous nineteenth and twentieth centuries, yet a great many marched on the winning side of liberal-national history: independence from Spain, anti-imperialist struggles against the United States and France, the rise to power of Benito Juárez and Porfirio Díaz, and, of course, the Mexican Revolution.

Guatemala's backwater colonial economy, in contrast, allowed for the consolidation and endurance of distinct indigenous identities centered on residential communities; the nineteenth-century coffee economy created an agrarian proletariat defined along racial lines. Indigenous communities were singled out as sources of labor; workers were conscripted through a series of extra-economic "incentives," including forced labor drafts, debt peonage, and vagrancy laws. Whole villages became captives of specific planters, who relied on them not just for labor but, unable to maintain a full-time labor force, to subsidize, through ongoing subsistence production, the nutritional needs of workers during the off-season. Indigenous peasants, in turn, used the wages they did receive to maintain and even revive community traditions and rituals—for example, *cofradías* (Catholic saint cults), *fiestas* (celebrations of specific saints), and *cabildos* (indigenous administrative institutions, associated with Spanish colonialism)—even as the land base that traditionally underwrote such activities was coming under intense pressure.

As a result, the concordance of liberal nationalism with a form of capitalism that deepened rather than dissipated racial identity generated a stable opposition: on one side stood indigenous communities allied with the Catholic Church, defending communal land and local autonomy; on the other were modernizing liberals pushing to alienate the corporate protections of both church and indigenous cabildo. When liberals took control of the state and its ideological apparatus in 1871, indigenous mobilization was uniformly portrayed as an obstacle to achieving their nation. In 1951, in the middle of Guatemala's "national-popular" decade, the historian Daniel Contreras (1951) did try to claim Totonicapán's Atanasio Tzul, who led a significant uprising in 1820, as a national *procer*, or statesman, paving the way to independence from Spain. This one exception aside, nationalist intellectuals nearly unanimously blamed the failures of Guatemalan liberalism—the fall of the first postcolonial liberal regime, the destruction of the highland Estado de los Altos, the collapse of the Central American Federation, the endurance of Rafael Carrera's conservative regime—on indigenous obstinacy.

The 1910 Mexican Revolution and the myths it generated inspired historians to search Mexico's agrarian past for the Revolution's origins and antecedents, yielding a rich historiography. Scholars set Mexico's revolutionary history within a context of long-term agrarian transformation, drawing on research done on other twentieth-century revolutions (Russia, China, Cuba, Algeria, various African nations, and Vietnam) and on concepts associated with peasant and subaltern studies. Guatemalan historiography, in contrast, came forth not in the flush of revolutionary victory but in the midst of counterrevolutionary terror. Starting in the 1970s historians and anthropologists, driven by an urgency to publicize and explain escalating repression against mostly indigenous peasants, produced studies that sketched out the history of the forced labor, stolen land, and militarized politics that formed the foundation of Guatemala's plantation regime (Smith 1990; Carmack 1988; Handy 1984; Cambranes 1985; Piel 1995; McCreery 1994). But subsequent scholarship failed to follow up on this work. While it is taken for granted that repression has played a central role in mediating community-state relations over the centuries, there is no long-frame rural sociology that examines how forms of violence, both oppositional and pacifying, changed over time, and how those changes indexed specific economic regimes and political epochs. As a result, accounts of Guatemala's post-1954 civil war tend to be either ultradeterministic (holding unspecified racism and exploitation responsible for the conflict) or ultracontingent (conflating the causes of the war with its most immediate provocation, often in one localized region).

Violence itself accounts for a lack of in-depth analysis of rural violence. No one in Mexico would think to explain the Mexican Revolution by trying to document whether it was the Zapatistas or the Federales who fired the first shot in Morelos, largely because the country has a vital intellectual class and a fully realized historiography that would render that exercise meaningless. But such an approach did consume much of the postbellum debate in Guatemala, where state terror had eliminated, either by execution or exile, a generation of scholars.

A case in point is the Guatemalan historian Severo Martínez Peláez, who in the 1970s had begun to sketch out a longue durée framework for studying rural violence. Martínez Peláez is best known as the author of *Patria del Criollo*, published in 1970, which today is often criticized for defining indigenous identity as something created whole cloth by Spanish colonialism. But it also was an early effort to take seriously the generative and repressive function of what he called "colonial language." "The colonial regime," Martínez Peláez wrote, "was a regime of terror," and needed to be that way (2009: 264). He had planned to follow up this book with a study of agrarian indigenous protest from the colonial period through independence, compelled to do so, as he put it, by the "current situation." At the time, violence against peasant activists, increasingly indistinguishable from the savagery inflicted on the urban opposition, was on the rise and about to enter a new stage with the 1978 Panzós massacre and the ensuing scorched-earth campaign. But he was forced to flee to Mexico at the end of the 1970s and therefore didn't go beyond surveying episodic and colonial indigenous *motines*, or riots — more often than not provoked by elite overreaction to peaceful petitioning of grievances. But extrapolating from Martínez Peláez's (1991) initial review, five dis-

tinct stages of agrarian mobilization and repression can be identified as playing a "decisive role," as he put it, in the formation of the modern Guatemalan
state, leaving the country on the threshold of the 1981–83 genocide.

1524–1712

Following the shock of the Conquest and the consolidation of colonial institutions—which included drastic demographic collapse and forced resettlement of survivors into controllable communities—Spanish rule in what is
now Guatemala, as it did in most of Mesoamerica, entered into what Friedrich Katz has called a *pax hispanica*, a period of notable quiescence and stability. In Guatemala, Q'eqchi's in the area of the Verapaces resisted Spanish domination for decades and retained a degree of brokered (through the
Dominicans) autonomy throughout the seventeenth century. For hundreds
of years the lowland Petén jungle, which extended east into what is now
Belize and north to the Yucatán, offered sanctuary to those who refused to
be incorporated into the colonial state; communities around eastern Chiquimula, as well as those in the far reaches of the Cuchumatanes, continued for
decades to withstand Spanish incursions (Jones 1998; see also Matthew and
Oudijk 2007; Restall and Asselbergs 2007).

   Yet in the core Mam, K'iche', and Kaqchikel highland zones, the Spanish established authority quickly. There existed no common language or tradition among these Maya, as in the more rebellious Andes, to unite sub-
jugated peoples. And within a generation of the Conquest, the complexity
that defined pre-Columbian politics and society in this region had been
muted. Noble lineages throughout the western and northern highlands continue to this day, yet by the middle colonial period *macehualization*—the erosion of aristocratic hierarchies and absorption of noble families into a more
diffuse population largely made up of *macehuales* (commoners) and led by
principales (elders)—had the effect of removing the nobility as an institution or symbol through which opposition to Spanish rule could be mounted
(see Pastor 1987: 323–44). Land for subsistence production was plentiful,
which allowed survivors to participate in the colonial economy on relatively
good terms. Forced labor in the mines of Huehuetenango and in the indigenous hinterland of the colonial capital, though onerous, was nowhere near
as central a colonial institution in Guatemala as it was in Mexico or Peru.
Many communities, including central ones like Santiago Atitlán, had a minimal Spanish presence throughout much of the seventeenth century, while
the presence of mendicant orders such as the Franciscans and Dominicans
helped buffer against too heavy *repartimiento* (forced labor) or tribute de-

mands levied by *encomenderos* (Spaniards granted a land concession settled by indigenous peoples), royal officials, and the secular clergy (not belonging to one of the orders, often associated with the Catholic hierarchy; van Oss 1986). Spanish institutions that did take hold often allowed indigenous leaders to take a stake in them. In K'iche' areas, for instance, descendents of precolonial lineages helped collect tribute, carry out censuses, organize work obligations, enforce church attendance, and adjudicate local disputes; principales from Quetzaltenango negotiated new rights, including the right to operate stores in the city plaza, in exchange for help in suppressing the 1712 Tzeltal uprising in Chiapas (Grandin 2000a: 45).

1712-1821

That uprising, which took place shortly after the ascension of the interventionist Bourbons to the Spanish Crown, brought the pax hispanica to an end. Provoked by intensified extractive demands, the revolt quickly expanded geographically through dozens of villages north and east of San Cristóbal. It also escalated ideologically, taking on a strong millennial cast as rebel leaders pledged their allegiance to an incarnate Virgin and proclaimed a "republic" beholden to neither God nor king. Language divisions among Chiapan Mayans limited the revolt, although rebels compensated by terrorizing neighboring towns that refused to join the insurrection, completely razing some communities and forcibly conscripting residents of others. Royal troops, with reinforcements from Guatemala, launched a punitive counterinsurgency, taking a year to completely pacify the insurrection. Martínez Peláez identifies this campaign as previewing one of the basic "modalities of repression" subsequently deployed by colonial and republican officials against indigenous mobilization, be they contained "riots" or transcommunity revolts: horrific, exemplary violence, including the wholesale destruction of insurgent communities and public executions of leaders followed by proclamations of forgiveness and often some concessions, including promises to rein in local abuses. Martínez Peláez locates in the suppression of this revolt, even more than in the violence of the Conquest, the elite race fear that would psychically structure state-indigenous relations for centuries to come. A hundred years after the event, he writes, *criollos* (Spaniards born in the Americas) were holding annual masses to thank God for the defeat of the Tzeltals; decades after independence, a panoramic painting could be found in Guatemala's old Audiencia, the royal administration building, depicting "massacres of ladinos, massacres of rebels, the torture and hanging of clergy and the torture of rebel leaders, towns burned to the ground by the insurgents, other towns reduced to ashes by the repressors, all presented with the most exact detail" (1977: 6).

The frequency and intensity of revolts increased throughout Mesoamerica in the century that followed, with each riot and uprising signaling that, as Martínez Peláez writes, the "limits of the tolerable" in any given community had been reached (1991: 7). Fifty serious indigenous riots took place in what is now Guatemala between 1710 and independence from Spain in 1821. (There were probably more, considering the poor communication of the time.) Plagues, famines, droughts, and other natural catastrophes could still, as they did in the earlier colonial period, instigate unrest, but increasingly the provocations were intrusive Bourbon efforts to strengthen colonial administration and regulate nearly every aspect of social life: alcohol, cockfighting, religion, education, burial rituals, dietary habits, and sanitation practices. Spain also demanded more and more taxes and tributes in order to fund its wars with other European empires. An expanding regional economy strengthened the power and wealth of local criollo elites, who took advantage of a royal state distracted by interimperial war to push their wheat and cattle haciendas deeper into municipal *ejidos* (common lands, often administered by indigenous cabildos) and step up their efforts to press labor, revenue, and land from indigenous communities. At the same time, the trend toward social secularization—due to migration and increased commerce—led to a growing class divide separating principales from commoners, beginning the unraveling of the patriarchal expectations of obligation and deference that bound together high and low, men and women, placing further stress on communities.

Starting around 1811, simultaneously with a massive, violent uprising (upward of half a million people lost their lives) led by the Catholic priests Miguel Hidalgo and José María Morelos that was spreading through Mexico's central valley, the pace of indigenous protests picked up in Guatemala. Riots and uprisings took place in Santiago Sacatepéquez (1811), Patzicía (1811 and 1821), Momostenango (1812), Comalapa (1812), Sololá (1813), Chichicastenango (1813), Santa Ana Malacatán (1814), San Juan Ostuncalco (1815), Quetzaltenango (1815), San Martín Jilotepeque (1815), Santa María Chiquimula (1814 and 1818), San Andrés Sajcabajá (1819), Santo Domingo (1821), and San Francisco El Alto (1821). And in 1820 in Totonicapán and surrounding communities a full-scale insurrection broke out.[1] Yet these protests did not coalesce into a movement similar in scope or intensity to the Hidalgo and Morelos revolt. Historians of that revolt describe distinct regional variation in the levels of support it received from rural communities; the rebellion was stronger in areas, such as Jalisco and Bajío, that had experienced the intensified commercial agricultural production that generated grievances as well as, by significantly breaking down community autonomy, the possibility of joining the kind of transregional, multiclass alliances that powered the rebellion. But Guatemala's situation corresponded more closely to those Mexican regions where communities still retained significant land and cultural integrity, where support for Hidalgo was either mixed or nonexistent. Bourbon-period pressure on rural community life in Guatemala did generate unrest, as did expectations of emancipation associated with the French Revolution and the 1812 liberal Spanish Constitution. But complaints remained localized. Furthermore Guatemalan criollos continued to remain loyal to the Crown, preferring, until Mexico's final break with Spain left them no choice, not to be left alone with a racially distinct majority population. This opposition of liberal-nationalists standing in fearful antagonism to rural society (as opposed to allying with rural society against a common enemy, be it the Crown, conservatives, or foreigners) would form the basic premise of Guatemala's counterinsurgent nationalism.

1821–1871

This period is marked by the steady erosion of the ability of indigenous communities, through their political representatives, to play off local and government elites to their advantage, as the Church's power was contained and regional and national interests moved toward convergence. The process was slowed somewhat during the neocolonial restoration of Rafael Carrera, but it intensified after 1871, as the coffee state mounted an all-out assault on communal autonomy.

For nearly two decades after independence from Spain in 1821, national politics was dominated by near constant conflict between liberals, generally composed of the urban and provincial middle class, and conservatives, mostly from Guatemala City's old colonial merchant and government aristocracy. Indigenous communities at first largely stayed out of interelite conflict and indeed used it to reestablish autonomy lost during the late Bourbon period. Yet once they got the upper hand on conservatives, liberals—both those based in Guatemala City and then in the short-lived highland separatist republic of the Estado de Los Altos, with its capital in Quetzaltenango—put into place an aggressive program designed to dismantle the Catholic and indigenous corporate protections, including efforts to alienate communal land and "extinguish aboriginal tongues," thus pushing many communities, particularly those in southern Quiché, Sololá, Chimaltenango, and Quetzaltenango, into open rebellion. Uniting in 1837 behind a revolution led by Rafael Carrera, within two years the Estado de los Altos had been forcibly reincorporated into Guatemala, and a long conservative restoration had begun (Taracena Arriola 1997: 314).

Carrera's assumption of power in Guatemala City had a contradictory effect on Indian-state relations. It led to at least a partial restoration of local indigenous authority, a respite augmented by a sharp economic downturn. His government abrogated liberal laws that sought to nationalize local authority, restored the tithe, and reinstated the colonial *Leyes de Indias*, which reestablished indigenous municipal autonomy. In towns throughout the highlands, principales re-erected whipping posts in town plazas and reconstituted their cabildos, which functioned as alternative sources of authority parallel to official ladino-run municipalities (Grandin 2000a; Ebal 1972). The government likewise reestablished the offices of the *fiscal protector de indios* and *corregidores*, colonial administrative posts that, nominally at least, defended the interests of indigenous peoples; communities regained the ability to appeal to a distant authority to settle disputes, with Carrera himself often personally intervening to grant land to aggrieved Indians.

Yet the regime dominated by Carrera and his allies for thirty-one years continued the movement toward secularization, as the state promoted private property, industry, and technological improvement, though at a much slower pace than liberals had previously attempted (Gudmunson and Lindo-Fuentes 1995). Limited indigenous resistance emerged against these changes, particularly against the growing number of ladinos in the countryside. In 1849 communities along the Polochic River protested against ladinos who had taken their land, leading to a minor uprising headed by a Poqomchi' Maya named Feliciano María; in the 1850s guerrillas roamed the Sierra Santa Cruz and harassed foreign settlers and government officials (Grandin 2004: 217). Following Carrera's death in 1865, some indigenous communities began to support dispersed liberal movements to unseat his conservative successors, suggesting some discontent (Bancroft 1887: 415–17). Carrera's rule also consolidated a centralized government, with an increased ability to monopolize fiscal and military authority, as well as the power to project that authority into heretofore remote reaches. (And he proved ruthless in putting down challenges, both from Indians and from elites.) Because Carrera repeatedly stoked fears of racial unrest (of the kind that had broken out with Yucatán's 1848 Caste War, to which Guatemalan elites paid close attention) to intimidate political opponents during his long tenure (and because he did in fact call out his indigenous followers on a number of occasions), he solidified the colonial equation, identified by Martínez Peláez, of race with terror.[2] And while the quasi-restoration of *principal* power did slow the proletarianization of rural society that had begun under the Bourbons, it also ensured that when export capitalism, along with its associated violence, did come with the second liberal state, its arrival would take place along sharply drawn racial lines.

1871–1920

The establishment of the liberal coffee state in 1871 marked the end of a pattern of resistance and rule that had governed Guatemalan rural relations since at least the 1712 Tzeltal revolt. The transformation of the western highland's regional elite—effectively the next generation of the same class who presided over the Estado de los Altos—into a national elite definitively ended the already withered effectiveness of protests, riots, and uprisings to check the aggression of nonindigenous provincials.

Coffee liberals built on the foundations laid down by Carrera to institutionalize and extend Guatemala's modern fiscal-military apparatus. New national legislation governing taxes and property holding hastened the privatization of communal lands, especially in the Pacific piedmont and coastal areas, in the Verapaces, and down into the Lake Izabal basin. At the same time, forced-labor drafts, taxes, military conscription, obligations to provide free or undercompensated labor on public works, and vagrancy laws forced peasants off their own small plots of land and onto plantations. And an expanding militarized bureaucracy made sure they stayed there. Leading to repression were efforts to discipline a workforce to the dictates of plantation wage labor in an economy in which capital was chronically short, wages dismally low, and the population still had at least partial access to subsistence cultivation. Telegraphs and telephones, a fortified ladino militia and military, a professionalized police force and prison system, department prefects, an expanded corps of judges and administrative officials, all funded by coffee revenue and an array of new taxes (that had the added effect of forcing peasants into the wage market in order to be able to pay them), tipped the balance of power definitively in favor of the state. A vicious cycle kicked in: rather than spending money on technological improvements of the means of production, the state and private entrepreneurs invested in the means of repression; rather than promoting technological innovation to further accumulation, capitalists came to rely on a coercive state to guarantee their profits.

The accommodation to this new order was gradual and often brutal. Both individuals and communities found ways to mitigate its worst effects. It was common for men to send their sons to a plantation or a public works project in their stead, or to give one name when they were conscripted and another when they arrived on the job, which meant that warrants dispatched for them when they escaped would be issued in the wrong name. And the archives are filled with letters from village leaders trying to negotiate with *jefes políticos* (department governors) for better terms or to forestall corvée requests. In regions with blurred jurisdictional lines, such as the boundary area separating the departments of Alta Verapaz and Izabal, families hopscotched from one side of the state border to the other, claiming to live in Izabal when agents from Alta Verapaz showed up and vice versa. Yet the absolute need for labor combined with the state's preponderance of force limited the effectiveness of such pleading and maneuvering and often led to violent retaliation. After the mayor of Huitán, a poor Mam community northwest of Quetzaltenango, protested that he couldn't supply any more workers since they were already conscripted, ladino troops arrived to terrorize the town. "They hit them as if they were beasts," the mayor wrote in 1884 to the jefe político in desperation, "[and] commit the worst abuses, robbing corn, poultry, food, and money, raping our wives and daughters" (in Grandin 2000a: 120). In the western highlands, evasive migration was difficult, since there existed little unclaimed land even in remote areas like the far side of the Cuchumatanes. In the northern highlands of Alta Verapaz, individuals, families, and sometimes whole hamlets sought refuge in the Petén or the Polochic lowlands into Belize. But by the end of the nineteenth century, flight became less effective as the state grew more capable of tracking down fleeing workers or debt evaders and as former areas of refuge became crowded and eventually fell under government control (and as its most fertile lands were titled to outsiders), leaving only inhospitable jungle lands as sanctuary.

Community-based protests continued through the first decades of liberal rule, building on anger that had gained speed during the last years of the conservative regime. A violent reaction by local troops to an 1865 protest in the town of San Pedro Carchá, which left eight Q'eqchi's dead, quickened an already established migration down the Polochic Valley to the area that would become the municipality of Panzós. Conflict also broke out in surrounding Alta Verapaz towns in 1877 and 1886. In 1877 in the K'iche' town of Sacapulas, hundreds of residents marched on the department capital, Santa Cruz del Quiché; they were met by the jefe político, who ordered troops to open fire, killing a number of the protestors (Najarro 2005). As throughout the colonial and early republican period, these disputes tended to be centered on material complaints concerning land, labor, and taxes. In Carchá it was over the encroachment of ladinos; in Sacapulas it was to contest the actions of a local planter. A rare instance when reaction took on a prophetic or chiliastic quality was in 1905, when an indigenous preacher traversed the Verapaz woods calling on Q'eqchi's to shed their clothes, embrace poverty, and burn coffee bushes. The liberal state responded to ongoing indigenous protest by arming the ladino towns that were strategically scattered throughout the highlands, turning them into militia garrisons by granting their residents generous land concessions in exchange for counterinsurgent reserve duty. In 1877 K'iche' Momostenango rose in revolt, launching what Robert Carmack describes as "full-scale guerrilla warfare" in reaction to having lost its best piedmont farmland to coffee (1983: 242). The government responded by sending in local ladino militias to "burn houses and crops in all rebel zones in Momostenango," summarily executing rebel leaders and forcibly resettling "many families suspected of aiding the rebels" (243); it was a campaign that both harked back to the pacification of the Tzeltal and previewed future counterinsurgent tactics. In 1898 Kanjobal residents of the remote Cuchumatán mountain town of San Juan Ixcoy, after years of frustrating land litigation fending off the advance of the neighboring ladino town of Chiantla, killed thirty ladinos. Chiantla's ladino militia, with reinforcements from nearby Soloma, responded by taking "ten Indian lives" for each "slain Ladino" (Lovell 2005: 212).

A key threshold in Guatemala's agrarian history had been crossed: after the 1870s, episodic violence not only did not bring about sought-for relief from abuses — as could reasonably be expected during the colonial and Carrera periods — but actually transformed local relations in a way that accelerated dispossession. The Ixcoy uprising was followed by what David McCreery (1994: 289) calls an "orgy of land grabbing at the Indians' expense," much of it by local ladinos who then resold the property to lowland *finqueros* to establish *fincas de mozos*, estates that existed solely to provide peasants access to subsistence land in exchange for their seasonal labor on commercial plantations. Upward of two thousand Momostecos were annually pressed into plantation work following Momostenango's pacification. State terror during this period also helped soften up communities for ladino infiltration, subordinating local indigenous politics and economics to the control of newly arrived, nonindigenous merchants, labor contractors, and politicians. (This subordination, in turn, would serve as a critical flashpoint of conflict during the waves of mobilization that marked the second half of the twentieth century.)

The (temporary) end of direct confrontation between indigenous communities and state agents led to new forms of oppositional politics. In 1884, for example, a widespread conspiracy extended throughout the highlands with the goal of overthrowing the government of President Justo Rufino Barrios (Grandin 1997a). Planned clandestinely and encompassing a wide geographical area, this movement was unique in its scope, as well as in its multiethnic, multiclass, and translinguistic character. (Up to this point, supracommunity mobilizations, such as the Tzul uprising in 1820 in Totonicapán or the Momostenango guerrilla war in 1877, tended to be restricted to one language group.) Tipped off about the plot—which involved providing coordinated support for an expeditionary force that would enter Guatemala from Tapachula, Mexico—federal troops easily repelled the invaders; local officials arrested 182 conspirators throughout the highlands, seventy-one from indigenous communities. Unlike the indiscriminate scorched-earth campaign launched against Momostenango seven years earlier, Barrios opted for more discretionary, targeted repression. In the past, preemptive reaction or punitive retaliation against indigenous protest was generally directed by local elites, whether or not they had the consent of faraway Guatemala City officials. In this case, the president opted to personally direct the *pacificación de occidente*, an indication of the merger of regional and national interests mentioned earlier. Barrios traveled by rail up the Pacific coast, ordering public executions in at least sixteen communities, whose geographic distribution, ranging from the coffee piedmont and the central highlands to the Cuchumatanes and the Mexican border, demonstrates the diversity of the movement: San Sebastián, San Felipe, San Andrés Villa Seca, Cerro Gordo, Santo Domingo, Cantel, San Gabriel, Cajolá, San Antonio Sacatepéquez, San Pedro Sacatepéquez, San Pedro Saloma, Todos Santos, San Pedro Necta, Ixtahuacán, Colotenango, and San Sebastian Coatán. Most surprising is the involvement of towns in thinly populated and remote Huehuetenango, where a punitive expedition ravaged the "entire department" with "fines and executions" (Watanabe 2000: 321–40). As in the case of Momostenango and Ixcoy, the violence both pacified and transformed social relations; in Cantel a heavy fine of 15,000 pesos forced residents, who until then had successfully avoided plantation labor, to the coast to take wage jobs to pay the penalty.

In addition to representing a deepening integration among oppositional forces, this 1884 conspiracy and its suppression reveal two trends building since at least the end of the colonial period. First, conflict was ever more driven by rivalries *between* communities, usually over land, as population growth, commercialization of agriculture, and ladino machinations placed sustained pressure on *campesino* (peasant) and communal holdings. Between 1830 and the end of the nineteenth century, in the K'iche' and Kaqchikel core of the western highlands, at least twenty-three serious disputes broke out between historic indigenous communities, at times involving pitched, deadly battles between opposing residents (McCreery 1994: 219). Second, conflict *within* communities, between competing individuals or factions, increasingly defined the intensity of protest. The pressures coffee brought to bear on Mayan peasants catalyzed these inter- and intracommunity conflicts, each feeding off and shaping the other. As with the earlier Bourbon reforms, the commodification of social relations and the growth of regional economies provided new opportunities for wealth accumulation, upward mobility, and corruption, which roiled internal community relations. What was now different was the sustained and growing pressure on subsistence agriculture, which strained internal communal hierarchies, since much of the authority of principales was founded on their ability to provide at least enough land for families to survive. In Cantel a decades-long land struggle against neighboring ladino and indigenous communities aggravated divisions within the community, between commoners who wanted to apply liberal law to privatize the town's ejidos and sell land to a group of investors to establish a textile factory and principales who opposed the sale. Elders who made up the latter group were those executed for their role in the 1884 conspiracy, betrayed by the leader of the arriviste faction who fingered them to Barrios's jefe político. Likewise the 1877 Momostenango insurgency revealed a community fractured with internal divisions since the second half of the eighteenth century, with one bloc joining the pacification campaign to put down their rivals.

This intensification of rural violence had the effect of lifting the veil of communal representation to reveal the multiple interests and contradictions lurking beneath. Rather than leading to a dilution of communal identity, this heated-up intramural competition deepened appeals to ethnic solidarity: rivalrous factions continued to rely, arguably even more than in the past, when community leadership was well-defined, on the language of community to establish their legitimacy. Yet at the same time, conflict within and between communities strengthened the state; even as contending factions invoked the name of *el pueblo*, the rapid constriction of subsistence agriculture made it difficult to establish intercommunal sources of authority through reciprocal relations of obligation and deference centered on the provision of land. As such, indigenous rivals increasingly called on government judges, politicians, and troops to back up their claims. This dynamic, by which community identification deepened even as state power increased, was especially pronounced during the two long periods of early twentieth-century dictatorship, presided over by Manuel Estrada Cabrera and Jorge Ubico, respectively.

1920–1978

The concurrent growth of the state and the spread of coffee capitalism caught rural peoples in a pincer movement. On the one hand, an expanding government bureaucracy put all of its local expressions—police, military, jails, telephones, telegraphs, roads, judges, and mayors—to the task of ensuring a plantation labor force. Taxes, military conscription, obligations to provide free or undercompensated labor on public works, and vagrancy and debt laws pushed campesinos onto the plantation. Once there they found themselves in a private zone of sovereignty, utterly dependent on the will of the planter. Plantations had their own jails, stockades, and whipping posts, and planters fought any attempt by the state to intervene in their labor relations or even to use their workers on public projects.

As traditional resistance strategies of protest or evasion proved ever less effective with the growth of the state, rural peoples increasingly engaged the rhetoric of liberal nationalism directly, working through an expanded bureaucracy and court system to contest abuses. Turning to ladino notaries, lawyers, and hired wordsmiths to draft their complaints, indigenous petitioners increasingly endorsed a hope that justice would be achieved not by a return to a colonial past but by the fulfillment of national and human development. Similar to other democratic movements of the late nineteenth century and early twentieth, indigenous protesters often used a distinction between *slavery* and *freedom* as a rhetorical gauge to measure this progress. "Since the French Revolution did away with lords and their privilege," forty indigenous peons wrote, with the help of a ladino lawyer, to the government in 1934, "slavery has been abolished everywhere on the planet. . . . The Indian should not be exploited to the point where he is converted into a slave as in days of old. . . . We are made to work for free as it used to be done for the feudal lords" (Schmölz-Häberlein 1996: 226–48).

In Guatemala forced labor was not a vestigial memory of a distant past. The most elemental promises of liberalism—the equality of rights and the denial of hereditary entitlements—were often floridly affirmed even as they were absolutely denied. This in fact made the rhetoric of freedom that much more potent and the contrast with actual practice more vivid, investing universal and abstract claims to citizenship and equality with the hope of release from the daily experiences of coercion, humiliation, and violence.

At the same time, with avenues of direct, violent action closed off, rural peoples began to channel their oppositional activities into organizations associated with modern mass-interest politics, and would continue to do so throughout the vicissitudes of the twentieth century. Community-based protest continued (the state exacted violent reprisals against oppositional activity in Nebaj in 1936, Tacaná in 1937, and Patzicía in 1944), but starting in the years after World War I politics was increasingly routed through vehicles affiliated with regional or transnational associations. In the 1950s and 1960s these included political parties, labor federations, and peasant leagues. After the 1960s these organizations were supplemented by cooperative and religious associations, cultural and human rights groups, and armed opposition movements. Status, religious, class, and political divisions that had emerged in the previous century were increasingly politically organized around these supracommunity associations and identifications. In turn, those associations and identifications served as the portals through which broad national and even international sets of ideas, alliances, and conflicts entered communities, linking what had previously largely been provincial tensions to larger political, economic, and ideological struggles.

Three critical conjunctures determined the history of rural violence during this period. The first started in the years after World War I, accelerated with the fall of Manuel Estrada Cabrera in 1920, and ended with the ascension of another dictator, Jorge Ubico, in 1931. The importance of this reform period, the country's first "democratic spring," has been underemphasized; it was arguably as consequential as the more celebrated 1944 October Revolution. The sudden emergence of multiparty competition opened the way for grassroots participation in civic life as never before, and political parties established affiliates throughout the countryside. Rural peoples, both those whose primary identification was rooted in a specific community as well as the country's growing agrarian proletariat, fully entered modern mass politics. Bringing together a diverse coalition that included artisans, laborers, peasants, intellectuals, middle-class and provincial professionals, and middling planters, the Partido Unionista best represented the democratic impulse of the 1920s. No Guatemalan Zapata rode forth from the Mayan countryside carrying aloft the banner of agrarian revolution, yet the rural highlands did simmer. Mexican *agraristas* and Salvadoran communists arrived to help organize *fincas*, and newspapers reported protests in a majority of rural departments among plantation workers (McCreery 1994: 296–300). Planters accused Unionistas of making easy and dangerous promises of agrarian reform and an end to forced labor to Indians and peasants, and the U.S. press charged the party with trying to "export" their revolution to Honduras. The three main areas of mobilization, including a sporadic series of strike waves, were the Pacific coastal and piedmont plantation zone, the foreign-dominated banana enclaves in the east, and the highland coffee fincas in Alta Verapaz. Strikes also took place on haciendas deep in the core K'iche' zone around Totonicapán, where workers demanded that they be paid in cash.

The second conjuncture was, of course, the October Revolution, particularly its 1952 agrarian reform. This reform was an attempt both to project the political and social reforms adopted after 1944 into that zone of planter power mentioned earlier and to bring about development through an extension of political and economic rights to rural peasants. The centerpiece of both objectives was the local agrarian committees, or CALs, for its Spanish acronym. Just as, a century earlier, the restoration of indigenous municipalities was the most defined expression of Rafael Carrera's political project—creating a parallel network of authority to weaken, or at least slow the advance of, rural ladino power—CALs were the thin edge of the wedge of the October Revolution's purest democratic impulse. They served both as the institutional front line in the struggle waged against the class power of the landed elite and an important arena of consciousness-raising. The five-person composition of the CALs ensured that they were always in the control of the local campesinos: one committee member was nominated by the department governor, one by the local community, and three by the local peasant union. Many times the president of the union and the president of the CAL were the same person, and little practically separated the two institutions. In other words, the leader of the peasant union petitioning for land was often the government representative charged with initially ruling on the petition. It was to these committees that land claims were made; moreover these committees were responsible for inspecting the disputed land, judging the validity of the claims, and then passing the decision up to departmental and national committees. By 1954 there were three thousand CALs operating throughout the country, and by the time of Jacobo Arbenz's overthrow, nearly 1.7 million acres were either expropriated or in the process of being expropriated.

The seriousness of the threat CALs represented was matched by the viciousness of the reprisals. In the months following Arbenz's resignation, the police, military, and ad hoc vigilante groups, either at the command of anticommunist committees or private planters, murdered between three thousand and five thousand Arbencistas (Grandin 2004). At the United Fruit Company plantation Jocotán on the southern coast, upward of one thousand plantation organizers were murdered after being taken into custody. In the plaza of the banana town of Morales, United Fruit's head foreman, Rosendo Pérez, executed over two dozen captured unionists, along with Alaric Benett, an Afro-Guatemalan union leader and congressman. These are the documented cases; most violence took place quietly, against troublesome yet less prominent activists who lived in remote areas not covered by the national or international press.

Land reform, both its application and its revocation in 1954, shaped the way many rural communities experienced the ensuing civil war. In the 1970s many of the peasant leagues that united to form the Comité de Unidad Campesina—the CUC, the most consequential indigenous campesino organization in Guatemalan history—could trace their roots back to the 1944–54 period, and the CUC grew strong in communities that witnessed high levels of mobilization during the land reform, such as Joyabaj, Comalapa, San Juan Sacatepéquez, Tecpán, and San Martín Jilotepeque.[3] On the coffee plantations of San Marcos the Rebel Armed Forces (FAR) in the 1960s and then the Revolutionary Organization of the People in Arms (ORPA) in the 1970s found support among plantation workers through the social networks created by the CALs. At times the connection between the CALs and the oppositional movements of the 1960s and 1970s was direct. In Cahabón, Alta Verapaz, the president of the CAL in the 1950s joined the Communist Party (PGT) in the 1960s. Most often the link was patrilineal. Juan Coc's father was the president of the CAL on Finca El Tesoro in San Miguel Uspantán, Quiché. Forced to flee after the 1954 counterrevolution, his family migrated to the Ixcán lowlands, and Coc became a leader of the region's cooperative movement, which was destroyed by the military in the late 1970s (Yoldi 1996). In Cantel, David Ordóñez Colop, general secretary of the peasant union, successfully obtained the return of over a thousand acres expropriated and given to the neighboring ladino town of Salcajá after the 1884 executions. An Arévalista in 1944 and an Arbencista in 1950, after 1954 Ordóñez joined a reformist political party and was elected mayor. In 1967 he successfully organized the town to stop the army from building a base on a site considered sacred, and in 1982, as an old man, Ordóñez was one of the leaders of a successful fight to reject the military's attempt to establish a civil patrol. Captured and tortured once in 1981, he was murdered by security forces in 1984. Ordóñez never joined the guerrillas, but his sons did. "I am a *revolucionario histórico*," Ordóñez would say to his impatient sons, while they regretted that he "never understood the armed struggle, the struggle of the masses" (Grandin 2004: 178). In Rabinal, a municipality that suffered over twenty massacres in 1982, the October Revolution produced successive generations of Achí militants. Emilio Roman López was an Arbencista and follower of Tomás Tecú Chiquito, a Communist Party militant during the October Revolution. Turned Evangelical pastor after 1954, López organized other Achís in a campaign of sabotage to protest the right-wing theft of the 1962 municipal elections. Under the pseudonym "Pascual," López took charge of FAR operations in Baja Verapaz. After his assassination in 1968, a number of his Achí followers were among the first group that crossed into the Ixcán to form the Guerrilla Army of the Poor (Ibarra 2000: 284–85; Macías 1997: 107–8, 121–23; Debray and Ramírez 1975: 265).

If much of the popular base of post-1954 oppositional politics could trace its immediate roots back to the October Revolution, so too could the ensuing counterinsurgency. In response to rural organizing, the military, the state, and private sectors in the decades after 1954 built their own institutional base of peasant support. In the 1960s and 1970s, through military commissioners, planters, and paramilitary groups, the primary vanguard of the counterrevolution, namely the National Liberation Movement (MLN), created a network of rural power in the highlands and on the southern coast, providing land to supporters and tapping into community divisions and hostility toward political liberalization (Velásquez Nimatuj 2002). After Arbenz's fall, instead of a wholesale restoration many finqueros associated with the quasi-fascist MLN opted to let certain families keep land in an effort to cultivate support. In San Vicente Pacaya, on the Pacific coast, Manuel de Jesús Arana reclaimed land taken from him under the Agrarian Reform yet granted small lots to thirty-three families, who went on to join the MLN. Throughout the 1960s tensions escalated between these MLN peasants and Arbencistas turned Partido Revolucionario activists (the PR was the only reformist—but barely so—party allowed to operate after the 1954 coup). Arana was the uncle of Colonel Carlos Arana Osorio, the infamous MLN commander of the Zacapa military base who became president in 1971 (Solano this volume). Immediately after his January inauguration, a detachment of troops occupied San Vicente for over a month. They raped women, captured and tortured dozens of peasants, and executed at least seventeen PR members, many of whom had been involved with the town's CAL or peasant union during the time of Arbenz. The violence destroyed the PR in San Vicente and ended all legal efforts to attain land.

The third conjuncture was the 1970s, when the political nationalization of local grievances described earlier catalyzed with a wholly new phenomenon: between 1954 and 1975 population growth and land enclosures finally closed off subsistence production as a substitute for, or at least significant subsidy to, wage labor. This situation meant that for the first time in the history of rural Guatemala, exploitation was no longer primarily instigated by the avarice and racism of local and national elites but rather by the abstract dictates of a global economy. Following the collapse of the Central American Common Market in 1969 and a decline in global agricultural demand in 1973, export production decreased and Guatemala entered a period of economic stagnation. This crisis intensified communal stratification and immiseration. Now tied through debt and reliance on fertilizer to a cash economy, many farmers increasingly migrated, either to the coast as seasonal agricultural laborers or to the lowland northern agricultural frontiers of the Ixcán and the Petén.

Communities found themselves divided as never before between a newly economically empowered bourgeoisie (involved in labor recruitment, commerce, manufacturing, and specialized agricultural productions) and an impoverished campesino class. Studies conducted during this period describe increasing inequality coinciding with a cultural and political rupture (see Brintnall 1979; Smith 1977). The most famous examination of this process is Ricardo Falla's 1980 work on San Antonio Ilotenango, where many of the new merchants embraced Acción Católica (Catholic Action)—a catechist movement organized by the Catholic Church in the 1950s to promote religious orthodoxy but which by the 1960s had aligned with progressive organizations—as a way to escape the onerous financial obligations of the cofradía system. The conflicts generated by the arrival of Catholic Action moved quickly from the cultural sphere—debates surrounding religious icons, for example—to the economic and political realm as its members organized cooperatives and ran for local political offices that had long been the domain of principales.

Around this time the forms and ideology of rural oppositional politics jumped scale yet again. Rural protest focusing on discrete grievances and comprising distinct organizing experiences (peasant leagues, unions, cooperatives, liberation theology, and the Christian Democratic Party) amalgamated in the 1970s into the nationwide, multiethnic and multilingual CUC, itself allied to both industrial unions and an escalating New Left insurgency that, by the early 1980s, had brought the Guatemalan state to the point of collapse. The alliances and interests that made up this movement, as well as the backlash against it, were diverse and shifting. In many places, particularly in southern Quiché and Chimaltenango, the "modernizers" described by Falla tended to be the social base of the CUC and its allies, while traditionalists supported the MLN. In other areas, like the Polochic Valley, where Catholic Action was weak and planter power strong, traditionalists supported the Left. Throughout the countryside the reasons any one individual, family, or community allied either with the insurgency or the counterrevolution were multifaceted, representing a new level of social complexity that, by allowing for sustained cross-class and cross-ethnic interests, made the moment explosive.

Considering the sweep of rural violence presented here, it is useful to compare the repression of this period to its counterpoint a hundred years earlier. In the 1870s government terror led to consolidation of the national state, the crystallization of an exclusionary nationalism, and the institution of ladino control on a local level. A century later repression in the 1970s had the opposite effect, propelling state dissolution. The massive infusion of U.S. counterinsurgent training and material in the decades after 1954 resulted in neither the pacification of the Left nor stabilization of the country. By investing in the most revanchist sectors of the governing and aspiring classes, foreign intervention led to a rapid erosion of a compromise-seeking center, which in Guatemala was a narrowly circumscribed place to begin with. It was, in a way, a classic crisis of overproduction, a concentration of *too much* repressive capacity in the state's hands, prompting a rapid and precipitous downward spiral of polarization. Facing increased mobilization and demands for reform voiced by a social movement that had united the city and the countryside, indigenous highland communities and coastal plantation workers, the state and the ruling class responded with untold violence and repression, provoking large segments of the population to join the armed movement. The military managed to regroup, launching a centrally orchestrated genocide that prevented a complete collapse. Yet the cataclysm nonetheless led to the dispersal of ladino power in rural communities and the emergence of a pan-Mayan movement that, while by no means eliminating the country's deep-seated racism, did make the political expression of that racism—ladino counterinsurgent nationalism—untenable as a political project.

Toward Genocide

The crisis of the 1970s led to the collapse of the monopoly of violence the state had managed to establish in the 1870s. In response, a cohort of young modernizing officers, who took power in a March 1982 coup, increasingly identified the kind of chaos that plagued Guatemala as an obstacle to national security. The pacification campaign they designed, which included hundreds of brutal massacres, in some ways marked a change from past strategies of violence: it was more centrally directed, sustained over a longer period of time, and executed with greater savagery than past repressive operations. Yet the campaign, ruled to be genocide by the UN Truth Commission, was ultimately different in degree, not in kind; it constituted a structured, historically informed response to a mounting threat, a culmination of anticommunist counterinsurgent state formation that built on long-evolving patterns of rural repression.

The justification for the massacres was based on a belief that indigenous communities were easily manipulated by outsiders, a manipulation made possible by their "closed," caste-like isolation. The killing, then, was specifically designed to cut off indigenous villages from the insurgency and break down the communal structures believed to be the seedbeds of guerrilla support. This explains the singularly savage nature of the counterinsurgency, which, while constituting the most rationalized phase of the war, was executed on the ground with a racist frenzy aimed not just at eliminating the guerrillas and their supporters but at colonizing spaces, symbols, and social relations deemed to be outside of state control.

As part of the pacification, the army placed the onus of keeping a community free of guerrilla influence on the community itself. It did so by requiring all adult men to serve in the infamous Patrullas de Auto-Defensa Civil (Civil Defense Patrols or PACS), responsible for local antisubversive policing (see Kobrak, González-Izás this volume). Repression carried out by PACS has received a good deal of attention from human rights advocates, yet few scholars have connected them to Guatemala's long history of popular participation in local militias, allowing for something of a popular Jacobin citizenship asserted through armed defense of the state (those who have include Kobrak 1997; Smith 1990). At least since the Bourbon reforms, if not earlier, factions within communities have sought institutional venues and ideological legitimacy so as to present their particular interest as community interest. The PACS were an extension of this process, allowing local leaders threatened by the popular movement and hostile to the guerrillas an opportunity to re-establish a power base within their villages, to impose order, and to make claims on the government, doing for the counterrevolution what CUC did for the Revolution.

Drawing on history, the military strategists who designed the 1981–83 genocide believed they could transcend history. Once soldiers had violently severed the relationship between the guerrillas and their social base, the military took charge of reconstruction so as to bring the final integration of Guatemala's rural indigenous population into national structures, thus hoping to finally end the centuries-long cycle of protest and repression. Officers like General Héctor Gramajo, a main architect of the army's 1982 turnaround, understood themselves to be presiding over Guatemala's first true national project, one that would not only remove the causes of rural unrest but would subordinate the private planter and oligarchic interests to a broader general national interest. "We brought government to the village," he boasted (Schirmer 1998: 64).

Victims of the genocide didn't feel history as transcendent, of course, but rather as the accumulated weight of what many had begun to call, around the time the civil war was drawing to a close, "five hundred years of repression." Meanwhile Gramajo's belief that the army would preside over a postwar national project has given way to what social scientists describe as a "captive state," controlled by organized crime, comprising competing factions of the established oligarchy and nouveau-riche military officers and corrupt politicians, involved in car thefts, bus robberies, illegal logging, and arms and drug running, along with more above-board enterprises, such as mining and large-scale planting of African palm for biofuels production. As the essays that follow indicate, a new postwar period of rural violence is well under way.

Notes

1. The definitive study of the Totonicapán uprising is Pollack 2005.
2. For references to events in Yucatán in 1848 and 1849, see Pollack 2005: 373–74.
3. San Martín Jilotepeque was one of the birthplaces of the CUC, and since the 1930s it had been a site of peasant organizing against the Herrera and Leal families, each owning dozens of fincas de mozos, many of which were expropriated but returned after 1954. Hat tip to Elizabeth Oglesby.

DIFFICULT COMPLEMENTARITY
Relations between the Mayan and Revolutionary Movements

In June 2000, the Coordination of Mayan People's Organizations of Guatemala (COPMAGUA) officially disintegrated. With it far more disappeared than simply the entity representing the political aspirations of organized Maya over the six-year implementation of the peace accords. Its dissolution also marked the end of a complex but close relation that had been forged between Mayan organizations and the revolutionary movements. This relationship originated in community organizing in the early 1970s, intensified during the most difficult moments of war and repression, and continued to grow through the following decades amid major transformations in Guatemalan politics. In this essay we tell the story of these relationships, focusing on Guatemalan politics from the perspective of *lo Maya*, in the difficult and ambiguous process of "transition."

The rise and consolidation of indigenous politics in Guatemala, later known as the Mayan movement, is deeply marked by its attachment to the revolutionary movement. In turn, one cannot understand the Guatemalan Revolution without tracing its articulation with the indigenous cause and the increasing legitimacy of an emerging identity: the Pueblo Maya as a People, not "just" an ethnic group. Between 1980 and 2000 these two projects traveled a long, tortuous road together, oscillating between aversion and recognition, sometimes allied with each other and at other times engaged in fraught struggles over leadership and political terrain. There are periods when it is difficult to differentiate the two, since the majority of the revolutionary organizations' bases were indigenous, and most indigenous organizations signed on to the revolutionary cause. Yet the Guatemalan National Revolutionary

Unity (URNG) took positions regarding indigenous issues that led many Maya to feel they were no longer represented there.

After the dissolution of COPMAGUA both the Maya and revolutionary movements were caught up in the flows of "post-peace normalization," with their leaders cozying up to spaces of power and in the process losing a great deal of their legitimacy and counterhegemonic standing. But the alliance between the two seems to be strengthening in precisely the places where it began: in the communities where Mayas, often led by former members of the URNG, are deeply involved in anti-corporate-globalization projects that are founded in transnational recognition of indigenous rights.

Prologue: From Origins to Polarization

The second half of Guatemala's twentieth century was marked by the efforts of various sectors of the population to gain access to the benefits of socioeconomic "progress" and by the enormous barriers the oligarchy, via state policies, threw in their path. Among them were indigenous people, increasingly unwilling to accept their lot of exclusion based on structural racism, and who began to demand equality and participation. Over years of gestation, mobilization occurred primarily in highland communities buffeted by the transformations brought by modernization, even as they retained their indigenous identifications (Brintnall 1979; Falla 1980). Out of these communities emerged a wide range of actions, leaders, and types of demands. For example, the Indigenous Seminars of 1972–79 brought together a highly diverse group of people, including catechists (Catholic lay leaders), linguists, organizers of the Indian Queen pageants of the patron saint festivals, health promoters, teachers, mayors and town council members, a few Catholic priests, and members of the Association of Indigenous Students (Arias 1985; Cojtí 1997), articulating the different political positions being created.

The increasingly restrictive political environment, however, limited how far these connected but divergent political actors could go. One example of the organizing dynamics was the huge enthusiasm for the Campesino Unity Committee (CUC), the peasant organization deeply embedded in communities and emerging from a unifying radicalized religious project, that rapidly gained ground with its calls for struggle against *los ricos* (the rich), even as mounting repression forced it to turn clandestine.

At the beginning of the 1980s increasingly rigid and authoritarian state policies had closed down the possibility for any civil society projects, leaving the revolutionary movement as the only contestatory political option. Indigenous communities became politicized, and in some places, through

FIG 2.1 An indigenous URNG member fixes her hair before lining up with her squadron in the Tzaval camp in Nebaj, where five hundred guerrilla fighters awaited their demobilization in March 1997. PHOTO BY JORGE UZON. USED WITH KIND PERMISSION.

making contact with revolutionary organizations, the mobilization took the form of peasant insurrection (Vela 2009). The state and army responded with repression and violence without limits. A Mayan activist called the harrowing spiral of consciousness-raising, repression, mobilization, massacre, insurrection, and scorched-earth policy "el periodo más oscuro" (the darkest time). The whole country descended into a chaotic whirlwind of unprecedented and brutal violence, leaving more than 200,000 dead and disappeared, primarily in the highlands (CEH 1999; REMHI 1998). The enormous pressures unleashed on these relatively young organizations sharpened the ideological differences that had always existed, leading in the early 1980s to a radicalization in which groups were either with or against the revolutionary forces that later joined to become the URNG.

One part of the incipient indigenous movement decided to also take part in the revolutionary project, whose political logics began to influence indigenous organizations more generally. The figure of the Maya-Ixil Pablo Ceto, aka Nicolás, who was a founder of the CUC and member of the leadership (Dirección General) of the Guerrilla Army of the Poor (EGP), best represents this option. But not everyone saw this as the best route. From the beginning some indigenous people had accused the guerillas of ignoring indigenous demands and treating them with the same racism endemic to the rest of Guatemalan society (MacLeod 2008). At the same time some in the guerrilla organizations accused "culturalists" of selling out or working for the United States. By 1981 the bipolar situation of being *with* or *against* the URNG was so strong that any intermediary efforts by *personajes bisagra*, or "hinge figures," became impossible, even as people kept trying to make connections, even in the most difficult moments of ideological polarization.

In this context the appearance of the Movimiento Indio Tojil is interesting. The Movimiento was an armed Mayan organization that was simultaneously revolutionary and nationalist. They managed to sustain political autonomy in a situation of all-out war, which transformed them into a target of *both* the army and other armed insurgent groups (Bastos and Camus 2003; MacLeod 2008; Uk'u'x B'e 2005). Although they failed militarily, they continued under the name Movement of Support and Mutual Aid (MAYAS) and in 1984 published the foundational document "Guatemala: From the Centralized Bourgeois Republic to the Federal Popular Republic," which proposed the creation of a sovereign "Popular Mayan Republic in federation with a possible Criollo Republic" (MAYAS 1990: 79).[1] The URNG responded dismissively, viewing the proposal within a logic of confrontation rather than of shared goals: "We shouldn't be surprised that in Latin America this tendency is not persecuted or rejected by the sectors that oppress and exploit us. . . . It is also not surprising that North American institutions linked directly or indirectly to the CIA or the Department of State have been promoting such ethnopopulist racism for quite some time" (URNG n.d.: 1) (Covert U.S. backing of the Miskito Contra army against Nicaragua's Sandinista government seemed to justify suspicion toward "divisive" indigenous demands.)

The term *Pueblo Maya* as a form of self-identification among those who understood the indigenous problem within a national perspective — meaning that the Maya are themselves a nation — dates from this moment and was, in part, a result of those polarized times. It arose from the need to differentiate themselves from the guerrillas, who referred to indigenous people as *campesinos* (peasants) or *naturales*,[2] and to emphasize the political character of the domination they experienced *as* indigenous people. Thus in the very heat and noise of insurrection and massacre, the early 1980s saw the beginning of a process of simultaneous love and hate, tension and complementarity, understanding and arrogance, hegemony and coordination that sets the Maya movement apart from other indigenous movements in Latin America yet also marks its similarity to other social processes in Guatemala.

Consolidation of the Dichotomy

With the political "transition" that, at least symbolically, began in 1986 with the return to civilian rule, some spaces were opened within the new logic that allowed various actors to begin pushing the process much further than counterinsurgency strategies had foreseen (Jonas 1994).[3] Although the repression unleashed against indigenous communities and organizations was meant to silence these "irritations," little by little indigenous activists began to emerge into public life, now as the "Mayan movement," with their own demands and strategies.

The movement was gaining maturity but also suffered serious divisions. Almost every aspect of indigenous mobilization, including the differences among the various organizations — from discourses and alliances to how they were organized, their funding sources, and international connections — was marked (and is still influenced) by the division between what were called *populares* and *mayanistas* (Bastos and Camus 1993). At that time, of course, it was impossible to claim any public connection to the URNG, but this public distinction reflected ideological differences based in these clandestine relationships. People began to take the increasingly rigid position of "being either with us or against us." It was a pressure-cooker time. Calls to militancy focused on being inside or out of the organization and demanded total loyalty based in well-founded terror of betrayal (as spies and infiltrators had caused overwhelming damage). In such a context, those activists who did try to unify both sorts of demands were rejected, and attempts at mediation got nowhere.

In the still repressive atmosphere of the late 1980s and early 1990s a number of new popular organizations were created, primarily by indigenous people participating in the new Coordination of Sectors Arising from the Violence, by taking up claims of being the victims of state violence and exploitation. They became the point of the spear for a regenerated popular movement, the "nucleus of a popular bloc" (Jonas 1994). With their demands, marches, and increasing public presence, they proved to other citizens and the political class that indigenous men and women were not bowed. They continued to demand their place and voice in national life in spite of the violence that had been unleashed against them. They were continuing the tradition of the mobilizations of the 1970s, and their principal aim was to have a national-level political presence. They were connected with the revolutionary organizations through an identity and sense of belonging to the bases of *la organización* (McAllister 2002) but maintained semi-autonomous leadership. Members of all of these groups developed an intense dedication to each other, based in strong emotional relationships and often at great personal sacrifice (Toj 2007). They carried out sustained and careful work inside communities and sectors, developing their own bases that could mobilize mass numbers of people. Taking decisive advantage of newly open political spaces, their concerns focused on land, poverty, and human rights violations, which brought them into direct conflict with the army. They were also part of the URNG's strategy to consolidate support and diversify its political struggle, which led to the creation of a constellation of organizations and individuals throughout the countryside, linked, to greater and lesser degrees, to different factions within the political-military leadership of the guerrillas.[4]

At the same time that these groups were questioning the deficiencies of the transition, other voices were being raised in the name of an oppressed Pueblo Maya. These were people who had not enlisted in the revolutionary logic but hoped to take advantage of the scarce but increasing legal openings for their projects. In 1984, the same year MAYAS published their document, several such organizations began meeting informally to better coordinate their efforts in the context of the Constitutional Assembly and the move toward civilian rule. They called themselves "Maya" and organized the Second Linguistic Congress, which called on the government to create a Mayan languages academy. Presenting themselves as independent from the URNG, they made cultural claims within a legalist framework. They organized differently, primarily through nongovernmental organizations created by Mayan professionals to carry out concrete and particular projects of cultural development.[5] Such aboveground activities allowed them to garner financing openly and to avoid state repression while working more independently from the URNG's hegemonizing pressures. It was a way to gain space without necessarily demanding national representation, given that they sought less to respond to a specific population or community than to promote cultural revitalization (language use, traditional clothing, spiritual practices) more generally, both in indigenous communities and as a pressing issue for a national audience. Over the course of many years of work they developed their own analysis of the ongoing colonization of the Pueblo Maya as a structural constraint, denying them the free expression of their particular lifeways. These activists and organizations coalesced around demands for such cultural rights as bilingual education and the creation of the state-based Mayan Language Academy (ALMG). At the beginning of the 1990s they created the Council of Mayan Organizations (COMG) to "coordinate, analyze, and reflect on the problems facing the Pueblo Maya" (Cojtí 1997: 110). While holding fast to their independence from the URNG, COMG represented such a diverse range of trajectories and ideological positions that it ended up including people who were linked to the guerrillas, but from a Mayanist position.

One early success of their struggles was achieving widespread use of the word *Maya* both as a term of self-identification and as the "correct" way for non-Maya to refer to them in the press, government documents, and everyday usage. This is perhaps the clearest symbol of the movement's consolidation on the national stage. Faced with overtly racist terms like *indio* or the colonially inscribed *indígena*, the use of *Maya* represents their own identity, which they themselves have chosen proudly, and marks their connections to a continuous and millenarian history. Thus to take on the identity of Maya is a profoundly political act that deeply questions the status quo of ethnic identifications in Guatemala. The term came into its own with COMG's 1991 publication *Rujunamil ri Mayab' Amaq': Derechos específicos del Pueblo Maya*, which called for recognizing the same rights for Mayas as enjoyed by the "Pueblo Ladino," which in turn would entail reformulating the state by ensuring ethnic parity in government organizations and creating territorial autonomy for the Maya.

Struggle for and over Spaces in "Favorable Conditions"

Over the 1990s these struggles, combined with powerful transnational efforts to legitimize the demands of indigenous populations, created favorable conditions for the consolidation of the Mayan movement. With the 1992 Columbus Quincentennial demands for a rereading of colonial history echoed throughout Latin America as part of the Continental Campaign of 500 Years of Indigenous and Popular Resistance, which brought together activists from the entire continent (Burguete 2010). In Guatemala, while Mayanists used the moment to focus attention on their demands and analyses, it was a group of popular indigenous activists who organized the national portion of the Continental Campaign. Their connections to the hemispheric project led to a sort of "Mayanization" of many people active in the "popular" organizations. They ended up creating the Mayan Coordinator Majawil Q'ij as an expression of more fully assuming their identity as a pueblo, in addition to and complementary with their identification as an exploited class. It was a turbulent period. On the one hand, at the Continental Campaign's second congress, held in Quetzaltenango in 1991, a sector of Latin American organizations, including COMG, dramatically walked out, openly breaking from the larger shared project, because they claimed the Left was trying to monopolize indigenous demands and was shutting down spaces for their critiques of continuing colonial domination (Warren 1998). On the other hand, these new, allied fronts in identity formation and terrains of struggle were strengthened by the campaign for and subsequent naming of Rigoberta Menchú Tum as Nobel Peace Prize laureate in the emblematic days of October 1992.

Also in 1991 the beginning of peace negotiations afforded a significant space for Mayan-revolutionary alliances. The URNG proposed, and the government accepted, discussion of a specific accord on "Identity and Indigenous Rights." Including this topic in the larger peace process forced popular and Mayanist indigenous groups to negotiate and work together. They increasingly encountered each other in different spaces and political moments where they were called upon to share their analyses or dispute issues. This led to the 1993 creation of the Mayan Negotiating Table within the Civil Sectors Coordination. It became the first ongoing space shared by disparate actors since the early 1980s. "One would have expected a lot of skepticism and serious reservations on all sides when faced with the necessity of working together again . . . but they put their fears aside and tried again" (Hale et al. 2001: 5). Relations were tense, however, and would give rise to new ruptures.

As the term *Maya* became more hegemonic through 1993, Demetrio Cojtí argued that one might already "consider many popular groups as Maya . . . because they adapted or added the ethnic demands to their traditional social demands and they claimed their identities as Maya. They have always been Maya, of course, but not in their discourses or their projects" (1997: 113). By accepting this term the URNG and its allies were acknowledging the importance of the claims of those they had formerly considered enemies. This transformation reflected the ideological changes of the historical moment with rising global demands for multiculturalism but was also due to tireless and ongoing Mayan struggles to gain recognition both within and outside the URNG's structures.

These were not the only changes afoot. Even while the guerrillas remained a clandestine force inside the country, with the peace process the URNG was transforming its military logic into one of negotiation, seeking political space through which to take a place within the state. This caused a number of tensions with leaders who were working publicly inside the country. The larger project of increasing indigenous autonomy within the popular organizations clashed with the war-based logics of clandestinity, verticalism, and hierarchy that continued to dominate the URNG and led to the near fatal schism of the CUC in 1992–93, perhaps the most important grassroots organization in Guatemala's history (Velásquez Nimatuj 2008 and this volume). But the crisis within the revolutionary movement also served to enrich and diversify the Mayan movement (Brett 2006). The dichotomy inherited from the 1980s began to relax as indigenous and other leftists who had broken with the URNG for multiple reasons, including dissent from particular strategies, began to return from exile and with discussions of new options, including a "third way" that would promote the creation of Mayan spaces in collaboration with state actors. Throughout this process a number of leaders, both men and women, and organizations with long-standing ties to the URNG, began to increasingly identify with the Mayan struggle as an end in itself, even as they integrated socioeconomic and human rights demands into the cultural work, and always with an increasingly Mayan focus. The presence of these former dissidents, however, reinforced a sense of distrust and suspicion among some within the URNG, leading to painful splits like those within CUC and the EGP (which also played out in the refugee return process; see Worby this volume).

Unity and Its Accomplishments: COPMAGUA and the Identity Accord

The high point of these "favorable (if tense) conditions" occurred between 1996 and 1999 and was a result of a process begun in May 1994, when Mayan organizations formed COPMAGUA as a unified front within the Assembly of Civil Society (ASC). Being included in the ASC was a national recognition of the enormous efforts of the previous ten years and was seen as an opportunity to win national recognition as a Pueblo—a People—with an active role in creating the Guatemala of the future. Again, leaving behind internal differences and the problems that had divided them before, the Mayan coordinators, representing a range of ideological tendencies, decided to formalize the project of COPMAGUA, also giving it the Maya-Ixil name Saqb'ichil, meaning "new dawn." Founding members included COMG and the by-then government-approved ALMG, representing the Mayanists; the Organization of Mayan Unity and Consensus, heir to Majawil Q'ij on the URNG side; and the new Permanent Assembly of the Mayan People, representing a "third way."

In record time they produced a consensus-based document presented to the ASC for use in the negotiations for the Indigenous Rights Accord. Titled *Qasaqalaj Tz'iij, Qakemoon Tz'iij, Qapach'uum Tz'iij* (Our Word Illuminated, Our Word Woven, Our Word Braided), the primary demands were for recognition of the Pueblo Maya, the granting of cultural rights and some level of self-government and territorial autonomy, and demilitarization and peace. The document (and the very existence of COPMAGUA itself) shows the compulsory solidarity imposed by the peace process on the different tendencies and outlines the parameters of basic consensus that would undergird further actions.

A year later the URNG signed the Accord on Identity and Rights of the Indigenous Peoples (AIDPI), which went far beyond what many Maya had even hoped for. It recognized the existence of the various indigenous Peoples: the Maya, Xinka, and Garífuna (Afro-Carib). It acknowledged that Guatemala is a "multicultural, pluriethnic and multilingual country" and proposed legal changes to institutionalize this recognition. The accord shows the level of pressure the Mayan organizations were able to exert, the more global legitimation of multiculturalism among international organizations, and its organic acceptance among central leaders of the URNG. For those who were negotiating, it was clear that the accord could not lower the bar that had been set by the recent protests over the Quincentennial and by the United Nation's Convention 169 on the Rights of Indigenous and Tribal Peoples. But the AIDPI also revealed the limits of acceptability of more structural demands, given its emphasis on cultural rights and reticence concerning autonomy and territoriality as expressly political rights and on ways to address ethnically shaped socioeconomic inequalities and the unjust distribution of land.

Times of Hard Work and Tension

After the final peace accords were signed in December 1996, the organizations in COPMAGUA were transformed into the central interlocutors with the government in putting the Identity Accord into practice. They would work through a series of commissions composed of equal numbers of government and indigenous delegates,[6] whose task was to propose legislative changes, including constitutional reforms, based on the needs of the indigenous Pueblos, which would then be debated and approved in Congress. Thus COPMAGUA became the official representative of the Pueblo Maya for implementation of the peace accords. This was the beginning of the "glory days" for the indigenous movement in Guatemala. They had achieved the unity they had so long desired and were negotiating directly with the state over concrete measures that would ensure respect for their specific rights. Despite normal jealousies and problems, between 1996 and 1999 practically all the energy, time, and creativity of leaders and interested international funding agencies focused on the efforts of COPMAGUA and the commissions. Hope was growing that they could finally transform Guatemala's long history of domination and exclusion.

But everything fell apart in 1999 and 2000. The reasons are complex, but here we concentrate on those connected to the special relation between Mayas and revolutionaries. In August 1996 COPMAGUA was reorganized to correspond to its new responsibilities as a participant in the National Permanent Commissions for implementing the peace accords. This meant losing its previous status as a coordinator of other coordinators. The changes led old tensions to flare anew as some of the Mayan organizations linked to the URNG tried to use the new structure to advance their interests, dropping the consensus politics that had been used up to that point. This was because the revolutionary Maya saw COPMAGUA as *their* project, since their sacrifices and willingness to risk their lives by going into the mountains to fight had created the necessary conditions for signing the peace accords in the first place. The move led to a new wave of desertions, however, as a number of Mayan cadres who had come to identify strongly with Mayan demands felt they could no longer sustain their loyalty to the URNG under the pressures coming from its leadership. For those who considered themselves "independent Maya," this was the apotheosis of URNG hegemonizing logic, taking over spaces meant to address the "ethnic question" that had been created by struggle and sacrifice from everyone. They felt the URNG, under cover of a discourse on democracy and inclusion, had appropriated the Mayan voice, subordinating it to their party and ideological interests.

Yet despite these disagreements, COPMAGUA did manage to function for several years, carrying out the tasks assigned them by the AIDPI and other agreements. All of the Mayan organizations contributed to the effort. Why? The answer is complicated. First, money was flowing freely from foreign donors, and most funding agencies didn't care what happened inside the Coordination, either administratively or politically, as long as the peace process seemed to be moving forward. Second, through COPMAGUA Mayan organizations and their concerns had gained a level of national attention they could only have dreamed of before, and no one wanted to risk losing it. Third, despite the rather chaotic situation, the process *was* working. The commissions managed to accomplish their mission and carry on negotiations with the government. Little by little, more here and less there, at different speeds and rhythms, they were achieving their goals. Legislation was being created that would recognize the Maya and their rights.

The End of the Illusion

It was decided, however, that all of these legal transformations would be approved as constitutional reforms via a referendum, the Consulta Popular. This decision transformed the happy ending so many had worked for so arduously into dashed hopes. As the campaign for the Consulta began, modifications contemplated in the peace accords ended up being deformed by counterinterests that also raised numerous barriers to their implementation (Azpuru 1999). Rather than supporting the Consulta, the political parties and the oligarchic interests behind them unleashed an aggressive and well-funded campaign against it, drawing on racist fears of the *indio* (Warren 2003). The only proponents of the "yes" vote were civil society groups of Maya, human rights defenders, and peasants' and women's organizations. These sectors did not have the same power to mobilize the population, and on May 16, 1999, with abstentions reaching 80 percent, the "no" vote won by a small margin of 55 percent, most coming from the capital city. And in the elections at the end of the year the Guatemalan Republican Front won throughout much of the country, giving its founder, the genocidal General Efraín Ríos Montt, almost presidential powers.

In the context of this thwarting of its labors, COPMAGUA's somewhat submerged internal contradictions began to emerge in full force and people's investments in unity for the sake of change began to collapse. When "the crisis of COPMAGUA" exploded, most saw the preceding period of unity, unique in the history of indigenous mobilization, as over and done with. Organized Mayas experienced the rupture as profound and definitive—emotions connected, of course, to the serious blow of the "no" vote in the Consulta. They felt deeply disoriented, suffering a sense of chaos and loss. These were symptoms of the larger crisis of representation they were facing along with the other members of civil society who had also worked so hard and so long for the structural changes denied by the "no" vote. Their hopes that unity could overcome the historic exclusion of Mayas from national power were shattered. It was the end of the illusion of peace.

At the same time the elections of 1999 completed the decade-long process of transforming the revolutionary movement from armed guerrillas to a political party. The constellation of rather diverse people and organizations that had circulated around the nucleus of the political-military organizations of the war years had slowly disintegrated as the peace process advanced. This collapse worked on two fronts. On the one hand, many leaders began to distance themselves as the URNG's developing role as the state's accomplice in the peace process decreased their spaces of autonomy and constricted their horizons for achieving their larger political goals. On the other hand, the political-military wing lost interest in the activities of many of its allied organizations because it no longer needed their support. Instead they were focused on calculating the various costs and benefits of the peace process, primarily as these related to their efforts to become a party involved in electoral politics. The URNG's policy of co-opting spaces for such ends was perhaps best illustrated with COPMAGUA, where it deployed its historic mode of clandestine manipulations behind a legal veneer. Yet by the time the crisis fully erupted in 2000 the central nucleus of the URNG was no longer interested in COPMAGUA. For the new party it was just another Mayan organization, made up of people linked to the URNG but not connected organically to its new political goals.

Twenty Years of Relations: The Difficult and Contradictory Complementarity

This "crisis of COPMAGUA" can be viewed as a final chapter. It was the closing moment of a process that began in the 1970s, survived the extremes of violence of the early 1980s and the regime change and peace process, that flourished anew with the signing of the accords in 1996, and began to falter with the Consulta Popular of 1999. It also marked the end of a whole way of doing politics in Guatemala, in which the polarization that accompanied internal armed conflict had made the free flow and organic development of political projects impossible, which led to the hegemonic role of the URNG not only within the Left but over all civil society. It was a period when the fate of the Mayan movement was linked, for better or worse, with the revolutionary movement, specifically the URNG — and vice versa. This meant that internal relations, ideological projects, and external connections were always mediated by being allied (or not) with this central actor.

Relations between the Mayan and revolutionary movements between 1980 and 2000 were quite ambiguous: at times complementary and other times contradictory. We saw how the events of 1980 produced internal divisions in the fledgling Maya movement between those allied or not with the revolutionary movement, and this duality endured for twenty years. The most strident critiques over the unraveling of COPMAGUA were denunciations of the URNG's arrogant attempts to co-opt the movement for its own ends. However, for years the same Mayan actors voicing these critiques had been deeply involved with and countenanced these same political practices vis-à-vis other groups linked to the URNG within the Coordination, and for the same pragmatic reasons that explain the entire trajectory from 1986 to 2000: because they needed each other.

One of the weaknesses of the Mayan movement during this phase was how little international presence they were able to achieve and their limited ability to pressure the Guatemalan state. This is precisely where they leaned on the URNG, well versed in confrontational methods and with its almost uncanny sense of how to open spaces for political negotiation at many levels. As Hale, Anderson, and Gordon write, the URNG "had an ability to follow and implement a political strategy designed to occupy key spaces of power and financing" (2001: 10). From the 500 Years Campaign to COPMAGUA, independent Maya depended on political spaces opened up through this strategy. In turn the Mayan movement provided the revolutionaries with a legitimizing discourse, especially necessary after the fall of the Berlin Wall and the supposed end of the socialist alternative. We see this fundamental contribution in the way the URNG developed the idea of "the Maya" over time. From the early 1990s the URNG increasingly took on the basic ideological premise that they were defending a colonized Pueblo's right to difference. The URNG inserted this issue into the peace negotiations and later fought for a version of the rights of indigenous peoples based on the principles defended by the Mayan movement. We might question how deeply this discourse was incorporated into their thinking, with all its possible consequences — territorial autonomy, lessening of ladino privilege — or was simply a tool to win political space and legitimacy. However, it did provide an essential support for these demands. And, despite everything, the URNG has proven to have greater understanding and flexibility in terms of ethnic issues than any other sociopolitical actor in Guatemalan society.

At the international level the revolutionary movement forcefully advocated for the ethnic dimension and importance of indigenous struggle in a number of fora, even as it tried to co-opt what "being indigenous" signified. For instance, while they added a socioeconomic dimension and insisted on respect for human rights within the indigenous movement, they also tended to delegitimize many cultural and identitarian aspects of Mayan demands, which were often soft-pedaled in international meetings. We must understand that claims for cultural difference were not easy to incorporate into revolutionary orthodoxy. The military logics forced on them by the state's counterinsurgency campaigns (and well-known army tactics like the use of spies and infiltrators) reinforced the most vertical structures and shut down spaces for disagreements or even discussion. In some cases this was enforced by killing those who challenged hierarchical authority, which in turn led to splits with indigenous leaders. Over time the revolutionary movement lost leaders and organizations and, with them, political power, to the Mayan movement. Hale (2006) suggests that this hemorrhaging of URNG dissidents, indigenous people with a revolutionary consciousness of the importance of the struggle for Mayan rights, was a boon for the contemporary Mayan movement as these people became its backbone.

But we might also read this relationship in a wider way. Many people joined the revolutionary movement from the Mayan side, and identities tended to fluctuate, often leaving no clear line dividing the actors. Many Mayan revolutionaries identified themselves equally as indigenous and as Maya, and it was always difficult to question the legitimacy of anyone's presence, discourse, or interests. Some who were not aligned with the URNG often distrusted these claims to identity, afraid they hid attempts to take advantage of "purely Mayan" interests that would thereby be drained of their Mayan meaning. However, from this perspective, "independent" and revolutionary Maya *were* involved in complementary projects throughout these two decades of ambivalent relations based in mutual need. The URNG facilitated action and opened lines of communication, spaces for action, and political power, which, from its end, offered the URNG legitimacy. Perhaps their political logics, their goals and aspirations (and quite clearly, their ideological motives) were not the same, but each side needed the other in the political struggle and never stopped being "natural allies."

This mutual need was strong, which is why they agreed to work together in COPMAGUA in 1994. The underlying tensions came through in their contrary understandings of the AIDPI, the Coordination's role, and the point of laboring in the commissions. For those involved in the Mayan movement from an independent position, the peace process was a *means*, a privileged space from which to advance their demands. The AIDPI was seen as a fundamental step and a powerful tool to work with, and the commissions were spaces where they could fight to obtain the best possible outcome. But for the URNG, the peace process was not a means but *an end in itself*, and the point was to fulfill each one of the accords they had signed, thereby ensuring their integration into Guatemalan politics. They felt it was their responsibility to implement the AIDPI and the rest of the accords just as they had been signed, and the commissions were seen as spaces to create a strong URNG presence in the state, via the institutions that created public policy and would carry it out. To accomplish this they needed to make sure the process developed as it had been planned, and they ended up clashing with those whose demands

were seen as too extreme, and who therefore put the whole process of implementation at risk.

Additionally, the entire aftermath of the war imposed a particular logic on
the development of the Mayan movement. First, of course, was the impact
of overwhelming repression, reaching genocidal levels. The scale of state terrorism, culminating in scorched earth and the succeeding militarization, is
fundamental to understanding the tactics and strategies of the indigenous
movement in Guatemala and its current configuration (Bastos 2010; Brett
2006; Sáenz 2003). Later the same polarization created the logics we have described here in the relations between Mayans and revolutionaries, whereby,
in the end, being for or against became more important that what they were
fighting for.

The entire peace process was a privileged space for the consolidation of
Mayan demands, but it also imposed its own rhythms, logics, and forms of
doing politics, especially given the extremely limited time frame in which to
work. A very short time, indeed, to even begin to address five hundred years
of indigenous exclusion, much less recover from a policy of genocide that
had killed so many leaders and so terribly disrupted the generational continuities necessary for developing people and projects. The price that was paid
for stepping into these fast-moving currents was accepting certain norms that
in turn shut down possibilities for mobilization and for making demands that
had been developed by Mayan organizations of all stripes in the first half of
the decade, before the accords were signed (Bastos 2006a). As a result of this
process the demands that were negotiated and given structure in the commissions ended up being decided by the Consulta Popular, which, by the
time it was carried out, had already lost legitimacy and responded more to
the immediate party interests of political players than to the future necessities of Guatemalan society.

The peace process laid heavy burdens of responsibility on the movement,
forcing it into a position of negotiation with the state — in what were supposedly horizontal relationships — when they barely had people with the basic
experience needed to hold their own, much less confront the total lack of a
constructive attitude on the part of the government's delegates. Such negotiations assumed an internal homogeneity of demands when, in truth, the appropriation of a Mayanist ideology was nowhere near consolidated and each
of the individual actors was immersed in his or her own logics and interests.
Perhaps it was not the best time for the Maya movement to stake all its claims
on the Consulta. They risked it all, and the time of "consolidation" paradoxi-

cally ended up becoming a disaster that clearly revealed the need to go more slowly, undertake projects with far deeper analysis, and achieve greater functional autonomy.

Epilogue: From Cosmetic Multiculturalism to Community Mobilization

Over the past decade Guatemala has supposedly been at peace. Despite the "no" vote in the Consulta, many Mayas, revolutionaries, and others who had worked so hard for peace with justice have continued their efforts at structural transformation from the spaces they have forced open in the state. But as time went on it became clear that successive governments were betting the house on insertion into the global economy along purely neoliberal lines, policies that, wherever they are implemented, have only served to increase the most profound historic inequalities. Thus while Guatemala's oligarchs grew stronger, political spaces for everyone else began to shut down, and everyday violence increased exponentially throughout the country (López García et al. 2009). In a situation so poorly suited to keeping hope alive, indigenous communities are nonetheless mobilizing to defend what little they have left: their natural resources. Almost forty years later a new alliance is being forged between revolutionaries and Mayanists working at local and regional levels. They are seriously challenging the government with claims for rights as indigenous peoples.

With the Peace Treaty the URNG became a political party like any other, although of all the parties it has the most militant indigenous members and most expressly supports Mayan demands. However, most of its former cadres have been reduced, via the party structure, to voters. (As of 2011 the URNG only has three congressional members and had to make alliances to even field a presidential candidate.) Given this, a relationship with the URNG is not a major factor in the Mayan movement, and new organizational forms and strategic projects have emerged, better representing the diversity of Mayan concerns. At the same time, the Maya have lost so much in the way of unity, public profile, and the ability to pressure the state that the anthropologist Roddy Brett (2010) doubts we should even call it a "movement" at all.[7] Much of the Mayan project has moved into the state, where spaces opened up as the government tried to paint itself as multicultural. It has made cosmetic changes to its policies and discourses and added the presence of Mayan faces to state organisms for Mayas, including the ALMG, the General Direction of Bilingual Education, and the Indigenous Development Fund (created before the peace accords), which in turn have given rise to the Indigenous Women's Defense

Office, the Culture Ministry's Sacred Places Initiative, and the Presidential Commission against Discrimination and Racism (CODISRA), among others, raising the number to almost thirty "Mayan" offices (AVANCSO 2008).

The problem with all these efforts, according to Cojtí, is that they are simply "institutional extrusions" on a state that remains resolutely "mono-ethnic," distracting people's attention and absorbing their energies while leaving in place the same policies, the same racist state structures, and the same exclusionary bases of Guatemala society (see also Uk'u'x B'e 2005; Cumes 2007; Hale 2006). And Mayan leaders who have decided to work in these spaces have found they have precious little ability to press for change. The same peace process that opened space in the state also distanced them from their supporters — especially left organizations — often leaving them divorced from the needs and experiences of people in the communities who are on the front lines of Guatemala's increasingly brutal encounter with neo-liberalism.

Nonetheless, while the URNG and the national-level Mayas have settled into a "post-peace normalization," there are many places where the indigenous population is mobilizing at the community level without counting (or depending) on those structures. On the one hand, local institutions like the Indigenous Mayors, which had been close to disappearing, have been reinvigorated through efforts to connect the idea of "ancestral authorities of the Pueblo Maya" with the right to self-governance and the application of Mayan law (Sieder 2011a).[8] On the other, since 2005 in provinces with a heavy Mayan majority, such as San Marcos and Huehuetenango, people are beginning to more actively confront the destructive effects of the mountaintop-removal mining increasingly used throughout the country (Solano 2005). Drawing on ILO Convention 169 and national legislation, including the Constitution and the Municipal Code, they are carrying out good-faith community referenda to show their opposition to these operations in their homelands. Despite being areas where the social fabric has been so diminished by war's violence and by the diaspora of massive migration to the United States, participation has been extraordinarily high and quite diverse, connecting, surprisingly, former civil patrollers, guerrillas, children, elders, Catholics, and Evangelical Protestants (Camus 2008; Mérida and Krenmayer 2008). The strong participation of women (over 50 percent) has been particularly noteworthy, even as they often lack the required identity cards to register to vote in formal elections — meaning that even though they are disenfranchised at the national level, they are engaged in local politics.

These mobilizations in defense of territory and, above all, in favor of re-

FIG 2.2 A woman votes with her thumbprint in a *consulta indígena* on mining in
San Ildefonso Ixtahuacán, 2007. PHOTO BY MANUELA CAMUS.

claiming the capacity to contest, speak out, and intervene have spread to
other struggles, like the rejection of an environmentally destructive cement
plant in San Juan Sacatepéquez and hydroelectric dams in the Ixcán, generating new forms of political action and mobilizing across ethnic lines. People
are holding referenda throughout the country — in sixty-three municipalities
as of April 2013 — in which almost a million people have been counted. While
there has been increasing repression focused on those involved, in 2009 the
Constitutional Court ruled, following Convention 169, that the referenda
were legally valid. In response, in 2011 the government tried to change the
law in order to limit their proliferation.

The majority of these actions, based in local communities yet with re-

FIG 2.3 A Waqib' Kej banner waves at a 2004 march against racism. PHOTO BY SANTIAGO BASTOS.

gional reach, are being coordinated by former members of the URNG, older Mayan activists with experiences dating from the 1980s or earlier. They are still working with and for their communities, now without the organic presence of revolutionary organizations but with the same "revolutionary identification" as always (Toj 2007). Faced with the exhaustion of a unitary discourse of class and pressure from younger generations, they are taking up a new kind of indigenous project that responds to a wider range of aspirations and necessities. It is not state-manipulated multiculturalism but the defense of their very lives against capitalist globalization, a parallel struggle to those developing throughout South America over the past decade (Burguete 2010).

This pressure from below, based in a revived revolutionary militancy acting at the community level, is giving new life to indigenous and popular mobilizations in Guatemala. Regional coordinators are being formed and national-level organizations are joining, though they need to update their discourse and practice to keep up with this emerging reality. For example, the Coordination of Pueblos of the Western Highlands (CPO), founded in 2006, emerged from departmental-level coordinators involved with the referenda. The 2007 Third Indigenous Peoples and Nations Summit, held at Iximché, Chimaltenango, gave rise to a larger group calling itself the National Mayan Coordination Waqib' Kej, which has become an important actor in antiglobalization struggles. The political system put in place by "post-conflict normalization" did not address the structural problems that currently face Guatemala, pushing it ever closer to the brink. The left parties have not known how or have not been able to respond to the challenges (Alvarez Aragón and Sáenz 2008; Torres Rivas 2007). The Mayan actors who took center stage in the 1990s also developed a politics that has not been able to resolve their people's problems or transform the structures generated from centuries of racism. These communities themselves, however, are challenging global capitalism and national impunity based in a vision of indigenous Pueblos that is managing to connect the difficult complementarities that once divided people. Together they are once again creating an alternative version of Guatemalan history.

Notes

1. Criollos are the direct descendents of Spanish colonizers. By using the term to demarcate this republic, the document's creators are sharply defining their understanding of power relations in Guatemala.
2. The term *natural* is also a colonial form identifying indigenous people as "originary." It was deployed by the Revolutionary Organization of the People in Arms (ORPA) as an alternative to *indígenas* or the overtly racist *indios*.
3. Indigenous issues were almost completely sidelined in the official transition. The slight acknowledgments contained in the new constitution could not hide the endemic racism and ladino-centrism of the new legal system (Solares 1993; Taracena et al. 2004). Political parties nominated almost no indigenous candidates for the new Congress. The late 1970s had seen increased indigenous participation in local government, including serving as mayors, but by 1986 these areas had not yet recovered from the Ríos Montt government's intervention into local power structures.
4. Since then the following groups have acknowledged these connections: the National Widows Coordination (CONAVIGUA), the National Council of Displaced People (CONDEG), and the Permanent Commissions of Guatemalan Refugees Representatives (CCPP), almost all of whose leaders were people who had been involved with the CUC (which was also returning to public life) and thus with the EGP. The Mutual Support Group for Families of the Disappeared (GAM) and the Council of Ethnic Communities "Rujunel Junam" (CERJ) were closer to ORPA, a group that incorporated the leaders of already existing groups as part of what was seen as a more selective or "elitist" strategy.
5. These included the Center for the Study of Mayan Culture, the Cakchiquel (*sic*) Coordinator for Integral Development, Cholsamaj Press, the Maya Center Saqbe', and the Mayan Library and Research Center.
6. Three *paritaria*, or equal representation commissions, were formed—Land Rights of Indigenous Pueblos, Participation on All Levels, and Educational Reform—along with two "specific commissions": Officializing Indigenous Languages, and Spirituality and Sacred Areas. Other commissions addressing development, the rights of indigenous women, and constitutional reforms also participated in the post-accord negotiations.
7. In *El movimiento Maya en la década después de la paz, 1997–2007*, we address different

aspects of this new phase of organization at the local, regional, and national levels (Bastos and Brett 2010).

8. Perhaps the case of Totonicapán is best known, where the mayors have been reinstated in all forty-eight hamlets of the municipality, but lately this has extended through most of the indigenous communities in the country (Reyes 1998; Ajxup et al. 2010).

TESTIMONIAL TRUTHS AND REVOLUTIONARY MYSTERIES

Genealogies of Testimonio

Doing fieldwork in the late millennial Guatemala of projects like the Recuperation of Historical Memory initiative of the Catholic Church and the United Nations Commission for Historical Clarification meant learning to take a *testimonio*. As a volunteer for a human rights organization working with survivors of the Panzós massacre, I was told that testimonios were critically important for acknowledging the suffering of victims, as well as for establishing the broader truth about what had happened in a context where forensic investigations were recovering far fewer human remains than expected. Nevertheless my initial attempts at producing testimonios were inadequate; my mentors were visibly displeased when, after a long day of interviewing victims, all I had come up with was a list of names, dates, and crimes. Watching them do their own interviews afterward, I realized that while such facts are certainly necessary elements of testimonio, they are not sufficient; to achieve its purpose, a testimonio must convey the "signs of harm" (Colvin 2004) that appeal to the compassionate imagination as well as the forensic judgment of its audience.

Producing such a narrative is a demanding task. Of the taker of the testimonio it requires gentle and skillful questioning to elicit a vivid sense of the violent event—how it unfolded, what was said, what was felt—in addition to the facts. This work must be accomplished within a period of time that is usually restricted by the presence of others waiting to give their own testimonio. Of the giver, it requires submission to this questioning and its conventions, which often include translation from a Mayan language to Spanish and always entail an uneven command of the communicative field and the time frames that govern it (see Ross 2003). These encounters can be just as collaborative and cathartic as intended, but they can also easily turn contentious. Field notes from the period of my apprenticeship in this art record testimonio-givers who were turned away for not really being "victims"; who insisted on speaking about current conflicts rather than past woes; who failed to remember dates and names or to understand the testimonio-taker's questions, even after translation; who came to the point of describing their victimization only after lengthy venting on apparently unrelated subjects; who became evasive or defensive about certain questions regarding the past; and who otherwise exhibited resistance to or confusion about what it meant to seek a witness for their stories. When I was once again entrusted with producing my own full-fledged testimonio, taken from a woman who had been sexually assaulted by soldiers over several weeks, her almost inaudible speech and profuse sweating deepened my doubts about this task. Eventually I became more proficient at taking testimonios, but I never felt entirely comfortable with their rigors.

The transformative powers human rights workers attribute to testimonio are called forth by a tradition that harkens to Jesus' claim to be the "new testament" of God. Testimonial accounts of events are only required, Paul Ricoeur (1980: 65) notes, when the truth is contested, put on trial in a struggle of opinions; consequently testimony affirms the truth rather than empirically verifying it. For the authors of what Christians know as the New Testament, the truth on trial was that Jesus' suffering and sacrifice on the Cross were the fulfillment of God's salvific covenant with His people. Their affirmation of this claim took the form of drawing typological correspondences between their stories of Jesus' life and the prophetical texts—known as the *testimonia*—of what thereby became the Old Testament, as a means to show that the "divine homogeneity of God's world-plot" culminated in the Crucifixion (Kermode 1979: 106). Christians who confess their faith in salvation thus bear witness not only to God's action in the world through Jesus Christ but also to the "transformed sense of time," the altered future, that this action inaugurates (Klemm 2008: 67).

The concept of trauma developed in late nineteenth- and early twentieth-century European clinics substitutes healing for salvation in enactments of this confessional tradition. Understood as a violent rupture in psychic processes of representation that leaves its trace in the form of silence, trauma is cured when its victims are able to narratively reconstruct the violent event in the presence of a witness, whose empathetic listening discharges their suffering by affirming its veracity (Leys 2000). In this therapeutic paradigm, secular acts of confession and witnessing liberate us from the past's weight on our present, orienting us toward a future in which we can finally "free the self we truly are . . . to make a project of our own lives, to fulfill ourselves through the choices we make, and to shape our existence according to an ethics of autonomy" (Rose 1998: 97). Technologies of social repair like truth commissions and historical memory projects have extended this paradigm from individual to collective psyches around the world, inscribing the capacities for self-actualization and compassionate identification in universal human nature by framing contemporary humanitarianism as a therapeutic practice (Fassin 2008).[1]

Proliferating critiques of the communicative and psychic imperialism entailed in these truth-telling technologies pose a challenge for scholars working with people who are the objects of humanitarian interventions, and thus in contexts saturated with testimonial forms of truth-telling. How can we produce accounts of the violence our interlocutors have suffered without simply becoming a cog in the humanitarian apparatus ourselves? One suggestion is to deploy other responses than what Veena Das (2007: 92) calls "careless invitations to . . . tell [us] what happened" when we encounter silence. Women who have survived communal violence in India, Das shows, use the conventions of ordinary gestural systems and kinship relations to enfold back into everyday life the "poisonous knowledge" suffering confers, a process that allows them to reinhabit worlds that would be rendered unlivable if this knowledge were spoken. She argues that collaboration in this process, not an injunction to speak, is the response their work of remaking demands. Nancy Hunt (2008) likewise listens to the "acoustic register" of the remembered screams and nervous laughter of sexual violence recorded in archival reports on the period of the rubber terror in the Congo as a counter to the "scopic economy" of humanitarian witnessing. Unlike the images of dismemberment that stand for this episode in humanitarian discourse, these nonrepresentational sounds permit the continuities between Congo's colonial past and its postcolonial present, in which rape is common but dismemberment is not, to emerge as potential objects for projects of reparation.

But expanding scholarship's sensorial range does not necessarily alter the identification of silence as the mark of language's inability to fully assimilate pain, nor the corresponding assumption that compassion is the appropriate scholarly response to silence. Even within testimonial traditions, however, other affective relations can obtain between those who testify and those who hear testimony. In Spanish the word *testimonio* refers to a literary genre as well as a humanitarian technology, one that bears witness to worlds whose existence the "lettered city" (Rama 1996) refuses to recognize, generally in the form of first-person life histories of members of subaltern communities (Beverley 1999, 2004; Saldaña-Portillo 2003; Yúdice 1991). Emerging in the context of burgeoning guerrilla conflict in Latin America, testimonio was cultivated by the Casa de las Américas, the cultural arm of the Cuban Revolution's relations with the rest of the so-called Third World, which in 1970 began to award an annual literary prize to the genre's best exemplar. Revolutionary testimonios are, like therapeutic ones, "exemplary narratives of personal transformation," in this case describing how their subject's consciousness, or *conciencia*, was born, and seeking the reader's affirmation of the necessity and universality of this process (Saldaña-Portillo 2003: 13). But the bond between the subject and audience of testimonial consciousness-raising is ethically and temporally distinct from that of testimonial therapy. As literary theorists have noted, the collective subject of conciencia—the fact that Rigoberta Menchú (Burgos-Debray 1984: 2), for example, tells the "story of all poor Guatemalans" in the first-person singular— disrupts the individualist precepts of bourgeois liberalism. But this collective subject's project for self-realization also subsumes the ethic of individual autonomy under one of revolutionary popular sovereignty (Beverley 2004). Invocations of revolution "spatially imply a *world revolution* and temporally imply that they be *permanent* until their objective is reached" (Koselleck 1985: 49). Oriented toward this horizon, revolutionary testimonio is a variety of romance, a genre David Scott describes as "moving steadily and rhythmically (one might even say, teleologically) in the direction of an end already in some sense known in advance" (2004: 70). Since the fulfillment of conciencia depends on reaching this future, revolutionary testimonio seeks less the compassionate identification of its readers than their passionate enrollment in the project of hastening it.

Strikingly, revolutionary testimonio exhibits these romantic features even when it narrates experiences of violence. For example, *La resistencia en Guatemala*, a 1989 collection of testimonios from the Communities of Population in Resistance, internally displaced communities that supported guerrillas, builds from charming tales of the beauties and difficulties of the life of resistance in the jungle to horrific stories like this:

> The army captured two orphaned brothers. . . . The army captured them, they dragged them out and killed the two of them together. With a stick or a machete they killed them, because they left them almost without heads. After killing them, the army burned the houses in the village. That was a

sad day for the community. The people began to cry and cry at seeing so much cruelty from the army. Carefully they gathered the pieces of the heads, the bones thrown around of the two brothers and all together they buried them. (Gurriarán 1989: 75)

Here we hear of the same horrific sufferings—inflicted, moreover, by the same perpetrators on the same victims—that were described in the testimonios I gathered. The story, however, does not end in suffering, but instead continues: "This is what the army does, what the people see, what the community sees. We want to work in freedom. Free in our work, free in our lives, free in our own land. This is what we want and this is why we resist. This is why we go on" (Gurriarán 1989: 76). This call to "go on" affirms suffering as a passion necessary to articulating the truth of testimonio (Asad 1997) rather than as an impediment to its articulation.

Latin American psychoanalysts, psychologists, and social scientists on the Left, themselves likely readers of literary testimonios, performed much of the labor of working up testimonial truth-telling into a globally deployed humanitarian instrument beginning in the 1980s (Hollander 1997). But as the bloody continental defeat of the Latin American Left over this same period began to cast the passionate purpose of suffering into doubt, the reiteration of testimonio as therapy began to exclude even the memory of its links to revolutionary futurity. Nowhere, perhaps, is this clearer than in Guatemala. Guatemala's revolutionary movements contributed actively to the development of testimonio, producing numerous collections of life histories of women, indigenous people, union activists, and refugees like the one cited above (e.g., Gurriarán 1989; Hooks 1991; Smith-Ayala 1991; Zimmerman 1991), as well as the award-winning *Days of the Jungle* (Payeras 1983; awarded the Premio Casa de las Américas 1981), and *I, Rigoberta Menchú* (Burgos-Debray 1984; awarded the Premio Casa de las Américas 1983). But in 1999, only shortly after Guatemala's guerrilla movements gave up their arms, commentators responding to attacks on the veracity of Rigoberta Menchú's testimonio by the North American anthropologist David Stoll had to remind him of the distinction between its standards of evidence and voice from those of the therapeutic or even juridical form of truth-telling with which he appeared to have confused it (see Stoll 1999; Rus 1999; Arias 2001).

More surprising than the amnesia of *gringo* academics is the absence of any hint of the revolutionary future in testimonios produced by those who are intimately acquainted with its call. Many contemporary Guatemalan testimonio-takers are also former participants in or collaborators with armed struggle and are deeply familiar with the revolutionary past of their practice. Some of those from whom they gather testimonios may share this familiarity, even perhaps having figured as the anonymous heroes of earlier testimonial collections. Yet as a rule postwar testimonio-taking steers clear of this shared experience. The convention that only trauma constitutes a true event in therapeutic testimonio facilitates this move by narratively relegating other goings-on to, at best, political or historical context. But even when references to testimonio-givers' experiences with revolutionary projects or the passions that informed them do somehow emerge in the process of testimonio-taking, they receive little uptake and tend to be omitted from the version that ends up circulating. In fact it is the process of ruling such reference out of context that generates many of the communicative difficulties that emerged during the production of testimonios in Panzós and elsewhere. The call to "go on" cannot sound in contemporary Guatemalan testimonio, focused as it is on restoring the integrity of victims' "everyday worlds."

The resulting silence, however, marks the presence of something less unspeakable than inaudible. Here I will argue that distinguishing between these two modalities of silence can help disrupt humanitarianism's claim on Guatemala's violent past and on those who wish to better understand it. As a number of the chapters in this volume demonstrate, evacuating revolution from accounts of Guatemala's war radically impoverishes not only our analyses of the armed conflict but also the genocidal acts it generated and their ongoing consequences. To rearticulate the links of the revolutionary past to Guatemala's present it is essential to recover a sense of the future toward which those participating in the revolutionary project were once directed. If the revolutionary call to "go on" can no longer be heard as a testimonial truth, overcoming our deafness to its call therefore demands we attune ourselves to nonhumanitarian forms of listening.

Truth and Mystery in a Postrevolutionary Guatemalan Village

My own process of attunement took place in Chupol, a Maya-K'iche'-speaking rural hamlet of Chichicastenango where I went to live after finishing my stint as a human rights volunteer. Chupol, which lies astride the Pan-American Highway at the southern tip of the Quiché, about an hour and a half by bus from Guatemala City, makes an excellent case for the importance of understanding the role of revolution in Guatemala's recent past. A site of early and enthusiastic conversion from *costumbre* (literally, custom, or what is now often called Mayan religion) to Catholic Action, Chupol found its faith (and convenient location) rewarded when the parish priest of Chichicastenango built a church and marketplace in the community in the late 1960s, providing ideas and infrastructure that accelerated Chupolense expectations for further change. By the mid-1970s the thwarting of these expectations, combined with the devastation wrought by the February 1976 earthquake, left Chupolenses receptive to the preaching of Sebastián Morales, a respected catechist placed in charge of the local church's distribution of earthquake aid.

A founding member of the Campesino Unity Committee (CUC), Morales convinced Chupolenses that the organization was their best hope for a better future. In the early 1980s, when the CUC merged with the Guerrilla Army of the Poor (EGP), Chupol became a bastion of EGP civilian support, with virtually every household participating in its *base social*. Among urban leftists, it was known as the *pueblo vietnamita* (Vietnamese village) for its reputed commitment to the EGP's Vietnamese-style anticapitalist and anti-imperialist revolution as well as its participation in a program to dig earthworks modeled on the Viet Cong's network of tunnels outside Saigon. After July 1981, when a series of raids by security forces broke up the EGP's safe houses in the capital, many urban cadres honored this reputation by taking refuge in Chupol's small adobe houses.

The army also considered Chupol an insurgent hotbed: Mauricio Héctor López Bonilla, a former colonel deployed against the EGP in this area (and, as of 2011, Guatemala's minister of the interior), told me that it was among the very "reddest" communities on the army's counterinsurgent maps (see Carmack 1988). In late 1981, after an army reconnaissance patrol stumbled upon one of the EGP's earthen traps, soldiers marched in to occupy Chupol's church, driving villagers out into the mountains on either side of the highway, where they were subjected to bombardments and lethal raids. During this period, hailing from Chupol marked one for death. Meanwhile Chupol's church became a "killing center," to which suspected subversives who were pulled off passing vehicles were taken to be tortured and killed. Only after the EGP told them the organization could no longer protect them did most Chupolenses decide to accept the 1983 amnesty that allowed them to surrender and return home.

Knowing nothing of Chupol's history except that it had been "badly hit" by the war, I arrived with the intention of investigating how the language and practices of human rights truth-telling engaged victims of violence. Although I never set out to gather testimonios, mentioning "human rights," "the war," or "the violence" invariably elicited deeply distressing stories about what Chupolenses had suffered. These stories rarely alluded to revolutionary organizations or actions, but gradually I gained some inkling of the revolutionary history I have sketched above, at first by piecing together things I learned from non-Chupolenses or nonresident Chupolenses. Eventually I began to ask Chupolenses in the village, but even once it was clear that I knew what I was talking about, many Chupolenses still denied any acquaintance with the guerrillas or spoke of them as shadowy, wild creatures, *ajxkay* (those of the weeds or untamed space), relegated to the nighttime and sensed only in passing. Their reticence on this subject was not very surprising. The war had ended only a year prior to my arrival, and Chupol was (and, at the moment of writing, is) still occupied by a platoon of soldiers—since 1985 more discretely quartered on a hill behind the resanctified church but still casting a heavy pall of surveillance over village life. Only after I had spent six months wandering along the highway asking my questions did Chupolenses decide— almost overnight, it felt like—to offer me the thoughtful accounts of their involvement with insurgent organizations that I had found myself seeking.

So far, so good: my patient inquiries and willingness to listen eventually allowed me to recover a Guatemalan history different than the one of helpless victimization and compassionate rescue that humanitarianism privileges. But recovering this history does not on its own mark a departure from the humanitarian truth-telling project. Let me explain by relating the shift I experienced in Chupolense storytelling to my earlier discussion of testimonio. The stories I heard at the beginning of fieldwork, which I will call "traumatic narratives," were clearly linked to the testimonios I had learned to collect as a human rights volunteer. They described the atrocities people had experienced, witnessed, or heard about, and they interpellated me, sometimes in so many words, as a *testigo* (witness). Chupolenses were among the first rural Guatemalans to participate in the Mutual Support Group (GAM), an organization for relatives of the disappeared, and many of those who told me traumatic narratives were members of the GAM or other organizations who had told their stories to human rights workers before me. To take note of this experience, however, is not to diminish the harrowing nature of these narratives or the force they exerted. People spoke as though they were reliving the events they described, often in gruesome detail and in long bursts, markedly varying their tone and pitch; sometimes they would stare, become glassy-eyed, or cry. Often they felt incapable of fully representing what had happened, trailing off with exclamations like, "Käx, käx, käx!" (It hurts, it is difficult).[2] Women were more likely than men to tell such stories, but when the stories involved sexual assault, a more authoritative speaker would often take over, as when a husband recounted how soldiers gang-raped his wife, resulting in the death of the infant she was carrying on her back as well as her own violation, while she sat silently beside him with her eyes downcast. After hearing such stories, I too felt compelled to give them voice and frustrated by my inability to do so. I sometimes had dreams about or even flashbacks to events I had heard described—by way, I imagine, of discharging some of their burden. But full discharge was impossible. When I told a friend about one such dream, he responded, "Yes, that's how it was," but even as he said it I knew it could not have really been so. Traumatic narratives identified Chupolenses as victims of unspeakable acts and me as their imperfect witness, drawing us all into the fraught space humanitarianism describes.

The stories I began to hear later in fieldwork I will gloss as "historical narratives." Even when I heard them from the same people who had earlier told me traumatic narratives, they bore few markers of their tellers' encounters with either unspeakable violence or therapeutic testimonio. These stories were not plagued by displacement or aporia; while men were more likely than women to produce them, they also tended to be their subjects, and they usually seemed in full control of their narration, calmly building arguments and adducing dates, names, and places to prove the points they wished to make about the revolutionary past. My requests for elaboration or clarification caused no controversy or discomfort. On the contrary, speakers frequently commented on their own narrative or asked for my opinion, using phrases like, "How do you see it?" or "This is what I think." Often these narratives took on an elegiac tone, sometimes colored by rumination or denunciation, but always engaging my powers of analysis rather than compassion.

Historical narratives evoked revolutionary rather than therapeutic testimonio in the sense that their subject was often the birth of conciencia. They usually told of the frustrating and hurtful state of relations between indigenous people and ladinos in the 1960s and 1970s and the speaker's dawning awareness, often through engagements with the revitalized Catholic church, that structural racism was responsible for this suffering. Frequently they described the head-turning rapidity with which Chupol became entangled with a series of revolutionary organizations that they saw as mobilizing the community to rectify this situation. Only then did they sometimes give way to traumatic narrative, when describing the mobilization's bloody dénouement.

But even when their content could have fallen out of the pages of I, Rigoberta Menchú, historical narratives ultimately failed to obey the critical conventions of revolutionary testimonio. Specifically they treated the revolutionary moment as past rather than future; these were tales of loss rather than appeals to "go on." Where romance emplots the inevitable unfolding of a better future, David Scott argues, tragedy "offers an agonic confrontation that holds out no necessary promise of rescue or reconciliation" (2004: 135), which suits it to voicing "a postcolonial present . . . drained of the fervor of the anticolonial revolution" (172). With its refusal to go on seeking freedom and simultaneous reluctance to lay the past to rest, the historical narrative locates Chupolenses and their interlocutors in this tragic postrevolutionary present.

Appreciating the postrevolutionary dimensions of the Guatemalan humanitarian context in turn frames the historical narrative as the revelation of a subjectivity that humanitarianism has displaced or even repressed, allowing Chupolenses to overcome a political silence in some ways as harmful as those imposed by their trauma. Witnessing the truth of their revolutionary past in this manner thus serves to challenge humanitarianism's circumscription of Chupolenses to their role as victims. The act of serving as witness to the lost revolutionary past, however, also returns me to the role of freeing Chupolenses to be the postrevolutionary selves they truly are, reclaiming the historical narrative, however involuntarily, for humanitarianism's therapeutic project and ultimately rehabilitating the story of Chupolenses' disappointed hopes for circulation as another sign of harm. Placing Chupol's revolutionary past under the sign of tragedy, in short, does not make the call of that past any easier to hear.

A third local genre of narrative about the war, however, did open my ears. From time to time throughout my fieldwork, I was surprised by something I will call the "heroic narrative." Where traumatic narratives speak of suffering, and historical narratives are "troubled by the hubris of enlightenment and civilization, power and knowledge" (Scott 2004: 13), stories in this third genre are jocular and boastful. Men, again, tended to be both the authors and the subjects of these narratives, although women also made jokes about wartime experiences to similar effect (McAllister 2010). Significantly I never elicited heroic narratives; the example below, like the others I heard, arose in the interstices of other discussions, some motivated by questions about "the violence" or revolutionary organizations, but some on unrelated topics.

On this occasion, around six months into my fieldwork, I was subjecting a sixty-year-old man I will call Max to a standardized survey that covered everything from the size of Chupolense landholdings to local perceptions of crime, passing through several fact-finding questions about the war. About two-thirds of the way through the questionnaire, I asked him where he and his family had gone when the army came. For Chupolenses, the arrival of soldiers in the community on August 15, 1981, marks the beginning of the war, so this survey question tended to launch respondents into traumatic narratives: we took refuge elsewhere; we were fine until the soldiers began to hunt us;

we had to hide in the brush; we lived and died like animals. Like many of his neighbors, Max began, "We went to hide in the mountains in the village of Lacamá," but then went off in another direction:

> One day I came upon some soldiers on either side of a man they were kidnapping. They wanted to take him to an avocado tree, where there were four other people sitting, surrounded by soldiers. There were also two women. "Why are you fleeing? Why are you afraid?" the soldiers asked these people in Spanish. The women didn't answer. I said, "Why are you asking them if they don't understand?" The army said they were helping them, that they went to get them from their house because they had escaped from the military base. I said, "We've got a lot of things to do, we're not afraid." They searched the women's bags and found two little rolls. "Oh, for your *compañeros* from the mountains," they said. Who could believe that about so little food?
>
> I said, "How could you think such a thing? You have no head. We should be praying." "What did you say?" they asked, because they heard that I'd mentioned God. The soldiers said, "You are *buena gente*, a good person, not *mala gente*, bad people, you'll help us. You have to come with us." I told the soldiers: "I am an *hijo de Dios*, a child of God. We are Christians. You are not children of God, you are animals. You come to kill people, you are *hijos de animales*, children of animals. Why don't you let us go?" They told me to get everyone together so they could kill them all at once. "Chupol has been swept clean but here hasn't. We have to leave this place leveled. We have to kill everybody to get rid of Lacamá as well." Then they tried to shoot me but the gun didn't go off. They gave me a date, but I didn't get everyone together. They kept asking the same questions: "Why did you escape?"

I congratulated Max on his bravery. "If you didn't talk, they killed you," he explained. "If you're nervous, then you must of course be a guerrilla. Since I was brave enough to talk, then, 'Of course he must know nothing,' they said."

Juxtaposing Max's heroic tale with traumatic or historical narratives brings out perhaps its most striking feature: while it is certainly presented as an eyewitness account, it doesn't seem particularly true. It is highly unlikely that Max insulted the normally trigger-happy enemy this clearly or that the soldiers' high-tech arms would all fail at once. But these improbable details serve to communicate the deeper truth that Max possesses heroic qualities as a defender of his people and a forthright speaker of his mind. Another Chupolense man who told me a similar story about confronting the soldiers on the day they arrived in Chupol (when, according to other accounts, they kidnapped and killed anyone they happened to encounter) summarized the claim Max makes here in stronger language: "They wanted to kidnap me but because I'm a *cabrón* [tough guy], I didn't let them."

Asserting these virtues establishes Max's authority to challenge the frame the soldiers have placed on their encounter with him. A critical element of army strategy was to convince Mayans that guerrillas were evil incarnate — bad people, or *mala gente* (see Levenson in this volume for what it means to be *malo* in the postwar). In Chupolense recollections of army propaganda, one of the principal manifestations of this moral turpitude was the guerrillas' propensity to behave like animals — for example, by freely sharing their women, a practice the army claimed was common in Cuba. In his brave defense of the women, Max turns this propaganda on its head: "I am a child of God," he tells the soldiers. "You come to kill people; you are children of animals." Moral questions have nothing to do with the *compañeros* from the mountains, he insists, but rather with how one behaves in this wartime situation. Max is a hero, he wants me to know, because he is a good person.

But such narrative jujitsu hints that Max's story also contains a metanarrative showing how good people should deal with bad or unreasonable demands, which is to use the appearance of going along with them as a means to avoid actually doing so. Of course, the soldiers make this feint easy to pull off, for, as children of animals, they are stupid: they don't know how much food it takes to feed a guerrilla army; they don't understand that the women don't speak Spanish; they keep asking the same foolish questions. "You have no head!" Max scolds them — even as he refuses to heed their repeated insinuations that he and the women are subversives. Max's heroism is proved by the foolish conclusion they draw from his responses. "Of course, he must know nothing," they decide. Max is a child of God, his narrative suggests, because he can keep a secret.

Given what I know (and was coming to know then) of Chupol's history, it seems likely that the secret Max is keeping from the soldiers actually does have something to do with the compañeros from the mountains. In fact when I asked him right after the story if he belonged to any "organization" while he was in Lacamá, he responded, "Yes, we were members — I mean, they warned us about things." It is not particularly mysterious why Max would want to conceal this relationship from soldiers engaged in a scorched-earth hunt for subversives. But in responding to my invitation to tell me his whereabouts during the war with a story about how stupid it is to ask questions about where people are going and what they are doing, Max's heroic narrative also encourages me to recognize that he is *still keeping a secret*, perhaps even from me. What purpose, almost two decades after the fact, does this insistence serve?

One way to understand it would be as a reproach to my overeager invitations to tell me what happened. Mayan sociolinguistic norms do not include the survey or the interview; overt inquiries are often preceded by an apology, *disculpe la pregunta*, to mitigate any threat to the addressee's authority or dignity. The war is also a delicate subject for any variety of talk; participants in a mental health workshop for survivors held at Chupol's church, lifelong neighbors who had suffered for years alongside one another, reported that they had never before openly discussed their wartime experiences or their sequelae. The local chapter of Neurotics Anonymous — which promotes mental health on the model of Alcoholics Anonymous and has a considerable following among poor Guatemalans — prohibited its members from speaking about the war, surely at least one cause of their neuroses. The combination of Chupolense aversion to questioning and reluctance to give voice to "poisonous knowledge" (Das 2007) often poses a challenge to therapeutic interventions, as the mental health workshop itself made clear. To the dismay of conveners, who hoped to instill a culture of compassionate witnessing in Chupol, participants universally preferred among three possible "listening strategies" the one in which someone who comes upon a sad friend says hello and walks on without mentioning her distress, instead of the conveners' preferred alternative, asking her what is wrong.

To treat Max's response as a demand for greater sensitivity to cultural norms for relating pain to language, however, is to gloss over the fact that he links my invitation to "tell what happened" to military aggression. In fact Chupolenses commonly include "Me hicieron muchas preguntas" (They asked me many questions) among the indignities they suffered at the hands of soldiers, and survey subjects other than Max also associated my questionnaire with that tense communicative context. A woman I will call Sebastiana was highly forthcoming on such topics as land, work, and religion but grew taciturn as we touched on issues closer to the war. When I asked her the same question that provoked Max's story, she responded only with voluble and seemingly irrelevant complaints about her neighbors' penchant for calumny. Although I tried not to press too much, by the end of our interview she seemed flustered. As we sat sharing a Coca-Cola, Sebastiana looked me in the eye and said accusingly, in the Spanish she rarely spoke, "You asked me many questions."

A chance encounter with a ladina woman I will call Pancha, who turned out to have worked for the army's notorious G2 intelligence service, sharpened such reproaches. Unnervingly chatty, Pancha told me with little prodding that she had been stationed in Chupol's occupied church during the horrific 1981–83 period, producing her own traumatic narratives about staying up all night with her fellow soldiers in terror of a guerrilla ambush, playing cards and sharing stories about ghost cows with eyes of fire wandering the highway. She left the military some years later after "overhearing" an incident, on which she did not further elaborate, involving a woman subversive held captive in the Escuela Politécnica. But despite these traumas, she was grateful for the experience of indigenous culture the army had given her and confessed that her dream was to put it to use working for an NGO in the countryside: "I know how to treat indigenous people. Now when I go to the Quiché I feel sad not to be working there anymore." She acquired these skills with indigenous people in a forty-day course called "Superior Psychological Relations in the Rural Area," which trained her to conduct herself as follows:

> A call would come in from Mariscal [the military base in the capital that controlled operations in this part of the highlands]: go to such-and-such a place to see if so-and-so is there. I would say I was a nurse or a teacher and find out if the information we had been given was true. Say it were you: I would follow you, make you my friend. I really identified with those humble people, indigenous people. I would sit on the floor, eat tortillas. I learned to make tortillas, learned words in Q'eqchi' or Kaqchikel. [People in this area actually speak K'iche'.] I would bring them gifts.

Minus the lying and the eventual demise of informants, Pancha's tactics for creating rapport were chillingly similar to my own.

These similarities suggest that it may be not just my questions but also the affect of compassion for "those humble people, indigenous people" apparently animating them that gave Max and Sebastiana pause. Chupolenses were often reluctant to accept the good faith of my desire to bear witness to their stories; a number of my surveys have notes on them like "He wants to know, what for?"[3] Like Max, these respondents are framing their silences as something *withheld* rather than something that cannot be said, as secrets rather than traumatic ruptures (Sommer 1991). By using his heroic narrative to point this out, Max asks me to abstain from compassion for his victimhood, at least for a moment. In troubling the assumption that the proper and exclusive end of my work in Chupol is helping Chupolenses work through their extraordinary hurts, his request may also chart a path beyond the humanitarian overdetermination of our relationship as one between a victim and his compassionate witness.

Heeding Parable in a Revolutionary Situation

Regarding the course this path should take, however, I can only fully attest that Max's insistence on secrecy means I have to figure it out. In *The Genesis of Secrecy*, Frank Kermode (1979: 23) explores the parables Jesus tells in the Gospels to explore the obscurity of "narratives that mean more and other than they seem to say, and mean different things to different people." In Mark, irritated at the apostles' failure to understand the Parable of the Sower, Jesus snaps that the point of his stories is not to illuminate the elect, who should already understand his message, but to bewilder noninitiates, "so that seeing they may see and not perceive, and hearing they may hear but not understand, lest at any time they should turn, and their sins be forgiven them" (Mark 4: 11–12, cited in Kermode 1979: 29). Such exclusionary esotericism seems to clash with the evangelical mission of spreading the Good Word, but Kermode argues that it insinuates an insistence on secrecy, the injunction that "nothing can become clear until after the Resurrection" into the heart of this mission (140). Seeing but not perceiving and hearing but not understanding is a fine description of the soldiers' reaction to their conversation with Max. In telling me a story that suggests that I, like them, am asking stupid questions, Max challenges me to shift from a hermeneutics of testimonio to a hermeneutics of parable, of secrecy.

What does such a hermeneutic ask of me, and how can I relate these responsibilities to those I bear for learning to hear the call to "go on" of revolutionary testimonio? Kermode notes that once we accept a division of the world into initiates and outsiders, we also accept that it is possible for the truth to finally be revealed, for ourselves to be initiated, which stirs in us "a passion for fulfillment, fullness, completion" (1979: 106). To serve this passion, we embark on interpretations, ferreting out the clues that will allow us to discover a narrative's secrets and bring it to its logical end. The clue to Max's heroic narrative seems to be his claim to be a child of God, someone who, as he told me a little later, has "always turned about to find where God lay." Where does this clue take me if I pursue it?

Max has long served as a catechist in Chupol's Catholic community, and in the late 1960s and early 1970s people who played this role were learning to find God in new places. One of the most controversial moves in the modernization of the Catholic church that began with Vatican II was Pope Paul VI's proclamation that the conscience (conciencia) is "man's most secret core, and his sanctuary [w]here he is alone with God whose voice echoes in his depths" (1965: 16). Understood in Christian moral theology as "God's abode in us," the spark of the Holy Spirit that allows us to witness and obey God's Word, the conscience is at once human and divine (Delhaye 1968: 85). Within Catholicism, this ambiguity makes the conscience an important locus of apostolic formation and governance, for the Church as the anointed community of Christ is the only place where relationships between God and the world can properly be specified (Delhaye 1968; Mahoney 1989). Paul's statement shocked because it privileged the moral instincts of the faithful over the Church's tutelary interpretation of those instincts, locating apostolic authority in the world rather than the ecclesiastical hierarchy.

Latin American liberation theology framed this authority as what Gustavo Gutiérrez calls "the right of the poor to think out their own faith" (1988: xxi). Affirming this right, however, did not mean accepting Protestant doctrines of personal revelation. If anything, the new responsibilities borne by the conscience demanded intensified apostolic attention to the formation of this moral faculty. Rethinking the relationship between the Church and the world means "articulat[ing] the discourse of society, of the oppressed, of the world of popular, symbolic, and sacramental signs, with the discourse of faith and the normative tradition of the church" (Boff and Boff 1987: 25). The method of articulation was *concientización*, a recursive process elaborated by the radical Brazilian educator Paolo Freire, that asked the poor to reflect on their knowledge of the world as a means of transforming themselves from spectators to, and objects of, a situation of injustice into self-determining subjects capable of understanding and transforming that situation. Within the Church, concientización used the prophetic and testimonial logic of biblical texts as a tool of reflection. Groups of poor and often initially illiterate lay Catholics learned to read the stories of Exodus and the Crucifixion as attesting that the "eternal salvation [God and Christ] offer is mediated by the historical liberations that dignify the children of God and render credible the coming utopia" (Boff and Boff 1987: 8–9). Concientización also required Christians to bear witness to this truth in their own historical action.

In Guatemala the principal vector of indigenous mobilization for revolution, the CUC, was formed through such a process of testimonial reflection. In the late 1970s groups of radical Jesuits in the Central American province formed a series of linked Centers for Research and Social Action to accompany the struggles for justice of the poorest and most oppressed members of their communities by integrating analysis and praxis. The Guatemalan center was informally known as the "Zone 5 Jesuits," a nickname referring to its location in a poor neighborhood of the capital, where researchers could be "more incarnate in reality [*más encarnada en la realidad*]" (Hoyos de Asig 1997: 50). "The objective that gradually gained priority" among the group, according to member Ricardo Falla "was popular organizing" (2000: 50).

By 1974 two young Spanish Jesuits, Fernando Hoyos and Enrique Corral, had moved from Zone 5 into Chimaltenango and the Quiché, where Catholic Action had produced a generation of indigenous catechists whose desires for change were difficult to address within a traditional ecclesiastical framework. One of the Bible study groups Hoyos established in Santa Cruz del Quiché was called Nukuj, a Maya-K'iche' term meaning, according to one participant, "preparation for the celebration" (Hoyos de Asig 1997: 134), but more literally, "training, rehearsal, or practice." To prepare, Nukuj members compared the attempts of local peasant organizations to liberate their communities with the efforts of Moses and Christ, inevitably finding them lacking. Nukuj and similar groups produced the indigenous leaders who went on to form the CUC, while Hoyos and Corral went on to become EGP commanders (for a fuller account of this process see Arias 1990; Le Bot 1995; Konefal 2010).

Given this history, hearing Max's claim to be a child of God as a coded reference to the birth of his revolutionary conciencia, and thus as a kind of encrypted revolutionary testimonio, would not be unreasonable. His insistence on encrypting this reference also links him to this very history. Insurgencies characteristically establish double worlds, asking their militants to maneuver between the aboveground of legality and the underground in which plans to overthrow the state can be developed and carried out before they are discovered. Training manuals for the EGP repeatedly hammer home the need to create spaces of clandestinity, where a revolutionary can hide in plain view by falsifying her identity, speaking in code, and otherwise concealing her true intentions and nature; and to practice compartmentalization, in which the revolutionary maintains her normal routine and relationships while conducting her revolutionary activities on the sly. The late 1970s EGP followed a mass organizational strategy that also required the broader group of nonmilitants it claimed as its social base to internalize these disciplines, both for their self-protection and for the viability of the struggle. The CUC was thus always a "semiclandestine" organization. Max was likely exhibiting revolutionary discipline when he encountered the soldiers, and perhaps he encodes the revolutionary testimonio he gives to me because he continues to keep faith with it.

But does understanding Max as possessed of conciencia mean I have heard the authentic indigenous revolutionary call to "go on"? A Jesuit I interviewed who ran a program in the 1970s to capacitate rural cooperativists at the Rafael Landívar Jesuit University, but who described himself as a "timid reformist," suggested that the existence of clandestine underworlds within Guatemalan Christianity inflected all Christian discourse with hermeneutic difficulties:

> In a situation of low-intensity war everything becomes polarized. Everything becomes so intensely black and white. We had to be careful with our words: *orejas* [informers, spies] would come. Anyone who went out in the hope of making changes, "Oh, they're communists," but people didn't even know how to pronounce the word. "*Comunistes*," they would say.[4] "Why are they killing us for that? What is that?" What do you explain to people who don't know how to read or write so that there will be no misunderstanding? We couldn't say *adiestrar* [training, drilling], because it could sound like weapons, or "revolutionary change"—revolution means turning things around, not necessarily a war, but you had to be careful, explain your words. We said we were giving people their *armas* [weapons], but for us they were intellectual ones, we never said that they were militating in anything. No violence. But people take what they want.

Once we agree that the meaning of a text needs decoding, Kermode (1979: 126) notes, we are also forced to admit that it is motivated by something other than transparent reference to the truth and thus that our pursuit of its "latent mysteries" to their ultimate source will eventually be disappointed. Inevitably, we are left to wonder if we too are just taking what we want. Perhaps Max's narrative is, at long last, the true story of all the poor people of Guatemala, or perhaps it's just something he said to get through our interview. I have no verifiable grounds on which to decide this question.

And yet, Kermode cautions, in matters of interpretation, the impossibility of verification is not necessarily a failure: "To see, even to perceive, to hear, even to understand, is not the same thing as to explain or even the same thing as to have access." Although we may despair at having to admit to "a measure of private intermittency in our interpretations" (1979: 126), the act of pursuing them nonetheless draws us into meaningful relationships with one another and with the world. These relationships may indeed be the point of interpretation, as the Landívar Jesuit then suggested. The Landívar, unlike other Central American Jesuit institutions, remained on the Right during the war, refusing, among other reactionary gestures, to let the Zone 5 Jesuits live in the university community. The Landívar Jesuit told me he rejected liberation theology and accused his Zone 5 brethren of endangering the groups with which they worked. Eventually, however, he told me that he thought their error had been less ideological than linguistic; they had made things too *explicit*. "I could see where [the Zone 5 Jesuits] were going, that liberating the people is good: the problem is how," he argued.

Shortly after, in language curiously like Max's, he boasted of using the appearance of candidness to frustrate understanding: "I had lots of books about Marxism at my house. If some ignorant person came to search my place they might think something, but since I taught sociology and Marxism was in vogue then, well, I had to have my references, right?" When I later recounted this conversation to a friend who is a former EGP militant, she told me she remembered the Landívar Jesuit from meetings of the organization. I said that she must have confused him with someone else, citing his institutional location and professed reformism, but she insisted that he had participated. I, and you, can take from this what we want.

Perhaps what the Landívar Jesuit tells us is that leaving room for people to take what they want is also a method of concientización. Sebastián Morales, the catechist who led Chupol's incorporation into the armed struggle (see Velásquez Nimatuj, this volume), had his first experience of concientización at a Jesuit-run Bible-reading workshop at the Landívar, where he claims (despite the Landívar Jesuit's protestations) that he was encouraged to emulate Moses and Jesus in leading his people out of oppression. But subsequent invitations to deepen his commitment came in the form of allusions and puzzles that awakened his love of fulfillment rather than providing him with instruction. He joined the CUC when his neighbor asked him for help with some "work." When pressed as to the nature of this work, the neighbor told him only that it was with an "organization" and for the "short term," without any further specification. This same neighbor moved Morales to join the armed struggle by telling him the following parable:

> What if there's a dog lying in the way, and we want to get that dog out of there? Are we just going to say, "Good dog, get out, go away?" He won't pay attention. And if you kick him, he'll jump on you and bite you, and stay anyway. Instead, if we make a good stick, and we tell that dog to respect us and to get out of there, and he doesn't want to go, we'll get him out with blows. And if he wants to jump on us, we'll answer him with blows.

Morales's story of revolutionary awakening is emplotted not as a romance with a known end but as an ever-deepening mystery, with each turn marked by the locution "And then I realized . . ." followed by a further question: "And then I wondered, why?"

The birth of the consciousness of other Chupolenses likewise meant learning not only to ask new questions but also to refrain from demanding answers. For Emilio, a young CUC leader who later served as Chupol's liaison with the national EGP leadership, initiation into the armed struggle came with an explicit injunction to hold its name and ends in abeyance:

A guy came and told me about a new organization. "It's a nice thing," he said, "This organization helps poor people, *campesinos*—it's related to the CUC." First they communicated with us to see if we were willing; bit by bit, if we thought it was a good organization we could join. "This organization is dangerous, clandestine—it can't be clarified [*no se puede aclarar*]," he said.

Like Sebastián and Emilio, most Chupolenses who are willing to speak about what it meant to mobilize for coming liberation describe at length their induction into the disciplines of clandestinity and compartmentalization and the mysteries it entailed. Incorporated into the organization as cells of four or five families, they faced heavy sanctions for discussing what they knew outside this group. Each cell member acquired a nom de guerre, which was taken from the limited roster of first names already used in the community, producing a reduplication of identities that even those in the know sometimes found difficult to follow. Conversation among cell members, who were also often neighbors, took place not in their homes but in what Chupolenses calls the *xkay* or *monte*, the wild space of the brush, at night, and through allusions, parables, and puzzles. This doubling over of quotidian existence into a daylight realm faced by a shadowy, secret one has left enduring traces on Chupolense understandings of what it means to have a conciencia.

Secrecy sometimes meant finding the mysteries of the organization genuinely mysterious. So many people made puzzling and conflicting allusions to a tree when telling me how their conciencia was born that I began to inquire into its meaning. Gregorio Chay, the national CUC leader who was likely responsible for introducing the tree into Chupolense discourse, told me it represented the "tree of exploitation," whose branches were the different government agencies responsible for making peasants' lives difficult, and which had to be cut down. Juana, a young woman who would have been seven years old at the time of the following incident, had her own interpretation of this image:

They put up a blackboard, they made drawings in the shape of a tree. "What we have to do now is tear up the root, and also cut off the branches." So, let's say, the tree is the government and the branches and the root are the armies [*los ejércitos*]. So they have to fight with the army and also with the government. In that example it's the government in the middle, in the trunk, exactly, so the little branches and the root are the army.

But according to Juana, most Chupolenses took the tree at face value: "They thought it really was a tree that they had to cut like that . . . but no, it's not, because they didn't understand that it was the government, like the enemy is the tree, you know, like an example." Conversations with Juana's neighbors on this subject tended to corroborate her assessment of their analysis. But despite the gap between the testimony this example was intended to bear and what Chupolenses were able to witness, the tree persists in Chupolense memories. Its persistence suggests that what pulled on Chupolense conciencias was the echo of a secret that could be heard in that gap; as in Emilio's case, the will to understand took temporal and moral precedence over knowing the truth.

Like the example of the tree, the intermittent echo thrown off by what may or may not be Max's conciencia in his narrative summons my interpretive labor toward a future that stretches beyond our meeting. It is thus in Max's refusal to speak of revolution that I am paradoxically able to hear a call to "go on" that resonates with that of revolutionary testimonio. Indeed the prevalence of latent mysteries over revealed truths in Chupolense accounts of revolutionary mobilization hints that conciencia may *only* be able to find refuge in parable when its promise to transform the future has yet to be fulfilled—that is, in a truly revolutionary situation. When I interviewed Enrique Corral, I pressed him to reflect on how the Catholic theology of the conscience had informed his involvement as a former Jesuit in the concientización of a generation of Guatemalan indigenous revolutionaries. He claimed he felt too theologically rusty to answer, for, unlike Fernando Hoyos, who remained in the Society of Jesus until he was killed by the army in 1982, Corral renounced his vows when he became an EGP commander. But as he described the ebbing of his vocation after entering clandestinity—not least because he began to fall in love with the woman who is now his wife—he brightened. "For me," he said, "clandestinity was the purest form of conciencia. No one knew who you were or where you came from, and you were free to act on your conciencia alone." The freedom and loving engagement that are the full exercise of conciencia cannot survive full disclosure while counterinsurgency seeks to contain their threat. If I try to understand rather than simply hear what Max is trying (not) to tell me, I allow the impossibility of finally determining the source of his story's echoes to teach me this, and thus to enact my own concientización.

This Is How My Consciousness Was Born (*Así me nació la conciencia*)

If all the available facts, including Chupolenses' own traumatic and historical narratives, suggests that we live in an age "drained of the fervor" of revolution (Scott 2004: 172), to what end is my conciencia born?[5] My argument that Max's secret participates in a particular revolutionary process should not be taken as a suggestion that he is holding out hope for a revival of the EGP or the CUC. On the contrary, while a surprisingly large number of Chupolenses remained in these and other organizations with roots in the armed Left even after they had been decimated by state counterinsurgency, by the late 1990s (and after the schisms documented in Velásquez Nimatuj and Bastos and Camus in this volume) many had grown weary with the leadership of these organizations and abandoned their ties to them. Nor should tracing the links between this process and debates within Catholic theology be understood as a claim that Max became a revolutionary because Jesus told him to. Attuning my ears to that which is inaudible in humanitarian testimonio no more gives me access to the Christian absolute than it enrolls me in a clandestine army of the poor.

But it does allow me to hear the call of a historicity that is not that of post-revolutionary tragedy, with its humanitarian "promise of being in the know, of being nonduped, of adequately accounting for, or reckoning" (Nelson 2009b: 30), a list to which we might add "of bearing witness." Fifteen years after the end of the armed conflict, the forces of injustice and violence that made revolution seem inevitable in Guatemala in the 1970s and 1980s are re-surgent, their ranks swollen with new members and their arsenals with new arms. Hemmed in by such forces, testimonial accounts of the past can only affirm as a truth the impossibility of conciencia ever finding its fulfillment in history. Max's refusal to attest to this truth, his insistence on awakening our love of fulfillment, and with it our commitment to the future, reminds us, in Freire's words, that the "unfinished character of human beings and the trans-formational character of reality necessitate that education be an ongoing ac-tivity" (2000: 84). Allowing ourselves to be educated in the enduring possi-bility of transformation is surely a project as worthy of collaboration as that of extending our compassion around the world.

Notes

The author would like to thank Malcolm Blincow, Elizabeth Ferry, Ashley Lebner, Laurie Baker, George Lovell, Ellen Moodie, John Beverly, two anonymous reviewers for Duke University Press, and of course Diane Nelson for their very helpful comments on this paper.

1. Authors who address these questions include Colvin 2004; Ross 2003; Fassin 2008; Das 2007; Hunt 2008; Wilson 2001; Theidon 2010; Sanford 2006.

2. When speaking in K'iche', Chupolenses sometimes use this expression to refer to the period of the war, that is, as "the hurt."

3. I hasten to note that these interviews were preceded by the appropriate obtaining of consent.

4. Guatemalan racist discourse commonly indexes the presence of an indigenous speaker with this erroneous substitution of an "e" for the final "a" or "o" of Spanish words.

5. The title of this section is the subtitle of the Spanish edition of *I, Rigoberta Menchú*.

PART II

MARKET FREEDOMS AND MARKET FORCES
The New Biopolitical Economy

DEVELOPMENT AND/AS DISPOSSESSION
Elite Networks and Extractive Industry in the Franja Transversal del Norte

Guatemala's Franja Transversal del Norte (Northern Transversal Strip) comprises the northern areas of Izabal, Alta Verapaz and El Quiché provinces and a small area of Huehuetenango, covering approximately 9,000 square kilometers. . . . It is a focal point of transnational investment due to its oil reserves and development possibilities in agriculture, cattle and lumber extraction; it is a source of speculation, enrichment, and dispossession for the new class holding power in the country.
Le Monde Diplomatique, October 1979

Cycles of Repression
In March 2011 over eight hundred mostly Maya-Q'eqchi' families were violently evicted from fourteen communities in the Polochic River area of Alta Verapaz. Antonio Beb Ac was killed, children and adults suffered from tear gas poisoning, their houses were burned or bulldozed, and hundreds of hectares of corn, beans, and other crops were destroyed. The families had been negotiating with the government and nongovernmental organizations for title to the land they were occupying, which is owned by the Widmann Lagarde family (owners of other large landholdings in the area). The families claimed the Widmann Lagardes had acquired it through questionable legal maneuvering. The Widmann family had installed the Chabil Utzaj sugar refinery there, but in 2009 they declared bankruptcy and abandoned the mill, raising residents' hopes of gaining title to the land. In October 2010, however, the Widmanns received new financing from the Central American Eco-

nomic Integration Bank (BCIE) to restart the refinery, and the violent displacements began.

Thirty years after *Le Monde* highlighted how enrichment and dispossession are entwined, such contradictions are being felt more sharply than ever. In this essay I argue that the Franja Transversal del Norte—that "focal point of investments"—is a useful place to understand the new economic and political world that is unfolding in the aftermath of Guatemala's civil war for peasants, indigenous peoples, and national elites. In many ways it is a microcosm of the issues, strategies, and actors that gave rise to the war and of the new economic and ecological system that is taking shape, a system that will affect Guatemalan national life far into the future.

The Franja is a large, mostly lowland region, stretching along the border with Mexico and historically isolated from, first, colonial and, later, national power centers by mountains and impassable jungle. It is a wild and inhospitable terrain (although rich pre-Columbian remains show it was once more heavily populated), and indigenous people fled there during the colonial period to escape the burdens of paying Spanish tribute, making the Q'eqchi' famously the last to fall under colonial dominion. Very sparsely populated, it remained an escape valve for political and population pressure through the beginning of the twenty-first century, even as it increasingly turned into a strategic zone for military governments after 1954. It was a central battleground in the post-1978 phase of the counterinsurgency war, inaugurated with the army massacre of Q'eqchi' peasants in Panzós, Alta Verapaz. The Ixcán and the Ixil areas, subregions within the Franja, saw intense violence, with the Ixil one of the four genocide cases recognized by the United Nations Commission for Historical Clarification. In the past ten years it has become ground zero for the intensive exploitation of nonrenewable natural resources and the production of so-called eco-friendly biofuels and hydroelectric energy, both controlled by political and business elites. This isolated but vital region has been transformed by these projects and the infrastructure needed to implement them, and is in turn transforming Guatemala's political economy.

As an economist and journalist, I have a perspective that may be more mid- and large scale than other authors in this book, but I am also strongly influenced by the work of the anthropologist Marta Casaus Arzú (1992) on family networks. In what follows I focus on who, among the small circle of elites, owns what and where, to describe how the Franja Transversal reveals an emerging model of postwar rural development. This requires following kin relations that twine through different industries, forms of production, financial, religious, and legal institutions, political parties, state offices, and

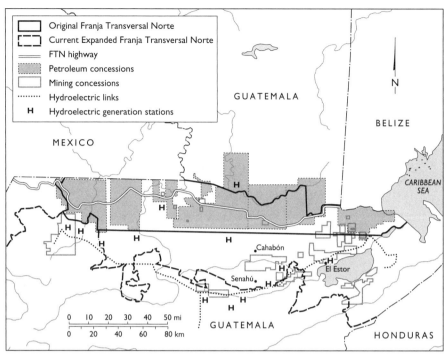

MAP 2 Map of Franja Transversal Norte.

military and paramilitary groups (including, increasingly, narcotrafficking), as well as global alliances, and how those ties enable increasing accumulation of the nation's riches in the hands of a few. The specifics I provide here of the family-industry-politics nexus involved in the Franja might seem, in their great and personalized detail, most useful for activists attempting to mitigate its effects. However, I argue that the *form* of this nexus organizes the exploitation of both persons and resources throughout Guatemala. These are central actors and key pieces in the jigsaw puzzle of Guatemala's recent history, and the density of connections between them is what allows these associations to thrive, while excluding the vast majority of Guatemalans from decision making about their futures. As readers will note, not a single Mayan name appears in these networks of power.

A Brief History of the Colonization of the Franja

Alta and Baja Verapaz were transformed by the coffee boom of the nineteenth century, when the liberal government essentially gave away land to primarily German plantation owners, thereby displacing large numbers of Q'eqchi' and Achi' from their plots and converting many of them into *mozos* and *colonos*, low-wage workers and sharecroppers. In the early twentieth century President Manuel Estrada Cabrera gave a 165,000-acre plantation in the Polochic Valley to the United Fruit Company, intensifying the violent eviction of local indigenous farmers (Grandin 2004: 140). Some of those dispossessed in these processes created small, isolated settlements in the northern jungles of the Franja. The 1954 counterrevolution also encouraged colonization of the Franja in place of the dismantled land reform of the Arbenz government, disregarding its shallow jungle soil as it was touted as an emerging "national breadbasket." About forty years ago, the first people to arrive in the Franja under this new regime were mostly ladino peasants from Chiantla, Huehuetenango. Desperate for land to cut their dependence on short-term migration to the south coast plantations during harvest season, they began to settle between the Ixcán and Xalbal rivers.

In the 1960s the Maryknoll and Sacred Heart orders of the Catholic Church organized a new wave of colonization after acquiring vast tracts of land through the state's National Institute for Agrarian Transformation (INTA). They brought Jakalteko, Mam, Q'anjob'al, Chuj, and K'iche' indigenous people, along with a few ladinos, to farm the zone. These priests, nuns, and farmers hoped to create what Beatriz Manz (2004) calls "a paradise" in this still mostly virgin forest, laboring to clear the jungle, build communities, and begin to plant with the goal of establishing not only a new economic system but also transformed social and spiritual relations. Although these utopian projects were later seen as a dire threat to the status quo, the state initially supported their efforts. It was eager to avoid, at any cost, even a hint at a land reform that might threaten the country's ossified agrarian structures. In the 1970s the government of Colonel Carlos Manuel Arana Osorio, with support from USAID, encouraged still further colonization by reconfiguring the Franja's administration and transforming its property-holding regime by declaring it an area of public interest and national urgency. Decree 60–70 established Agricultural Development Zones over a large area that included the municipalities of Santa Ana Huista, San Antonio Huista, Nentón, Jacaltenango, San Mateo Ixtatán, and Santa Cruz Barillas in Huehuetenango; Chajul and San Miguel Uspantán in El Quiché; Cobán, Chisec, San Pedro Carchá, Lanquín, Senahú, and Cahabón y Chahal in Alta Verapaz; and all of Izabal.

The unexpected consequence of the backbreaking labors of peasants desperate to create a better world for themselves and their families was that it drew attention to the immense natural riches of the area. They ended up almost literally paving the way for other interests — powerful economic groups burrowed deep within and parasitical on military rule — to move in and benefit from the very processes meant to address the agricultural needs of indigenous and peasant populations. Even as they encouraged people to move to this "paradise," Colonel Arana and subsequent military governments began to build a highway system connecting the entire region, part of a plan for more independent national development under strict military control. In the mid-1970s military commanders and their political and economic associates began a merciless campaign to accumulate territory for fine wood and lumber extraction, cattle raising, and oil and mineral prospecting, especially nickel, which culminated in the massacres of the early 1980s. By the mid-1960s there was an established guerrilla presence in the Sierra de las Minas, just south of the Franja, and the Franja itself was a stronghold of the Guerrilla Army of the Poor (EGP) and the Rebel Armed Forces (FAR) in the later 1970s. As a zone of "subversion," the Franja also became a site of strategic military importance for the army, which implemented its most devastating violence and most sophisticated social and political control in the area. Thousands were killed, entire communities were emptied, and tens of thousands took refuge, either in the forests as the Communities of Population in Resistance, or in refugee camps in Mexico (see Worby this volume). The Franja became a "paradise in ashes" (Manz 2004; see also CEH 1999; Falla 1992). Scorched-earth counterinsurgency was later transformed into return and resettlement of many of those affected, restructuring and redesigning local relations in ways that generated new problematics around landholding, increased agrarian conflict, and created new sites of struggle over the control of territory.

Although the military's ambitious road plans were interrupted by the rise of the guerrilla and the subsequent scorched-earth campaigns, postwar civilian governments are again working on the highway as a fundamental element in the new economic model gestating since the end of the civil war and galvanized with the signing of the peace accords. Both before and after the war, military, economic, and political groups drew on strategic and privileged information to appropriate and distribute lands they knew were rich in oil and minerals, beginning a transformation in the nation's formerly agrarian-based process of accumulation. This led to another expansion in the official borders of the region to encompass the Polochic River area in Alta Verapaz and the municipalities of Chajul and Uspantán in Quiché, all principal theaters of the counterinsurgency war and scene of the majority of the massacres. The Franja now constitutes 20 percent of the national territory, with 10 percent of the total population; 75 percent are indigenous, comprising thirteen ethnolinguistic communities. There are twenty-four municipalities, 80 percent of which are poor or extremely poor, registering chronic malnutrition and less than 50 percent literacy. These statistics have led postwar civilian governments to claim that reestablishing Agrarian Development Zones in the Franja is again of "public interest and national urgency" and to promise that the new highway and other infrastructure projects will alleviate the extreme poverty suffered by residents and victims of state violence. But this "agrarian development" is starkly different from the paradise the early arrivals envisioned. Governments in the twenty-first century are returning to the heavily militarized economic blueprints of the 1970s, which had sought to industrialize the country via the incipient Central American Common Market, focused first on forest extraction and cattle, and subsequently on oil drilling, mining, and hydroelectricity. I argue here, however, that these development plans are not innocent and that the highway is not a simple road. It is a strategy.

New Model, Old Associates

The new model for the Franja may, like the old one, be of "national urgency," but unlike the old one it can make few claims to operate in the "public interest." Its foundations lie in so-called megaprojects and in encouraging new economic activities based in extraction and exploitation of natural resources that will attract foreign investment (although, perhaps surprisingly, on much less favorable terms than under the nationalist military governments of the 1970s), benefit national elites, and increase competitiveness on the global market. Since 1996, with the end of the war, the Franja has seen the construction of massive hydroelectric facilities, mountaintop-removal mining, oil drilling, large-scale clear-cutting for new plantations of "megacrops" like African palm and extending sugarcane cultivation — both for the emerging biofuels markets — along with "megaroad" construction and the creation of ports, free trade zones, and corporate-controlled tourism infrastructure. Accompanying and facilitating these enormous interventions in the physical landscape is the deepening "liberalization," or privatization, of the markets in telecommunications, electricity, and financial services. All of these transformations, moreover, are anchored in the formation of new alliances between national and foreign capital under the sign of increasing corporate conglomeration, such that large businesses, both national and transnational, dominate the processes and investments that are reconfiguring the country's historic agro-export economy. This model enacts a kind of internal neocolonialism in which transnationals, governments, and economic and military elites are allied in search of the biggest profits, while sustainable development and social needs remain missing in action. The heirs to the transnational counter-insurgency projects that have violently reshaped Guatemala over the past sixty years have seized upon this advantage to embark on new processes of accumulation at previously unimaginable scales of profitability and social and ecological devastation. The Franja is becoming the central nervous system of an increasingly exclusionary Mesoamerica-wide system.

To understand how this scaling-up of prior formations of capital is taking place, it is crucial to understand the particularity of the links among sectors of the Guatemalan elite, state projects, academic-political ideological formations, and transnational extractive corporations. Global capital does not encounter a blank field in the spaces where it chooses to invest. It confronts not only local political and social histories but also already functioning markets and legislation, all of which must be contained or transformed to ensure conditions of sufficient profitability to "justify the risk" of investing in what are, thanks in large part to the operations of global capital itself, increasingly "unstable places." Success depends on the connections corporations are able to form with national elites, who can help them negotiate their entry into national markets — acquiring land and labor, for example — as well as reforming local governance to suit their needs. The rewards for national elites willing to play this role are significant: transnational investment represents an extraordinary opportunity for restaking their interests in the new global economy as well as consolidating their power over competing elite sectors and the country as a whole.

The reopening of postwar Guatemala and particularly the post-genocide Franja for transnational business began with President Alvaro Arzú (1995–99) and shows how these connections have helped ground transnational extractive industries in Guatemala's most violent and exclusionary legacies. Arzú was the fourth president of Guatemala after the return to civilian rule in 1985, and his government signed the peace accords with the Guatemalan National Revolutionary Unity (URNG). Nonetheless he had long-standing ties to right-wing terror. Earlier in his career Arzú was a member of the professional wing of the Movement for National Liberation (MLN), the self-proclaimed party of organized violence, which played a central role in the 1954 overthrow of Arbenz and later spawned the infamous Mano Blanca (White Hand) death squad. Arzú was also the director of INGUAT, the state's tourism office, during the regime of General Fernando Romeo Lucas García (1978–82). He later distanced himself from this sanguinary past, winning the presidency with the new National Advancement Party (PAN), overtly representing business interests. His government mounted the largest campaign for international investment in Guatemala's history, much of it focused on the Franja. The peace accords conveniently supplied a central element of development strategy by offering "the necessary political stability" for investor confidence.

One of Arzú's major backers was the García Granados family — Arzú's first wife was Silvia García Granados de Garay — which has links to right-wing terrorist groups (Raúl García Granados de Garay was a founder of the Mano Blanca, and several other family members served with Arzú under Lucas García) and to oil and nickel mining. One of the PAN's key legislative projects was to privatize the national electric company and reform the Mining Law, reducing royalties from 6 to 1 percent.[1] Together with their relatives in the Skinner-Klee family, the García Granados family had been active for years in arranging agreements with the military on oil and other mining matters. Indeed in a 1979 interview given just before he was assassinated, the progressive presidential candidate and former Guatemala City mayor Manuel Colom Argueta called them "the great de-nationalizers of our natural resources. [Jorge Skinner Klee] is the lawyer who has written each and every one of the anti-patriotic laws in this country. He was the United Fruit Company's lawyer, he is the author of the laws that destroyed the Agrarian Reform, and those that gave away the oil to foreign interests. . . . I know him well, I know all the details, and that is why they hate me" (*Latin America Political Report* 1979). Collaborating with these families in the postwar "de-nationalizing," Arturo de la Cruz, a PAN congressman and retired general from Alta Verapaz, pushed through mining reforms that opened the door for a number of foreign (primarily Canadian) companies to be granted exploration licenses.

Also deeply involved in the privatization project, having been appointed by Arzú's predecessor President Ramiro de León Carpio as president of the De-monopolization and Privatization Commission, was Manuel Ayau Cordón, a man with long and deep connections to mining, oil, and hydroelectric energy as well as to the intellectual and academic labors aimed at installing a fully "liberalized" economy in Guatemala over the past sixty years. A proud member of the MLN, Ayau Cordón founded the Center for Economic and Social Studies in 1957 to hoist the flag of laissez-faire economics, which became the incubator for the private Francisco Marroquín University, which opened in 1972. The university's founders include members of the Campollo (sugar and energy generation), Herrera (sugar), Berger (sugar and now African palm), and Novella (cement) families. Ayau Cordón also represents a subsidiary of Exmibal, the nickel-mining concern that began working in the Franja in the 1970s. When he built a private dam on his property in Izabal he managed to negotiate a higher price per kilowatt from the Serrano Elías and de León Carpio governments than any other company received, perhaps facilitated by his previous experience as vice president of the National Electricity Institute (INDE).

These same families were the beneficiaries of Arzú's investment–friendly policies, as they used the capital they had amassed from agro-exports to invest in newly opened extractive opportunities. For example, the Arzú government authorized the formation of the Atlantic Petroleum Company (CPA), a new national oil company that was capitalized by the Campollo Codina family (sugar producers powerful in the electricity sector, some of which uses sugarcane for generation) and in whose businesses Arzú is a major shareholder, according to sources in the petroleum sector. The government also agreed to accept royalties in kind from the Basic Resources oil company— meaning asphalt, which was used to improve and extend the road system (much flaunted in the PAN's election propaganda and also key to extractive industries).

Basic Resources is an energy company founded by John Park, the retired U.S. Air Force officer who had created Guatemala's 1955 petroleum legislation. Its history is a veritable paradigm of the conspiratorial relations between the most strongly anticommunist sectors of Guatemala's business elite and the emerging extraction sectors, and the role these link[age]s played in the development of the Franja.[2] In 1970 Basic Resources began working in the Franja region, specifically in Alta Verapaz and Izabal, mining magnesium, copper, and nickel through various subsidiaries and exploring for oil along the Mexican border. It began drilling oil in Chinajá, Alta Verapaz in 1977 and the Ixcán in 1978, and by the early 1980s had installations in Yalpemech, Caribe, Tierra Blanca, and Rubelsanto. Until 1980 the oil was transported by tanker truck (via a company owned by Ayau Cordón and others) and mostly bought by Cementos Novella (later Cementos Progreso), owned by the Novella family, which has long held a monopoly on cement production in Guatemala (and controls the country's most important bank, the Banco Industrial). It was in 1980, while doing undergraduate research near San Pedro Carchá, Alta Verapaz, that I first encountered the penetrating odor of crude oil leaking from the tankers stranded by the side of the pot-holed dirt road, or wrecked in ravines. Demands for better infrastructure to transport the oil led the INTA, the state's agrarian branch, along with the army's Engineering Battalion and Shenandoah Oil, to begin the first trans-Franja road in 1975. A few years later Basic began planning an oil pipeline through the Franja to Puerto Barrios. While production increased substantially, from only 2,400 barrels in 1974 to 1.5 million in 1981, the rise of the guerrilla caused a sharp reduction. However, with General Efraín Ríos Montt's coup d'état against Lucas García (supported by the Reagan administration), production increased to 2.5 million barrels by 1983.

The correlation of the national production of crude oil with the movements of counterinsurgency during the bloodiest years of the war (1977–83) is no coincidence. The oil industry not only contributed to economic struggles among the groups in power but also helped finance the counterinsurgency strategy carried out by the military and paramilitary apparatuses and contributed heavily to its ideological justification, both nationally and internationally, through support of neoliberal economic theories. Basic Resources shared a building with the Francisco Marroquín University for that institution's first two decades. University president Ayau Cordón has moved in and out of public roles with the company, while serving twice as president of the Mount Pelerin Society, a global club for what Marta Harnecker (1999: 164) calls "franco-masonic neoliberalism" that counts Milton Friedman, Karl Popper, Ludwig von Mises, and Friedrich Hayek among its members, and which evolved into the World Economic Forum. Enrique Novella was also one of the first directors of Basic Resources, using crude oil to generate electricity. With Roberto Alejos Arzú, Juan Maegli, and others, Ayau Cordón helped contribute $10 million to the 1980 presidential campaign of Ronald Reagan and oilman George H. W. Bush through the Association Amigos del País.[3] Through Basic Resources Ayau Cordón also developed connections with Dick Cheney's family, stakeholders in Union Pacific Resources, which later acquired Basic. Ayau Cordón's Fundación Francisco Marroquín (headed by Elliott Abrams in 2000–2001) is also a major player in the academic, oil, capitalism, neoliberal ideology, political power matrix that I have been sketching here.[4]

As extractive industries come to play an increasingly important role in the Guatemalan economy, the close personal, economic, and political relations established in the 1970s through this matrix have been extended into new generations, opening new opportunities. Early in the twenty-first century Manuel Ayau Cordón's nephew Antonio Minondo Ayau (who is also related to the Herrera sugar family) took over Basic in Guatemala and, with his brother, also runs several hydroelectric plants for the industrial gas company Fabrigas, which is owned by their uncle. In 2001 Basic was bought by the French transnational firm Perenco, and Minondo Ayau remains as head of public relations and operations. Perenco now holds the largest oil contract in Guatemala, operating, despite great controversy, inside the Laguna del Tigre National Park, which is supposed to be an ecological bioreserve. (Perenco has been frequently denounced by national and international environmental activists for its multiple violations of national laws.) These same families are also connected to major private security firms (one of the few growth industries in Guatemala) and to the Grupo Multi Inversiones, which is perhaps the most powerful economic entity in the country. It is headed by the Bosch-Gutiérrez family, which includes Dionisio Gutiérrez, a well-known talk show host and purveyor of the most powerful Guatemalan brand of all: Pollo Campero (a fried chicken chain). All are investors in Basic Resources.

These relations also tie this sector of the elite to the military. During Arzú's government Marco Tulio Espinosa Contreras, an army general (and U.S.-trained oil engineer), was named head of the Presidential Guard, a position from which he was quickly promoted to minister of defense. The general had pushed transnational-friendly petroleum legislation in 1983, during the military governments and under the open tutelage of Basic Resources ("New Law Eases Terms in Guatemala" 1983; "Operators in Guatemala Propose Changes in Hydrocarbon's Rules" 1983). While he was head of the Presidential Guard both Bishop Gerardi and the petrochemical businessman Edgar Ordoñez Porta were assassinated. Gerardi, who oversaw the Catholic Church's REMHI human rights report, had been a target of the extreme Right since the 1970s for his activism in the Church's social doctrine programs. Ordoñez Porta's murder has been linked to his crude oil business's competition with Basic Resources and to his brother Hugo's newspaper, *elPeriódico*, which criticized the Arzú government. Amnesty International denounced Ordoñez Porta's assassination, the later threats to his family, and suspicious property destruction as the work of a "corporate mafia acting as a parallel power, representing a noxious alliance among traditional sectors of the oligarchy, new businessmen, army and police elements, and common criminals attempting to control lucrative illicit affairs and to monopolize the legal sectors of the petroleum industry" (2002: 1). When Alfonso Portillo came to power in 1999, Arzú was elected mayor of Guatemala City. (The Constitution prohibits reelection to the presidency.) He apparently maintained his associations with the Atlantic Petroleum Company, and Espinosa Contreras stayed on as his right-hand man, developing, according to *elPeriódico*, a telephone spying station in the basement of City Hall.

Although the Portillo government approved the highly controversial Glamis Gold mining license for the Marlin project in San Marcos, which has since been bought out by the Canadian transnational Goldcorp, Portillo was far less interested than Arzú in promoting extractive industry and even annulled a CPA contract to drill around Lake Izabal. With the 2003 presidential election of Oscar Berger, however, the drive to attract international investment resumed with new force. Berger's GANA Party was a splinter from Arzú's PAN and represented many of the same interests, including Berger family investments. His administration signed a number of petroleum and mining leases and began serious work on the Franja highway, which was hailed as a Marshall Plan for the Franja, meant to improve commerce, land values, and tourism and support the Plan Puebla Panamá for regional integration,[5] as well as the area's impoverished indigenous population. In addition to the road, a major aspect of this plan was promoting African palm production for cooking oil and biofuel. Throwing state backing behind industrializing African palm production was not a disinterested move for the Berger government. The business group behind the monocrop includes the Bolaños Valle and Arriola Fuxet and various branches of the Torrebiarte family (old agro-export families, connected by descent and marriage with the Novellas and Lantzendorffes). These families were major financial supporters of the GANA government, and many of its members were appointed to important ministries, including Minister of the Interior Adela Camacho de Torrebiarte, whose family is a major cardamom exporter from Alta Verapaz and is related to the Bolaños Valle family (with large banana and African palm plantations). Family members are also involved with the highly contested Montana/Marlin gold mine.

So we shouldn't be surprised that in 2004, just after assuming the presidency, Berger inaugurated the AgroCaribe plant for palm oil extraction in Izabal, which at the time was owned by the Arriola Fuxet family in association with the Bolaños Valles. They had forged ties with companies in Mexico (the major consumer of cooking oil in Latin America) and with Palmas del Ixcán, a subsidiary of the U.S. firm Green Earth Fuels, which is based in Houston and was created jointly by the Carlyle Group, Riverstone Holdings, and Goldman Sachs.[6] The Berger government also supported exploration and exploitation of the Franja's oil fields.

Although President Hugo Chávez of Venezuela invited Guatemala to join his reduced-price oil program, Petrocaribe, and the Alvaro Colom government (2008–12) showed interest, the agreement was never finalized, and Guatemala has been hard hit by the sharp increases in oil prices throughout the new century. This led Colom to seek increased oil licensing (a familiar "Drill here, drill now" logic) and to transform Guatemala's energy matrix by a massive increase in hydroelectric plants. While self-identified as social democratic, the Colom government had to respond to heterogeneous interests and the pressures of economic elites who sometimes directly, other times indirectly, co-govern.

In fact from Arzú through Colom (1994–2011, and surely into the foreseeable future) we see the same people who were active in the 1970s and 1980s and their heirs—the Ayau Cordón, Delgado Wyld, Novella, Torrebiarte, Berger Widmann, Maegli, Arzú, Campollo Codina, and Bosch-Gutiérrez families—expanding their holdings in the Franja with investments in oil, mining (especially nickel and minerals for cement), hydroelectric, African palm, and sugarcane. Their capacity to make these investments is grounded in landholdings acquired fraudulently during the military governments, leading to a joke popular in the 1980s that plays on the double meaning of *ganado* as "cattle" and as "won" or "earned." The joke goes: A tourist is going through the Franja Transversal and is impressed with the great expanses of the pastures full of cattle. He stops to take a look, and the owner comes up. "Wow!" says the tourist. "Is all this *ganado*?" (meaning cows). The owner, Colonel Arana, snorts with laughter. "*Ganado*?! No, It's all *robado* [stolen]." These same families have also *ganado* (won) by selling their less productive lands at inflated prices back to the state, to then be resold to returning refugees and other landless peasants, maintaining the market as the only reply to the growing demands for real land reform and seriously indebting these already vulnerable communities (see Velásquez Nimatuj this volume; Hurtado Paz y Paz 2008b). Finally, these same families are behind continuing violent (and illegal) evictions like those of March 2011, described at the beginning of this essay. The connections and investments that I have traced here simultaneously reproduce ties among these families and maintain their dominance over the industrial and finance sectors of the Guatemalan economy, even as they reproduce and expand their access to local and international capital. Basically these are the people who design and implement the economic policies of the state—for their own benefit and that of their transnational allies.

"A Complex Region Where Two Visions of Agricultural Development Compete"
SEGEPLAN

What do these dense networks that link kin and money through violence and "seizing opportunity" mean for peasants dreaming of a better life, who have also made their homes in the Franja? The government's planning agency, SEGEPLAN, plainly laid out the prospects for these dreams in their 2009 report on the Franja's future. "Peasant development" entails "returnees and peasants with historical roots in the territory, with needs for state support in agricultural development principally understood as a motor for food security and small scale production" (SEGEPLAN 2011a: 75). In some ways the hopes that the Franja would become a breadbasket for Guatemala have come true as local farmers provide an important percentage of the national corn and bean markets. On the other hand, SEGEPLAN (2009: slide 14) explains, there are simultaneous "extractive processes that, in reality, have little impact on local development and include African palm, sugar cane, oil, hydroelectric and cattle." Peasants, many heavily affected by the war and displacement, seek to fortify local production and need technical and financial support from the state as well as improved links to the regional and national economy. The competing logic pushed by business elites covets the territory for extractive activities alone. Which logic is likely to prevail?

Both projects justify massive government investment in highway construction (even as education, health care, and other social services go begging, as Worby shows in this volume). For communities directly connected to or near this corridor, the government predicts benefits like increased local productivity, better access to markets, improved mobility, tourism, and more connections among communities. For big capital, the Franja highway is vital for the future investments they foresee, which will require transport of inputs and products, and for the inexorable expansion in profitable land transactions that will undoubtedly result from the intensification of production. A highway would also respond to the opportunities opened by the Central America Free Trade Agreement. This includes increased commerce with Mexico (both licit and illicit, for the Franja is a central zone for both drug production and transshipment), already a major market for the isthmus and a potential bridge to the U.S. economy, as well as deepening connections among Guatemala, El Salvador, Honduras, and Belize. The immediate beneficiaries are the actors introduced in the previous section: oil companies like Perenco, linked to the Ayau and Berger families, and the CPA, whose largest shareholders are the sugar baron Campollo Codinas and, it is rumored, the Arzús. The Berger Widmann and Herrera families, with their stakes in sugar, are also central players in biofuel production, owning plantations and the Chabil Utzaj mill in the Polochic Valley (site of the 2011 evictions). The Guatemalan Nickel Company, a subsidiary of Russia's Solway Group with links to the Bergers, also holds licenses in the Franja and thus has a strong interest in the highway being built. Along the Franja highway, therefore, we can see a new set of tendrils extending out from the networks we have been tracing.

Road building is itself big business, and in 2007 the $672 million contract was awarded to the sole contender, the Israeli company Solel Boneh International (SBI). Like so many of the actors in the Franja, SBI is closely connected to the military governments of the 1980s, having accompanied the Israeli counterinsurgency advisors who aided the Lucas García regime (1979–82) in training and equipping the army, providing arms and transport, developing military technology, and advising on development plans for the Franja (Rudenberg 1986). Beginning with apartment construction under Lucas García, SBI has become the principal contractor for the Guatemalan state and enjoys extremely close relations to business elites. For example, in 2007 SBI signed a private contract worth $227 million to build a hydroelectric dam on the Xacbal River on the Finca La Perla in Chajúl Quiché, which is scheduled to become one of the largest in the country. La Perla is owned by the six Arenas Menes brothers, sons of José Luis Arenas Barrera, the infamous "Tiger of the Ixcán" who was assassinated by the EGP in its first public action in 1975.[7] One of the brothers was director of immigration in the Arzú government, and Berger personally promised them a paved road would be built from La Perla to the Franja highway to incorporate their plant into the Central American Electricity Interconnection System, itself a central element of the Mesoamerican Project (formerly known as Plan Puebla-Panamá). The dam is connected to the Grupo Terra, a powerful Honduran conglomerate linked to the coup d'état against President Manuel Zelaya in 2009.

Despite these ties to friends in high places, SBI was sharply criticized by members of the Congress and human rights groups for paying bribes and inflating prices, challenges that led to the cancellation of the original contract in 2009. It was renegotiated and approved, however, even as the six independent congresspersons who voted against it denounced secret negotiations behind the scenes and declared that they had experienced intense pressure to change their votes. The final cost will be $203 million, financed completely by the BCIE and administered by the Louis Berger Group (no connection to the Berger Widmanns), one of the world's largest construction companies (also heavily involved in the Iraq reconstruction).

Even as the infrastructure for extraction was being developed, the new Foundation for the Production of Natural Resources and Sustainable Development of the Polochic River Basin was created in 2007, purporting to address the concerns of "peasant development" highlighted in the SEGEPLAN report. Aiming "to improve sustainability [*autogestión*], production and investment in order to reduce the low levels of development in the Polochic area," the Foundation claimed it would intervene in "negotiations of community conflicts to establish responsible dialogue in search of solutions," according to Regina Rivera, spokesperson for the Guatemalan Nickel Mining company in 2007 (Solano 2008: 50). The government showed its support when

Vice President Eduardo Stein attended its public launch, and community organizations hoped it would shift the balance of power in the region. It turned out, however, that the Foundation consisted of many of the very same actors responsible for the conflicts, including CGN mining (then a subsidiary of HudBay); Mayaniquel S.A. (a subsidiary of the Canadian Anfield Ventures, which holds over forty licenses for exploration and extraction of nickel); the Widmanns' sugar refinery Chabil Utzaj; the Guatemalan companies Baleu (rubber producers), INDESA (the only palm biofuel producer in Guatemala, owned by the Maegli family), and Maderas El Alto (a lumber company owned by Carlos Meany, minister of energy and mines under Colom and a major donor to Colom's party); and the Luis Augusto Turcios Lima Foundation, run by the former guerrilla commander César Montes, aka Julio César Macías. Montes is a well-known columnist in the right-wing newspaper *Siglo XXI*. While he has worked with Rigoberta Menchú and the state-run Land Fund, he has also been severely criticized for his role in heightening several rural conflicts and for his close ties to big business.

Public relations promises of "responsible dialogue" and "solutions" notwithstanding, the Foundation seemed to be another front for familiar oligarchic practices, another node in the circuits of accumulation by violent dispossession. Tracing the connections of just two of the families involved provides yet another point of entry into the complex webs linking these wide-ranging histories of economic and political interests and influence. The sugar-producing Widmann family and the Maegli family (owners of INDESA, after 2011 known as Grasa, S.A.) descend from German and Swiss immigrants who benefited from the state's land giveaways of the nineteenth century and from land grabs in the late 1950s counterrevolution as the Arbenz reforms were overturned. Walter Widmann Luna, a millionaire banker and sugar and coffee baron, was one of three laymen who helped found the Guatemala branch of the anticommunist Catholic sect Opus Dei; in 1966, along with Juan Ulrico Maegli Mueller, he helped refound the eighteenth-century Amigos del País Association, a powerful right-wing group that supported the MLN Party and the Mano Blanca, and later supported and then lobbied President Reagan for backing in the "anticommunist struggle" and to burnish the image of the genocidal Lucas García government.[8] The Association also included Roberto Alejos Arzú, whose plantation was used for training the Cuban exiles involved in the abortive Bay of Pigs invasion.

In the late 1960s Widmann Luna acquired the Finca Chaculá in Nentón, Huehuetenango to raise cattle, a strategy supported by the beef export policies of the Arana Osorio government. The plantation was abandoned in 1981 following claims that Widmann Luna had ordered assassinations in local communities, which made him a guerrilla target. It was sold to the state in 1990 for resettled refugees. He was also identified as a principal actor in the murders of Belgian priests and local catechists in Escuintla, where he had extensive sugar holdings. His son, Carlos Widmann Lagarde, is also a member of Opus Dei and is a brother-in-law of former president Berger (whose own son, Oscar Berger Widmann, directs Continental Energy Corp. and has a brother who married into the Köng family, the country's largest producers of oil and edible fats).

As mentioned earlier, the Widmann family received a $32 million loan from the BCIE to reactivate the Chabil Utzaj sugar mill, in return for which they promised to invest in health, education, roads, water, and latrine projects. The bloody evictions of hundreds of Q'eqchi' families, however, occurred just before the loan's announcement. The mill also received financing from the Pellas Chamorro family of Nicaragua, the largest cane ethanol exporters in Central America. Oscar Berger Widmann directed the Banco del Quetzal, now part of the Banco Industrial, when the Banco del Quetzal was administering the loan for the Chabil Utzaj sugar mill. The Widmanns also have kin connections to the Marroquín family, who own and operate the most important newspapers in Guatemala.[9]

The Maeglis are a Swiss family that started in coffee then expanded to other crops. In the 1950s, feeling threatened by the Arbenz land reform, they also became one of the main funders for Opus Dei, thereby forging connections with economically powerful families like the Widmanns and Novellas. Juan Maegli married María Marta Julia Novella Wyld in 1954 and became president of Cementos Progreso in 1996. Like the Novellas, he was in the MLN and openly financed paramilitary death squads beginning in the 1960s (Bogdan 1982; Solano 2011). The Maeglis bought United Fruit Company land in Escuintla and in the 1970s invested in plantations in the Polochic to take advantage of the military government's support for cattle ranching. Under their ownership, local Q'eqchi' subsistence farmers were gradually displaced and converted into day laborers. In the mid-1990s this veteran businessman converted his holdings into African palm and began to develop vegetable oil extraction plants in alliance with the Urruela Köng and Köng Vielmann families. In addition to the cement monopoly, they and their children are connected through family ties to the Banco Industrial and other financial institutions and the Tecún Group, which produces and distributes agrochemicals, farm and construction machinery, and cars. They are also involved in regional businesses through COPRONSA, which unites Guatemalan, Salvadoran, Nicaraguan, and Costa Rican capital investments in edible fat, and is in alliance with German financing to produce soap, detergents, cleaning supplies, and cooking oil.

As the recent investments of these families suggest, the cutting edge of capitalism in the Franja lies in the biofuel sector.[10] Accordingly African palm has become the government's primary community development project in the Franja. The Colom government has encouraged small-scale independent farmers to retain their landholdings by growing African palm, a policy that creates a production base favoring the monocrop's largest investors. The best example of this dual use is the state's Rural Development Program (Pro-Rural), which allied in 2008 with the Palmas del Ixcán company to promote "independent" production in Ixcán, Cobán, and Chisec, where the company already planned on planting twenty-five thousand hectares. Until early 2011, ProRural was the central axis of the country's rural development policies; its director was Roberto Dalton Aceituno, of Disagro, S.A., the primary purveyor of fertilizers for the Guatemalan state. An important associate in Disagro was Carlos Enrique Carmelo Arriola Torrebiarte, whose son, Enrique Arriola Fuxet, was the president of Palmas del Ixcán until 2010.

Through Colom's ProRural plan peasant farmers—currently the primary source of basic grains in the area—are supposed to become independent African palm producers, assured of a market, as the company promises to buy their entire harvest. The company in turn gains political stability, a captive production force (in addition to the thousands of day laborers already delivered by decades of displacement), access to land they could not otherwise acquire, and guaranteed levels of production for their export markets. Unfortunately, however, this strategy for development puts food security at risk for thousands of peasants as they transfer their land from the production of staples to African palm. This repeats a pattern established in the 1970s and 1980s, when the government heavily promoted growing cardamom, a spice popular in the Middle East, only to leave many small-scale producers bankrupt after international prices plummeted. Once again private companies are drawing on state resources to pull independent producers into their commodity chains, leaving the most vulnerable to shoulder all the risk.

Another actor in this process is AgroCaribe, which buys palm fruit from independent producers and has close to nine hundred hectares in production in Izabal. The company was part of the African Palm System created in 2008 by the Presidential Commission for Local Development (CPDL), which also includes the private agency Fundasistemas. These private companies have benefited from the National Fund for the Reactivation and Modernization of Agropecuarial Activities, which gave land to over two hundred families in Izabal. These families are now being transformed into "independent" palm producers. The Fund said its goal was to have new landowners participate in a crop system that would "encourage both individual entrepreneurship and collective projects, including the benefits accruing to interactions among communities, government, and the private sector" (in Solano 2010a: 56). The CPDL signed a contract with AgroCaribe to guarantee purchase of their palm harvests for twenty-five years, while Fundasistemas flaunted the company's "green" credentials and the all-around benefits of the agreement: "Agro-Caribe is an important company dedicated to producing cooking oil and biofuels to satisfy the growing demand for 'clean' energy provided by crops that are carefully grown to protect the environment." The government commission, in turn, is lauded for "facilitating the creation of a system of holistic development, in a context of harmony with nature and Guatemala's cultural riches. Thanks to these connections the communities are benefitting from the company's aid in financing and technical training, improving their use of the land" (www.agrocaribe.com). Palmas del Ixcán planned to incorporate eight hundred families planting 9,800 acres, and ProRural began a similar project involving five hundred small farmers to get over 5,000 acres in African palm.

ProRural's African palm projects were financed by the state's Develop ment Fund with $6.5 million for the first three years to buy fertilizer, herbicides, and pesticides (presumably from DISAGRO, the state's principal provider). The state also buys seeds from Palmas del Ixcán for its own greenhouse in Chisec, which are provided in turn by the Grupo Numar, the primary producer of African palm in Central America. All of this financing comes from the government's food security program, which is supposed to increase the production of corn, rice, and beans. Including palm production in the program seems to be aimed at winning the trust of small farmers to more easily convert them into producers for agribusiness. (An earlier attempt by the Berger government to encourage palm production in Petén foundered precisely on people's lack of faith in the process.)[11] Of course, these sorts of agreements make the local producers totally dependent on the buyer, forcing them to accept any price the buyer sets.

In the hands of Guatemala's elites, through state-private collaborations like this or the Polochic Foundation for development, mentioned above, the logic of local development and sustainable peasant agriculture in the Franja is paradoxically deployed to foster monocropping and embed a renewed logic of agro-exportation still deeper in the Guatemalan state's agrarian policies. Although the Polochic Foundation broke down in 2009, unable to align its many divergent interests or to interest transnational actors in its projects, it remains a prototype of how the discourses of community solidarity and development inherited from projects that challenged the rapacious Guatemalan oligarchy and its international supporters in earlier generations are being deployed by new extractive industries and their local representatives to further their own, perhaps even more rapacious purposes. The Foundation's very existence, moreover, which papered over the significant divergences among members of the elite to present a united defense of profit extraction in the Franja, suggests just how potentially rich those profits are perceived to be.

Dreams for the Future: By Way of a Conclusion

Indigenous peasants must confront the dilemma of acquiescing to this model and becoming totally dependent on it or seeking alternative development paths that will defend natural resources and their means of survival. Many communities are in favor of developing the Franja but sharply question the elite's vision of what this means, clearly aware of its foundations in dispossession and plunder. But many communities are also being subtly tied in to the new model, becoming small-scale palm producers via state support and pressure, and thereby increasingly dependent on the big companies. As investments rise, the highway pushes on, and drug trafficking increasingly infects and undermines local politics, community structures, and property relations (as cartels buy up or steal territory), land is increasingly concentrated in fewer and fewer hands, and agrarian conflicts proliferate.

All of the national and international sectors supporting biofuel, hydroelectric, and other new investments in the Franja portray their projects as "green": ecologically sound and environmentally friendly. But for those who are forced to live every day with their consequences, these projects are revealed as nothing more than the same old attempts to squeeze the greatest possible profit from lucrative natural resources — sustainability be damned — and for the benefit of a very limited number of people. While biofuels are vaunted for cutting dependence on carbon-based energy sources like oil and gas, African palm and sugarcane plantations require clear-cutting, which contributes to climate change and destroys habitat for the wide diversity of flora and fauna native to the Franja, as well as heavy use of pollutants like pesticides, herbicides, and fertilizers. Agribusiness has profound effects on local water supplies, draining aquifers and contaminating what's left of them with chemical run-off, leading to soil depletion and desertification. New illnesses have begun to affect human and other life in the area. Fish die-offs, depletion of animal life, and the loss of edible plants both undercut biodiversity and the access to forest nutrition that many families rely on to get through tough times. Meanwhile, as people lose access to land they also lose locally based food security, and the planet loses the small-scale producers globally recognized as engaging in truly environmentally friendly production, who are also storehouses of biological knowledge. Thus replacement of the Lacandón rainforests by these biofuel mega-monocrops is not really a viable response to global warming, however much "greenwashing" its proponents deliver. Similarly, many environmentalists have championed hydroelectric power as an alternative energy source, but the reservoirs formed behind the dams and the rerouting of rivers and watersheds wreak terrible destruction on local ecosystems and human lives.[12] All of these "progressive" alternatives are displacing thousands of people, many of them Maya, and thus combine ethnic with ecological marginalization.

As the networks I have sketched here suggest, the profoundly exclusionary nature of decision making in the context of plans for developing the Franja and, by extension, all of Guatemala makes it almost inevitable that the multimillion-dollar projects enacted by the state with support from the international community will confer their benefits in deeply unequal ways. Likewise the tight collusion between local agro-industrial-finance capital, transnational corporations, and the state, regardless of their ostensible local development programs, also makes it very difficult for nonelite actors to intervene in these plans. Nonetheless protests and denunciations of these effects of "development" and national and transnational investments are gaining ground, sustained by the clear and present dangers people face. Due to drastic loss of land and natural resources, many communities are simply disappearing as their individual members are converted into day laborers overnight—the very reality their parents and grandparents worked so hard to escape when they undertook the backbreaking work of colonization in hopes of a "paradise." And the descendents of the same south coast bosses (*patrones*) for whom their parents and grandparents labored are the ones taking over the Franja today, albeit hidden within the entrails of impersonal and impenetrable corporations. Many residents of the Franja see clearly how land loss has accelerated over the past ten years as more and more people are violently evicted or forced to sell off their parcels under immense market pressures. In response, they are opening new spaces for increased organizing as they insist on imagining different plans and projects than those of the government and the neoliberals. A paradigmatic case is resistance to the Xalalá hydroelectric plant by a Community Good Faith Referendum (Consulta) held on April 20, 2007, in which 90 percent of the twenty-one thousand

FIG 4.1 Ten thousand people march to Guatemala City in 2012 to protest increasing violence and call for recognition of anti-mining referenda. PHOTO BY JAMES RODRÍGUEZ / MIMUNDO. ORG. USED WITH KIND PERMISSION.

voters from dozens of communities opposed the dam and other extractive projects in their area. The Consulta forced the government to step back, and it is now considering cancelling the project altogether.

The second colonization of the Franja, therefore, may not go as smoothly as elite forces hope. Struggles over land, labor, and water, increasing social conflict, legal uncertainty around peasant landholdings, and environmental impacts, along with fights within the groups holding economic power, raise the possibility of still more violence and repression in the Franja if more inclusive decision-making processes are not developed. Guatemala's future is in play in this supposedly remote region. At stake is not only the installation of a new economic model and its consequences for thousands of families but also the sustainability of the natural resources on which the entire nation depends. To escape the specters of the Franja's recent history, its communities must be included in decisions about its future. And these decisions must be respected.

Notes

1. The mining code of 1965 was far more progressive, requiring a 53 percent income tax.
2. Basic Resources is also linked to the Vatican Bank and Propaganda Due (a far-right Italian organization with ties to the mafia), which apparently laundered money through oil production, and to trans–Latin American rightists like Roberto D'Aubisson of El Salvador, the Argentine military officer Carlos Suárez Mason, and members of the Nicaraguan contra. For more information, see Solano 2005: 53–60.
3. Basic had hired the former CIA subdirector and retired general Vernon Walters (a member, along with Roberto Alejos Arzú, of the Knights of Malta) to negotiate improved terms with the military government of Lucas García.
4. For more information on Ayau Cordón, the Amigos del País, and Basic Resources' links to transnational anticommunist terror organizations, money laundering, the Italian mafia, and drug trafficking, see Solano 2005: 52–60, 84–85.
5. Initiated by President Vicente Fox of Mexico, the Plan Puebla Panamá included all the governments of Central America and Colombia, with the aim of converting the region into a strategic economic zone for transnational capital by taking advantage of its proximity to U.S. markets. More limited aims led to its being renamed the Proyecto Mesoamérica, which is primarily focused on energy and road building.
6. These links were dissolved in 2010, when Palmas del Ixcán became wholly owned by Green Earth Fuels and the Arriola Fuxet family cut its ties with AgroCaribe. Regarding the relation of Goldman Sachs to Green Earth, in "The Great American Bubble Machine," Matt Taibbi outlines the firm's "green investments," including $3.5 million to lobby around climate issues, their holdings in technologies that will prosper when the government forces energy producers to use cleaner energy, and in the emerging market of carbon offsets. Similar to the argument here, that what seems good may actually be good for only a small number of people, Taibbi writes, "Well, you might say, who cares? If cap-and-trade succeeds, won't we all be saved from the catastrophe of global warming? Maybe — but cap-and-trade, as envisioned by Goldman, is really just a carbon tax structured so that private interests collect the revenues. Instead of simply imposing a fixed government levy on carbon pollution and forcing unclean energy producers to pay for the mess they make, cap-and-trade will allow a small tribe of greedy-as-hell Wall Street swine to turn yet another commodities market into a private tax collection scheme. This is worse than the bailout: It allows the bank to seize taxpayer money *before it's even collected*" (2010: 8).
7. Arenas Barrera founded the Party of Anticommunist Unification in 1952 and worked with the counterrevolutionary governments of the late 1950s. He enjoyed close relations with the military and with the owners of other plantations, like San Francisco in Huehuetenango and San Luis Ixcán. Along with La Perla these were the sites of some of the most dramatic massacres during the war (CEH 1999; Falla 2011).
8. Juan Maegli and Alfonso Castillo were invited to the 1980 Reagan inauguration.
9. For more on the Berger Widmann family, see Solano 2011.

10. It is worth mentioning that while Guatemala remains a small-scale oil producer, its petroleum companies have enjoyed very active support from the U.S. government, the only consumer of Guatemalan oil exports. One government after another of the Colossus of the North has backed oil exploitation in Guatemala, with U.S. political and economic elites forging close ties with their Guatemalan collaborators, creating a political, juridical, and economic framework that ensures dazzling corporate profits. The same goes for mining companies: although the majority of those functioning in Guatemala are Canadian, many of their shareholders live in the United States and are angling to benefit from the current bonanza in mineral prices created by the demands of the People's Republic of China and the economic downturn, which made gold worth close to $2,000 an ounce.

11. However, the Olmeca company did take advantage of the first few palm producers in the Sayaxché area to begin pressuring other landowners to sell and now has bought up and displaced various communities in the area.

12. While one arm of the state seeks ecosystem preservation with the creation of bio-reserves and national parks, others, in collaboration with the elites detailed here, are destroying them, as with the San Ramón Biological Reserve (now a site of African palm production) and the Mayan Biosphere (now being drilled for oil), both in Petén.

"WE'RE NO LONGER DEALING WITH FOOLS"

Violence, Labor, and Governance on the South Coast

Scene 1: Guatemala's Pacific Coast, February 1980

On February 18, 1980, the Campesino Unity Committee (CUC) launched a labor strike on the Tehuantepec sugar estate in Guatemala's fertile Pacific coast region.[1] It was the harvest season, and within days the work stoppage spread to encompass eighty thousand workers at eighty sugar plantations, more than a dozen cotton farms, and eight sugar mills, escalating into one of the largest and most strategic labor actions the country had ever seen. The CUC strike climaxed years of rural organizing in the indigenous highlands and on the southern coast (Albizúres 1987; CEH 1999, vol. 1; Fernández Fernández 1988; Forster 2001; Grandin 1997b, 2004; Handy 1994). Resident agricultural workers joined forces with temporary day laborers and seasonal migrants, an unprecedented alliance, and in the heady atmosphere of those few days, a wider popular insurrection seemed possible, even imminent. One *campesino* leader recalled the strikers' ebullient mood:

> The *chopper*s were circling above us, boom, boom, boom, boom. They might have fired on us, except that we had taken over the vehicles of the *finca* [plantation], and the army didn't know if the *administradores* were in them. Any driver that said no to us, well, the young ones would just slash the tires! There were so many people! We even took over the Pepsi truck! We went from finca to finca; people kept joining, and the groups from the highlands went with us. . . . God, what a caravan of cars and trucks and tractors we had! And people stood on the side of the road and applauded.[2]

Scene 2: Guatemala City, August 2005

On August 5, 2005, three days after President George W. Bush signed the Central American Free Trade Agreement, more than a hundred Guatemalan business elites gathered in a hotel ballroom in Guatemala City's posh *zona viva* for an event billed as the country's first forum on "corporate social responsibility." Present were executives from Guatemala's most powerful industries, including sugar refineries and coffee plantations, cement manufacturers, and Central America's largest *maquila* textile factory, as well as President Oscar Berger, the minister of labor, various international diplomats, and representatives from the United Nations Development Program and the International Labor Organization. Panel discussions throughout the day grappled with the significance of corporate social responsibility and what it might mean for Guatemala; there were speeches on changing global market conditions, international codes of conduct, and consumer demands for higher quality, "ethically produced" goods such as fair-trade coffee and "no sweat" apparel. ("We're selling smiles," remarked one coffee executive.) But global market pressures weren't the only item on the agenda; participants also queried each other on how a social responsibility motif could be used to build worker loyalty, influence state policy, and help forge a more stable society (more "disciplined," as one moderator commented). In short, the day-long event was, in the words of President Berger, an exercise in linking corporate social responsibility to a long-term project of governability, as envisioned by some of the most influential members of the Guatemalan private sector.[3]

These two moments bracket the story I want to tell in this chapter. In early 1980 Guatemala appeared headed toward all-out armed revolution: guerrilla organizations were active in the capital city and in wide areas of the countryside; Mayas and poor ladinos from different regions were organizing together; the rich were evacuating their wealth; and in the halls of the National Palace there were whispers of an impending insurgent victory. But what looked imminent in 1980 was demolished in three short years. In the Pacific coast region the peasant and union organizations that had directed the February 1980 strike were crushed in its aftermath. The military government retaliated by hunting down the CUC activists, and hundreds of workers were fired. Only a handful of strike leaders survived the violent backlash of the next several years, and the plantation labor unions crumbled.[4]

Guatemala's abortive revolutionary experience failed to bring about systemic change, but it did alter the social relations underpinning the country's agro-export economy, as indigenous mobilization exploded into view. By uniting the various groups of rural laborers, the 1980 CUC strike upended plantation labor management that had been based on the manipulation of ethnic divisions.[5] For planters it was a dramatic sign that something had changed in Guatemala, perhaps irrevocably. The owner of a small sugar mill expressed this view to me in 1994: "Before, workers from the highlands were subdued [eran callados], but we're no longer dealing with fools [ya no se trata de gente tonta]."[6] This brief period of rural insurrection helped usher in consequential, if unintended, changes in labor relations in the coastal region, as planters sought to regain control.

From the mid-1990s to the early years of the twenty-first century, I interviewed some seventy-five representatives of Guatemala's sugar plantation sector, including the owners and top managers at most of the country's sugar mills (sixteen in the 1990s, now reduced to thirteen). At first I wanted to know simply how the Guatemalan agro-export elite had survived the political and economic changes of the 1980s. In contrast to El Salvador, where the civil war and economic reforms precipitated a shift in power from the traditional landed oligarchy to new commercial and financial sectors (Segovia 2002), in Guatemala the landed elite still holds sway over the prime agro-export region along the Pacific coast, even as they have diversified into many other economic activities, such as real estate, banking, and financial speculation.

Indeed between 1985 and 2005, Guatemala's land area planted in sugarcane more than doubled, while overall production tripled, even as the U.S. Agency for International Development was trying to steer producers away from plantation-style crops into new specialty exports like snow peas, broccoli, and processed fruit (McCleary 1999; Fischer and Benson 2006). Guatemala rose to be the third largest sugar exporter in Latin America, after Brazil and Cuba, and fifth in the world. By the end of the 1980s Guatemalan sugar producers had emerged as the core of a revitalized private sector. With the rapid increases in sugar production for ethanol during the early twenty-first century, the role of these producers in national life remains key (as Solano makes clear in this volume).

In the aftermath of the 1980 strike, sugar mills on the southern coast initiated a far-reaching program of managerial change that encompassed every aspect of production but that was explicitly geared toward recapturing control over the rebellious harvest labor force. New methods of labor control originated at Pantaleón, Guatemala's largest mill, where top executives studied the weaknesses of the harvest system following tense years of labor unrest between 1976 and 1980. Pantaleón's managers experimented with changes in the harvest labor process and in labor recruitment, and by the 1990s they were actively encouraging other mills to adopt similar policies.

It soon became clear to me that the story of the *azucareros* (sugar producers) is about more than just the sugar mills and their satellite plantations. The larger story is about how a powerful group within the Guatemalan private sector seized the initiative on a broad array of policies, using the discourse of corporate social responsibility to chart a new project of rule in the postwar era. After the 1980s, "corporate social responsibility" and "strategic development alliances" became ways for Guatemalan plantation owners to rationalize control over the labor force, influence national development debates, and ultimately attempt to shape the nature and scope of Guatemala's democratic transition.

The first part of this chapter describes the sugar plantations of Guatemala's Pacific coast after 1980. I argue that the late 1970s and early 1980s marked a rupture in the mechanisms of rule on the part of a sizable sector of the agro-export elite. Internal managerial changes underpinned the spread of sugar throughout the Pacific coast region, as the plantations sought both to respond to changing global conditions and especially to regain control over their labor force. In an effort to create what Rose (1999) calls "productive subjects," or new sorts of subjectivities linked to labor discipline, these sugar elites resurrected, in a sense, a classic nineteenth-century liberal dilemma of how to integrate Guatemala's indigenous populations into the "productive order" while deepening existing patterns of accumulation.

In the second and third parts of the chapter, the analytical lens shifts from the plantations themselves and the micropolitics of labor control to the broader institutional change set in motion by the azucareros. By the 1990s, the National Sugar Foundation (FUNDAZUCAR), which began on the south coast to manage the plantation labor restructuring, had grown into a prominent NGO participating actively in national and international fora and advocating for an elite-led model of "public-private development alliances." At the core of FUNDAZUCAR's expanded efforts was a struggle over influence in the postwar landscape of civil society (Oglesby 2004). By the first decade of the twenty-first century, FUNDAZUCAR had morphed into the Center for Corporate Responsibility (CENTRARSE), based in Guatemala City. The Center tries to shape economic policy and create a new ideological consensus, a vision of a future of "enlightened"—and unchallenged—elite rule.

This chapter traces the causal dynamics of this new hegemonic project, as well as its incompleteness. Certainly multiple elements came together to create the rupture of the 1980s: global market shifts coincided with the rise of a new generation of organic intellectuals among the business class (including among the azucareros and their high-level management). But what often gets ignored, especially in structural analyses of global change (e.g., Robinson 2003), are the ways the revolutionary upsurge, and particularly the labor strife on the south coast in the late 1970s and early 1980s, demanded a rethinking of both the micro and macro techniques of rule and their interconnections.

I am influenced here by Gidwani's (2008) concept of the "government of work," a framework that combines a nuanced analysis of the management of the labor process with a broader examination of governance in its various social, political-economic, and institutional milieus. This framework draws upon Foucauldian ideas of biopower, in the sense of limiting labor's power as a political force while maximizing its potential as a productive force (Foucault 1977; Rabinow 1984; see also Rose 1999), and of governmentality as "governing the conduct of one's self and of others" (Burchell et al. 1991). It is an approach that looks carefully at the concrete mechanisms of power as these are exerted upon the bodies of workers, who are induced to become complicit in their own management.[7] But it is also influenced by a Gramscian notion of hegemony as a contested process fought out in multiple social spheres (Roseberry 1993b). Perhaps for the first time since before the nineteenth-century coffee boom, agro-elite sectors in Guatemala are developing a hegemonic project of rule. How are the azucareros reworking the boundaries between coercion and consent (and why)? How does this project fit into the postwar context, in which the Left has reemerged as a potential (albeit vastly weakened) political contender? And how does all this affect the lives of working people in Guatemala, on the coast and in the highlands? These are the questions that motivate this chapter.

The View from the Plantations

Pantaleón is an imposing agro-industrial complex that looks like a small city on the edge of the Pacific coast highway about fifty miles southwest of the capital. The mill's primary owners are members of the Herrera family, whose wealth dates from the nineteenth-century coffee boom. The mill earned fame in the late 1970s for its turbulent labor history, including a bitter labor strike in 1976 and the participation by Pantaleón workers in the famous 1977 miners' march from Ixtahuacán, Huehuetenango to the capital (Levenson-Estrada 1994). When the 1980 strike erupted, for management it brought to the fore a broader weakness of the mill's operation, especially vis-à-vis the suddenly intractable migrant labor force. This was also a period (1982–83) when international sugar prices fell and the United States imposed harsh new import quotas, factors that contributed to the mill's search for greater efficiency. Beginning after 1980 the most astute top executives at Pantaleón were given free rein to implement changes in all aspects of the production process.

Pivotal in the process was the general manager, Julio Herrera, a family cousin and minority shareholder who had lived most of his life outside Guatemala (indeed he speaks Spanish with an accent) and who joined Pantaleón in the mid-1970s. By all accounts, Herrera possessed a modernizing vision when he assumed leadership of the mill, and technical changes got under way early in his tenure. After the labor conflicts heated up in the late 1970s, Herrera lobbied other relatives and board members for carte blanche powers to create a hand-picked management team led by an industrial engineer, Miguel Fernández, who would later become a sort of organic intellectual of the self-styled "progressive" wing of the private sector. Herrera told his confidants that he wanted "a big project, he didn't know what exactly, but he wanted a change."[8]

Eliminating labor friction by doing away with the harvest labor force was not an option for the mills. Several natural features of sugarcane cultivation in Guatemala prohibit full mechanization of the harvest, including undulant fields, rocky soils, and high winds that leave the cane stalks tilted at odd angles.[9] The goal, then, became how to mold a labor force that could be both highly productive and also stable and disciplined.

As a first step, Pantaleón converted to a system of "computerized migrancy,"[10] whereby electronic databases record daily worker productivity and the year-to-year labor history of each cane cutter. In a typical yearly evaluation, cane cutters receive a weighted score based on productivity (40 percent), work quality (40 percent), and "attitude" (20 percent), and these records are the basis for a more sophisticated selection procedure designed to recontract individually with only the most highly productive and cooperative workers (as opposed to the previous system of using labor contractors to indiscriminately round up migrant workers). In a ranking system called "qualifications of conduct," workers are given positive points for "labor stability," "maturity," and "development potential" and negative points for poor attitude or otherwise being conflictive. Blacklisting is not new, of course, but the ability to track and select workers electronically is a qualitative extension of management power.[11]

Profiling is used to characterize "desirable" and "undesirable" workers. For instance, the decision of whether to recruit from the Indian highlands or from the periurban shantytowns on the coast is a determination loaded with racially charged ideas about what makes a "good" worker.[12] The labor profiling has clear political dimensions as well, as entire municipalities are depicted as producing good or bad workers depending on the particular histories of labor recruitment and political struggle and the perceptions of managers. The ratio of coastal to highland harvest workers thus varies from mill to mill, but overall more than half of the sugar harvest labor force comes from the highlands (Oglesby 2007b: 178).

The harvest labor process was reorganized along Tayloristic time-and-motion principles to radically increase worker productivity. The process of cane cutting is broken down into precise stages, and each stage is catalogued. "Monitors" (usually cane cutters who have been promoted) teach cane cutters the appropriate steps: which rows to cut first, how many cane stalks must be cut with one swing, and how to lay the cane on the ground correctly. Cane cutters are scored based on quality criteria: how close to the ground the cane is cut, whether the rows are cleared of stones, roots and stumps, or how straight the cane is laid, and numerical measures of quality become part of a worker's permanent record, along with the average daily productivity. The work of the monitor is also regulated, and monitors receive training about the production process as well as in applied statistics and motivational psychology.

Gender is a central component of the sugar mills' strategies to enforce labor discipline by reshaping worker identities. The mills primarily recruit young men between the ages of eighteen and thirty for the arduous job of cane cutting.[13] The masculinization of the plantation labor force is not only about recruiting men; it is also about creating new ideas of masculinity among harvest workers. The new work regimes seek to deflect workers' class-based identities (sharpened during the era of civil conflict) and strengthen a particular notion of masculinity linked to labor discipline. Ideas of masculinity are promoted to enhance productivity, so that cane cutters come to view themselves as "champion" workers. Notions of the ideal masculine worker are used to encourage workers to view themselves as stable breadwinners or, in the case of very young workers, as a way to encourage this aspiration.

Desired output levels are high, and there is intense interest in buffing up workers' bodies. New diets were developed for these migrant workers; these are supposed to provide 3,700 calories daily with a balance of proteins and carbohydrates. At Pantaleón mill managers refined the cutting system by carrying out time-and-motion studies. They videotaped the best group of cutters and observed their movements: how close to the cane stalks a worker stood, how wide an arc he made with the machete, how the cane was laid on the ground. They measured workers' muscles for ongoing nutritional experiments. A 2000 promotional pamphlet by the Guatemalan Sugar Association claimed grandly that cane cutters are "treated like true Olympic athletes."

Workers are expected to cut at least six tons of cane a day. (An average worker in 1980 would have cut one ton a day.) At Pantaleón by the mid-1990s one-quarter of the workforce cut over nine tons a day. The increase in output is linked both to technological changes (including heavier machetes) and the mechanization of cane loading, but it is also about getting workers to work harder and longer. "Champion" workers are rewarded with prizes that range from T-shirts and tape recorders to bicycles and household goods. Managers emphasize their success in building up relationships of trust with workers over time. Middle and upper-middle managers highlight the good rapport they have with workers: they visit the migrant camps regularly, eat and drink with workers, and listen to their concerns. One manager at Pantaleón joked that workers call his human resources office a "human rights" office (a play on the UN and other human rights agencies that sprung up in the countryside during the peace process).

Trust, according to management, comes about because workers know the mill and the mill knows its workers. Under the old system of labor contracting, which managers describe as too porous to ensure political stability, this was not the case: "The *contratistas* (labor contractors) needed a certain number of people, say a hundred people. Who were those people? I don't know, but there they were. With this system, the contract is with the individual. I contract with you because I know you. You know me. You know the conditions here."[14]

This building of knowledge about workers is a major area of activity of the human resource departments. Attention is given both to workers on the coast and in the highlands, although the most intense effort is focused on indigenous migrants from the highlands, whose "otherness" creates a potential communication gap from the perspective of management. The kind of information valued by the mills entails keeping track of workers' bodies during the course of the harvest season; it also means making the individual and collective psyche the object of study. The databases that the mills maintain on harvest workers are extensive; Pantaleón, for example, keeps files on workers' marital status, ethnicity, religion, land tenure relations, and off-season occupation in an ongoing effort to develop a profile of the "ideal" sugar worker.[15]

FIG 5.1 Cane cutters. Three young male cane cutters in front of a burned sugar cane field. PHOTO BY DANIEL HERNÁNDEZ-SALAZAR, © 2000, WWW.DANIELHERNANDEZSALAZAR.BLOGSPOT.COM. USED WITH KIND PERMISSION.

FIG 5.2 A worker gathers up an armful of cane on the El Baúl finca in Escuintla, 2002. PHOTO BY JAIME PUEBLA. USED WITH KIND PERMISSION.

The ideal worker not only exhibits physical prowess but is mentally adaptive, because the presumption is that the desired physical traits can be instilled. Supervisors put a lot of energy into rectifying perceived flaws in worker behavior, for example, making sure workers understand the rules of hygiene and conduct that are enforced in the migrant camps. They must use the correct utensils while eating and stack their plates neatly when finished; they are instructed to use the latrines correctly, to bathe and wash their clothes daily, to line up without fuss for the bus, and to always be on time. There are slide shows and videos to promote the desired conduct among workers. The emphasis is on discipline, on the production of compliant working bodies, but also on the promotion of positively defined characteristics as a way of socializing workers into internalizing attitudes that management deems more "rational" and that, in turn, the plantations believe will help forge a broader work ethic among cane cutters.

Both material and psychological incentives are used to recast the meaning of plantation work and build worker loyalty to the mills. At Pantaleón a training supervisor makes the rounds of all the harvest groups once a week with a computer printout that lists the leading work crews from the previous week, as well as the top individual cane cutters and their scores. Managers believe that an emphasis on this "psychological contract" between the mill and the individual worker helps build worker allegiance and has a direct impact on productivity. For example, after a careful observation of top cane cutters and "so-so" workers, Pantaleón determined that there was little technical difference between cutters who cut ten tons of cane a day and those who cut less. The critical difference was a psychological one, managers concluded. The more productive laborers had a different attitude toward work, a more goal-oriented outlook that let them meld more easily into the mill's production system. In a classic replica of early twentieth-century Taylorism, a human resources supervisor described the mill's efforts to observe workers by taking sample groups and studying their movements: "The most noticeable difference was in the psychological attitude. [Productive workers] have an attitude when they start the day of 'I am going to achieve this,' while the others just get here thinking, 'Let's see how it goes.' We're studying how to foment the former."[16]

This assessment of worker disposition (which is evaluated more critically at the end of this chapter) has broad implications for the structuring of the plantation labor market. The quality of harvest labor is now seen as crucial, and this depends on the individual attributes of migrant and seasonal laborers. The harvest labor cycle turns not only on the ability to hire and fire workers "flexibly" but on the year-to-year recruitment of the best workers. In other words, there is a tension between the "flexibilization" of labor (to lower costs) and its stabilization (to boost productivity).

FUNDAZUCAR was created as a way to manage this tension by helping the mills develop a social buffer zone in the agro-export region of the south coast. In fact the emergence of the subsequent corporate social responsibility discourse in Guatemala has its origins in this effort to micromanage labor markets on the coast as well as to confront other postwar political projects (a feeble, but for elites still irritating, state pseudo-populism and an also weak but still latent project of popular mobilization).

Beyond the Gates: FUNDAZUCAR, Corporate Social Responsibility, and the "Privatization of Development"

"Property is Development" is a sugar industry slogan for its worker housing projects on the coast. As a dictum, it sends a double message: it reminds us that the mills are committed to breaking the "feudal" schema of labor relations on the coast by relocating plantation workers to periurban lots, and it incants the central message that the motor for national progress will come from within the core of a private sector secure in its leadership position. "We have two main areas of work," the Guatemalan Sugar Association's public relations director told me in 2000, "from the gates of the sugar mill inward, and from the gates of the sugar mill outward."

By the mid-1990s Pantaleón had expanded to become the largest sugar mill in Central America, with twenty thousand acres of cane under its own administration and another twenty-four thousand under supplier contracts. Worker output in the cane harvest at Pantaleón soared 700 percent between 1980 and the mid-1990s, measured in terms of how many tons of cane a worker cut in one day.

Other sugar mills, and reportedly even some members of the Herrera family, at first ignored the strategic import of the shift in policies and reacted with suspicion, as one of the architects of the mill's strategy described:

> What attracted the most criticism was giving meat and chicken to the cane cutters. The other mills said, "You guys are crazy, why are you giving that food to people who aren't used to eating it?" Some of them told me it would do harm to the workers; how can you believe that feeding someone is going to do them harm? But there were these incredibly backward ideas. They said we were half communist! I'm sure some people thought I was a little bit Red [medio rojito].[17]

Pantaleón's spectacular growth and apparent labor acquiescence were strong advertisements for these reforms, however. In 1985 Julio Herrera and his team hosted a seminar for sugar executives at the Camino Real Hotel in Guatemala City, and shortly thereafter managers from other mills began to request advice on how to implement similar reforms. Pantaleón's idea was to socialize its experience in order to spur the sugar sector to organize itself into a powerful interest group and to jointly invest in labor stabilization programs. After domestic sugar prices rose in 1990, each sugar mill contributed Q1 million to create FUNDAZUCAR to standardize the programs started by Pantaleón: "It was difficult to convince ASAZGUA [Guatemalan Sugar Association] to change, to do things as a bloc. Pantaleón did a lot of lobbying. Miky Fernandez helped a lot; really, the private sector owes him. Because there was this mentality: 'This is a finca; the administrator is in charge.' People went around carrying pistols."[18]

An important backdrop to these private-sector organizing efforts was the tentative start of peace talks between the government and the Guatemalan National Revolutionary Unity in the late 1980s and early 1990s. For the private sector, this raised the question of how to ensure its influence on the peace process, and it became urgently important for the business class to articulate and promote a vision of national socioeconomic development whose basic tenet would be the preservation of private property rights.

"We are NOT talking about distributing wealth," declares a poster in the entrance to FUNDAZUCAR's office in Guatemala City, "but about creating opportunities so people can generate their own well-being." The Foundation's mandate is to "work from the gates of the mill outward" through several strategic goals: (1) generate human capital in order to make the industry more competitive; (2) show corporate responsibility; (3) achieve the long-term stability of the sugar sector; (4) be a facilitating agency for aid money for the Pacific coast region; (5) generate changes in state policy; and (6) show congruence with the peace accords.[19]

Housing was one of FUNDAZUCAR's first ventures. In the early 1990s the agency channeled international aid and credit to facilitate the removal of the resident workforce out of the plantations and into new *colonias* on the urban fringes of coastal towns. This was a priority for the sugar mills, in order to reduce the cost of maintaining a year-round workforce on the plantations, while still having access to a nearby trained labor force. In education the Foundation's efforts focus on administering a USAID-funded public-private educational project, called PRONADE.[20] The Foundation also runs teacher-training workshops, and the industry emphasizes the reorientation of educational institutions to respond to the skilled labor needs of the sugar mills. Several initiatives have focused on "domestic science" programs for women in the new coastal colonias, with the goal of teaching women to create "orderly" households through programs in hygiene and to learn to stretch their husbands' now seasonal wages.

Health is the area where FUNDAZUCAR has had the most visible and controversial presence. The most prominent project has been the remodeling of the national hospital in the Pacific coast region. The Foundation provides ophthalmologic, pediatric, surgical, and general medical services in these facilities; the idea is that this project will serve as a prototype for a restructuring of health services within Guatemala and in Central America. The plan is not privatization per se, as a purchase of public installations, but rather what the World Bank calls a "transfer of authority;" in this case, FUNDAZUCAR lobbied for a change in state regulations to allow it to administer the outpatient wing of the public hospital with a fifty-year lease. On the coast FUNDAZUCAR is associated more than anything else with the restructuring of the hospital, although the process has been contentious (see below).

The Foundation's work with municipal governments focuses on strategic planning workshops with local mayors, with the stated goal of creating a class of "municipal managers."[21] This focus is consistent with efforts to promote the decentralization of governmental authority and to reframe development issues as technical problems to be solved by increasing managerial competence and improving the flow of information and communication with local communities. For example, malnutrition problems among children are posed primarily as a lack of knowledge on the part of mothers, which can be corrected, in this view, by educating women in matters of hygiene and nutrition.[22]

Working out a plan for local governance is crucial for the industry not only due to the current push for political devolution away from the central state but because of the history of political organizing and unionism that existed on the coast prior to the 1980s. In the municipality of Escuintla, for example, the election of a social democratic mayor in 1978 helped to articulate a potent popular movement on the coast that linked rural and industrial labor unions with university and political activists. Union-sponsored literacy and popular education classes were held inside the town hall, until an assassination attempt in 1980 forced the mayor to flee the country.[23]

FUNDAZUCAR's self-defined role is to act as a "facilitator and accelerator" of the programs of structural adjustment and to project its "clear and futuristic vision" to the rest of the private sector and the society. The combined force of these discursive projects is aimed at constructing an invigorated notion of nationhood that the business class pledges to defend—and define. In 1992, for example, during the commemoration of the Spanish Conquest, a broad range of indigenous groups met in Guatemala for a summit called "500 Years of Resistance." FUNDAZUCAR printed its reaction in the editorial pages of *Costa Sur*, alongside an article appositely titled "500 New Housing Solutions for 1993." But more than new projects, the editorial claimed, what Guatemala needs is a "change in attitude, a positive, constructive attitude . . . instead of always demanding, criticizing, condemning and complaining":

> If 500 years have taught us anything, maybe it's a good pretext to look for a renovation of spirit and national consciousness; we should reorient our efforts toward a positive mental attitude. . . . It's time to enter a new century as a just and dignified nation, *la patria grande*, as was the dream of our Central American patriots. Five hundred years of resistance hasn't left us much in the way of positive. Maybe it's time to stop resisting ourselves and begin to integrate a nation proud of its roots [that are] indigenous, creole, mestizo, mulatto or whatever, but which today make up a new Central American identity. (Fundazucar 1992: 2)

During the 1990s more than a dozen peace agreements broached issues ranging from indigenous rights to socioeconomic reforms (Jonas 2000). Although sugar executives took a cool view of the peace accords themselves (since they conferred legitimacy on the Left and called for an expansion of state social programs), the sugar sector has strived to show "congruence" with the peace process, as noted earlier. In one report several years after the signing of the final peace accord, FUNDAZUCAR (1999: 18) published a table showing point by point how the industry's "business framework" was strengthened by the accords' mandate for improved education and health coverage and the strengthening of municipal autonomy.

A large part of this political offensive around the peace accords was directed at gaining the trust of international donors involved in raising and channeling postwar economic aid (aside from the World Bank and the various branches of the UN system, this included USAID, the European Union, and, to an increasing extent, Japan). ASAZGUA and FUNDAZUCAR organized numerous tours of the Pacific coast plantations for diplomats and UN functionaries to encourage these institutions to step in to support industry-sanctioned programs there.

The South Coast since the 1980s

What does the south coast look like a generation after political violence destroyed the plantation labor movement? Sugarcane dominates, from the
skirts of the volcanoes in Esquintla all the way to the scorching flatlands near
the sea. Just before the coastline, rusty cotton gins are strewn about the fields,
and the old United Fruit–era *galeras* (bunkhouses) are mostly empty; down
there, African palm plantations have replaced cotton, and the palm plantations need relatively few workers. Around Tiquisate some banana plantations have returned for the first time since the 1950s. Otherwise, genetically
engineered sugarcane stretches across the south coast like giant swaths of
AstroTurf. During the *zafra*, or cane-harvesting season, the air on the coast is
choked with smoke and ash from the burning cane fields, combined with the
sticky-sweet odor of cane juice being boiled down into raw sugar.

Virtually the entire (formerly) permanent plantation workforce has been
relocated to periurban neighborhoods on the fringes of the major south coast
towns. Some of these settlements were constructed by FUNDAZUCAR, while
others are spontaneous settlements. Residents of the post-1980s sugar industry colonias that ring Escuintla and Santa Lucía Cotzumalguapa speak
favorably of some changes; for example, workers no longer have to walk the
long distances to the fields during the zafra, since now the mills' buses come
right into the colonias every morning to pick up cane cutters. But for many,
the shock of sudden proletarianization meant losing a community that might
have existed for several generations, along with the access to land for planting and raising animals that existed on the plantations. (When I first visited
these settlements in 1994, I saw corn and beans planted on these tiny urban
lots, but by the early twenty-first century these lots had mostly disappeared,
as houses expanded to accommodate growing families.)

Near the departmental capital of Escuintla, although the new colonias have
names like Cañaveral I–IV (*cañaveral* means cane field), many of the original
residents have left, unable to make the loan payments on their houses (echo-
ing the classic experience of other company towns, such as Chicago's Pull-
man Village and Guatemala's postwar market-driven resettlements, as Velásquez Nimatuj details in this volume). The neighborhoods were opened up
to workers from other industries and to middle-class buyers.[24] The working-
class families here are a mixture of skilled mill workers (electricians, mechanics, etc.), harvest workers (mostly young men), maquiladora workers,
and others. Salaries in the formal sector are well below poverty levels even
in these established colonias, however, and the informal economy has bur-

FIG 5.3 Former agrarian reform land parcel, Escuintla, 2000. Campesino residents were driven out in the early 1980s. PHOTO BY ELIZABETH OGLESBY.

geoned.[25] Many women work in domestic labor or run sidewalk vending activities out of their homes, and men work as day laborers or as vendors in town.

Those who can hold on to their lots in the sugar colonias are among the most secure people on the coast, but in other areas, the question of land tenancy has smoldered for a generation or more. The different types of settlements on the coast — squatter settlements, *parcelamientos* (land projects created during the era of the agrarian reform in the early 1950s), and periurban shantytowns — have in common a history of struggle to carve out an existence in the crevices of an expanding agro-export sector. Even in areas that have been settled for decades on former finca land, many people still do not have title to their lots. In the *parcelamientos* that interrupt the coastal horizon like islands in a sea of cane (one *finquero* described them as "pockmarks" on the landscape), few of the original 1950s-era beneficiaries remain; they either left through attrition when the export economy expanded in the 1970s or were driven out by the violence of the early 1980s. Most of the people I interviewed on the coast were either renting their lots or were enmeshed in an arduous process of trying to pay off the purchase price.

The loss of land area for planting is compounded by the environmental changes on the coast. Older workers tell of how they used to combine wage income with hunting and fishing, but this is difficult if not impossible today.

Aside from the occasional giant ceiba tree that rises spectacularly above the fields, and a few new rubber and African palm plantations, there is little forest left on the coast. And the intensive use of pesticides and fertilizers over several decades has turned rivers, streams, and estuaries into toxic sewers. The crisis for coastal workers, therefore, is how to survive on wages that are still below subsistence levels, while negotiating the erosion of the social wage (meager benefits and small parcels of land on which to plant corn and beans, which the fincas used to provide to permanent workers but no longer do).

In contrast to the mobility of highland migrant workers, labor markets on the coast are relatively fixed geographically. The sugar mills have mapped out their respective zones of influence, and they recruit coastal labor from within a set circumference. In the maquiladora sector, both male and female workers from around Escuintla can commute to factories located just outside Guatemala City, but other areas of the coast are excluded from these essentially urban labor markets. Around Santa Lucía and to the west, workers are more likely to travel seasonally to Mexico for the coffee harvest or to carve out a precarious existence as day laborers or street vendors or, even shakier, by collecting and selling wild herbs. Prostitution, even child prostitution, is common.

Labor migration to the United States is not seen on the coast to the same degree as in many parts of the highlands. In part this probably reflects the ways transnational recruitment networks developed in the highlands, but it is also rooted in the patterns of poverty on the coast and the fact that most working-class people there do not have any land to borrow against to pay a coyote's fee.

The sugar mills have a delicate relationship with local governments on the coast. On one hand, the overall weakness of the state financial system creates a public sector dependent on private sources of credit; municipal authorities sometimes have to borrow money from the sugar mills to cover short-term payroll expenses. On the other hand, even after the dampening of social protest, municipal governments are still key arenas where local conflicts are broached and, at times, fought out, such as conflicts over environmental pollution and local taxes. Sugar mills are required by law to pay a surcharge per sack of sugar directly to local governments, but in the past municipal authorities have enforced this statute only laxly, partly because of their dependent position vis-à-vis the private sector. The mills loan money, and they extend their machinery and technical expertise to local governments, which "lack the moral authority to press them on the tax or environmental questions," according to one municipal employee.[26]

The technical approach, and the rapprochement with the municipalities, would seem to resemble what Ferguson (1994) called an "anti-politics machine," or a way to depoliticize social development discourse. Many people involved in social organizations on the coast see the private sector policies in this light, as an elite effort to occupy the spaces of the local state and civil society that were wrested from the Left in a bloodbath during the 1980s. In this view, FUNDAZUCAR's aim is "to crush the spirit of workers [aplastar los ánimos de los trabajadores]."[27]

Yet these initiatives are not simply a way to create social buffer zones around the sugar mills, although this may have been the original, more limited intent. They are not just a project of "anti-politics" but a particular kind of politics that admits popular participation, as long as this is channeled in ways consonant with the industry's goals. The message FUNDAZUCAR and the sugar industry would like to instill is that class warfare is a scourge of the past, and workers, empresarios, and local communities can join in common purpose.[28] It is a proactive project to create new sorts of subjectivities linked to work discipline.

Perhaps the key point in analyzing the azucareros' model is that the wage structure underpinning the new corporate social responsibility discourse in the plantation zone is not very different from previous eras when the real cost of labor was externalized through minifundio (subsistence parcel) subsistence production.[29] Piece-rate sugar harvest wages (paying workers by the number of tons of sugarcane they cut) are well above the rural minimum wage, but they continue to be below subsistence costs. With partial mechanization and improvements in labor productivity, the harvest season has been reduced from six months to just over four months (roughly from early November to mid-March). Migrant workers from the highlands can return to their villages for corn-planting season and augment plantation wages with subsistence production (the minifundio system). As noted earlier, however, resettled plantation workers have lost access to the small plots of land where they used to be able to plant crops and raise animals. The extreme "flexibilization" of labor on the coast (removal of the permanent workforce from the plantations and overall shortening of labor contracts in other sectors to avoid paying benefits) means that far fewer workers receive prestaciones, or social wage components such as health care, severance pay, and retirement benefits, which are vital sources of support for workers given the precarious wage levels.[30]

Access to infrastructure and services in the new coastal semiurban colonias is another critical issue. FUNDAZUCAR claims to have a presence in more than fifty communities on the coast, but in the urban fringe neigh-

borhoods of Escuintla, where I conducted collective and individual interviews in 2000 and 2001, the only contact residents claimed to have had with
FUNDAZUCAR was through an occasional education seminar (for teachers)
or through sewing or cooking classes (for the wives of mill workers). These
programs were viewed positively as worthwhile pastimes, although they did
not address the most serious concerns for workers: low incomes, insecure
land tenancy and employment, lack of community infrastructure, and crime.
In the sugar industry colonias, FUNDAZUCAR has a more engaged presence
(running a nutrition center in one colonia and administering a privatized
water service in another), yet even here residents spoke of the local municipal government and the public-sector social security administration as being
the key institutions to which they appealed for services.

Access to services is one of the most pressing issues in these colonias. For
one local development committee in a colonia built on land that a sugar mill
turned over to its workers as severance pay, it has been difficult to formally
establish institutional responsibility for infrastructure goals. A community
leader described efforts to secure basic services: "The municipality has helped
a bit, but it's difficult because we don't have official recognition as a colonia.
FUNDAZUCAR has not helped; they say we have to go to the *ingenio* [mill],
but the ingenio hasn't responded." One resident of a large Escuintla shanty-
town expressed a disparaging view: "FUNDAZUCAR is like one of these hens
that lays an egg and then goes strutting around crowing about it. But even
after all the noise, it's still just one egg."[31]

The debate over development policy is played out nationally in the relationship between FUNDAZUCAR and other nongovernmental organizations.
In some limited ways, these different institutions meet on common ground
vis-à-vis the state. For example, FUNDAZUCAR led an effort to amplify the
tax-exempt status of NGOs. On more substantive issues, however, the institutional alliance breaks down. The Foundation wants to use its experience
on the coast to press for a broader restructuring of social services, urging, for
example, a total privatization of the national social security system, while for
other NGO federations, particularly ones with historic ties to social movements, the priority is to preserve and improve the sphere of state action as a
motor for development.[32]

FUNDAZUCAR's role in the hospital in Escuintla is one of the Foundation's most controversial arenas of activity. Services are improved, but
patients' costs have risen steeply. Moreover, since the agreement transferring
authority to FUNDAZUCAR was signed in high-level negotiations between
the Ministry of Health and the azucareros, grievances generally are not dealt

with on-site but are referred to authorities in the capital.[33] Disagreements over FUNDAZUCAR's role in the hospital have on occasion escalated into showdowns between the Foundation and the union, including an attempted blockage of the outpatient wing by hospital workers, making these "alliances" appear more like power struggles. "They don't negotiate," objected one hospital employee, "they send us psychologists instead."[34]

The development alliances promoted by FUNDAZUCAR can, at best, be characterized as technical partnerships rather than political alliances. A key question is whether popular-sector organizations and communities can leverage any meaningful social space from the corporate responsibility model. In the late 1990s the UN's peacekeeping mission and its Development Program organized public events on the coast to discuss aspects of the peace process and the specific social problems of the region. National leaders of the sugar industry participated in these initiatives, even though it put them face to face with community activists. In some of the rebuilt plantation communities, a second generation of community leaders has emerged, one that uses the private sector's own idiom of public-private alliances to press their case to FUNDAZUCAR for expanded community services and a resolution of environmental problems. A few years after the signing of the peace accords, a national leader of the CUC expressed cautious acknowledgment:

> When the latest human development report on Guatemala came out, they held a forum where a representative from CACIF [representing agricultural and industrial elites] spoke. I think it is a positive sign that they are willing to discuss these issues. I think it's true that there is a new generation of empresarios now, and maybe the sons are not as bad as the fathers were. But we have to see what changes in practice. The problem in Guatemala is that the private sector has never been willing to let go of any power.[35]

From Biopower to Biofuel: Consent and Coercion in Guatemala's Cane Fields

In December 2011 a spate of news stories pointed to a disturbing trend in Central America: men are dying of preventable kidney disease in alarmingly high numbers. According to data from the World Health Organization, since 2005 deaths from chronic kidney disease have risen almost 30 percent in Guatemala and more than 40 percent in Nicaragua (where sugar production increased after Pantaleón purchased the large Monte Rosa sugar mill in Chinandega in 1998). Epidemiologists trace the spike in kidney disease to dehydration and heat stress, caused in large part by the strenuous labor of cutting sugar cane (Chavkin and Greene 2011; Sheehy 2011). In the cane fields along Central America's Pacific coast, men are literally working themselves to death.

The reports of cane cutters' broken bodies square with ethnographic information I collected in Guatemala among sugar workers in the early twenty-first century. In Joyabaj, El Quiché the town pharmacies stock a dozen brands of Vitamin B injections, and migrant cane cutters start buying them weeks before the sugar harvest starts, at half a day's wage for one shot. Eighteen-year-old Sebastian and his twenty-four-year-old brother, Santiago (pseudonyms), described working in the cane fields:

> Sebastián: We start at six in the morning. We have to get up at four if the cane field is far away. We finish at about seven at night, but sometimes later. Sometimes, we can't even see any more where the machete is going. The buses come, but instead of picking us up, they shine their headlights into the fields so we can keep working! The only way I can take it is because of the injections. I pay for my own injections: Nervión, Nerotrópica, Tiamina, and Sin Sueño.[36] You don't feel the sun that way. You don't get tired. One pill lasts about two or three hours, but an injection lasts fifteen days.

> Santiago: The old people, especially, are the ones who take vitamins, people over thirty. Young people still have good bodies and we don't need them as much. People take other things too, things that make them talk like crazy people, and they walk around like drunks. The ones who cut ten or twelve tons a day, many of them take drugs. Not just vitamins, but real drugs, then you can't work without them. Those people don't think, but I do, it's not worth it. You can die if you don't realize you've had too much sun. I know some people from here who are so burned out that they can't work on their land anymore.[37]

Mill doctors are cognizant that the effects of these vitamin shots are as much psychological as physical; in fact their main value is to make workers feel ready to put their bodies into overdrive.[38]

Both of these young men, and other cane cutters I interviewed in El Quiché, talked about the labor competition in the cane fields in self-mocking, even sardonic tones. "It's like a race," said Sebastián. "In the morning, we all start out even, in a row. Then you begin to watch who pulls out in front. You're always looking around, making sure you stay ahead."

Sebastián's neighbor, another cane cutter, did a comic imitation of a worker walking around with his chest swelled with pride to parody how workers react to the engineers' depictions of them as champions: "The empresarios [owners, or, in this case, their representatives] come to the camps every week to tell us how great we are, that we're ahead of all the other workers."[39] On the other hand, "some people get crazy with the competition," said this worker, seasoned at twenty-six. "It's like when they put up a greased pole at a fair. Even though you know you can't win, you have to try."[40]

The tone became less jocular when the young cane cutters talked about the darker side of workers pushing the limits of their physical endurance. The twenty-six-year-old who was clowning around with us said he had chronic back and shoulder pain from his previous year on the coast that made it difficult to work in his own cornfield, despite having spent quite a lot of money on pain injections.

Are workers "disciplined" by these labor practices? These "vanguard" cane cutters are pushed to compete with each other to reach production goals by both piece-rate wage incentives and psychological pressures, including the manipulation of masculinity and notions of machismo. All this doesn't make workers dislike cutting cane any less or erase class consciousness, but when it is cross-cut with an emphasis on the recruitment of youth, it does create a separate group of workers for whom labor migration to the sugar plantations of the south coast is a rite of passage and a stepping stone to aspirations of future U.S.-bound migration (trading cutting cane for "cutting chickens" in southern U.S. poultry plants, in the case of these youths from Joyabaj; Oglesby 2001, 2003).

What has changed in the south coast region since the violent labor repression of the 1980s, and what has not changed? Through increased labor surveillance, a piece-rate wage system, new "human resource" programs, and the removal of the permanent plantation workforce, the mills have been able to raise worker output spectacularly and keep labor unions off the plantations. These changes are not a complete transformation in plantation labor relations; they should be seen instead as a new layer of labor control, one that builds upon, incorporates, and remakes prior methods. The structure of production in Guatemala is redolent of the nineteenth century: large landholdings still control the Pacific coast, and while nominal wages have risen, real wages remain below subsistence levels for most of the harvest workforce.

The sugar sector has been very successful at garnering international aid money for its programs on the south coast, winning awards and large grants and loans from the World Bank and other international donors. The positive aspect of these initiatives is that, as a World Bank representative put it to me, leaders of the powerful sugar elite are "coming out of the trenches" with a project of governance that is not based wholly on the use of death squads. Much caution is needed, however. For example, the azucareros have projected the vision that FUNDAZUCAR and other private-sector initiatives are resolving the question of poverty on the coast, yet as this chapter shows, livelihood conditions on the coast are even more precarious than in the highlands, even though most development organizations work in the highlands.

Much more research is needed to understand contemporary social conditions on the coast, and particularly to gauge the fragile spaces for participation by local communities and the state. If these programs are to be called "alliances," the state's role must include at minimum an enforcement of labor laws and the creation of effective mechanisms of redress for labor abuses as well as environmental damages. It is important to consider a state role in promoting income-generating programs that might be compatible with seasonal wage labor. The state must also comply with the obligations assumed under the peace accords to extend basic services such as education and health care; private partners may participate, but they cannot substitute in this endeavor.

Sugar production continues to increase, especially with the growth of ethanol as a biofuel (made from cane refuse). In 2007, for example, Pantaleón received a $50 million loan from the World Bank to increase ethanol production at its mill in Nicaragua, and in 2010 the mill announced a planned 200 percent increase in ethanol production in Guatemala. (By the late 1990s Guatemalan sugar mills already produced 20 percent of the electricity consumed nationally; International Finance Corporation, World Bank Group 2007; Central American Business Network 2010). Since the south coast cannot accommodate the growth of the biofuel boom, cane production by at least one mill has spread to the Polochic Valley, with its history of violent land evictions dating from the 1970s (see Solano this volume).

Is the discourse of corporate social responsibility at odds with this scenario of "accumulation by dispossession" (Harvey 2003) or a cover for it? Given how cane cutters are succumbing to the arduous work regime, if *biopower* is defined as the "administration of bodies and the calculated management of life" (Foucault, cited in Rabinow 1984: 262), what we are seeing in Guatemala's cane fields might more accurately be described as a "bloody Taylorism" (Lipietz 1982: 40) of harsh labor demands and ongoing primitive accumulation, lubricated by the language of corporate social responsibility. At the same time, however, a new logic came into play on the plantations of the south coast in the aftermath of the social mobilization of the 1970s and early 1980s, one that attempts to shift the balance between consent and coercion. Only a fine-grained and agile analysis can capture the ways powerful sectors of the Guatemalan elite assessed and responded to this history of struggle and the significance of their postwar project of governance. Whether or not any meaningful social space can be won from these changes remains to be seen.

Notes

1. In Guatemala this region is called the "south coast," and it includes the departments of Escuintla, Suchitepequez, and Retalhuleu.
2. Interviewed in Escuintla, January 7, 2001.
3. I attended this forum in 2005. A video of the forum, and subsequent annual events, is available from the Centro para la Acción de la Responsabilidad Social Empresarial en Guatemala (www.centrarse.org).
4. The Commission for Historical Clarification documented the assassination or disappearance of twenty-eight union leaders from the sugar industry between 1980 and 1983 (CEH 1999: 4:106).
5. On the history of forced labor in Guatemala, see McCreery (1994, 1995). Debt peonage and labor drafts in Guatemala did not end until the 1930s and 1940s, respectively. A number of studies document how plantations later used ethnic segmentation as a form of labor control, for example, by giving nonindigenous permanent workers a series of benefits, and then, when these workers organized into unions, by seeking to replace the permanent workforce with Maya migrant laborers from the highlands (Pansini 1977; Bossen 1982; Cabarrús 1978).
6. Interviewed in Retalhuleu, November 1994.
7. In addition to a large body of work in this vein within labor history, the more recent field of critical management studies draws upon critical theory and poststructuralism, in particular the writings of Foucault and the relation to human resource management. See, for example, Legge 1995; Storey 2007.
8. Interview with a former Pantaleón top manager, Leonel Borja, Guatemala City, November 2, 2000. After his tenure at Pantaleón, Miguel Fernández went on to become a partner in KORAMSA, a textile maquila established jointly with Korean investors. KORAMSA became the largest maquila plant in Latin America, until the Koreans pulled out their capital in the twenty-first century.
9. Mechanization of the sugar harvest has increased in recent years, with the signing of the 1996 peace accords and the elimination of the Guatemalan National Revolutionary Unity as a military threat, making it less costly to producers to take the political risk of displacing workers. Industry sources told me in 2000 that about 25 percent of the cane harvest was fully mechanized, yet, they stressed, full mechanization will probably never encompass more than 40 to 50 percent of the harvest.
10. I have borrowed this term from Jonathan Crush's (1992) study of electronic monitoring of workers in the South African gold mines.
11. While it is enticing to see this information system as a "superpanopticon" (Posner 1990), it helps to bear in mind that it is, in actuality, a simple Excel program subject to disruptions. One year, for example, a technical supervisor left the mill and took the database with him. In 2000 I heard that several Pantaleón supervisors had been held up at gunpoint while on their way to give a PowerPoint presentation in one of

the migrant camps. The highway robbers stole a laptop computer on which the year's labor information was stored, much of it with no backup files.

12. I heard various views on the composition of the harvest labor force. Some mills claim that workers from the highlands are not as physically capable as ladino workers (nonindigenous or second- or third-generation migrants) from the coast, and their presence "retards" the region's development. Others shun highland workers because they believe indigenous workers won't assimilate as easily into a labor regime that emphasizes individual competition around production quotas; in this view, Mayan workers by "nature" tend to act collectively, and this is not an especially desirable trait should a labor dispute arise. Others, however, maintain that indigenous workers are more disciplined than workers from the coast; they come to work, and it's easier to get them to stay for the entire harvest, as opposed to the more "rebellious" coastal workers.

13. In January 2012 the Guatemala online journalism project, *Plaza Pública*, published an exposé on child labor in the cane fields (Arce 2012). My sense is that this phenomenon occurs mainly in independent cane farms and less so in the plantations connected to the sugar mills, which are attempting to recruit young men who are physically powerful enough to handle the grueling work regime.

14. Mill interview 21, Pantaleón, October 12, 1994.

15. The question of "peasant" or "worker-peasant" consciousness was, of course, a subject of protracted debate during the 1970s. As Roseberry (1993a) notes in one of the best reviews of this literature in the Latin American context, the debates were profoundly political as well as theoretical. What strikes me about the ways the sugar plantations are striving to build knowledge about highland migrant workers is that it seems a mirror image of what the Left was trying to do twenty or thirty years ago, that is, an attempt to identify the structural position of workers and to correlate these typologies with particular sorts of behavior, to determine what makes not an ideal revolutionary, but a model worker.

16. Mill interview 47, Pantaleón, November 29, 1994.

17. Interview with Leonel Borja, Guatemala City, November 2, 2000.

18. Interview with Leonel Borja, Guatemala City, November 2, 2000.

19. FUNDAZUCAR 1999; interview with María Silvia Pineda de Sajché, former executive director of FUNDAZUCAR, Guatemala City, December 1999.

20. PRONADE is a program run out of the Ministry of Education, whereby local committees (*coeducas*) and "facilitating agencies" like FUNDAZUCAR hire, train, and monitor the performance of teachers who are hired in a parallel, lower cost (nonunionized), and theoretically more "locally controlled" educational system.

21. Interview with María Silvia Pineda de Sajché.

22. Interview with María Silvia Pineda de Sajché.

23. See CEH 1999, vol. 1 and Illustrative Cases.

24. The price of lots and housing construction rose steeply after the first wave of resettlement. In one case in the late 1980s, Doña Margarita, a woman with a forty-nine-year work history at one of the mills, received Q6,500 in severance pay when the resettlement started (around $2,300 at that time). The value of her ten-by-thirty-meter lot was discounted at Q3,800, and she received the rest in cash, along with a bank loan to finance construction of a new house. In a poignant twist, Doña Mar-

garita's new lot, indeed a large part of the new colonia, is set on land that had actually been her own *parcela* during the fleeting seasons of the agrarian reform in the early 1950s but which she was now forced to pay for. South coast interview 16, Escuintla, October 7, 2000. Later on, in the newer colonias built after 1990, the cost of lots rose from Q25,000 to Q40,000, and with inflation construction costs for an average-size house climbed from Q10,000 to around Q75,000, according to community leaders.

25. In the same sugar industry colonia, community leaders showed me a survey they had conducted that estimated average yearly income in the formal sector at Q12,000, or just about bare subsistence wages at the time. South coast collective interview 6, November 17, 2000.

26. South coast interview 45, January 18, 2001.

27. Interview with a unionist, South coast interview 12, Escuintla, October 7, 2000.

28. These quotations from Pantaleón's "Permanent Values Campaign" were published in FUNDAZUCAR's newsletter, *Costa Sur* 2, nos. 2, 3, 4, and 7 (1992). Note what is included — and omitted — in the evocation of justice:

    My conduct reflects who I am. I carry out my duties. I act with DISCIPLINE.

    I am part of an enterprise that I respect, because I belong to it. I believe in being committed to my work. I believe in LOYALTY.

    There is more than one way to do something. I will always find a better way. I use my CREATIVITY.

    Everyone has the same right to the sun, to the night, to the rain, to work, and to life. I believe in JUSTICE.

29. According to my interviews with cane cutters in the highlands and on the coast, mean sugar wages in 2000 were about Q1,300 a month (about $170), while "champion" cane cutters earned up to Q2,000. The cost of a family basket of goods for the same period, according to the National Institute of Statistics, was Q1,200 a month for food and Q2,100 for food, clothing, health, education, and transportation. Workers inside the mills started at about Q1,600 a month; in comparison, a maquila worker earned about Q1,500 a month.

30. Data from the Guatemalan Social Security Institute (IGSS, *Informes anuales*) indicates that the percentage of coastal workers covered by social security plunged 60 percent during the 1980s. A remnant of the 1940s reform period, IGSS provides health care coverage for full-time workers. A worker must be employed continuously for ninety days in order to receive health benefits.

31. Collective interviews 3, Escuintla, November 7, 2000, and 12, December 21, 2000.

32. The analysis developed in this section is taken from an interview with a leader of the National Forum of Guatemalan NGOs, Guatemala City, January 12, 2001.

33. Interview with hospital union representatives, December 21, 2000. Grievances include, for example, holding the agency responsible for its part of the official agreement to contribute to hospital maintenance costs. Unionists believe this part of the agreement is purposely neglected in order to accentuate the difference in appearance between the rundown state infrastructure and the newly remodeled wing that FUNDAZUCAR operates, to provide a rationale for a further privatization of health services.

34. Interview with hospital union representatives, December 21, 2000.

35. South coast interview 40, November 20, 2000.

36. The first three are Vitamin B shots; Sin Sueño is an over-the-counter stimulant.

37. Interviews 30–31, Joyabaj, July 2000.

38. A similar morale booster was sought through the oral rehydration drinks given to cane cutters each morning; as one of the original engineers at Pantaleón told me, the mill decided to add red coloring to the drinks to make them look like blood, thus giving workers the sensation that they were getting a potent transfusion.

39. I'm not sure exactly when workers began to use this word to refer to plantation owners, as opposed to the more plainly class-conscious *ricachones* (rich ones, fat cats), but it's now widespread. The term *empresario* is sometimes used interchangeably with *ingeniero* (engineer) when referring to mid- and upper-level management or people who, in workers' minds, are part of the company. It was interesting to me that workers chose the word *empresario*, which translates to the image of "businessmen" that the sugar mill executives project, over *finquero*, or landowner.

40. Interview 36, July 14, 2000.

"A DIGNIFIED COMMUNITY WHERE WE CAN LIVE"

Violence, Law, and Debt in Nueva Cajolá's Struggle for Land

We thought that if evictions occur on the farms, in the capital they don't, so we came to ask our government to solve our problem, since we came with the full backing of the law.

Rural Maya-Mam activist, July 1992

"Where were you in 1992?" If you were a Maya-Mam peasant from Cajolá, Quetzaltenango, you were occupying the Central Plaza of Guatemala City with five hundred other families, people who had been fighting since 1989 for land their community was promised by President Justo Rufino Barrios in 1872. They came, as they said, to "ask our government to solve our problem," after years of making legal claims and taking other peaceful actions to obtain the land they needed to feed their children. The Cajolenses in the Central Plaza appear in the iconic image of the Columbus Quincentennial in Guatemala, "Meeting of Two Worlds" by Daniel Hernández-Salazar. Taken on July 22, 1992, the photo was published in newspapers and continues to circulate in posters, books, and postcards; it shows Mam women of different ages, some carrying their small children on their back, all dressed in their distinctive regional clothing of red *güipiles* (blouses) and blue *cortes* (skirts), standing in front of the heavily armed antiriot police. The women's courage is evident. No one is backing down or even showing fear. They are unarmed, while the police have shields, clubs, guns, helmets, and tear-gas bombs. It is a highly condensed image of gender, race, agrarian struggle, resistance, and potential violence. As the man quoted in the epigraph suggests, these men

FIG 6.1 "Clash of Two Worlds, 1492–1992. A group of indigenous peasants face Guatemalan police members." PHOTO BY DANIEL HERNÁNDEZ-SALAZAR, © 1992, WWW.DANIELHERNANDEZSALAZAR.BLOGSPOT.COM. USED WITH KIND PERMISSION.

and women brought their hopes from the far reaches of the country to finally be heard in the capital.

A few hours after the photo was taken, however, the people of Cajolá were brutally removed from this public space. In this essay I explore how their violent removal both extended and complicated their struggles, to show how indigenous *campesinos* "with the full backing of the law" can nonetheless find their demands blocked and (perhaps unrecognizably) transformed as they become enmeshed in neoliberal aftermath (for more detail, see Velásquez Nimatuj 2008). When their claims on lands ceded to them in the nineteenth century became entangled in corruption, the women and men of Cajolá pressed their claims by turning to direct action: squatting on the land and taking over the Central Plaza. The state argued that these tactics constituted "actions outside the law" and responded with its own illegal actions. This dynamic suggests that the Cajolense struggle participates in the "cyclical ritual of mass protest–negotiation–agreement–failed promises–mass protest" that Petras and Veltmeyer (2003: 232) describe. Cajolense experiences also support Charles Hale's (1998) argument that the effective participation of indigenous people within international organisms and the state is determined in the last instance by force, the power to call forth members, and the established capacity of the organizations that are leading the struggle. But even when Cajolenses successfully deployed these tactics to get a response from the state after being removed from the plaza, it was a highly constrained "solution" based in the World Bank's more global project of "land reform" via market mechanisms, which has ended up drowning the community in debt and obliging Cajolenses to extend their cycles of protest indefinitely. The exhaustion the community began to suffer had devastating effects on the later stages of this struggle, even after they won the land titles they sought.

As I argue here, Nueva Cajolá shows the utter inadequacy of neoliberal solutions to demands for agrarian justice. I also suggest just how difficult it is to achieve any complementarity among peasant, indigenous, and revolutionary struggles (see Bastos and Camus this volume) as they work through the often unpredictable effects of past and ongoing physical and structural violence. This chapter uses the complex messages frozen in Hernández-Salazar's photo to explore the following questions: How do organized groups like the Cajolenses challenge the country's racial hierarchy as they confront the economic inequalities it has created? How do Mam peasants confront a historically racist nation-state weakened by globalization, especially in its judicial and social service functions, yet still willing to respond to the claims of poor indigenous people primarily by deploying force? To return to the central figure in the photo, how far can Mam women go, even as they are central actors in the struggle for agrarian justice and for access to land, in addressing the multiple axes of gender, class, and race inequalities that both structure and exceed their agrarian struggle?

Speaking Collectively

I began working with the community after a complex series of negotiations with the National Indigenous and Campesino Coordinator (CONIC), the organization that had supported the Cajolenses through much of the process, and several of whose leaders are from Cajolá. The experience of gaining entry and then beginning to work in the community taught me that it wasn't enough to be a Mayan anthropologist myself or to stand in solidarity with their struggles, but that patience during fieldwork, respect for the internal decisions of organizations, and an unwavering commitment to support the struggles of my Mayan brothers and sisters were key, because little by little they allowed me to acquire a wealth of experiences. One methodological challenge I faced while living in the community arose when I proposed interviewing leaders one by one. They answered that they were not interested in doing individual interviews. "Look, *compañera*," they said, "it's better to speak collectively. As many times as it takes, we will form a circle. You ask, one of us will take the word, and we will all listen to what each one of us says. We are going to add what has not been said and what is important. You see, there are names that I no longer remember, but this *compañero* or another one might, so it's better to speak collectively. Also, something that one cannot say in Spanish,[1] someone else will be able to explain. Do you understand me?"

This methodological proposal made me reflect on the value of indigenous peoples' forms of knowledge and interpretation. The campesinos of Nueva Cajolá, I understood, were insisting on the very epistemologies that have been marginalized in classical anthropology. I understood the message, and we conducted several rounds of collective interviews, some with only men or only women and others mixed. It also made me think about how deeply influenced I was, as a Mayan woman, by Western research methodology. It hadn't even occurred to me that fieldwork might allow me to be educated within my own cultural frameworks. For that reason, it cheered me when the Cajolá leaders recognized me as a Mayan woman and had the confidence to tell me how they wanted to work. As I address below, however, the meanings of this "speaking collectively" were still more complex than I understood at the time.

Rightful Claims

In 1989 more than five hundred Mam families presented a demand to the state for land known as Pampas del Horizonte, based on a property title granted to them in 1870 as payment for military service in the liberal army of Justo Rufino Barrios by the community of Cajolá. In 1884 Cajolá was stripped of its communal holdings as the same liberal regime expropriated land in support of the incipient coffee economy. The community immediately sued to regain those lands and for access to Pampas del Horizonte. Then as now the demand for land they considered rightfully theirs was understood as vital to the community's prosperity and its ability to guarantee a good and dignified life to its future members. After twenty years of pressure, in 1909 President Manuel Estrada Cabrera ordered that Pampas del Horizonte in Coatepeque, Quetzaltenango be awarded to the militiamen and their families. But the order gave them only twenty-two of the promised forty-five *caballerías*, and, despite presidential approval, the families never took full control of the land because local power brokers, specifically the ladino owners of neighboring farms, prevented them from settling in. People today remember their grandparents struggling with the lack of infrastructure and roads. Those who did try to settle were struck by an illness that killed many people, finally forcing the survivors to return to Cajolá.

In the late 1950s cutbacks in seasonal hiring on the local coffee plantations increased land pressure, leading families to turn back to the lands promised them in 1870. Meanwhile the land had been annexed to the Coantunco farm, owned by members of the powerful Arévalo Bermejo family. The first attempt at recovery foundered on people's lack of economic resources for travel and legal representation, their inability to speak Spanish, and the violent context of the post-1954 counterrevolution. A second attempt in 1967 likewise failed due to lack of resources, monolingualism, and the upswing in the state's counterinsurgency violence. Finally a third movement arose in December 1988, in the midst of the armed conflict. At the time, the army considered the *municipio* of Cajolá to be a "red zone," a military stronghold and support base for the Revolutionary Organization of the People in Arms (ORPA). While ORPA operated in the region, however, leaders insist that their land struggle was organized independently of any guerrilla group.

Returning to their claims within the 1910 title, the families founded the Pro-Land Peasant Movement of the Mam People and began seeking support from regional institutions and from the capital. They visited the recently elected Maya-K'icheé congressman for Quetzaltenango, Rolando Colop, a member of the then-official Christian Democrat Party, and a few days later Colop confirmed the title's authenticity and passed it on to the National Institute for Agrarian Transformation (INTA). This led to a series of visits to find boundary markers and make surveys, legal preliminaries necessary to take possession. Meanwhile the Arévalo family insisted the land was theirs and cultivated allies in elite organizations like the Coordinator of Commercial, Industrial, and Financial Associations (CACIF) and the National Agropecuarial Union (UNAGRO), which published ads warning of anarchy and chaos in the countryside due to campesino disrespect for private property. With the war still very hot, the oligarchy, the Arévalo family, and much of the mass media talked about the families of Cajolá as a mass of "usurpers of private property," and as "manipulated by the Communists" and "by leaders who do not show their faces."

Pressing Claims

Despite this pressure, on April 1, 1989, the president of INTA gave the green light to move in, and 250 families, with support from the priests of San Juan Ostuncalco, Quetzaltenango set up camp. In response the headlines of the major newspapers warned, "Property Invaded!" The occupying families immediately had to confront health problems resulting from the change in climate from cool highlands to tropical heat, a lack of food, and the resistance of the Arévalo family and their workers. Soon after they arrived, the state arrested their leaders, who had to pay a Q3,000 fine, while intense pressure from economic elites led two of the families' allies—Congressman Colop and the INTA president—to publicly retract their support. The Cajolenses did receive support, however, from the Campesino Unity Committee (CUC), the National University Student's Association (AEU), the Diocese of Los Altos and Father Andrés Girón (leader of a campesino struggle for land nearby on the south coast), and a number of international nongovernmental organizations. But despite working with local legal representatives and the Congress, in September 1989 the state sent antiriot squads to evict them. Hoping to avoid violence, the families retreated peacefully and occupied the nearby highway.

From the beginning, women were an essential part of the struggle to recover the land. Rosario explained to me that when the organization began, she was single and accompanied her father to the meetings. After she married, she supported her husband. She said, "I left with my husband and took my children with me when we occupied our farm that Arévalo had, and when we were removed by the police, we moved to the highway with everything, and with my little children. There I was, and I said, here I'll remain, and here I am." Marta also reconstructed those events: "When we occupied the high way, there were times when we didn't have anything to eat; the food ran out. The little food we could get, we gave it to our children. In spite of enduring hunger, we wouldn't get desperate. We never told our husbands, 'Let's go back!' On the contrary, we saw all the things the men did. They came and went. At times they left at dawn without even drinking a little bit of coffee to make the rounds in [the cities of] Xela, Guate, to any offices. How were we not going to support them?!"

They spent two months on the highway before President Vinicio Cerezo Arévalo, strongly pressured by the Catholic Church, agreed to see them. He promised a solution within fifteen days, but (perhaps due to his family ties) seventeen months later the Cajolenses were still on the highway. The lack of food and water, the heat, and outbreaks of disease killed twenty children over that year and a half. Fourteen years later the women's eyes still filled with tears remembering their lost children, who remain buried by the side of the road. (Lacking resources, the parents have been unable to transfer their remains.) "Nobody is going to give us back our children. There was no one to help, no medicine, not even water for the fevers, and much vomiting. But perhaps the greatest pain is that our community's children are still there. We never brought them to our cemetery, we left them there."

Nine months after the meeting with President Cerezo, the state proposed they renounce their claim to Pampas in return for land in Barillas, Huehuetenango, or Alta Verapaz. According to Damián Vaíl, one of the community's leaders (and an active member of CUC), those lands were too far away, and the families did not want them. Not only was their claim based on legal property titles, but for the Mam culture, historical feelings tied them to that farm because it represented the struggle of their ancestors. However, they were willing to accept another farm of equal size on the south coast, as long as other poor campesinos were not evicted, and they proposed several alternatives, but the government's answer was always silence. "We got tired of going and coming. It was like we didn't even exist."

To push their case, some families organized a ten-day march that reached the National Palace on August 9. They presented their demands and drew attention to the serious health conditions affecting women and children, which led INTA and the Labor and Popular Action Unity (UASP) to help find a provisional farm. Identifying Santa Inés in Retalhuleu as a good prospect and with an owner willing to sell, they petitioned the president to facilitate the process so the campesinos would "not have to spend Christmas on the highway" (Roldán Andrade 1994: 47).

Once again, after receiving no response from the president, the families took action. Announcing that the government had deceived them, fed up with hunger, disease, cold, and death, and within their full rights to their motherland, they occupied the farm on December 22, 1990. The government granted it to them in January 1991, but it only included 4.5 caballerías (approximately 450 acres), without water, latrines, or even shacks to live in. Costing Q900,000, the land would provide only twenty *cuerdas* (approximately 3.5 acres) each to eighty-nine families.[2] The credit that the government offered them so they could plant corn and sesame seed arrived late and was less than what had been agreed upon. But the campesinos accepted the farm as long as Coatunco was surveyed and with the understanding that Santa Inés was a provisional measure because it left over four hundred families landless.

In May 1992, in the context of the peace process and Quincentennial pressures around indigenous rights, these families took over part of Coatunco for the second time, erecting seventy provisional houses and planting approximately 680 acres of corn. They were supported by the CUC, of which the Cajolá activists Damián Vaíl, Cruz Vaíl, and Fidel Huinil were members, and Cajolá demands were included in a huge CUC march, which had been in the planning for several months, scheduled for May Day. The marchers left Huehuetenango on April 25 and entered the capital on May 1, covering 272 kilometers on foot. Approximately ten thousand mostly indigenous peasants participated, including children and elders. The CUC, despite being decimated in the 1980s and amid continuing armed conflict, ensured that the government of Jorge Serrano Elías felt the massive presence of indigenous people and campesinos, who, organized and peaceful, took over the downtown. They demanded a state response to agrarian problems, including higher plantation wages; respect for the human rights of indigenous people, widows, and orphans of the war; attention to displaced communities and refugees; demilitarization by disbanding the civil patrols; and ending forced recruitment of rural young men for the army.

Difficult Complementarity: The CUC Split and the Birth of CONIC

Most participants in the march considered it a great success and were not prepared for what happened fifteen days later. Members of CUC were summoned for an apparently ordinary evaluation meeting only to be confronted by an Extraordinary Assembly, where members of the CUC Board of Directors—Juan Tiney, Pedro Esquina, Juana Vásquez, and Federico Castillo— were accused of wasting money on an ineffective seven-day march, using the march to negotiate individual privileges with the president, and betraying campesino struggles by sitting down with the government. According to Isabel Solís of the Women's Commission:

> When the assembly began, the conflict against the Board of Directors started. They said that they had sold out. They even showed a picture of leader Juan [Tiney] next to President Serrano Elías. I requested the floor, and asked, "Why are we fighting? If this is not our goal . . ." Suddenly a woman pulled my hair, and said, "You do not have anything to talk about. If our plan is not carried out, it will be your fault." Then I kept quiet. I remember that it was the people from the Quiché who said the board was bad, that it had sold out, that they were corrupt.

When I interviewed Juan Tiney ten years later he told me:

> At the evaluation meeting, we were accused of selling out to the government and the army, and they demanded that we leave the CUC. For the national directors of the EGP [Guerrilla Army of the Poor] our crime was to promote indigenous demands along with agrarian demands. Our "strategic error" was to engage in a dialogue with the government on those topics. According to the EGP, that was the responsibility of the leaders of

the URNG [Guatemalan National Revolutionary Unity] at the negotiating table, not ours. . . . The accusations created confusion among the people attending. When the trouble occurred, people were on the verge of attacking each other with machetes. It was very dangerous, and we saw no need for that. We had always worked in a conscious and sacrificing way, without pay, out of our conviction of revolutionary consciousness, not to stay in power. So we stepped down. We became ordinary members, representing communities of grassroots activism. One is not a leader forever, right? (Interview, June 2003)

To avoid violence, Tiney, Esquina, Vásquez, and Castillo retired as directors of the CUC, to be replaced by Rafael González, Maria Toj, Rosario Pu, and Sebastián Morales. Confused by the accusations and dismayed by the lack of clarity about their future, members returned to their communities.

Damián Vaíl could not hide his sense of betrayal, surprise, and frustration. He left the hall in Villa Nueva, Guatemala with Cruz Vaíl and Fidel Huinil, Cajolenses who were occupying a different farm, and walked to the main highway to wait for a bus to Retalhuleu and then to their separate destinations. While they waited they talked about the sudden removal of their leaders. Damián was the most disturbed, repeating what he had publicly stated during the assembly: "Look, *muchá*, so much gossip, so much shit, a poisoned tongue is worse than a bullet! Who knows if everything said inside there is true. Fidel, do you believe that Juan and Pedro already have a farm?" Fidel, a little calmer, answered him, "Look, I don't believe it. I think that the ones who created all this confusion just want to break us apart, divide us, and they did it. Well, they really screwed us!" A worried Damián added, "*Muchá*, I have so much pain that I do not know how I am going to explain all this mess to the people back on the farm. What are we going to do without the support of the CUC? Without a lawyer?"

These concerns of Damián, the Cajolá representative to the CUC, were justified. The families had occupied the Coatunco farm just a week before, counting, as they had during the past years of struggle, on the CUC's political and legal expertise. And now, when eviction orders, death threats, and attacks in the national press made legal support most urgent, those who had provided the bulk of that support were gone. But as Fidel Huinil said, "We decided that our struggle must go on. It can't end here."

How can we explain this well-articulated and well-planned but unexpected political maneuver to dismiss respected leaders who had worked for seven years—first in clandestinity and then publicly—to rebuild the CUC after its brutal destruction in the 1980s? The CUC division of 1992 might be understood as an internal dispute between indigenous leaders who decided to sit down and negotiate with the state, and senior ladino leaders who decided to remove them for betraying the principles of the revolutionary movement. But that would be too simple. The rebuilding of the CUC, begun clandestinely in 1984 and going public in 1988, differed from its founding in that those involved were now active members of the EGP. That rebuilding was part of the EGP's strategy to expand their struggle in the legal spaces opened by the 1985 Constitution and ongoing peace process. Nevertheless 90 percent of the EGP's national leadership was ladino, educated, middle class, and male, and they wanted to control organizations like the CUC. That leadership clamped down on CUC leaders' attempts to organize based in the specific characteristics and needs of their base communities within a particular national political moment. But there is another element here. The coup d'état was ordered by the only two indigenous men on the EGP's National Directorate. I propose the concept of "shifting boundaries of solidarity" (Pandey 1988) to analyze the confrontation between indigenous leaderships, even as they were all indigenous, all members of the same guerrilla organization, and all working for a common objective: to strengthen political struggle and transform the structures of the state in order to improve the material and cultural life of the indigenous and poor ladino sectors of the country.

To return to the question of the "difficult complementarity" among indigenous and popular strands of organizing, in short, we must remember that "peasant consciousness is a contradictory unity" (Chatterjee 1993: 167). There *was* unity in people's awareness of their historical exploitation and servitude through the colonial, republican, and contemporary eras enacted by an exclusionary elite that transformed the state to maintain their economic, racial, political, and cultural privileges. Both sides in the CUC split were rejecting this subordination. Nonetheless a contradiction arose from the different forms they adopted to transform it.

The CUC leaders Tiney and Esquina were following a path demanded by their bases: to directly negotiate with the state to obtain land and thereby confront the conditions of hunger, labor injustice, and racial inequality. Their tenacity, creativity, and flexibility in moving among forms of protest and struggle suggest that they strategically and sensitively deployed the "cyclical ritual of mass protest–negotiation–agreement–failed promises–mass protest" to maneuver among the forces arrayed against them and respond to conjunctural possibilities. Following this logic, they met with President Serrano to insist on the urgency of campesino and indigenous rights and to push for resolutions of specific agrarian conflicts like Cajolá. Also according to this logic, they did not discuss this move with the leadership of the EGP, who were not in the country, and at a time before cell phones or the Internet.

But those members who took over the CUC, following EGP orders, saw no contradiction in their own disciplinary actions against these leaders because they understood that the equality peasants were demanding could be obtained only through the larger revolutionary project offered by the EGP. Meeting with Serrano posed a threat to that larger project. For Pablo Ceto, "that was a government where the military had control, in spite of having a new Constitution, and it was dangerous for EGP security." These fears arose in a context where the EGP had lost the military war and was hemorrhaging members, even as the organization's survival depended on its ability to make dramatic achievements in negotiations with the state and position itself as a progressive political force. Antonio Argueta, a lawyer and counselor to UNSITRAGUA (the labor federation that sheltered the CUC during its rebuilding) and the Cajolenses' advisor, sees the coup d'état as the result of CUC's "creating a new way to address popular demands about land ownership, which became a political, ideological and procedural shock for the EGP." The organization's commanders were afraid "that the popular and public arm could be separated at any moment." The reconstruction of CUC, which in turn helped create other organizations like the indigenous widow's group CONAVIGUA and the anti-PAC activism of CERJ, fortified the EGP, but also raised the specter of those organizations becoming autonomous. For maximum political influence at the negotiating table, the EGP needed greater unity among its bases.

The split in the CUC thus suggests that the indigenous peasant movement's everyday practices exceeded the vertical principles of the EGP, which ended up becoming a straitjacket, limiting their flexibility in responding to a dynamic reality. For example, the EGP's attempts to maintain control from abroad were simply unrealistic. Peasant leadership could not wait fifteen days to safely communicate with the EGP's commanders to execute a strategy. But perhaps most limiting was the way the military wing dominated the political wing of the organization, making it difficult for the EGP to separate combat logics from the work of the CUC, which demanded open and public participation. The EGP's discourse of democratic participation and attention to indigenous demands was ultimately stymied by its desire for control. It did open space for two indigenous men, Pablo Ceto and Gregorio Chay, but could not acknowledge the racism in which its organization, ideological doctrine, and leaders were immersed.[3] In this, the EGP acted like many other guerrilla organizations that rejected or reduced racism to class oppression. But racism runs parallel to class oppression and will not be resolved (even if it is somewhat mitigated) by achieving socioeconomic equality. Racism requires its own analysis and actions. The EGP's reluctance to address this issue forced one of the most influential campesino and indigenous organizations in Guatemalan history to basically commit suicide.

In the meantime, for the Mam who were occupying Coatunco once again, far more pressing than these larger strategic questions were the eviction and arrest orders that had been issued against their leaders. Damián Vaíl, Fidel Huinil, Eulalio Vaíl, Daniel Huinil, and Cruz Vaíl, mostly Mam and almost illiterate, sought out Tiney and Esquina for help and found that the lawyer Antonio Argueta had also left CUC in solidarity with those expelled. Together with other members, such as Isabel Solis, they were forming a new peasant organization, the National Indigenous and Campesino Coordinator (CONIC), founded on July 16, 1992, in Santa Inés, the new community they had helped establish with the Cajolenses. Given the urgency of the national-level peace treaty negotiations, they made it absolutely clear that they were not competing with the URNG leadership but were responding to the need for political action beyond the peace accords, for example, in state offices where campesino leaders could negotiate more local demands. They gathered the fruits tossed out by the CUC into a new movement, less vertical, with fully indigenous leadership, relatively active women's participation, and that took Mayan culture and spirituality, which had been denied and displaced by the EGP's Marxism-Leninism, as a priority. These were the impulses behind CONIC.

One Cycle Culminates, Another Begins: Eviction, Purchase, and Debt

The new organization's birth, however, came too late to save the community from the three hundred riot police who were sent on June 15, 1992, to evict the "invaders" from Coatunco. The police burned the shacks containing the people's few possessions, along with the four hundred *manzanas* of corn. Again the families left peacefully and returned to occupying the highway. From there they and the fledgling CONIC tried to pressure the government, but it was hard to both feed themselves and sustain their struggle. So, as Damián remembers, "We all decided to go to the capital and sit in front of the National Palace until the president received us and our petition for our farm."

And go they did. Arriving at the Central Square, the campesinos remember, "We felt nervous because the antiriot police had surrounded the entire plaza, [and] we entered with our women and our children." They were finally received, "reluctantly and in a bad way," by the president's private secretary,

Antulio Castillo, and even the mainstream newspapers noted the racist attitudes of the government:

> A commission of campesinos from Cajolá gave a petition to Mr. Castillo, who with great arrogance refused to let them enter his office, and only spoke with them in one of the corridors of the National Palace, perhaps thinking that they were going to leave the scent of sweat in the atmosphere, or that they could stain the armchairs. The attitude of Castillo demonstrates that in this country there are still two classes of people: indigenous and ladinos. We are sure that if well-dressed people, smelling good with their lotions and imported deodorants, had arrived to see him, this state official would have opened the doors of his office and even offered them coffee. But no: they were those Indians who only serve to make trouble, according to state officials, because they demand land that now belongs to an illustrious family, the Arévalo Bermejos, who have given so much to the country. It seems like a joke, but it is the truth. Here there is one attitude for ladinos and another for indigenous people. (*Prensa Libre*, July 22, 1992)

Meanwhile the government was already planning how to evict them from the public square.

First, heavily armed security forces surrounded the Central Plaza to intimidate them. But a participant remembers, "We were already tired of being ignored for such a long time as they sent us from one place to another, and nothing—nothing ever got fixed, so we had all talked before leaving, and it was decided among us that we would not move from the Central Park; we would not move, not the women, not the children, no one." Then at 5:20 p.m. on July 22, 1992, the antiriot squad moved in, attacking men, the elderly, women, and children alike with guns, tear gas, and clubs. Over twenty wounded were admitted to the hospital with serious injuries, and everyone was affected by the tear gas. According to Julia, the harshest blows fell on women:

> We were all attacked, but they hit the women more, perhaps because we are women, because we could not run as fast as the men, we had our children. What were we supposed to do, leave them? We could not run. On our heads, our arms, our backs came the blows from the police and we didn't have anything to defend ourselves or our children. They struck us until our blood ran; our *güipiles* and our *cortes* were stained.

The protestors took refuge in national university buildings in Zone One. National and international condemnation was swift and powerful. Ramiro

de León Carpio, then human rights ombudsman, deplored government in-
tolerance, and many sectors expressed indignation at the scenes on television
amply demonstrating police brutality (*Siglo XXI*, July 23, 1992). While the
state had carried out massacres in hundreds of highland indigenous communities, for many capital-dwellers it was novel to see such violence taking place
so close to home. Scenes from the hospital also revealed the high indices of
malnutrition suffered by the women and children of the community and an
outbreak of conjunctivitis. By a stroke of luck, the United Nations' human
rights expert, Cristian Tomuschat (who would later lead the UN Commission for Historical Clarification), was in Guatemala and witnessed the state
repression. He visited the campesinos at the university, publicly denounced
the police actions, and described the case as "very complex, because they
have two problems. . . . One is the lack of land, but this is a subject that the
government needs to solve. The other is the violent eviction carried out by
police, which was a violation of human rights" (*El Gráfico*, October 24, 1992).[4]

National and international outrage combined with pressure from the
Archbishop's Office and other human rights organizations to force the executive branch to order INTA to finally survey the Coatunco Farm. Only then
did they request the file from 1872. "We were very hurt by the blows, *compañera*, but quickly, with the aid of lawyer Antonio Argueta and other people,
we formed a commission and went to the palace," a member remembers.
Only days after being brutalized, they were willing to put aside their suffering to sit down and have a dialogue with the state. "We came to ask our government to solve our problem, since we came with all the backing of the law"
(*Siglo XXI*, July 23, 1992).

After five months camped out on university grounds and negotiating
through a multiparty commission, in December 1992 the state urged the families to accept a loan to buy the Santo Domingo farm and its annexes, located
in the south coast *municipio* of Champerico, Retalhuleu, with enough land
for all five hundred families. The price of the farm was Q27 million plus taxes,
and the families agreed to pay the loan over ten years. One of the leaders
explained why they accepted the government proposal: "Because we were
already tired of being in the capital and saw that the president wouldn't give
us another option, so we said it's okay, we accept the loan."

They named the community Nueva Cajolá, and on December 23, 1992,
they moved in. The government committed to support them with three years
of technical, social, economic, and bookkeeping assistance and basic foods
for the first three months, and to build temporary shelters to later be used as
a communal hall, school, and health center. Although they did not obtain the

land first promised their ancestors in the 1870s and promised again to their grandparents by Estrada Cabrera in 1910, they did have a piece of land to begin a new life. Joy and relief prevented the families from seeing that raising up this new community would be as challenging as the century of legal and political struggle that had finally concluded.

Each family received five manzanas of land and 10 percent of the finca was dedicated to forest, and sixty manzanas were set aside for the town center and for roads. The land, however, was clay soil that had been severely damaged during its previous existence as a cotton plantation. Excessive use of pesticides and herbicides had destroyed the little organic matter it contained, making it susceptible to various diseases and insect infestations. The area also turned out to be drought-prone, in part because of heavy deforestation. To produce, the land would require heavy investments in time, labor, and financial resources. These issues were not considered by the INTA in their financial or technological studies or in the assistance they agreed to provide (Roldán Andrade 1994: 55).

Women were key actors in the struggle for land and in constructing the new community. They participated in local and national demonstrations, they confronted violence, and they agreed to initiate a family and collective life without even minimum services: "When we arrived, there was only dust and heat. We did not have a place to grind our corn. We ground *masa* [dough] on a grinding stone, and those that could bought a hand mill." Maria commented on the lack of water: "It was difficult. We could not wash our clothes. We had to walk to wash. The men began to make wells, and from that water we drank, because there was no other source, but our children became ill, because that water has cotton poison. It was hard, very hard." And it got harder.

To begin, they planted corn to guarantee their food supply and sesame as a cash crop to pay their loan. But the poor land and lack of technical support and of adequate loans to finance production were compounded by the drought of 1994 that destroyed almost the entire corn crop and 75 percent of the sesame harvest. They had received the loan to pay for the land through a financial cooperative that in turn had borrowed from commercial banks. When the Cajolenses were unable to pay, the cooperative also fell into arrears, and the community lost its only line of credit.

In 1994 Nueva Cajolá began showing the first symptoms of the famine that later afflicted much of the country. Losing the corn harvest meant there was nothing to eat. In addition, the community lacked potable water, electricity, housing, a school, and medical aid. People remember, "The anemic condition of the campesinos caused so much desperation that several wanted to commit suicide. The governor requested that they stay calm and that together they would look for a viable solution, like support in dealing with governmental institutions and international organizations. The suicide attempts were a consequence of the accumulated levels of frustration." This was a community that had maintained a tenacious struggle for the return of their land, only to end up acquiring a loan of more than Q27 million. Once they had the land after so many struggles, nature showed no mercy. On top of that, most state actors ignored them. One person I interviewed at the end of 1994 said, "Yes, we wanted to take our lives, because how were we going to pay for what we borrowed? If everything was lost, nothing grew, we are only leaving our children indebted." Total losses for the 1994 harvest were Q1.3 million, not including the families' labor.

Despite its commitments, the state never fulfilled its promises, although several institutions visited and evaluated their needs, including UNICEF, INTA, FONAPAZ, CRN, INDE, and the Ministries of Agriculture, Communications, Education, and Health. All concurred that by the end of 1994, of the forty-six short-term projects that the state had promised, only 48 percent were under way, while all of the long-term projects were pending.

The community was legally constituted as an association and organized commissions for infrastructure, women, health, discipline, festivities, and education. They continued to apply pressure at the regional and national levels, and the new president, Ramiro de León, even visited the community in November 1994 and promised housing, electricity, a school, a road, and a health center, but these promises all evaporated when his term ended.[5] Without even a road, the community was isolated, unable to travel much less transport out or bring in products; in emergencies, a patient would die before reaching the nearest hospital.

Then in 1998 Hurricane Mitch destroyed all of Nueva Cajolá's harvests. The community received economic support and food from CONIC but could not cover the loss of harvests, animals, homes, and possessions. Mitch destroyed the few hopes the community had left, and as one of the older members of the community emotionally explained, "Many young people and adult men decided to emigrate to the United States, and other families decided to leave the community and return to Cajolá." More than half the families who had struggled for so long abandoned Nueva Cajolá, leaving only 250. By the middle of the first decade of the twenty-first century a quarter of these were dependent on remittances sent from the United States. Yet even with far fewer people, Nueva Cajolá was not sustainable.

By 2000 Nueva Cajolá owed more than Q32 million. Supported by CONIC they continued to petition the state, now headed by Alfonso Portillo, to fulfill its long-standing promises. They reiterated their demands for a health center, housing, water, and the road as well as support for their Mam culture and agrarian technical assistance. They also proposed that the debt be paid from a fund the Taiwanese government donated after the eviction in July 1992, and from government reparations for the violent eviction from the Plaza and for loss of the twenty children by the highway. Finally the Portillo government agreed to reduce the loan and turn the land over to the community. In 2001 each family symbolically paid Q352.

Land, Free and Clear?

Removing the threat of constantly growing debt from their horizon has allowed the community to concentrate its resources on infrastructure. As one woman said, "Well, now we have water, which is a blessing. We only open the faucet and there it is, but we had to request it, and come and go until we were tired and we thought the blessed water was never going to come." Now the women are organized in a Women's Commission that worked with CONIC to obtain a corn mill at a cost of Q12,000. "The mill is for the entire community, and the price that we charge is lower because it is not private. We only need to cover operating expenses and the rest is paying for the loan," one of the members explained to me. They received the mill and were trained in its handling and cleaning. But the mill did not last long because it had a factory flaw: "Look, we already went and we told the association of the community and CONIC, we have done a lot, and they said that it cannot be fixed nor can they give us our money back." In 2003 the women lamented the slow advances in their demands because they hold no power in the community association.

The Women's Commission also created a grocery store with a loan through CONIC, meant to provide basic products at reasonable prices for the community. They were able to pay the loan but now face competition from other stores nearby, authorized by the town, which has led to a sharp decline in profits. This occurred because the Board of Directors believed the Women's Commission was too attached to CONIC (a point I'll return to), so it withdrew its support.

These problems were compounded by women's generalized conditions of oppression. In surveying the community I found that of ninety-six women, 74 percent said they are illiterate, compared to 39 percent of men. This educational disadvantage allows men to justify handling the projects and deciding on community priorities (see also González-Izás this volume). Members said that participation in the Women's Commission "does not grow," because husbands do not allow their wives to participate in activities outside the home. Others explained that they wanted to participate: "[But] we cannot because we have work in the house, and if we participated there is no one to take care of our children, and why are we going to fight with our husbands?" With an average of three to four children per woman and without support for child care, it is difficult to take on other responsibilities. To be clear, I am not arguing that Mayan women should have fewer children, but I question why they are the only ones to care for them and the home, leaving little time for individual and collective activities. It remains a challenge to break the cycle that prevents women from participating in the construction of the kind of community they desire, as women, mothers, Maya-Mam, and rural people. Limited education for women denies them full participation in the collective construction of their community and limits their political possibilities, both locally and nationally, in terms of participation in CONIC or other institutions.

People in Nueva Cajolá agree that during the process to recover their land, the contribution of women was key (just as in refugee communities before the return, as Worby shows, this volume). It would seem that during that stage, the community patriarchy became flexible and allowed them to emerge as actors. But after obtaining land, although the struggle of women continues to be important, patriarchy reinstalled itself in families and in the community and now restrains women from participating fully in their new community. Making patriarchy flexible, not just during certain conjunctural moments but permanently, remains a challenge for the community.

The triumph of debt cancellation also led to friction between CONIC and the community's Board of Directors. Once the debt was gone, several families on the Board—especially those who left the community after Hurricane Mitch—decided they wanted individual property titles so they could sell their land. Other families, backed by CONIC, wanted the land to remain collective. In the end, privatization won and individual titles were created, allowing several families to abandon the community, the very out-migration CONIC had hoped to avoid.

Later I learned that the methodological demand that the Board had stipulated when I arrived, "Look, *compañera*, it's better to speak collectively," was not only the "Mayan" collective answer to a "Western" individualizing of communal experience. It was also their attempt to control what stories filtered out to me, someone who arrived under the aegis of CONIC, given that the community was deeply divided over the question of property and titles, with CONIC playing a role in the division. While in part the struggle over private versus collective was ideological, it also arose because families were exhausted by the struggle to make the land produce. Many of the men and women now in charge were born in the midst of the struggle and find it increasingly unbearable to wait for improvements that never seem to happen, no matter how hard they work. The current divisions are the results of indebtedness, frustrations, and losses that have accumulated for decades. Both the land and the people are exhausted.

Learning from Nueva Cajolá

The existence of Nueva Cajolá is a harvest of many violences. It arose from a nineteenth-century land claim based in military service. And, while the Mam peasants went to Guatemala City in July 1992, certain they would find an audience because they had the "full backing of the law," they suffered public brutality at the hands of that law. The excessive nature of that violence, in the context of the build-up to "peace" and a climate of demands for respect of human rights, forced the government to, first, cede terrain to the community, and, second, forgive its debt. These victories and the joy and high hopes they produced, however, were thwarted by other, more subtle and long-term forms of violence, like the mistreatment of the ecosystem in Retalhuleu, government policies that have actively denied education and justice to Mam people for generations, and especially to women, along with the more modern indifference of a racist neoliberal state.

To some extent the cyclical rituals of dialogue and direct action were successful in securing land in Santa Inés and Nueva Cajolá, in spite of the physical, emotional, and economic toll they took as people struggled to maintain their demands under repression and through conflicting understandings of how to press their case. Local organization and external legal, technical, and economic support (lacking in the first two attempts to recover Pampas in 1955 and 1967) made it possible—after three intense years of struggle, the loss of twenty children, extensive police brutality, and emotional abuse—for more than five hundred Mam families to use the state option to buy land, but only by taking on an enormous debt. Continued lobbying, again with the support of CONIC, finally managed to get the state to forgive the loan. CONIC continues to support Nueva Cajolá by looking for technical support for new crops in hopes of getting those exhausted lands to produce. This is because, as CONIC has stated, despite all its problems Nueva Cajolá is a school of campesino experiences through which other collectives can be nourished.

But the historic conjuncture that transformed the repression in the Central Square into land for peasants was very brief. If Nueva Cajolá is a school for campesino experience, one of its more enduring lessons is that it is extremely difficult for campesinos to extract any advantage from the land market imposed by the state and the World Bank. The Mames of Western Guatemala have been violently implicated in the global coffee trade since the nineteenth century, when Cajolá lost much of its land and government policies forced Cajolenses to harvest the beans first as debt peons and then for the most pitiful of wages. The decisions taken over various decades in the late twentieth century to occupy land granted in 1872 were also linked to the vicissitudes of the coffee economy, as wages and hiring on the plantations steadily decreased. In 1989, the same year the Mames renewed their struggle for Pampas del Horizonte, the Berlin Wall fell and the United States withdrew from the International Coffee Agreement, a cold war artifact that had controlled the price and supply of coffee in order to avoid the "advancement of communism" (Boteach 2002). This withdrawal left coffee prices in the hands of the market, which ended up being controlled by four companies that, worldwide, began to pay less and less.

Philip Morris, Sara Lee, Procter and Gamble, and Nestlé worked to stimulate competition among producing countries by incentivizing production through World Bank loans and purchasing low-cost and low-quality coffee. In the mid-1990s Vietnam and Brazil broke into the world market with low-quality sun coffee, creating massive overproduction that led to steep price declines, culminating in 2002, when coffee sold for its lowest price in one hundred years. The "coffee crisis" in Guatemala, where *finqueros* left beans to rot on the trees because the prices would not cover the cost of the harvest, devastated the Mam highlands. Global political and economic changes in the market monopolies had inhuman impacts on indigenous and poor ladino families in some of the remotest parts of Guatemala. No longer able to survive on the coffee plantations, people faced unemployment, migration, prostitution, and increasing crime—including organized mafias and narcotrafficking—all contributing to family breakdown, starvation, and death.

In this emergent global context, nation-states wield reduced power in the face of transnational market interests. But the Guatemalan state was additionally unwilling or unable to confront national coffee elites who refused to meet their obligations to their workers and instead took advantage of the crisis to transform themselves into finance capitalists. The school of Nueva Cajolá suggests that landowners, struggling in brutal neoliberalized markets, "outsource" their problems to campesinos and the state. In this context, the land market is not an option for solving agrarian conflicts because productive lands are not for sale, and the policy of facilitating the purchase of damaged lands only exacerbates the poverty of the groups that acquire these lands, because they receive none of the tools—working capital, access to loans, technical advice, training for diversifying production, or access to national or international markets—they would need to make the lands produce sufficient returns to justify the price paid for them on the market. The loans from the World Bank provided to communities to buy land have instead provided finqueros with significant capital, allowing them, with the collusion of the Guatemalan state—especially its legal apparatus—to transfer its resources into other, safer and more remunerative economic sectors (see Oglesby this volume; Solano this volume). This process is occurring just as the Central American Free Trade Agreement opens Guatemala to cheap foreign corn and other crops, making them less profitable to produce inside the country, shredding peasant subsistence strategies (and food security more generally), and freeing up cheap labor for assembly plants, organized crime, and emigration. Internalizing these lessons, half of the five hundred families that founded Nueva Cajolá have abandoned the community, weakening its leadership and making it difficult to transfer experience to new generations, while reinforcing the oppression of women and generating friction with the institutions that have accompanied residents for over a decade of struggle.

But the school of Nueva Cajolá also necessarily speaks to those extraordinary moments in 2002 and 2003, when thousands of indigenous and ladino families occupied more than one hundred farms in different regions so that they would not starve to death. The courage of indigenous and campesino movements in taking such risky direct actions is a tactic in local and national struggles to force the state and elites to submit to justice. These campesinos seek the constitution of a rule of law for everyone equally, and that is why they understand such "illegal" tactics as correct and moral responses to ongoing crises and increasing inequality. Massive and organized campesino marches, farm occupations, highway shutdowns, and seizures of public offices do not occur just because campesinos are challenging exploitation, but because the system of exploitation has stopped working altogether, leaving campesinos stranded, without the most basic necessities of work or food.

The crisis caused by the changes in the global economy created another type of relation in which agriculture may no longer be a solution for either finqueros or campesinos. Perhaps this crisis represents the end of a long cycle of colonialism, from 1524 to 2000, which was based on agrarian exploitation. As this cycle concludes, campesinos are allowed to access land through the market, but the struggle for the land has changed in form and meaning, because it has been surpassed by the same history of exploitation. Now the yearning of campesino sectors is no longer just for an agrarian reform that allows them access to productive land, but is also for the ability to incorporate themselves into a global economy from which they are ever more radically excluded.

Notes

1. I speak Maya-K'ichee', not Maya-Mam.
2. Land in Guatemala is commonly measured in the old Spanish units of the *cuerda*, the *manzana*, and the *caballería*. The cuerda varies from region to region, but as a general rule, ten cuerdas make one manzana, and sixty-five manzanas make one caballería, which is approximately equivalent to one hundred acres or forty-five hectares.
3. Tiney, Esquina, Vásquez, and Castillo remember the 1991 pre-Quincentennial Hemispheric Meeting in Quetzaltenango (see Bastos and Camus this volume) as a breaking point that transformed their consciousness and influenced the path they later took with CUC. They say the event was like an X-ray showing the serious ideological differences and inequalities in power and control between the popular and indigenous movements. For example, only 10 percent of the delegates were indigenous (Delgado 1996); popular leaders clearly subsumed indigenous claims within the demands of class; and the popular movement acted in typical vertical fashion, preventing it from valuing the diverse indigenous struggles and demands being generated across the Americas.

   Juana Vásquez, from El Quiché, relates her change in consciousness to her experiences as a Catholic nun in the 1970s and her experiences in exile where, together with Federico Castillo, a Maya-Poptí, she created the CUC's Commission for International Relations and later resigned from the Catholic Church. As she and Federico worked to reconstruct the CUC, they began to reflect on Mayan spirituality. Their work influenced Tiney, Esquina, and others to take Mayan spirituality more seriously and even include it as a political demand.
4. To give a sense of the surrealism of the state's reaction to indigenous resistance it is worth quoting the national police chief's description of the event: "The indigenous people provoked the anti-riot police: luckily no one was injured, and if anyone was, it was because the demonstrators fell when running, because police did not strike anyone. What's more, the campesinos moved their heads towards the clubs of the agents. . . . Outside people convinced parents to force their children to cry, because it is obvious that it was fake weeping. . . . The campesinos grabbed the tear gas canisters from the police and triggered them, and this is why the police threw them" (*Siglo XXI*, July 23, 1992).
5. A Kafkaesque letter the road crew sent to the community explained the suspension of the road project: "In view of the fact that their truck tires were in bad condition, which represents a danger and limits their trips as they waste more time repairing them, making their work yield low, we must also inform you that the replacement parts for the machinery designated for that road have not been obtained because out of the eight months of the year so far, the ministry has only authorized the budget for one month."

PART III

MEANS INTO ENDS
Neoliberal Transparency and Its Shadows

CHAPTER 7 | *Deborah T. Levenson*

WHAT HAPPENED TO THE REVOLUTION?

Guatemala City's *Maras* from Life to Death

The vivacity of the popular and democratic movement for radical social change permeated Guatemala City in the late 1970s, even in the face of state violence. In 1977 over 100,000 city residents turned out to greet and support eighty Mam miners who had walked for days from the highlands to the capital to publicize their struggle for a union in a tungsten mine. One year later, in October 1978, students, private and public sector workers, young and old barrio residents, and almost everyone else in the city brought it to a complete stop to oppose an increase in the bus fares and to demand higher wages. On May 1, 1980, some fifty thousand marched in the last massive urban demonstration of the twentieth century, faces covered, under banners that read "For a Revolutionary Guatemala," and "Nicaragua Today, Guatemala Tomorrow." It was unimaginable that by 2010, juvenile gangs, and not revolutionaries, would so infuse the city's imagination and its dynamics.

The uproar about juvenile gangs came on the heels of the military's breakneck defeat of that possible future of popular revolution. The maras made their first public appearance in 1985 as part of a student demonstration against a bus fare increase. The massive publicity generated by the media, politicians, and the National Police about the presumed dangers of these new gangs contrasted sharply with the complete silence surrounding the peak of the military's ongoing genocidal war in the early 1980s, when hundreds of villages were destroyed and over 200,000 people slaughtered in the most sadistic acts of terrorism military leaders could devise.

In 1987, wishing to make sense of this abrupt emphasis on juvenile crime in a nation racked by extraordinary state violence, three researchers from the new Association for the Advancement of Social Sciences in Guatemala (AVANCSO), Nora Figueroa, Yolanda Castillo Maldonaldo, and I, studied these new maras. We interviewed dozens of *mareros* (gang members) about family, work, school, and their views on life and their gangs. Our findings, published in 1988 by AVANCSO in a monograph titled *Por Si Mismos: Un estudio prelimar de las Maras en la Ciudad de Guatemala* (On Their Own: A Preliminary Study of Gangs in Guatemala City), showed that the maras offered clues, but not danger, to the world around them. Gang members had grown up within a city permeated by the popular movement's visions and interpretations. Although anxious about life, they celebrated it, and they concerned themselves with the communities that surrounded them. Their "us" included the poor; the "asshole wealthy" or *burgueses* constituted their "them."

By the time of the 1996 peace accords, these maras had become violent worlds unto themselves; their "us" had become the gang, and their "them" was everyone else, including the poor. Although they are doubtless accused of far more crimes than they commit, into the twenty-first century many mareros have become the victimizers they were originally wrongly accused of being. In addition, and even more common and striking than their violence, is their obsession with death. According to their own version of themselves, they now kill to keep control, punish, defend, prove themselves, and earn a living; in turn they expect to be murdered before they reach their mid-twenties (Demoscopía 2007).

In what follows I describe the gangs of the mid-1980s and contrast them to those of later years. I suggest that the mareros' growing violence and their use of death as a fundamental resource are in part rooted in the military's successful use of "excessively cruel" violence to massively murder Guatemalans as the means to finish off fifty years of unfinished history in which radical political movements polarized Guatemala in a battle for its destiny.[1] The shift in the urban maras is also, again in part, the consequence of one of the military's major accomplishments: the destruction of an urban barrio culture of class solidarity, a culture that was reflected in the earlier maras' social imaginary.

The 1980s: Gangs to Live For

In September 1985 students from Rafael Aqueche High School in Guatemala City took to the streets to protest an increase in bus fares, and for days thousands of young people burned buses and engaged the police before the municipal government rescinded the price hike. The police termed bands of roaming youth *maras*, which, according to the head of public relations for the Guatemalan National Police, comes from *Marabunta*, a plague of red ants that relentlessly devours humans.[2] A marero named Victor, who hung out with his friends at Plaza Vivar, a rundown mall on Sexta Avenida in the city's dingy downtown, remembered, "The guys from the press and the cops said 'Here comes the Marabunta!' And that's how it came to us and we started the Mara Plaza Vivar Capitol."[3]

By 1987 boys and girls ranging from fifteen to nineteen had created over sixty maras, with names that represented a place or suggested fun, mischief, or toughness. Altogether Mara Los Garañones (stallions), Tigresa (tiger), Las Brujas (witches), Los Angelitos (little angels), Nice, Relax, Miau Miau,[4] 3 de Julio, Las Cobras, Mötley Crüe (from the heavy metal band), and Mara FIVE included as many as one thousand children and teenagers who joined together to financially support themselves and their families and to dance, socialize, have sex, steal, and live with a style, attitude, and personality of their own.

Figueroa, Maldonaldo Castillo, and I found that most of the young people with whom we spoke were surprisingly calm—given their bad reputation—articulate and thoughtful. Concerned about love and acceptance, they did not want to be misunderstood by us or the media, and they were eager to talk. The teenagers we surveyed came from families like most in the city: ladino and either poor or lower middle class. Their parents labored in the informal and formal economies as vendors, laborers, and domestic servants. These youth often described their home life as tense because of financial and emotional strains. Their discussion of emotional problems centered on male figures: the most dangerous person in these families was either the father or the stepfather. Young women and girls told of fathers and stepfathers who raped or deserted them. Young men and boys spoke of fathers and stepfathers who beat them or in other ways failed them. Strikingly, gang members who spoke well of their families were usually referring to those without men in them; the "disintegrated family" so feared by social workers and by the growing Evangelical movement. Maritza, a nineteen-year-old from Mara de la 4, related with pride, "My mother is a seamstress, she also makes ice cream to sell and with that and what I bring in we do OK. You know how hard it is to get steady work? My father, who knows? He left long ago. He was useless."

These young people wanted better families, not traditional ones. They slept at home most of the time, and they created new kinships inside their maras, which they referred to as "family." Yolanda, a fourteen-year-old member of Mara Belen, who lived with her mother and father, said, "Like the others say, for me the mara is my family, the best one in the world. There you have someone who loves you and tells you so." Alejandro reported, "It's like family, but nicer, because no one bawls you out. Instead each person is like they are, and that's all there is to it." Herman also commented on family and mara in terms of freedom: "I think that family puts a lot of pressure on you, and because of that you seek your own group, a new family, so you can be as free to be what you want to be and not how others want you to be." Maritza, whose Mara de la 4 was at one point all-female, explained, "I joined because there was emptiness inside me, a little loneliness, a bit of sadness. Maybe we are all alike in this. I joined through a bunch of girlfriends with whom I was very heavy [*pesado*]. We've shared sorrows and joys. I think the mara is a group of people who need affection. Most of us want to escape the mess in our homes. Sometimes we think we can create a new world." To not have a dysfunctional—as distinct from a disintegrated—family, to have one of affection and empathic peers, was Maritza's wish.

This new mara family did not disapprove of sex for young people. Inside the maras sex flourished as exploration and conversational theme. A silent truth elsewhere—that some girls choose to have sex before marriage—was not hidden. Moreover one of the few spaces for youth that accepted open heterosexuality and homosexuality was within maras. Herman cheerfully described the mara in his working-class neighborhood as "twenty-eight guys and two dykes." His own lover was male. He said, "The heavy thing is that in the mara you learn to be freer in every sense. So, if a guy has sexual relations with a guy, no big deal. Same thing with the girls." Maritza, who had had an amorous relationship with another girl, described her greatest wish: "[To] find a girl or boy who in all honesty loves me and loves that I love her or him."

The gang members contributed financially to their two families, mara and blood kin. Many had worked in the informal and formal economies at one time or another. Maritza, for example, had picked coffee and taken in wash alongside her mother. Rafael said, "I worked in everything. Can you believe that when I was a little kid I collected plastic bags in the garbage dump? After that I gathered old newspapers and sold them in the market. After that I worked as a mechanic, which is very tiring work, and after that in a supermarket."

But in the effort to generate cash for two families and for themselves as well, they quickly found out—often from adults who supplemented their wages in the same way—that more money could be made by stealing than in either the formal or the informal economy. When the Pepsi-Cola Company employed Alejandro, a seventeen-year-old Mara Las Cobras member, at Q15 a week, he discovered he could make Q15 a day stealing and selling crates. In 1987, as a full-time thief who "worked" tourists traveling to Antigua, he earned as much as Q800 during the Semana Santa Easter holiday. These youth specialized, some in opening car locks, others in slitting pocketbooks or fencing goods. They were proud of their expertise. The milieu of the illegal economy, the new social relationships within it, its language and skills, all generated a new identity and power, and the illegal economy kept them in a comfortable traditional role within the family wage economy. They could provide new necessities for their new selves and old necessities for their families and maintain their accustomed selves. Herman explained, "I have money for my father's cigarettes, and I get what I want too," as he waved a handsome gold wristband around. Stealing provided a way to get something for oneself without hurting family members. Lupe provided cash for her mother and sunglasses for herself.

These young people wanted the new consumer articles of global youth — but not rapaciously, not at the expense of their accustomed obligations. They expressed solidarity with the poor, and they made intelligent critiques of society. Silvio, an eighteen-year-old in Mara FIVE, had been a part of an openly political association in public school at the close of the 1970s. To answer a question about his school, he explained that he was expelled because of his membership in the student association, but he was more interested in pointing out that school was a waste of his time: "I want a different education; something that was really helpful and not a lot of crap that, what the hell do you want to waste your time with it anyway? It would be great if the teachers taught in an interesting way and not just by dictation after dictation. You get tired and then you lose interest in your studies because you are treated as an object that should not talk, move, or think — that basically should not really exist."

Their explicit political and cultural opinions and choices were another example of their proximity to the popular movement. *La Historia Oficial,* an Argentine film about the dirty war, was a favorite movie. They unanimously described Ronald Reagan and President Vinicio Cerezo of Guatemala in negative terms — Cerezo as "a greedy asshole." They dismissed Madonna as empty-headed and Michael Jackson in negative terms because he rejected his roots. They selected Rigoberta Menchú and Che Guevara as "people [they] admire." One marero had an artistically arranged scrapbook, which he regularly updated, of clippings about the Sandinistas.

In 1987, when a few trade unionists attempted to hold a May 1 demonstration, the first since 1980, they approached Mara Plaza Vivar Capitol about it because this mara was close to the route and the final rallying point of the march in the city's Central Park. Plaza Vivar Capitol told the labor activists,

"The mareros are from the working class and we would never harm the working class." When poor people occupied urban lands in 1986, gang members supported them (AVANCSO 1993: 86). And after a coup attempt against the civilian government in May 1988, Mara FIVE ran a classified ad in the newspaper *elPeriodico* that read, "This business of wanting to put an end to government is no good. Youth wants peace, not violence. When will we be heard? Mara FIVE."

As I wrote at the beginning of this chapter, these youth grew up in the late 1970s, within the social imaginary of the popular movement that predominated in Guatemala City's barrios. In their minds their victims were burgueses (rich), and their "crimes" had a class justification; as mareros they had moral élan. Calixto, from Las Cobras, put it this way: "Look, the only people I steal from are people with money, because robbing from my equal would be evil." Rafael, a seventeen-year-old from Mara 33, said, "I've taken what I need and I have robbed from the rich. Taking from the burgueses is like taking a strand of hair from a cat, and you have to survive one way or another." Lupe, a fifteen-year old Mara Piranas member, explained, "I knifed [the pockets of] two burgueses.... I took stuff from some others as well.... Last year I bought my mother a pair of shoes for Christmas so she doesn't have to use sandals anymore.... We in the mara, we have to steal from the burgueses because they have things we don't have, and it doesn't affect them."

When Berlin explained the origins of his small local mara, he made clear the connection between thievery and their senses of necessity, narrating the mara's class nature:

> It all started when we played soccer on the Barrio San Antonio team [in 1985]. We qualified for the juvenile championship, and we were supposed to play in the final, but we didn't have decent sneakers or the money to buy them, so we decided to steal them from some burgueses who had a couple of pairs each. We watched them, and then we jumped them, and we took their shoes and some other stuff.... After that we met and played soccer but not with the same illusions. You begin to realize that even soccer is only for the burgueses.... We got to know other guys, and we started to get together to talk about the problems each one had.... The problems were the same—we were just a bunch of poor people! Then we felt this unity and a lot of desire to stick together. When one of the guys was really down, we helped out, but all of a sudden, we realized that we could have everything that was in style by ripping it off, or as they say, "borrowing." (AVANCSO 1988)

Berlin draws together many elements of lower-class life in the city in the 1980s. It was virtually impossible for members of the working class to carry out their lives, even the simple leisure activity of soccer, without some sort of struggle. But bereft of movements to raise wages or to change anything at all, gangs became one of the few avenues through which working-class youth could obtain material improvement, albeit through stealing. Berlin's mara was a local organization devoted to meeting needs defined in part by the dramatic rise of advertising for youth consumer goods in the 1980s.

As appealing as the young people were with whom we spoke, we concluded our 1987 study without too much optimism. Despite the powerful critiques and commentaries about life, love, family, and friendships that the gang members made, they were not trying to transform the already rapidly changing worlds in which they lived. The moral affirmation of stealing from the burgueses and of giving to themselves and others as poor people was important to the identity of the maras in the 1980s, but we knew that they knew that they were not always stealing from the rich to give to the poor, and that when they talked about stealing particular car or truck parts for the black market, they had no idea whom they defrauded. These were offspring of a revolutionary movement that still held the ethical high ground, but not much more. Moral flair and a Robin Hood discourse did not protect or orient these gangs of teenagers in a world in which hope for social justice was dying a painful death.

Moreover, in the mid-1980s powerful adults treated these youth terribly, both representationally and physically. The media stigmatized them as irrepressibly violent, the Evangelicals named them devil worshippers, and the police consigned minors to adult prisons, where they experienced violence and developed solidarities with adult criminal rings. In addition, neoliberal cutbacks shredded the few existing organizations for addressing youth issues. For example, the Juvenile Court judge lost her staff, forcing her to rely on the Direction for the Treatment and Orientation of Minors' youth facilities, which could house no more than 250 children and adolescents and were overflowing in 1987.[5] That year, the Juvenile Court joined with UNICEF to create the National Commission for Action for Children, an alliance of governmental and nongovernmental organizations. Evangelical NGOs—with funding from abroad, staff, long experience in gang ministry around the world, and ongoing cooperation with the Guatemala military's social engineering projects in the highlands—became the Commission's most active members. For example, under its auspices a well-known Evangelical psychologist set up a home called Casa Shalom for mareras. He had a cold manner, used corporal punishment, and developed close authoritarian relationships with the girls. His associate, a Nicaraguan nicknamed Panamá, went into the streets "where Satan works" to save youth. He would tell me nothing of his life beyond his own narrative of sin and salvation: he had been a Contra in Nicaragua, and then a member of a Guatemalan death squad, but he had a revelation, met Christ, and left the death squad, although it remained unclear to me what he understood as "sin." I toured a few Evangelical centers with Panamá over a period of months. All proposed an Evangelical regime of self-love and self-improvement proceeded by self-hatred and punishment. Physical penalties accompanied the psychological chastisement of acknowledging one's sins. "Unruly" youth, Panamá explained, were locked up in small spaces. He was a shrewd, physically strong, well-fed, politically smart young adult and a self-confessed killer. At some point it occurred to me that he might have kept his ties with Army Intelligence, which maintained an excellent relationship with the Evangelicals, and I stopped seeing him.

Years later, as I continued my research, I learned that Army Intelligence (G2) used some mareros from the moment the gangs started in 1985. Army Intelligence made all the moves in the city in the 1980s. In response to anxieties about gangs, it could have destroyed the maras, but it did not. In 2002 Victor, a founder of Mara Plaza Vivar Capitol, told me that in 1985, G2 "kidnapped" some of their members, including him, from a street corner in Zone 1 and brought them to an army base "to train [them] to fight." The military then took the boys to the Ixil Triangle and dressed them as members of the Guerrilla Army of the Poor (EGP), in "long hair and cheap rubber boots."[6] According to Victor, they traveled under the guidance of a Cuban and a Nicaraguan to a small Mayan village, where they gathered the community together and began lecturing them on, as Victor described it, "social justice, Marx, Lenin, all that stuff": "We had a *mitin* [political rally], like what the EGP always did." Then the soldiers came down and "massacred the people." After the army "discharged" him and other gang members back to the place from which they had been kidnapped, plainclothes men — "in other words G-2" — seized them again, put them in a van without license plates, murdered them and tossed their mangled bodies into a ravine the following day. Victor said he survived because he had crossed the street to buy a fresh fruit drink right before the vehicle showed up. He fled to Mexico where he got work with La eMe, a Mexican drug ring with connections throughout California's prisons system.

This discovery that the military utilized *mareros* does not negate our 1987 findings that the maras were groups young people could *live* for, but it clarifies the complexity of the panorama in 1985 and helps explain the turn towards extreme violence taken by the maras in the 1990s and beyond. What emerges from Victor's story is that the military had connections to the gangs at the same time that it used them as a scapegoat. This deliberate manipulation, however, was only a part of the larger landscape in which the maras evolved,

The 1990s: Gangs to Die For

In the years following the 1996 Peace Accords violence increased dramatically in the forms of domestic violence, lynching, homicides, *feminicidio*, robberies, theft, "war" taxes on bus drivers and businesses, kidnappings, and all manner of extortion and blackmailing, and finally, narco-trafficking, Guatemala's most thriving business.[7] This violence has been labeled "depoliticized," but its multiple causes *are* political (Savenije and van Der Borgh 2002). The accords did not address the social and economic roots of violence at a time of worsening economic crisis. On the contrary, the structural violence that led Guatemalans to rise up in the first place intensified with neoliberal policies, and more so because rural and urban organizations that might have countered the violence by winning better pay, benefits, and rights had been destroyed or had turned inactive (with notable exceptions) nationally.[8] The postwar governments' refusal to take up the burning problem of impunity has encouraged the current renaissance of local and international organized crime. Impunity has authorized violence. Veritable monsters such as Efraín Ríos Montt and the other generals who ordered genocide and war—deeds far beyond what any gang could do—have legitimatized roles in society. Practitioners of extraordinary mass violence have hardly been the losers.

Politics also underlines the "depoliticization" of youth, including those in maras. By the end of the 1990s the Guatemala City I knew in the late 1970s and into the 1980s had gone up in smoke. What revolution? What radical movement? The language of popular culture that used concepts and terms such as *exploitation, class, bourgeoisie,* and *capitalism* had vanished, and as the twenty-first-century advances, discourses of the Left have not returned. It is not that the generations that experienced the radical urban movement do not remember those terms and times. Rather they have been afraid—notwithstanding important exceptions—to communicate them, to elaborate on lessons that would allow them to move forward, or to publicly invoke the era of popular protest. Over time these fears deform those very memories, and the richness of this past is lost to the subsequent generation. The dominant discourse, the new "official story," has converted state violence and revolutionary armed struggle into *la violencia* as if it were simply an inexplicable natural force, and analytical thinking loses ground.[9] This does not mean that all young Guatemalans know nothing about this period. However, they seem to have heard more about the bizarre and ultraviolent feats of the *kaibiles* (army special forces) than about the goals of ordinary people who joined the revolutionary fronts. In other words, youth who joined the gangs in the 1990s and later grew up within a new subjectivity engendered by the defeat of critical consciousness and of human solidarity as widespread practices. The transformation of schools from cauldrons of activism to establishments that promote individualism, self-promotion, and competition between students is the most obvious example of a radical change in the lives of young people. No one attending public school in the early 1990s had anything resembling the experiences of students from the 1940s to the early 1980s. The transformation was that fast and that profound.

The neighborhoods where these youth grew up also changed precipitously in the 1990s. Although Guatemala City was no longer the zone of economic attraction it had been between the 1950s and 1980, old barrios grew and new settlements such as Mezquital appeared, in part due to the arrival of war migrants. This meant that people who at one time would have articulated themselves in the city by virtue of their rural hometowns were secretive instead and marked as "refugees," "victims," "ex-soldiers," "survivors," "widows," or "orphans." Even if and perhaps especially when they did not talk about the massacres for fear of reprisals, or spoke of them in ways that disguised blame and personal connection, these new residents carried within them the deep trauma, despair, and anger of their war experiences (Bastos and Camus 1994; Gellert 1999).

The presence of this dispersed and disorganized war-related migration has been one shift in urban life. Another has been that neighborhood involvement has become almost exclusively tied to the infrastructure of global NGOs since the 1990s.[10] In many areas vertically structured civic life has replaced the horizontal political life of the earlier period. The number of global NGOs, from the Lions Club to World Vision, has increased dramatically. Structural adjustment programs have meant the decline of state services such as medical clinics. In contrast to the 1970s, grassroots organizations have become few in number and only local in perspective. That means everything that went with grassroots agency—from starting from scratch in someone's front room and getting up the nerve to go door to door, to developing analysis, strategy, and tactics in relation to the Guatemalan state and its agencies—has all but died off. Community-improvement committees generally seek financing and advice from vertical, not horizontal, agencies with international ties; they are often entangled in trying to win changes "from above" rather than in mobilizing "from below." With many NGOs working in barrios, competition for funding from these agencies often divides community leaders. Communities have tended to become further depoliticized because the international NGOs encourage them to resolve their problems through the medium of the NGOs, instead of bringing them to the attention of the broader public and the state, as did *poblador* (squatter) groups in the 1970s, when neighborhood residents boldly inserted themselves into national politics (Gellert et al. 1999).

To further confound this new absence of horizontal solidarities, violence has shattered the Catholic Church's previous role in urban barrios. In the 1970s Catholic lay workers and clergy spread the tools and language of liberation theology to develop strategies to end what was understood as human-made oppression and exploitation and to create "God's Kingdom on Earth." After the devastating earthquake in 1976, for example, a liberation theology priest led the land invasion that settled a large urban area with displaced people. He and other community members called the new neighborhood of hastily built homes Tierra Nueva I (New Land) because they planned for it to be a religious socialist community. That vision was destroyed by the military as well as by nongovernmental financing of alternative projects, including Evangelical ones.

By the 1990s dozens of Evangelical churches dominated neighborhoods such as Tierra Nueva I. Trucks mounted with sound systems blasted taped messages of sin and salvation incessantly to summon residents to services that went on for hours during the day and evening. Unlike liberation theology adherents, many Evangelical pastors opined, in the words of one, "The poor will always be with us. The poor choose to be poor."[11] For the most part Evangelical pastors emphasized that nothing could be done about the fact that life is hell, and this portrayal of earthly impotence and hopelessness resonated in the wake of the defeat of the human project for social change (Nuñez 1996: 167). The Evangelical message underscores the constancy of crisis. Nothing could have seemed truer in the 1990s. These churches grew like wildfire.

The history of Tierra Nueva II illustrates these changes. In 1985 the teenage son of a religious left-wing organizer of the original Tierra Nueva launched Tierra Nueva II with his friends. Two of the newly emerged socially aware maras of the mid-1980s, Nene and Las Cobras, were born with the invasion; they were part of its "heat," as one participant described their support for the new community (AVANCSO 1993: 86). But within a few years the combination of well-funded NGOs and selective state violence undermined the power of the original organizers and their visions for a community-run Tierra Nueva

II. Death threats forced one organizer into exile and others out of activism. A rivalry between Maras Nene and Las Cobras, once confined to break-dance contests, became violent over "territory" that included neighborhood streets and young women's bodies. Las Cobras destroyed Mara Nene at the end of the decade.

By 1990 Las Cobras was one of many local maras that had become violently abusive within and without—within the gang, in the neighborhood, and in the city.[12] In 1991 crack consumption skyrocketed, the drug apparently initially supplied by dealers in the old barrio El Gallito in Zone 3.[13] In the following years the U.S. Immigration and Naturalization Service (INS) started to deport undocumented and imprisoned gang members back to their home countries. Over the years the INS sent hundreds of members of Mara Salvatrucha (MS-13) and Mara 18 (M-18), two gangs formed in Los Angeles, into the urban sinkhole of Guatemala City's depoliticized and demoralized neighborhoods.

What were these Los Angeles gangs? They came out of poor LA neighborhoods teeming with the tens of thousands of Central Americans who had fled their countries as a consequence of the wars in the 1980s and 1990s. Salvadorans started MS-13 in response to racism and exclusion from Latino gangs; among its founders were ex-soldiers and, besides Salvadorans, many Guatemalans and Hondurans joined it. M-18 was an older Latino gang that Central Americans came to dominate. At some point a fierce rivalry started between MS-13 and M-18; their fights and their violence seemed, by most accounts, to be distinctly more brutal than those of the many gangs in the area (Hayden 2004). In one way or another, these youth "knew" Central American war and state terror, either through their parents' experiences or their own. They were not only "LA gangs," a term used by journalists, security agencies, and a handful of scholars to identify the maras.[14] In an interview, Ernesto Miranda, a Salvadoran ex-soldier and founding member of MS-13 in Los Angeles, explained, "[In Salvador] we were taught to kill our own people, no matter if they were from your own blood. If your father was the enemy, you had to kill him. So the training we got during the war in our country served to make us one of the most violent gangs in the United States."[15]

By contrasting them to the Mexican gangs in Los Angeles, an astute LA gang member explored what he saw as the uniquely Guatemalan and Salvadoran quality of MS-13 and M-18:

The difference between the Mexicans and Salvadorans or Central Americans in general is this: Mexicans usually come from states like Michoacan. They live in a small town and are mainly agricultural. They do have violence from feuds, drug war, or now LA barrio violence. They, generally speaking, are not initially violent when they come to the U.S. El Salvador and Guatemala is another story. [There] it was common to see a street splattered with brain particles and blood. People in Guatemala were getting kidnapped and tortured to the point of insanity. In the main university in Guatemala City, students were forced to give classes due to the fact that all the professors had gotten smoked, one by one. . . . In El Salvador if you reach the age of fifteen without having to identify [the body of] a relative you were blessed. . . . These people [Guatemalans and Salvadorans] saw carnage that even the *Faces of Death* [snuff videos] chose not to use.[16]

However much influenced by LA subcultures, as well as by unemployment and racism within LA, these youth came from milieux in which "carnage" beyond the sick imagination of a snuff filmmaker predominated, and at least some of them had the skills and experiences of ordinary soldiers involved in extraordinary wars against their own kind of people: poor people.

MS-13 and Mara 18 consolidated in Los Angeles, but the gangs' "foundational map" starts in Central America's wars, zigzags through crime-ridden Mexico, and crosses the border into Los Angeles and into California's multinational prisoner population, where gang members made important contacts. Once deported to Guatemala or El Salvador, these mareros took over local maras, which then became MS-13 or M-18 subgroups, or *clikas*. Without necessarily maintaining ties to LA, MS-13 and Mara 18 in Guatemala City carried on the LA legacy of deadly rivalry and, without doubt, some of their ties to the changing scene of Mexican drug lords.

Victor's saga is illuminating. By the time he crossed into Mexico to "run away from G2" in 1985 at age fifteen, after participating in a massacre and having his friends' bodies turn up mutilated, he was a changed teenager. He rode on the tops of trains until he reached Mexico's northern border. Some of the Guatemalan teenagers he met along the way went on to Los Angeles, where they were drawn into either MS-13 or M-18, ending up in jail, and from there, according to Victor, they were deported back to their countries. Victor stayed on the Mexican side, where he "met the eMe, lived in DF" (Mexican gangsters and lived in Mexico City), and learned to "live in the street, to steal, to rob, to kill." When he came back to Guatemala after the 1996 peace accords, he knew "all the knowledge, the structures — the *veteranos*, the *palabras*, the laws and the reasons for them, the colors, who were the enemies."[17] By then MS-13 and M-18 had a presence in Guatemala. He found the maras in Guatemala City "more sophisticated, Mara FIVE had joined MS-13 and [his own] Plaza Vivar Capitol was with M-18." He explained, "Everyone saw themselves as soldiers serving *el barrio* [the gang] in a war against the world and without any Geneva Code." By then a man in his late twenties, he joined M-18, lived in cheap hotels in Guatemala City, "distributed *bolsas* [drugs] at the corners," and got paid in either cash or goods. A small cog in a flourishing enterprise, he saw himself as "bad," and his "place in the world" consisted only of areas of the city held by M-18.

Even through MS-13 and M-18 are transborder gangs, their stake and sway lay in local neighborhoods. In the 1990s residents described the maras as opening a new chapter in barrio life. The newness was not so much violence itself but the explosion of violent crimes by the poor against the poor. Death squads, not youth, murdered neighbors in the "old days." In one neighborhood a woman said, "Ten years ago you could come in [to the area] at 9 at night," but by 1995 that was impossible, and in addition between 8 p.m. and 4 a.m. there was constant gunfire and screaming. In this barrio, every social space had become dangerous. Rival maras came to "own" the basketball courts, street corners, fields, and plazas. Residents described acute changes in daily life that made mistrust and fear realistic reactions and the acquisition of weapons a necessity. Gang members broke up community events such as dances and meetings, their presence divided people along the lines of their offspring's affiliation in rival maras, and their constant warring with one another made walking around nerve-racking and sleeping difficult (AVANCSO 2000). By 2001 gun fights between rival maras led to fires in neighborhoods where firemen refused to enter because police had been unable to maintain substations there. By 2002 maras had enough power in some areas to regularly tax merchants and bus and delivery truck drivers. Afraid that their children would be beaten on their way to school, families sometimes kept them home and, for fear of the gangs and fear that their children might be forced to join them or be killed for refusing to join, even sent their children abroad to live with relatives. They have reconfigured neighborhoods and the routines of everyday life.

To many, the maras seem unassailable. The late Jesuit Padre Manolo Maquiera spent years building sports and art workshops in which supposedly reforming gang members had the responsibility of teaching young children in a neighborhood of Zone 6, only to discover that all the while they had been recruiting the kids into Mara 18. After ten years he judged the mara members beyond rescue and redemption.[18] He, like others, turned away from the maras and instead concentrated on "children at risk," a term for children who had not yet joined a mara or been killed by them.

The first time I met members of MS-13 was in the late 1990s, when I was sitting with a Casa Alianza street educator doing medical checkups in a makeshift sleeping quarters for homeless children.[19] Two mareros came in to shake the children down. Straight out of a photograph, with tattooed arms and dressed in black, the two looked muscular and healthy, even jaunty, and they contrasted with their prey, the malnourished, drugged, and sick street children who huddled on filthy mattresses. After one marero directed the street worker to look over a wound, the two retreated, to return only after we had departed.

Later that day street children who lived in the Casa Alianza crisis shelter told me that mareros forced them to take drugs and demanded money from them. But the same children prized the MS-13 and M-18 signs on their bodies, and one small boy drew MS-13 in block letters on a piece of paper as he sat with me waiting for lunchtime. Ten-year-old Minor from Zone 6 reported proudly, "MS-13 paid me to run errands" and "knew how to get things done." What things? I asked. "Defend themselves," he replied. In an essay on the topic "what I wish my family were like," a twelve-year-old named Rubén wrote that he wanted his older brother to be head of Mara 18 so that everyone in his family would be "safe, and the men feel strong," and his mother would be "happier and less sad." Carlos, a seven-year-old whom street educators had found in the bus terminal, looked forward to being in a *mara clika* (subgroup) when he was "stronger." These children knew the maras for better and worse, and the gangs seemed to represent an inevitable pathway and source of violent defense against an evil world of violent parents, police, and other adults. At least they could join the maras. Everyone else disapproved of them. In the same shelter I spoke with ex-mara members who stayed there to escape either the gang or the police. Sixteen-year-old Eduardo had been leaving his home on and off since he was four years old. From a family in one of the most impoverished *colonias* in Zone 18, he remembered that when he was hungry, his brother gave him drugs to stop his stomach pains. He said, "[I] went with 18 from the start, I was convinced that they would help me." He stayed for a few years, until he witnessed the death of two youths in a fight with a clika from MS-13 and left, horrified. Because the penalty for leaving would be death without trial, he said, he had entered the shelter. Seventeen-year-old Luis Arturo described himself as a "professional" drug salesman because he did not take drugs and insisted on cash payment. A muscular body builder who regularly worked out in a gym in Zone 1, Luis Arturo spoke about his barrio as a sales region, one he had killed several sellers from other clikas to protect. He normally lived alone in a "so-so" hotel, but he now stayed in the shelter because the "involvement of the National Police in the trade" had become a "permanent threat" to his life.

One striking difference between youth in the 1980s and those of the postwar period is that the former were eager to talk about almost anything, often took the conversational initiative, and hoped to present themselves as "good" within the framework of a class struggle between rich and poor. The latter teenagers did not. They framed most of their thoughts in relation to their own and "society's" inherent evil and, as if to resolve this evil, around killing and death.

Repeatedly, without pride, young men in the maras described themselves as *malos*, "evil, bad." They had little to say about being malos, except to indicate that it was the way of all flesh. Seventeen-year-old Edgar put it poignantly: "We are bad, like life, and that's why we have to be bad." José Josué saw being malo as part of his occupation; he told me that "life demands malo." He left home when he was thirteen with his fifteen-year-old brother, and together they started to steal radios out of cars and sell them to pay for a Q30-a-week room in a hotel. The police captured him after a Mazda he and others had stolen crashed into a pole, and they sent him to jail. There he made friends with malos. His initiation into MS-13 happened in jail, where thirteen other members beat him thirteen times. After he left prison, he bought baggy pants, which he said symbolized freedom from prison, as well as the rank of having been a prisoner, a proven malo. He found MS-13 on the outside, resumed a life of "robbery," and continued to live in a small hotel. He did not comment on his gang activities beyond saying "Somos malos." It had no ring of the "Bad is cool" of U.S. gangs.

Somos malos— "We are bad," the phrase I heard again and again—started to sound like an indispensable, pragmatic manner of being. Given that life is evil, their evil needs no explanation. What was there to discuss? Life is bad, period. Fourteen-year-old Venado told me, "[Because] they [are] malo, we have to be." Who are "they," I asked. "*La gente, la sociedad* [people, society]." What does society do? "Mistreat us." Like other researchers and outreach workers, I found the gang members had little to say about "society," except that it did not accept them because of their tattoos and general manner. Gang members neither talked about burgueses nor the social justice of stealing, nor could most place the name Rigoberta Menchú. A young man explained to the sociologist Anneliza Tobar Estrada, "Society isn't ours, it belongs to others. . . . When we join the gang, we look with indifference at the rest of the world" (2007: 46).

Violent death seemed to weigh heavily on their narratives of their own activities and trajectories. Everyone I met said that friendship was what initially attracted them to the clikas of MS-13 and Mara 18. But the internal life of the maras had shifted away from good times, to use that expression in a general sense, to the intense matter of fighting the rival gang. Several explained to me that MS-13 and Mara 18 had become bitter enemies because of a "very serious and unknown incident" in Los Angeles, which no one could describe. This repeatedly mentioned legend gave MS-13 and Mara 18 their identities and defined their mission as being enemies of one another. Gang members constantly referred to themselves as "soldiers" in a war to the death against rival gang members. Hundreds of young men and boys and a smaller number of girls from similar backgrounds and with similar troubles composed each other's enemy. One young man explained, "We dedicate ourselves to killing gang members who aren't from our barrio, and that's it, day after day, someone dies every day, every day our life is the same except it's different, the person who dies, one day one of theirs, one day one of ours." Another described himself as a "calm, cool fighter." He had killed to defend "mi barrio," a term referring simultaneously to his gang and its *territorio*, or space, without which the gang is not a gang. Because he had killed, he had been promoted to the status of *veterano*. Thirteen-year-old CC, a member of Mara 18, described how one day he would die in a gang fight, "*matando a ellos, matado por ellos* [killing them, killed by them]," to live and kill for the gang, to be killed soon. Gato told me that he had "nothing to do with anything except kill 'rivals'": "We die one day to the next."

Amiable, fifteen-year-old Abel, a member of a clika of MS-13, explained that he had been forced out of his home "because of poverty" and went directly to the National Airport because he thought he could sneak onto an airplane. Instead he met a kindly cleaning woman who paid him to help her, and eventually she took him home. She tried but could not maintain him, so she brought him to the Casa Alianza crisis shelter, which, because he was stable and did not take drugs, placed him in a group home for boys ages thirteen to fifteen where, he says, he discovered drugs and MS-13:

> They [MS-13] offered me a barrio. I wanted one, and they had asked me so I joined. To join I had a baptism. They took turns hitting me, hard, thirteen times, thirteen seconds each blow. . . . You need the mara to defend you, you need friends for fights; they say "If someone touches you they are

touching everyone." There isn't a night without a fight. The ambulances don't come; nobody comes. I fight. I am prepared. I don't have obligations. If I die, so what?

Later killed in a gang fight, a former street child recounted his experiences in MS-13 this way: "A bunch of us little [street] kids entered the MS-13 together. One of us was five years old. The majority of us are dead now. They [MS-13 leaders] killed them. . . . Five people died at my hands. The last time I killed was in 2003. I gave a coup de grace in the forehead, right here" ("Revista Domingo" 2005).

These youth had a "text." They knew they were the bad kids with tattoos all over themselves who coolly killed—even if they did not. They knew that they would burn in hell, and they all loved their mothers, but they loved above all their gang, and they killed and were killed for it because that is the way it is. They presented this seemingly airtight argument over and over, without spontaneity. Often tattooed, but sometimes covering their tattoos with neat, almost preppy clothes, speaking about the "rules," accepting being beaten and beating others, killing and being killed, they spoke as if they had complete control over their destiny: death.

As poor as they were, they generally did not live in the mode of poverty-bound Guatemalan neighborhood youth. Whether they stayed in cheap hotels or remained inside their neighborhoods, they severed themselves from *esa vida*, "that life" of the poor, as if their mara identity, with its special style of handshakes, graffiti, tattoos, palabras, and codes, liberated them from the classic class identity of worker and the "ethnic" identity of ladino, both of which increasingly signal powerlessness.[20] Questions about their personal social milieu of family went unanswered; what they wanted to highlight was that *they* had broken with their families, even if, in fact, they still slept at home. Victor articulated this in stark terms. When I asked him where he was born, he replied, "I was born with the mara, without it I am nothing."[21] When I asked Fredy, a sixteen-year-old member of MS-13, about his kin, he replied that his mother thought that he was malo, and he thought that she was not part of his *vida*. These youth might well have supported families, but that was not part of their story. What they communicated was that even though they were bounded by poverty on all sides, the life that they lived in the mara severed their identifications to poor people's lives—and perhaps, tragically, with life itself. Initiations sometimes involved being raped or raping or killing a known person such as a neighbor or a rival gang member's relative, or, in the most stunning break with tradition and morality, an elderly person.

After she left the gang and went into hiding, twelve-year-old Rosa gave a social worker at Casa Alianza the following account of the internal life of a mara:

> At first I was happy in the mara, but when I saw them rape a girl . . . I felt like crying. It felt like they were doing it to me. The girl is dead now; they killed her in front of me, because they were afraid she would turn them in. They shot her, and she just kept quiet, she didn't say anything. Her name was Elisa. She had already left the mara. I was ready to — ready to kill my-self. My heart ached and I felt like I really needed to get out of the maras, but I just couldn't.
>
> After joining the mara, I killed an old woman because they told me I had to kill somebody and to sacrifice their blood. . . . I pushed her, and when I touched her afterwards, she wasn't breathing any more. She was a sixty-year-old woman who lived with her grandchildren. They were from the Brekera Mara [a rival clika]. I felt so bad, like I had killed my own grandma. . . . I don't remember exactly what happened. The mara has also tried to kill me — once with a gun, once with a knife, and another time with a car.

According to the social worker Rosa felt sick and lost.

For these "soldiers," there appears to be no "cause" except a rivalry none can explain. Whether or not they recognized themselves in each other, M-18 and MS-13 have become involved in suicidal homicide, just as in the war, wherein the common soldiers, usually forced Mayan and ladino "recruits," were taught to hate an enemy similar to them in social and cultural background without any clear reason, except that they were "other" — when they were not. This killer/killed persona is the warrior, the winner of the contest to decide Guatemalan history, who was also a loser, a dead warrior.

As the gangs have become more violent, the proportion of males to females has shifted. There were far fewer young women in the early twenty-first century than when the maras started in the mid-1980s. A certain male-ness now prevails. Masculinity's many meanings — ranging from courtesy, breadwinning, and bravery to mindless brute physical violence — have shriveled to the latter. This is the violence of the solider, who, unlike the violent general, has no idea why he is fighting and only the knowledge that he will kill and die. The male fighter was valorized in Guatemala and in "world" youth culture long before the military's triumph over the revolutionary movement, but I am arguing that the loss of a class, community, and humane language and practice and the normalization of the ability to maim, wound, and kill as

INTRODUCTION The Internet abounds with dread-inducing "gangster" images of menacing tattooed young men in maras. The Guatemalan photographer José Manuel Mayorga reaches beyond the politics of provoking fear *of* mareros by instead evoking the fears *in* which they and others live: the common reality of weapons used by adults, here by a parking lot attendant; a child who works assisting a bus driver in a space that belongs to criminals; and a small calling card suggesting that Guatemala City is "finished"—in such disarray as to be defunct—and inviting us to visit and see for ourselves.

FIG 7.1 *The Pistol and the Defeat*, 2011. The pistol, carried "just in case," is a quotidian feature of many Guatemalan lives. The "Red Defeat" of the headline here refers to the frustration of the national soccer team's hopes of qualifying for the World Cup. PHOTO BY JOSÉ MANUEL MAYORGA. USED WITH KIND PERMISSION.

FIG 7.2 *Streets of Fear*, 2011. Ciudad de Guatemala. Boarding a bus, no one can be sure they will leave it alive, if the driver will be shot dead, if passengers will be held up. PHOTO BY JOSÉ MANUEL MAYORGA. USED WITH KIND PERMISSION.

MAYORGA   GUATEMALA

FIG 7.3 *Carte de visite: Bitter Boulevard*, 2006. With a public transportation system in collapse, people seek the security of solitary travel to their destinations, even though private vehicles can also be held up or stolen; pickups are particularly coveted. PHOTO BY JOSÉ MANUEL MAYORGA. USED WITH KIND PERMISSION.

a form of power within urban life did not happen until the postwar period because before then, a praxis of solidarity flourished.

By the mid-1990s humble, often domestically abused, and increasingly disconnected urban boys and girls for whom *ladinismo* and Mayan ethnicity continually depreciated into a cultural nothing, without jobs or aims and within communities without internal cohesion, were drawn or forced into the imaginary of the power of violent death over life. Within the gangs' understanding of the world the line between victim and victimizer, once as clear as crystal, became blurred in a messy intertwining of ruled and ruler. There existed only one side: the absolute of violence, the killer's side. The effective identity of mara came to flow as lifeblood from the power to hurt and kill. Their everyday lives became everyday life or death, nothing in between, and death, their own deaths, would win because death is supreme. In the late 1990s one significant tattoo signaling mara membership in Guatemala City was three small dots between the thumb and the index finger that, a young man explained to me, stood for hospital, prison, and morgue. The feisty 1980s maras belonged to the period of political fight; those of the 1990s and later belong to the postslaughter, the all-is-over time. Neither rebels nor conformists, orphans of the world, and not only of Guatemala, criminalized by adults and even by the U.S. Department of Homeland Security for all manner of evil, the mareros have become a variation of those whom Hannah Arendt (1951: 276–302) once called "the most symptomatic group," the leftovers, "forced to live outside the common world," who, in this case, futilely reproduce the traumas that cast them out, to end those in death.

Notes

1. The Commission for Historical Clarification (CEH) repeatedly uses this term and others like it to refer to sadistic acts, including those inflicted by the military as well as forcing others to commit and witness.
2. The term *mara* was already used to refer to groups of friends in at least Guatemala and El Salvador.
3. Author interview with Victor, Guatemala City, 2002.
4. Named after a famous Puerto Rican gang in New York.
5. Author interview with Direction official, 1987.
6. The Ixil Triangle is made up of the three Maya-Ixil townships of Nebaj, Cotzal, and Chajul, designated a site of genocide by the CEH.
7. In 2009 the United Nations Development Program (UNDP 2010: 10) declared Central America "the most violent region in the world," and "Honduras, Guatemala and El Salvador . . . between three and six times" more violent than other nations in the region. Currently 88 percent of the cocaine consumed in the United States passes through Guatemala.

8. There has been a resurgence of activism among banana workers, schoolteachers, and villagers affected by land loss, mineral exploration, and megaprojects.

9. The origins and use of the term *la violencia* in the Guatemalan context are complex. During and after the war, many Guatemalans employed it (or *la situacion*) to refer to state violence without getting into trouble. But for many in subsequent generations *la violencia* refers to a past that is not explained. The military, politicians, and unfortunately much media and many NGOs and even social scientists use the term without explaining who does "it" or why "it" occurs.

10. NGOs were in the neighborhoods in the 1970s but did not replace more organic groups.

11. Author interview with Juan Miguel Fuentes, Guatemala City, 1997.

12. One of assassins of the AVANCSO founder Myrna Mack was recruited from Las Cobras.

13. Author interviews, El Gallito, 1992 and 1996.

14. Violent gangs grew significantly in Honduras between 1985 and 1989, which was before the INS began to deport gang members (Salomon 1993).

15. Miranda 2005. In 2006 he left MS-13 in Los Angeles and returned to El Salvador, where he was murdered for having quit the gang in LA.

16. Angelface website, accessed May 2004. *Faces of Death* is a series of snuff videos that show moments of real violence and pandemonium, such as actual scenes of death squad killings in El Salvador, the slaughter of dolphins, the napalming of Vietnamese, a massacre at a Colombian wedding, electrocution, rape, and a train wreck in India. The videos are snapshots of violence without context or narrative.

17. Author interview with Victor, 2002. According to Victor, the status of *veterano* is earned by killing someone. *Palabras* connect different *clikas* within the broader gang structure.

18. Author interviews with an unnamed Inter-American Development Bank (BID) representative and Padre Manolo Maquiera S.J., 2005.

19. Connected to New York City's Covenant House, Casa Alianza opened in 1981 in Guatemala City. For years its extraordinary staff aided street children and exposed police brutality against them. The Guatemalan National Police, as well as the so-called parallel powers of state repression, made life extremely difficult for Casa. Several of its staff were killed in the years before it closed.

20. The population of Guatemala City — poor and largely ladino — should put to rest the pernicious stereotype of ladino as homogeneously or even primarily middle class. If this were the case, almost half of the Guatemalan people would be middle class, and this is not the case (see González Ponciano this volume).

21. Personal communications with Padre Manolo Maquiera and members of the Equipo de Estudios Urbanos and AVANCSO; interview with Victor, Guatemala City, 2004.

THE LONG WAR IN COLOTENANGO
Guerrillas, Army, and Civil Patrols

In Colotenango, Huehuetenango, a highland Mayan community caught up in Guatemala's armed conflict, indigenous Mam residents were both the objects and agents of violence: many supported or joined the armed guerrillas; others served the army in the civil patrol system, including some who attacked neighbors who opposed military rule. Colotenango illustrates two central issues in recent Guatemalan history: how a struggle between government forces and a small rebel movement came to take the lives of as many as 200,000 civilians (CEH 1999: vol. 2:15) and how a geopolitical conflict took the form of neighbor attacking neighbor. This paper examines one killing and its legal aftermath, a case that became a critical challenge to impunity and an important moment in the development of Guatemala's postwar regime of "human rights," even as it involved a form of collective punishment of poor people that felt alarmingly similar to war. This history of struggle between Colotenango's civil patrols and their opponents in a revitalized Campesino Unity Committee (CUC) demonstrates the difficulties of confronting Guatemala's legacy of political violence and the ambiguities of "democratic" state functioning.

The Long War

Rebel groups were functioning in Guatemala by 1962, but it took twenty years for the armed conflict to arrive in Colotenango. In early 1982 the Guerrilla Army of the Poor (EGP), the largest rebel group in the Guatemalan National Revolutionary Unity (URNG), began its biggest offensive of the war. The

EGP's strategy was to provoke wide insurrection in the isolated western highlands, overtax the army, and create the conditions for a final guerrilla victory on urban terrain. Central to the guerrillas' plan was Huehuetenango, a mountainous department along the Mexican border. To take Huehuetenango, the rebels had to control the Pan-American Highway, a stretch of paved road that runs through Colotenango along the narrow canyon of the Río Selegua. The army established a series of outposts along the road, but EGP guerrillas moved easily through the area, blowing up bridges and ambushing army caravans as they moved along the highway.

In a series of visits to the municipality of Colotenango in 1999 and 2000, I asked residents about the rebels' early organizing work.[1] Villagers recall that guerrillas' speeches promised a better future, in which a revolutionary government would undertake massive land reform and divide up the country's huge coffee and sugar estates among rural supporters. The message went over well on the steep slopes of Colotenango, where arable land is scarce and the soil is dry and sandy and where the Mam-speaking population — neglected by the government and exploited by plantation owners and a small local ladino elite — had little to gain from the status quo.

The guerrilla-army struggle exploded into the open on March 11, 1982. Rebels ambushed an army transport truck at Rogelio Bridge, a few hundred meters below the hamlet of Ical. Villager testimonies leave it unclear whether the EGP's newly formed local peasant cadre helped rebels carry out the sabotage. What is certain is that many in Ical supported the guerrillas and that the army, through its local agents, knew it. Moments after the attack, army troops followed the guerrillas' path up the steep mountainside and into Ical but found no sign of the armed insurgents. In what had become a typical army response to guerrilla activity, troops fanned out and killed thirty-six local residents, among them ten women and six children.[2] Such indiscriminate massacres punished the rural poor for the deeds of the elusive guerrillas and appeared designed to dissuade them from ever supporting the rebel army again. The strategy worked in much of the highlands, but in Colotenango army violence turned many more strongly against the government.

Nor were guerrilla actions always popular. Two weeks after the massacre in Ical, rebels occupied the center of Colotenango and burned down the municipal salon, a distinctive alpine-style building in an otherwise shabby town. This act of arson was part of an EGP effort to destroy every symbol of state power in Huehuetenango. For one town resident, the Army of the Poor erred in destroying what little Colotenango had. "Why didn't they go to the coast," he wondered, where *los meros ricos* (the truly rich) had their plantations? Rebel sabotage would allow Colotecos to view both army and guerrillas as agents of destruction in the years that followed.

Just as the violence reached its peak in Huehuetenango, General Efraín Ríos Montt took power in a coup in Guatemala City. At first Ríos Montt continued the policies of his predecessor, General Romeo Lucas García, massacring peasants and burning villages in areas of guerrilla activity. But in June 1982 Ríos Montt changed the terms of engagement, declaring an amnesty that gave rebels thirty days to turn in their guns and civilians thirty days to organize into antiguerrilla militias, the civilian self-defense patrols (PACs, in their Spanish acronym). In Colotenango rebels stayed on the offensive, killing two town residents who had encouraged their neighbors to form a PAC. Few villages did as the army ordered, as residents feared guerrilla retribution or believed rebels would protect them from the army.[3]

For the time being, the government's attention lay elsewhere. Its July 1982 scorched-earth campaign focused on rebel strongholds in northern Huehuetenango and included large-scale massacres of unarmed civilians.[4] The offensive gave new strategic importance to the Pan-American Highway, and guerrillas used it to harass troop transports as they passed near Colotenango's hamlets. The EGP seemed to welcome a showdown with the army over its civilian support. On July 27 guerrillas blew up the Chanjón Bridge near the village of Tixel, and the ensuing EGP communiqué openly claimed its local supporters had participated in the sabotage.[5] Residents recall a municipality divided: some feared drawing the army's attention; others remained committed to the guerrillas' cause.

On August 7, five months after the government's terror campaign began, soldiers fanned out on the paths leading out of the town of Colotenango. Passing themselves off as guerrillas, they invited villagers returning from the Saturday market to come with them to a camp to receive guns to fight the army—exactly what many unarmed guerrilla supporters had been waiting for. When the villagers went to get their weapons, however, they were seized by soldiers. Those who resisted were killed on the spot; those who did not were taken to an army outpost. Soldiers forced their captives to dig a pit, then strangled or shot them one by one before dumping the bodies, thirty-nine in all, into a common grave (CEH 1999: vol. 7).

This time army killings had the desired effect. Guerrillas fled the region, leaving unarmed supporters to fend for themselves. Elsewhere in Huehuetenango and Quiché, the EGP encouraged its partisans to flee en masse to Mexico or deep into the jungle. But Colotenango was not near any jungle or border, so most sympathizers stayed put. Cut off from guerrilla contacts, residents of rebel-organized villages had no choice but to accept the army's demand that they form pro-government civil patrols. With the army in control, the massacres soon ended, but the conflict would continue.

The Civil Patrols

In just a few months the Guatemalan army secured the collaboration of hundreds of thousands of villagers and a lesser number of town residents. Every male Coloteco between eighteen and fifty-five—and quite a few younger boys—was forced to perform a regular twenty-four-hour turn in the civil patrol, each village guarding a highway bridge or other government installation. Armed with only sticks or machetes, patrollers were still a poor match for the guerrillas, who could continue to blow up bridges. But the army could then easily take vengeance by punishing patrollers, among them many former rebel supporters.

The patrol obligation turned out to be an efficient way for the military to impose its rule and establish authority in the Guatemalan countryside. It gave the army an easy way to distinguish those willing to patrol, who had accepted government authority, from those who had fled or refused to patrol and whose loyalties remained questionable. It separated rebels from civilian supporters, which undermined the rebels' mobility and allowed the government to recall most of its troops from the region. Patrol commanders also reported on their neighbors' activities, enhancing army intelligence and making active support for the guerrillas increasingly dangerous.

Rural militarization often turned villagers against each other. The army compelled patrollers to inform on guerrilla collaborators and patrol resistors, and in certain regions forced or encouraged patrollers themselves to torture or kill local suspects. Though many villagers tried to prevent the patrols from dividing their communities, too often militaristic patrollers turned on their neighbors with a vengeance, carrying out the army's demand that they purge their communities of political opposition (Americas Watch 1982; CEH 1999: vol. 8). Patrollers were also called on to attack communities that had yet to accept army rule. Villages that did not do the army's bidding could become the object of an army massacre (Americas Watch 1982; CEH 1999: vol. 8).

I spoke with Colotecos about their long years laboring for the army, without pay, in the civil patrol system. Most recall the patrols as an onerous burden and say the army forced the patrols on them. Days spent guarding a bridge, after all, was time they could have dedicated to tending their fields or earning money laboring on the plantations. Cold nights spent staring at an empty highway would have been more comfortably spent asleep in their beds with their wives. Nevertheless many patrollers in the department of Huehuetenango recall the patrol obligation as an improvement over the fear of army violence, and some were happy to see the guerrillas gone (Kobrak 2010).

As the army demanded that villagers identify with the civil patrols, it was aided by guerrillas' attacks on communities that had turned against them. In Colotenango the EGP claimed it killed six "army collaborators" in the hamlets surrounding the town in the months before the civil patrols had formed. After the patrols were imposed, the rebels attacked the villages that most enthusiastically accepted the army's call to organize. Villagers in La Barranca recall four EGP killings in 1982; in Xemal rebels are said to have killed another four local men, part of an EGP strategy in Huehuetenango to treat civil patrollers, both on and off duty, as military targets. A decade later civil patrollers in Xemal and La Barranca would be accused of killing local guerrilla supporters. While apparently none of these guerrilla acts of violence was denounced to Guatemala's Commission for Historical Clarification (CEH 1999: vols. 7 and 8), the CEH's database on Colotenango included approximately 130 killings and forced disappearances committed by the Guatemalan army and thirteen committed by civil patrollers.[6]

The civil patrol system was the centerpiece of the army's plan to make villagers into loyal government subjects. It created a hierarchy of discipline and ideological control, reaching down from regional army base commanders, through the municipal military commissioners, to village-level patrol chiefs, who frequently met with their superiors. In indoctrination sessions the army told villagers that rebels had started the violence and denied the social origins of the armed conflict. In its telling, the army, together with the civil patrols, had pacified the countryside and made it safe again for people to stay "on their land, with their families," a mantra I often heard years later from patrollers themselves.

Even as the patrol system involved rural indigenous men in state repression, it also made many feel newly enfranchised in the Guatemalan nation. Patrollers were part of a patriotic effort against enemies of the state, whom the army labeled "communist subversive delinquents." In some villages patrollers received guns from the army. Though the presence of arms made villages into guerrilla targets, it also represented an unprecedented display of government trust toward the Mayan poor. Patrollers benefited materially from this new state attention as long-ignored communities received development aid designed to address the sources of rural insurgency (but see González-Izás this volume).

In most of Guatemala, active fighting between government and rebel forces ended in 1982. But in much of rural Guatemala, the patrol obligation continued day and night into the 1990s. The Guatemalan army—first through massacres, then through the civil patrols—had convinced many in the countryside to never again support or tolerate any sign of political opposition. Living under army control, many guerrilla supporters learned to forget they had ever been attracted to the struggle at all. But not in Colotenango.

The Campesino Unity Committee

After 1982's holocaust of state violence, opposition groups in Guatemala had difficulty finding anyone willing to organize with them. With the army in control, anyone mixed up in *la política*, which included making human rights demands, could become a target of government death squads. When the military dictatorship gave way to civilian rule in 1986, however, Guatemala's "popular movement" tried to reestablish its presence in the still militarized countryside. Among its few successes was Colotenango's strong show of support for the CUC.

The CUC first emerged in 1978. It pledged to fight for the interests of the poor by uniting indigenous and ladino, highland farmer and lowland plantation worker. In 1980 the group attracted international attention when it occupied the Spanish Embassy to protest state repression in the department of Quiché, only to have government security forces attack the building. In the ensuing blaze thirty-nine people, protesters and hostages alike, died. Later that year a CUC strike succeeded in bringing the country's sugarcane harvest to a halt. After the strike a number of CUC leaders were shot down, forcing the group underground. Many remaining members joined the EGP rebels, if they had not already.

By 1986 CUC organizers surfaced in southern Huehuetenango, a region where they had little previous organizing experience. The group presented itself as a human rights organization focused on the need to end the civil patrols. "The end of the patrols became the first of our struggles," said Rafael González, CUC's general secretary. "The patrols impeded the free movement of the people and they made the movement of the guerrillas difficult." González and other CUC leaders are now forthcoming in discussing the deep connection between their group and the EGP guerrillas. The CUC was an unarmed organization "of the masses," but it shared political interests and overlapping leadership cadres with the Guerrilla Army of the Poor (see Velásquez Nimatuj this volume; Bastos and Camus this volume). In Huehuetenango this connection went even further. Soon after the CUC began local operations, the EGP began to use the CUC's organized base to recruit a detachment of local rebel fighters, the Zonal Guerrillero "Fernando Hoyos," named for a Spanish Jesuit priest turned EGP combatant (see McAllister this volume). The Zonal had its greatest recruiting success around Colotenango, where "weekend warrior"–style guerrillas reestablished a rebel presence—hanging banners on footpaths, painting graffiti on bridges, and occasionally assisting with guerrilla sabotage or in combat against the army.

Organizations like the CUC gave guerrilla supporters a degree of security they had lacked in 1982, when the EGP tried to quickly expand its presence from strongholds in Quiché to the rest of the highlands; in Huehuetenango this had made it easy for neighbors to identify rebel allies and denounce them to the army. Now, working more carefully, the EGP used the CUC to shield its political base. Indeed many CUC recruits were unaware of the group's links to the guerrillas. The legal, pacifist face of the CUC allowed armed guerrillas to regain a foothold in a region where both the memory of army violence and the presence of the civil patrols made people afraid to identify with the armed insurgency. "The people still feared the guerrillas, so they used CUC to mask the organization, to make its work easier," said Félix Méndez Ruiz, a former CUC and EGP cadre leader in Colotenango. "The army knew what we were doing. But it never found out who was directing all this."

Leaders in the CUC and the EGP counted on constitutional rule and Guatemala's desire to end its status as a human rights pariah to limit the army's freedom to attack guerrilla partisans. But the army would not stand by and let its dominance be eroded by groups like the CUC acting in the name of human rights. So the army called upon civil patrollers to do what it could not: find and neutralize leaders of this growing opposition.

Tixel

In October 1987 Guatemalan guerrilla and government representatives met in Madrid, in secret, to discuss a negotiated solution to the country's armed conflict. As a precondition, URNG representatives demanded the army dissolve its civil patrols. Army negotiators refused. The military command saw the continuing presence of the patrols in the countryside as its greatest bargaining chip in future discussions with the rebels. Weeks later the army unleashed its "year-end offensive," a military assault on pockets of resistance designed to show guerrillas and their supporters who was in control. The rebels responded with a show of their own power in Colotenango. Reestablished cadres blew up four bridges on the Pan-American Highway, slowing military transports and contributing to the offensive's failure.

One of these destroyed bridges was Puente Chanjón, the destruction of which had provoked the army massacre in Xemal five years earlier. Civil patrollers from Tixel were guarding the bridge one night when guerrillas arrived to blow it up. They told the patrollers to get out of the way. Patrollers obliged, and though they failed to act against the guerrillas, the army did not punish them. Soon Tixel would be the first village to openly challenge army rule.

Like most of Colotenango's villages, Tixel sits on the steep slopes of a narrow stretch of the Selegua Valley. In the early 1980s many local residents had collaborated with the EGP until army killings and the guerrilla retreat left them disconnected from the rebels. When EGP fighters reappeared in Tixel as CUC organizers, they faced the hostility of their former collaborators. One organizer told me he often heard this complaint: "First you talked about seizing power, then we heard nothing from you. Why did you abandon us? Why didn't you give us guns?" Rebel organizers persisted, and despite feeling forsaken by the guerrillas or fearing a repeat of army massacres, many in Tixel rejoined the struggle, both as CUC members and as EGP recruits.

Colotenango is one of the few places in the Guatemalan highlands where the guerrillas reestablished their presence after 1982. Success in Colotenango is likely due to the CUC's determined efforts to organize the population and the fact that rebel supporters stayed in their villages instead of taking refuge elsewhere. Amílcar Raymundo Cedillo, a former guerrilla organizer in Colotenango, observed that in nearby municipalities like Cuilco and La Democracia, better-off coffee farmers opposed the guerrilla presence early on, while in Colotenango, where almost everybody is poor, no one opposed the guerrilla return until the army encouraged civil patrollers to do so. Raymundo also noted that earlier army repression in Colotenango, though terrible, never approached "the criminality in Quiché," where government violence had depopulated entire regions. During the patrol era, internecine violence was also more extreme in Quiché, where CERJ, the Council of Ethnic Communities "Rujunel Junam," led the fight against the civil patrols and lost twenty-five members between 1988 and 1993, many of them killed by civil patrol loyalists (Americas Watch 1989; Robert F. Kennedy Center 1993).

Still, by the late 1980s peasants throughout the highlands had grown weary of the obligations of patrol duty, still typically a twenty-four-hour turn once every week or two for each male villager. The 1985 Constitution clearly specified that civilian militias were voluntary, but few openly challenged the army by refusing to patrol. The army, fearing a guerrilla resurgence, pressured villages in strategic regions to continue the militias. When a handful of communities in Quiché successfully petitioned the army to allow them to suspend their patrols by citing economic necessity, the CUC decided to use the tactic in Colotenango.

A number of Tixel's families were secretly organized in the local chapter of the CUC. Encouraged by CUC organizers, they decided to take over the village civil patrol and bring it down from within. Brothers Romelio and Alfonso Morales Jiménez became Tixel's new patrol commanders in a community vote.[7] During a visit to their home, I was told, amid much laughter, how they spent over a year loyally attending patrol commander meetings at the Huehuetenango military base. Meanwhile they kept a low profile as CUC affiliates quietly working to convince their neighbors that it was time to end the patrols.

In 1990 Tixel residents agreed overwhelmingly to stop patrolling. Romelio and Alfonso returned to the Huehuetenango military base to present an act signed by villagers saying that they had dissolved their civil patrol. Officers were taken aback by this show of independence in Colotenango, and they did not demand that Tixel continue to patrol. But army troops began to regularly drop by the village, convening the men to ask them if they really wanted to stop patrolling. The answer was always the same: the patrols had become a burden and villagers wanted to stop.

The CUC's victory in Tixel aided its organizing in other Colotenango villages. In one village after another, men decided to stop giving their time to the army—first Tojlate, high on the mountain, where the guerrillas had once roamed; then Ixconlaj, also a previous EGP stronghold. In Ical villagers laid down their machetes after army soldiers shot a local patroller who had fallen asleep while guarding a bridge (ODHAG 1991). The shooting showed another reason not to patrol: spending all night guarding a highway was dangerous. And of course, no one was getting paid for his efforts.

The CUC had begun to challenge the mind-set of submission the army had tried to establish through the civil patrols. Membership in the CUC and the EGP appealed to village youth who had been too young to join the guerrillas in 1982. The army also targeted young men from poor, outlying villages through its forcible military recruitment system. The EGP told supporters that if they were caught in an army sweep they should stay around for the three-month basic training, then desert to become guerrilla fighters. Patrol loyalists, however, worried about the opposition's advance. Tensions grew in Colotenango as the CUC became a more obvious, public organization, and the EGP increased its military activity.

Xemal

In Xemal the terrain is thick with coffee trees and sugarcane, but, as in other villages, families are large and few have enough land. To make ends meet, most residents work on the coastal plantations or on government road crews. In the early 1980s some residents collaborated with the guerrillas. But when the army insisted they form a civil patrol, the village became a government stronghold and a target for the guerrillas. Neighbor turned against neighbor.

In January 1992 Alberto Godínez, Xemal's longtime patrol commander, encouraged fellow villagers to vote to disband the militia. He then publicly proclaimed his membership in the CUC, and would later claim to be a guerrilla. Godínez told me that for years he played "both sides," leading the patrols and working with the rebels.

Villages that independently disbanded their militias worried the army. An army patrol visited Xemal and accused villagers who no longer wanted to patrol of being guerrillas. Godínez and his allies refused to resume the patrol, but another group agreed.

The new patrol commander was Efraín Domingo Morales, a young man studying to be a teacher and thus one of the most educated persons in Xemal. Efraín's family had been affected by both guerrilla and civil patrol violence. In 1982 guerrillas killed his father, Juan Domingo Morales, after he led the formation of Xemal's civil patrol. Then, one night in 1990, patrollers under the command of Alberto Godínez severely beat Efraín's younger brother, Remigio, when they heard what they thought was rebel gunfire and found Remigio and another teen showing off a pistol to girls in a nearby hamlet. Godínez's critics say he ordered patrollers to attack the boys with machetes; Godínez claims he tried to dissuade his patrollers from killing the boys for being guerrillas. Frantic, Efraín ran down the mountain to summon the municipal patrol chief. When they arrived, the boys lay bloodied and near death. At dawn, patrol commanders summoned army officers, who told patrollers to take the boys to a public hospital and explain that they had wounded each other in a machete fight. Efraín pressed his brother's case wherever he could, and the Catholic Church's Human Rights Office detailed the incident in a number of reports (ODHAG 1990, 1991, 1992). In the end, the army never punished patrollers for the attack and the courts refused to intervene.

Two years later Efraín was in charge of the re-formed Xemal civil patrol, while Godínez and his allies supported the CUC. Previous patrols carried only sticks and machetes, but now the army provided Xemal with a set of M-1 and Mauser rifles. The army said the rifles were to help deter guerrilla attacks, but they were mainly used to intimidate neighbors into joining the patrols. The patrols grew quickly. When I asked one villager if he had given his time to the new civil patrol, he said, "Yes, I was in it. Why would I lie? But the commanders told us that they would kill those who didn't patrol. Some say the army was behind them, making the commanders make us patrol."

The guerrilla-army fight was now expressed in tensions between hamlets where most men participated in the patrols and those where residents joined the CUC and its sister organization the National Coordination of Guatemalan Widows (CONAVIGUA). The guerrillas and their supporters grew confident. In the town marketplace, residents shouted "Long live the URNG" when protesting army recruiting (ODHAG 1992). In Xemal CUC banners proclaimed, "Down with the civil patrols." Guerrillas no longer attacked the civil patrols directly, as they had in 1982, but some Colotecos accused combatants of keeping everyone on edge by shooting their guns from the forest. Former guerrillas insist they never fired their weapons near patrolling villagers and suggest that patrollers shot off their rifles to create fear of the guerrillas.

In August 1992 government and URNG negotiators signed a peace accord in which the army agreed not to form any new civil patrols. But in Colotenango the army issued more guns to the remaining civil patrols. That same month, armed patrollers from La Barranca set up checkpoints at Los Naranjales Bridge to see what residents from villages higher up the mountain were buying in the market and confiscated goods from those suspected of bringing supplies to the guerrillas. In Xemal patrollers conducted illegal house searches to look for arms caches, confronted CUC members with physical and verbal intimidation, and occupied a hamlet whose residents had ceased patrolling (Inter-American Commission on Human Rights 1993; ODHAG 1993). Both the CUC and CONAVIGUA denounced the intimidation campaign to the government, but neither Guatemala's army nor the police did anything to rein in patrollers.

With authorities passively looking on, the civil patrol dispute in Xemal turned deadly. A couple in the village, Pascuala Sánchez Domingo and Santiago Domingo Sánchez, had refused to send their son Juan to patrol. On the afternoon of July 5, 1993, unknown men entered their house and killed the couple and their son with gunfire and machetes, then looted the premises (CEH 1999: vol. 8: 589).[8]

The Death of Juan Chanay Pablo

Police were reluctant to investigate the triple homicide in Xemal. So on August 3, 1993, the CUC and other popular organizations held a mass protest in

Colotenango's town square to denounce the violence and demand an end to the remaining civil patrols. The protest represented a major mobilization of the opposition and a show of popular force against the army. Thousands of Maya came from all over Huehuetenango, while national and international human rights activists came out from the capital. Colotenango had become a human rights cause célèbre.

Protesters invited the mayor, the governor, the government human rights ombudsman, and the commander of the Huehuetenango military base, Colonel Luis Felipe Miranda Trejo, to their march to hear their grievances. When the colonel did not show up, protest leaders sent a commission to the army base to demand that Miranda Trejo dissolve the patrols in Colotenango and retrieve their guns. The colonel dismissed their demands and told protestors to direct their complaints to the president.

Protest leaders returned to Colotenango to inform the crowd that the army would not disarm the patrols. The sun was going down, and, fearing a confrontation, protesters began returning to their villages. Those who lived below the town would have to pass over Los Naranjales Bridge, which was lined by forty patrollers from La Barranca. Most patrollers carried sticks, rocks, or machetes, but a few bore the army's Mausers and M-1s. They taunted passing families, yelling out "Guerrillas!" or "You don't want to work, you're all loafers," an accusation the Guatemalan Army routinely leveled at rebels and their supporters.

One protestor, Rafael Vásquez Simón, stopped to speak with his neighbors. "Brothers," he recalled saying, "we aren't guerrillas. We're just here to demand our rights."[9] Protest leaders arrived in a Jeep driven by a Belgian solidarity activist, Karel Op de Beeck, who began taking photos and shooting videotape of the scene while berating patrollers in broken Spanish. Patrollers, annoyed, shook their machetes at Op de Beeck and those who had stopped to watch the confrontation. The crowd grew until a patroller fired his rifle into the air, scattering protesters from the bridge. At that moment, according to CUC witnesses, armed patrollers took aim at those fleeing down the highway. Three protesters were shot in the leg and fell to the blacktop. Their comrades managed to spirit away a wounded young man and a teenage girl. But the third victim, Juan Chanay Pablo, a sixty-four-year-old CUC member from the village of Tojlate, was left on the highway, where he died of shock.

Questions remain about exactly what happened at Los Naranjales.[10] What is certain is that patrollers on the bridge meant to violently intimidate anti-patrol protestors and that the army had encouraged such violence. Hours after the shooting, an army contingent from the Huehuetenango base arrived in La Barranca. According to a resident sympathetic to the CUC, officers were upset with patrollers for killing an old man; had the victim been younger, they said, they could have claimed he was a guerrilla. Juan Chanay Pablo's body still lay by the highway, waiting for examination by the justice of the peace; army civilian affairs officers apparently took the opportunity to plant a revolver and fragmentation grenade in his shoulder bag to make it appear that he was a rebel combatant killed in an exchange of gunfire (CEH 1999: vol. 7: 375).

In Juan Chanay Pablo the CUC and the EGP had an attractive martyr: an elderly indigenous man from a poor village, apparently shot dead by an army-sponsored civil patrol after a peaceful protest against the abusive patrols. A week after the killing, CUC leaders presented an accusation against fifteen La Barranca civil patrollers for the death of Juan Chanay. The case would test the limits of impunity long enjoyed by Guatemala's security forces. Not one military officer had ever been convicted for any of the tens of thousands of extrajudicial killings of civilians in the 1980s; only a handful of low-ranking operatives had ever been brought to trial.

The violence in Colotenango continued. A month after the Naranjales killing, the Xemal patrol commander Efraín Domingo Morales was ambushed while marching in an Independence Day parade at his school in nearby Ixtahuacán. The smoothly executed assassination appeared to be the work of trained combatants. Two weeks later, in an apparent reprisal, two vociferous CUC members, Andrés Godínez Díaz and María Pérez Sánchez, were killed while working in their fields above Xemal. In the valley threats from patrollers guarding the bridges and paths into town created a de facto evening curfew for anyone from a village without a civil patrol. Threatened with death, CUC and CONAVIGUA leaders could no longer safely visit the town during the day or night.

The army openly intimidated patrol opponents. Its lawyers filed trumped-up countercharges against witnesses for the prosecution and tried to have CUC and CONAVIGUA tried for sedition. When two of the accused civil patrollers were detained, the army brought truckloads of civil patrollers to demonstrate outside their preliminary hearing in Huehuetenango. The National Police told plaintiffs that they were afraid to go to Colotenango to carry out arrest warrants against the other accused.[11]

Guatemala's new president, Ramiro de León Carpio, had called for the end of the civil patrols while serving as the government's human rights ombudsman. However, soon after he became president, his cousin, the politician and newspaper publisher Jorge Carpio, was killed on a rural highway in an ambush carried out by civil patrollers working for the Quiché military base. Just days after Juan Chanay was killed, de León told a gathering of ten thousand patrollers at the Huehuetenango military base that he supported the civil patrols and asked for their support in his efforts to purge members of Congress and the courts. To the president, the civil patrols were no longer a human rights problem but an electoral base (*El Gráfico*, August 20, 1993).

The Trial

The case against the La Barranca civil patrollers stalled until 1995, when the army began preparing to sign a final peace agreement with the rebels. The civil patrols, a bargaining chip in preliminary negotiations, suddenly represented a liability to the military. The army stopped pressing villagers to patrol. Instead, former minister of defense Julio Balconi told me, the army worried about how to get hardcore patrollers to turn in their guns.

Officers from the Huehuetenango army base convinced nine fugitive La Barranca patrollers to turn themselves in to the police, telling the accused that it would arrange their defense and that they could expect to go free in a matter of weeks. In a brief April 1996 trial, the judge refused to order an exhumation of the cadaver or to accept as evidence the photos of the incident taken by Karel Op de Beeck and disqualified all prosecution witnesses who had participated in the protest. He ruled for the defendants. The prosecution appealed, and the defendants returned to jail.

In August 1996 the civil patrols were formally dismantled. The government of Alvaro Arzú held the first demobilization in Colotenango, choosing an emblematic site of civil patrol abuse. The government representative Marta Altolaguirre openly denounced the violence of Colotenango's civil patrols. The government, Altolaguirre made clear, would punish patrollers for their wartime actions. Impunity had to end "so that justice and the rule of law predominate in all Guatemala, including Colotenango." General Otto Pérez Molina, head of the army's Joint Chiefs of Staff (elected president of Guatemala in 2011), bluntly redefined the army's position: "We don't deny that patrollers engaged in illegal actions, but this was never part of army policy" (*Siglo Veintiuno*, August 10, 1996).

European countries that were funding the peace process pressured Guatemala to bring the Juan Chanay Pablo case to trial. In early 1997 the Guatemalan government accepted civil responsibility for the shooting at Los Naranjales Bridge before the Inter-American Court of Human Rights in Costa Rica and agreed to pay for a series of development projects for Colotenango's villages and provide $50,000 to those individuals affected by the civil patrol

FIG 8.1 Bus passengers watch civil patrollers prepare to disarm in Aguacatan, Huehuetenango, in preparation for the 1996 signing of the peace accords. PHOTO BY JORGE UZON. USED WITH KIND PERMISSION.

violence. The government also promised to speed a new trial in Guatemalan courts.

Thus in late 1997 twelve of the fifteen patrollers who had originally been accused of Juan Chanay's murder once again faced trial. This time protesters' testimony was heard and each defendant was placed on the bridge. The criminal complaint stated that all fifteen patrollers had fired on the protesters. However, photos taken by Karel Op de Beeck showed that some of the accused were carrying machetes or no weapons at all and could not have shot Juan Chanay Pablo. The prosecution's attorney Julio Arango asked the court to find all defendants guilty under a seldom-used "crime of the multitude" clause in the penal code, arguing that guilt should be shared among them. The court agreed, finding each defendant guilty of "simple homicide" (nonpremeditated murder), and sentenced each to ten and a half years in jail. When army lawyers appealed the sentence, the appeals court reaffirmed the decision but increased the sentence of each ex-patroller to twenty-seven years in jail, appearing to forget that punishment for "crimes of the multitude" is supposed to be distributed among defendants. The decision found them all guilty of killing Juan Chanay, not as accomplices to murder, which might have been the sentence within a justice system that insists on establishing individual guilt or innocence.

The Colotenango case was celebrated as a landmark victory for the victims of state violence in Guatemala. Nonetheless it could also be seen as
another instance in which poor rural indigenous people—in this case civil
patrollers—suffered the brunt of pain and punishment produced by the
armed conflict. In 1982 the army had indiscriminately burned or massacred
whole villages in the guerrillas' zone of operations. Now, through the courts,
the state had collectively and, in a sense, indiscriminately punished a village
paramilitary group, whose voluntary nature could be questioned, rather than
establishing individual responsibility.

A Constitutional Court official told me in 1999 that neither the earlier acquittal nor the guilty verdict had much to do with the facts of the case: "It's
rare to find a magistrate in Guatemala whose decisions stick to the law. Too
often they are influenced by political pressures, by public opinion, or by the
will of the international community, which now reigns in Guatemala." The
army once protected Colotenango's civil patrollers as important elements in
the counterinsurgency; now their function was to show the world that someone would be punished for decades of systematic state terror. But imprisoned
patrollers did not quietly accept this role. Following another Guatemalan tradition for doing justice, they took matters into their own hands.

The Jailbreak

During their lengthy legal process, twelve La Barranca civil patrollers spent
four years in the decrepit Huehuetenango jailhouse until a judge ordered
their transfer to sturdier prisons. Adding insult to injury, he sent many to the
other side of the country, where family visits would be difficult. Family members appealed to human rights authorities in Huehuetenango. The United
Nations' observer mission to the peace process (MINUGUA) arranged a
meeting with the judge so villagers could protest the transfers. But supporters in Colotenango had had enough of protocol; they decided to bust their
neighbors out of jail.

Early on the morning of April 30, 1999, close to a thousand villagers from
Colotenango traveled by truck to Huehuetenango to free their condemned
neighbors. Their timing was remarkable: it was the last day that the jail would
be under the control of Guatemala's notoriously corrupt National Police before the new, better paid National *Civil* Police was to arrive in Huehuetenango. The caravan checked in at the army base, then drove to the center of
town. With prisoners' wives and children leading the way, protestors marched
to the police station and, facing little resistance from the police, liberated
their neighbors from the jail inside. The crowd, with the fugitives in the

middle, marched unmolested through Huehuetenango and boarded trucks for the trip back to Colotenango. There the former patrollers held a tearful homecoming with their families.

What the crowd had done was clearly illegal, but when protesters returned to Colotenango they approached the office of the justice of the peace and asked him to write up an act acknowledging the fugitives' freedom. The judge refused. The incident, however, illustrates how many rural Guatemalans relate to the rule of law: justice is for those who go out and take it, and if the poor want justice, they must organize and gain strength through numbers, as patrol opponents achieved through the CUC and patrollers did by organizing the jailbreak. Furthermore, for village people, few of whom are functionally literate, decisions must be codified in writing, such as by having a judge write an act. Rural communities spend inordinate amounts of time writing acts, an inheritance of a particularly Byzantine form of Spanish colonialism.

To excuse its inaction, the police played to urban fears of the angry peasant mob (see Burrell this volume). Police testimonies described a ferocious crowd, violent and unstoppable. They claimed protesters beat them with sticks, took away an agent's rifle, and broke down the jail door while officers cowered in the bathroom. But police officers showed no bruises and the flimsy chicken-wire door to the cells remained intact. The warden had apparently handed the keys to protesters. At the time, the local police chief was under house arrest for abuse of authority, and few Huehuetecos would have been surprised to learn that the National Police received a bribe to let the prisoners go. Furthermore officers may have felt a debt of gratitude to patrollers: in 1982 rebels killed six urban police in Huehuetenango and neighboring Chiantla, but when the civil patrols formed, the guerrillas' mobility was curtailed and police killings ended (*Noticias de Guatemala*, nos. 79–82).

A United Nations press release repeated a rumor that army soldiers had marched with the demonstrators and actively aided the escape (MINUGUA 1999). While this appears to be untrue, the army did have a column of soldiers patrolling near the jailhouse, part of a plan to dissuade an escape on the eve of the police transfer. When the squad reported the protesters' arrival, the base commander ordered them to withdraw, supposedly to avoid a violent confrontation. Army reinforcements arrived after protestors had left the police station, and threw tear-gas canisters to disperse the crowd, but only once the fugitives were on their way to Colotenango.[12]

The Aftermath

After four years in jail, Colotenango's fugitive former patrollers kept to their mountainside hamlets, lying low, planting corn when the rains began, and trying to put their families back on firmer financial ground. Despite the outburst of press coverage and the existence of Guatemala's new, better-equipped police force, the escapees had little to fear. Police never attempted a recapture.

For many in Colotenango, this was just fine. Patrollers had already done their time, despite what the courts said. Twelve patrollers had each spent four years in jail. According to a local calculus, often repeated to me, "Twelve times four — they already suffered forty-eight years for just one person." Even CUC leaders questioned the appeals court's sentence. "Juridically, sentencing twelve persons to twenty-seven years each is a problem," said Alfonso Morales Jiménez of Tixel. "But in the armed conflict as a whole, the civil patrols committed lots of crimes." His fellow Colotecos, he acknowledged, paid for the sins of the many, even though they were only following army orders. The CUC and other popular organizations, which had protested so many times before, never demonstrated against the jailbreak, which had provided a solution for all concerned: condemned patrollers were free, but power had shifted in favor of the political opposition. Once CUC leaders had been afraid to come to town; now former patrollers were running scared.

For Guatemala's organized Left, Colotenango was a success story. After the December 1996 peace signing, the EGP declared Colotenango its *pueblo simbólico*, and in honor of its civilian martyrs, held its ceremony marking the end of armed struggle in Juan Chanay Pablo's village. In 1997, when guerrillas formally demobilized, Colotenango had one of the highest concentrations of returned guerrilla fighters in the entire country, confirming what civil patrollers had long suspected.

Colotenango's former civil patrol enthusiasts told me they had little desire to return to patrolling and that there was little love lost between them and the army. Juan López Ramírez, La Barranca's patrol commander at the time of the Juan Chanay killing and later head of his village's development committee, told me villagers had served in the civil patrols for their own reasons: "We did it to protect our families, not to protect the army." Ramírez, whose father was abducted and disappeared by the guerrillas in February 1982, denies that ex-patrollers still identify with the military. "They [the army] have their salaries — and us, what did we get? The patrols were not a development project."

In one sense, guerrilla-government peace negotiations had been about each side delivering the goods to its supporters. While ex-patrollers initially got nothing, each guerrilla fighter received a compensation package. International aid flowed to refugees and the displaced, many of whom identified with the rebels. European aid organizations worked in Colotenango villages identified with the CUC, while villages identified with the civil patrols were limited to government development aid.

This postwar bonanza provoked conflicts, and not just between former guerrilla and army supporters. Following a Mother's Day celebration, Xemal's former patrol commander Alberto Godínez was rousted out of bed by a group of drunken men. According to Godínez, they demanded a share of the $700 compensation he had received as a demobilized guerrilla. He refused, and he says the men attacked him with machetes. MINUGUA reported the incident as a politically motivated attack by former patrollers on a former guerrilla. Three young men from Xemal were sentenced to five years in prison for the attack. When I spoke to them in the Huehuetenango jail, they said they had never served in the civil patrol. Two were former guerrilla fighters who never received compensation because they had left the EGP and the Xemal CUC after their fathers feuded with Godínez.

This violent dispute between former guerrillas does not compare with the violence of Colotenango's civil patrols. But in this paper I have detailed different kinds of political violence to understand why patrollers turned on the army's local opponents. To do so, I have also tried to describe the relation between guerrillas and the civilian population. For many years, human rights reporters and others sympathetic to the suffering in Guatemala were loath to mention the guerrillas in too much detail. The army was still in control and its discourse still too threatening. But now the armed conflict is over and former guerrillas and their allies are telling their own histories. After years of army propaganda that demonized them, rebel supporters openly take pride in their militancy.

But after keeping quiet for so long about their guerrilla participation, some do not want to recognize that the years of systematic state and civil patrol violence were, above all, an attack on the guerrillas and their supporters. When I interviewed the Colotenango CONAVIGUA leader María García Domingo, she began by saying, "Here, the army killed us simply because of our culture, the clothes we wear, and the language we speak." Perhaps this is how García presents the conflict to foreign visitors, and I understand why she wants to cast the struggle in this way. But in Colotenango the violence was mainly a product of an army-sponsored assault on the political opposition, one that included both popular organizations and the armed guerrillas that promoted these unarmed resistance groups.

In Colotenango CUC and CONAVIGUA members correctly distinguish their organizations from the armed guerrillas. But to former patrollers, the guerrilla struggle and the struggle for human rights did often appear as one — as in efforts to end the civil patrols — and they were not mistaken in thinking that many CUC members were also guerrilla fighters. In their interpretation of local history, influenced by army propaganda, ex-patrollers felt threatened by the guerrilla expansion in the late 1980s and early 1990s. Tellingly the civil patrols continued longest and were most violent in La Barranca and Xemal and the central town of Colotenango, communities where the guerrillas killed numerous residents in 1982.

The human rights movement that the CUC and CONAVIGUA belong to, and that the guerrillas supported, was crucial in establishing the right to democratic participation for all Guatemalans, not just for rebel sympathizers. There is no necessary contradiction between demanding one's human rights and at the same time supporting an armed struggle for state power. But to understand the violence of the civil patrollers, it is necessary to point out this guerrilla connection, one seldom specified in Guatemala.

Though the civil patrols were created and controlled by the Guatemalan Army, former patrollers make up the bulk of security force members punished for crimes committed during the armed conflict.[13] In Colotenango the army encouraged patrollers to attack the rebels and gave them arms as the war was winding down. It is unclear how often after 1982 the army specifically told patrollers to attack guerrillas' unarmed allies or those who refused to patrol — but that is clearly what the army wanted them to do. When patrollers did use violence, the army protected them, until patrollers no longer served the army's larger strategic interests.

In Guatemala both the army and rebels used rural communities for their own purposes. The army press-ganged a million peasants into the civil patrols and made these unpaid militias the first line of defense against the guerrillas. In Huehuetenango the guerrillas openly claimed civilian participation in their campaigns of sabotage and ambush, helping the army justify its slaughter of unarmed villagers. The EGP attacked unarmed or lightly armed civil patrollers, even as they knew patrollers had little choice whether to serve. That said, the guerrillas' level of abuse and manipulation of civilians never came close to that of the army.

Acknowledging the guerrilla presence helps us comprehend Guatemala's counterinsurgency. But it does not make it defensible. Since the U.S.-

sponsored coup in 1954, the Guatemalan Army, with the support of much of the business and plantation elite, has chosen to deal with political opposition, armed and otherwise, through ruthless and destructive means. Unarmed civilians, both real and potential bases of opposition support, were slaughtered. Survivors were forced into the civil patrols, bringing the costs of the war to bear on Guatemala's most vulnerable population: its indigenous peasantry.

Nevertheless some rural Guatemalans came to see the army and its civil patrols as their salvation. In late 1999 the Guatemalan Republican Front (FRG), whose leadership includes a number of former army officers, swept national elections, even in areas hard-hit by army violence. The FRG used the figure of its founder, Efraín Ríos Montt, the army dictator who expanded the civil patrols throughout the highlands, to gain the rural vote, including the vote of hundreds of thousands of former patrollers. Ríos Montt became the president of Congress.

Meanwhile the guerrillas' political party has struggled in the postwar period. Colotenango has been a rare URNG electoral success story as the CUC and the guerrillas turned their once-clandestine organization into an electoral base. In 1999 Arturo Méndez Ortiz, the lead plaintiff in the Juan Chanay case, ran for mayor of Colotenango on the URNG ticket and won easily. Shortly before Méndez took office, a banner appeared in the Colotenango marketplace. It proclaimed, "We don't want guerrillas in the mayor's office" and listed acts of rebel destruction: the burned buses, the destroyed town hall and bridges. But despite years of antiguerrilla propaganda, many Colotecos continue to identify with the struggle. Méndez and the URNG won reelection in 2003 and 2007, by which time Colotenango's was the only town hall in all of Guatemala controlled by the ex-guerrilla party.

In much of the highlands, villagers appear wary of the guerrilla project and are more focused on migration to the United States. The civil patrol obligation, though missed by few, can still occasionally serve as the basis of rural organization. Throughout the early twenty-first century, former civil patrollers, demanding compensation for their long years of service, frequently shut down the same stretch of Pan-American Highway running through southern Huehuetenango where guerrillas used to ambush army caravans, trying to gain recognition and recompense in the new Guatemala.

Notes

1. This chapter is based on those informal conversations, interviews with members of Guatemala's army and rebel and popular movements, and press and archive sources.

2. *Libro de Defunciones*, Municipalidad de Colotenango, March 11, 1982; author interviews.
3. *Libro de Defunciones*, Colotenango, June 30 and July 4, 1982; author interviews.
4. On July 17, 1982, army troops killed 302 villagers at the Finca San Francisco, Nentón, on the Mexican border north of Colotenango, in one of the biggest massacres of the war.
5. *Informador Guerrillero* 12 (August 1982). The communiqué referred to the supporters as *zapadores*. The EGP appears to have taken this name from the early twentieth-century work battalions in which peasants were subject to military discipline and forced by government authorities to labor on roads and state buildings (Adams 1970; McCreery 1994).
6. The CEH report gave voice to survivors, but received testimonies did not give a complete picture of the violence in Colotenango. Opposition organizations encouraged their members to present denunciations of government atrocities to the UN-sponsored Commission, but their local opponents, including relatives of guerrilla victims, appear to have stayed away. According to guerrilla accounts presented in *Noticias de Guatemala* 85 and 86 and corroborated by Colotenango's *Libro de Defunciones*, EGP killings in La Barranca include those of Sebastián López, Lorenzo Vicente Sánchez, Cecilio Díaz, and Pascual García Gómez (La Barranca's first civil patrol commander). In Xemal reported EGP victims included Marcos Sánchez Godínez, Juan Domingo Morales, Andrés Domingo Pérez and his son, Alberto Domingo López. Alleged EGP victims near the town include Sebastián Pérez, Augusto López Pérez, Antonio García Morales, and military commissioner Rito Gerónimo López and his four sons—Gildardo, Miguel, Santiago, and Antonio. Though the EGP claimed responsibility for the killing of Rito Gerónimo's four sons, the Comité Pro-Paz y Justicia (1983: 223) claimed it was the work of an elite army counterinsurgency force, the *kaibiles*. Between July and September 1982, during the initial formation of the civil patrols, the EGP claimed to have killed between 155 and 180 patrollers or army collaborators in Huehuetenango (*Noticias de Guatemala* nos. 81–86).
7. After the 1986 Constitution prohibited forced militias, the army renamed the civil defense patrols Voluntary Civil Defense Committees, or, in army shorthand *comités voluntarios*. The Huehuetenango army base permitted villages to select their own commanders in a bid to recast this military obligation as a popular community institution.
8. Villagers in Xemal told me the triple killing was the result of a land dispute with neighbors rather than an attempt to force recalcitrant villagers to patrol. However, a land dispute had never caused a triple homicide in Colotenango, and the victims were active in both the CUC and the EGP, lending credence to the claim that the killings were a response to the struggle between patrollers and opponents.
9. This quote and much of the detail for this section come from court testimonies.
10. Residents who live near the bridge told me that the first shots they heard, presumably when patrollers fired their rifles in the air, made a booming sound, as an M-1 or Mauser would, and that subsequent gunfire made a popping noise, as though it came from smaller guns. Other witnesses saw smoke coming from the trees near the highway, suggesting that the bullet that killed Juan Chanay Pablo may not have come from patrollers on the bridge. No bullet was ever found during the autopsy.

11. At roadblocks near Colotenango, police detained a number of men with names similar to those listed on the arrest warrant, none of whom belonged to La Barranca's civil patrol. The two captured La Barranca civil patrollers were released on bond, then escaped to Mexico and never again presented themselves to the court (ODHAG 1993; Inter-American Commission on Human Rights 1994).

12. Breakouts had become a routine part of Guatemala's justice system, even from high-security prisons. The newspaper *elPeriódico* reported that over 130 prisoners had escaped from jails during the tenure of penitentiary system director Joel Torres (July 30, 1999). In early 2000 twenty-seven more prisoners escaped (*Nuestro Diario*, February 25, 2000).

13. Punished former civil patrollers include three from Rabinal, Baja Verapaz, who were sentenced to death but whose sentences were later commuted; those convicted in the death of Tomás Lares Cipriano in Joyabaj, Quiché; Rubén Cruz, who led repression of the Comunidades de Población en Resistencia; and patrollers from San Pedro Jocopilas and Saquillá, Chichicastenango, Quiché.

CHAPTER 9 | *Jennifer Burrell*

AFTER LYNCHING

This chapter is about lynching in Guatemala, particularly one lynching. More specifically, it is based on an ethnographic account of the aftermath of a lynching that occurred in April 2000. In a collection that interrogates how war has been interpolated into everyday life and national visions and shaped possibilities for imagining collective and individual futures, this moment and many others like it provide a basis for understanding the violence of the past in the present and the multitude of contexts in which it is articulated and animated.

On April 29, 2000, Saison Tetsuo Yamahiro, a Japanese tourist, and Edgar Castellanos, a Guatemalan bus driver, were lynched by an angry mob during the Saturday market in the Maya-Mam town of Todos Santos Cuchumatán in northwestern Guatemala. Rumors of an international satanic cult gathering in the nearby departmental capital of Huehuetenango had contributed to a panic that was fueled by local radio stations and word of mouth. In the tense atmosphere that resulted, villagers attacked Yamahiro when he reached out to calm a crying child nestled on his mother's back. Castellanos, who ran away when villagers boarded his bus to look for children they suspected were hidden there, was presumed guilty, caught on the far side of town, beaten, and burned to death.[1]

The death of a tourist, particularly from Japan, a country that figured prominently in the postwar reconstruction effort, focused national and international attention on this lynching in a way that previous incidents over the years had failed to do. In this chapter I place this lynching case within a larger national context while attending to the particularities of this specific incident. Between 1994 and 2001 I spent thirty-four months living in Todos Santos. I was not present for this incident, having left the village just two weeks before. However, sickened by media portrayals of "backward" savages left behind by modernity—these were not the people I had lived and worked with for years—and with deep concern for the townspeople who had shared their lives and opened their homes and worlds to me, I returned several months later to try to understand the complex aftermath of this case. I also returned to address what was, critically, often absent from news and human rights accounts of the incident: I listened to myriad stories told by Todosanteros about what happened and explanations of why it had happened. I also paid close attention to the understandings that people brought to their explanations of the aftermath of the lynchings, an exercise that opened a rich history of long-term community conflicts, their register in the present, and how they figured into imagined futures.

What I found is that in the weeks and months that followed, villagers engaged in a collective process of mourning the victims. As a host of historically rooted grievances and antagonisms circulated in the aftermath of the lynchings, some Todosanteros made a series of strategic choices not only about representing themselves as a community but also perpetuating and strengthening notions of community and shared practices and histories for themselves. Immediately after the lynchings, wooden crosses were erected on the spots where Yamahiro and Castellanos died. Villagers prayed during the week following their deaths, left flowers from their gardens, and lit candles. The public process of mourning culminated nine days later with a mass in the Catholic church during which Todosanteros remembered their Japanese and Guatemalan brothers and vowed that never again would such a thing happen in their town. Following the mass, over Q900 (U.S.$150), the monthly salary of a teacher at that time, was collected for the widow and children of Castellanos, and approximately two hundred people accompanied civil and religious authorities to the place where Yamahiro had died. There they gathered the dirt that was still soaked with his blood, placed it into a wooden casket, and carried it to the cemetery. The ceremony was repeated in the place where Castellanos died.

At the same time, they struggled to make sense of the cooperation of some villagers in state investigative procedures that directly implicated other community members. In the process, a host of past and present grievances that Todosanteros held against each other and the state surfaced, taking new form as they joined the forceful currents of transitional justice and neoliberal governance. The period immediately following the lynchings, they emphasized, was *como el ochenta* ("like the '80s," or during the war) in its arbitrariness and terror; villagers could never be sure whether they might be implicated and called upon by investigators and state functionaries searching for those responsible for the deaths. Just like during the worst period of the civil war, neighbors and family members often found themselves on different sides of the conflict. "We were scared to leave our houses," people told me. One person commented, "I could never have imagined that my family would be involved in such a situation."

At the forefront of the violence that has come to define the postwar period in Guatemala, lynching presents a particular challenge to democratic rule of law and state power. The prevalence of lynching has given rise to a number of explanations—it's barbarism, popular, grassroots, or local justice—that attempt to account for the logic, ambiguity, criminality, and tensions associated with these forms.[2] Lynching is also connected to specific histories of power and struggle in local communities, resurrecting competing versions of events and challenging dominant narratives that have come to inform how the war and the postwar period are understood. While the lynching of Yamahiro and Castellanos in Todos Santos is hardly representative of all lynching in Guatemala, its aftermath provides a way of beginning to understand some of the connections between tropes, hopes, and discourses of transition; realities of neoliberal governmentality; and local contradictions, experiences, and struggles. In this case, I look to a moment infrequently considered in relation to lynchings: What (if anything) happens afterward in places where forms of "popular justice" have been used? I argue that the answer to this question affords us a singular glimpse of one community's encounter with what Sieder refers to as the top-down efforts of "rule of law construction [or strengthening]" in the democracy building that animated the early postwar period in Guatemala (2007: 68).

Postwar Contexts and the Guatemalan State

Between 1996 and 2004 MINUGUA (2004), the UN Verification Mission in Guatemala, recorded 580 incidents of lynching in the country, with more than a thousand victims, of whom 255 died as a result. Many of these incidents have occurred in the areas of Guatemala that were hardest hit by the war, particularly the rural and indigenous western highlands, where the genocidal campaigns of the 1980s were followed by the paramilitarization of villages in the form of civil patrols (see Kobrak this volume; Remijnse 2002). These numbers must be understood within a larger context of postwar crime in Guatemala that has resulted in the highest murder rate in Latin America and one of the highest in the world (Inter-American Commission on Human

Rights 2005). While it is common to argue that people have reached an advanced state of desperation in relation to the rule of law, there is an emerging understanding that this hopelessness extends to deep-rooted structural problems that keep the majority of the population living in poverty, with lack of services like water and power and lack of access to land (Velásquez Nimatuj 2008; Burrell 2010; Nelson 2009b). Crime statistics in Guatemala have skyrocketed from already high levels as the effects of worldwide economic crisis and the slowdown in remittances are experienced throughout the country. The marginalization sown with the failure of redistributive peace and justice is now contributing to an unwelcome harvest of violence.

But the statistics are only part of the picture. Citizen security has also become an overriding concern of all Guatemalans. In addition to rising numbers of separate instances, some commentators suggest that recent cases of lynching often add a new level of brutality to an already cruel form of violence, one wherein townspeople have been known to arrive early with snacks and drinks to witness organized lynching spectacles ("Anatomia de un linchamiento" 2009). Three people were lynched in Camanchaj, Quiché, in January 2009 as close to one thousand people gathered to watch.[3] In December 2009 in Panajachel, Solola a man was beaten to death by a mob for allegedly robbing a vendor of $850 (Escobar 2009). In the resulting standoff between the police and the mob, four police cars were torched and three women, supposed accomplices of the victim, had to be rescued. Just days later, in Huehuetenango, four men were burned alive for a supposed kidnapping. Other incidents have involved victims tied up in barbed wire, dragged by cars, and stoned and beaten by mobs. While a statistical downturn in the number of lynchings in the beginning of the twenty-first century had suggested that antilynching campaigns, local capacity-building efforts, and democracy-training workshops were potentially producing fruit, they have surged once again, with some 119 incidents and forty-seven people killed in 2009 alone and bountiful evidence to support that this upswing continues.[4] This particular harvest of violence now appears to grow increasingly bitter.

When I first wrote about lynching in the immediate aftermath of the Todos Santos incident, I mentioned the difficulty of prosecuting it as a crime and the fact that lynch mobs were historically known to use the anonymity of the crowd to avoid the selection of individuals to stand trial. As a result, authorities were stymied in their attempts to prosecute anyone for these incidents. But this is best considered within a larger national context: only 2 to 3 percent of the perpetrators of any crime, from human rights atrocities to robberies and murder, have been prosecuted since the cessation of the war (GAM

2009). In turn, widespread corruption led to the dismissal of the leadership of the National Civil Police in 2009 and Carlos Castresana, the director of the International Commission against Impunity in Guatemala (CICIG), re-signed following a carefully orchestrated campaign to remove him. Given these contexts, the inability to prosecute or difficulty of prosecuting those who lynch is hardly outside the everyday judicial profile for the country as a whole. Impunity reigns at both the upper reaches of governmental and non-governmental organizations and in daily life. While some observers speculate that at the start of the lynching phenomenon the government failed to take a strong stance because of the initial perception that "lynching was a way to deal with common crimes and the victims were 'just criminals'" (Elton 2000), it is probably true that it became more difficult to seek out individuals for punishment as many Guatemalans began to lose faith in the rule of law. As the CICIG has stated, this failure of the state to bring perpetrators to jus-tice has surely resulted in the state's lacking legitimacy in the eyes of many of its citizens.[5]

Arguments that the Guatemalan state is "weak" or "failed" are frequently at the center of explanations for why people lynch and why lynching has be-come so prevalent. While this may very well be true, exploring lynching in general and the particular case that I discuss here encourages a more nu-anced consideration of this assumption. First, lynchings have occurred in a number of countries in Latin America (especially Mexico, Ecuador, and Bolivia, where people express varying degrees of popular support for the state), usually in marginalized places (although these need not be rural), and often in indigenous communities or areas that have majority indige-nous populations.[6] As Vilas (2003) suggests, in some Latin American coun-tries the terrain of justice is complicated by such factors as competing legal systems, indigenous forms of judicial administration, and the fact that rural populations often feel excluded or ignored by the state. The state's presence across national territory is certainly uneven, but this patchiness should not automatically be equated with weakness. Rather, as Das and Poole (2004) explain, the production of marginalization relative to the state is a mecha-nism of governance. In elaborating the concept of neoliberal multicultural-ism Hale (2005) has shown that it operates with very particular techniques of exclusion and inclusion in Guatemala. Intrinsic to this project are the lim-ited inclusion of cultural rights and the governmental institutionalization of racial ambiguity. As Maya work to build and sustain ongoing movements and economic stability, they are ever vulnerable to the charges of "asking too much" or, as the news articles surrounding the 2000 Todos Santos lynchings case indicated, not being fully worthy of entering modernity. Indeed a common theme in the debates surrounding this case was that lynching a tourist was a vital threat to the economic "goose that laid the golden egg," as the tourism sector was called, and significant government funding immediately thereafter was directed toward international campaigns assuring that Guatemala was safe for tourists (Alonso 2000). Failed or weak states, then, may very well be likened to the "failed" development projects studied by Ferguson (1994) and others that have produced unarticulated but desired goals. While failing in one realm, the Guatemalan state may indeed be prospering in another; for instance, the opening of international markets, the privatizing of publicly owned concessions, increased remittances due to elevated rates of out-migration, soaring wealth concentrated in fewer hands—all of these are consistent with the goals of neoliberalism and the production of neoliberal democracy.

In the aftermath of the lynching in Todos Santos, what became clearer were the kinds and limits of inclusions and exclusions being perpetrated by the postwar transitional state. Crime involving tourists, particularly crime reported in international news outlets (I first read about the lynchings in the *New York Times*, and then my phone starting ringing as friends called to check on my safety), was to be prosecuted and investigated with all the due process of the fledgling rule of law. At the same time, Todosanteros themselves were seen as profoundly outside the flows of modernity. The dominant argument that initially circulated in the media was that Todosanteros, among the most photographed people in Guatemala for their scenic mountain locale and the colorful *traje* (hand-woven traditional clothing) worn by men and women, had lynched because they believed that taking photos robbed the children of their souls. This "explanation" was based on reports by an anthropologist who had lived among them in the 1940s and was conveyed with authority and expertise by Monseñor Victor Hugo Martínez, president of the Episcopal Conference of the Catholic Church. It is unclear whether Monseñor Martínez ever set foot in Todos Santos. Yet by 2000 at least 25 percent of the population, if not more, had already migrated to the United States and many traveled back and forth over the course of each year. People "left behind" in the national-level modernization projects of the striving-to-be-multicultural Guatemalan state were at the epicenter of its hypermodern form of transnationalization. Indeed as rumors circulated in the aftermath about those individuals responsible for the lynchings, several potential suspects left for the United States.

The argument that lynching occurs where the rule of law has failed must also be placed within the larger context of the neoliberal project of decentering law, currently promoted internationally as part of a transnational trend. Sieder (2008: 79) and others have pointed out that while this project has increased the autonomy of some indigenous communities, it simultaneously decreases state responsibility within the legal realm. The onus for compliance with the law then falls to communities, which often enjoy few if any official resources for complying. In Guatemala the peace accords, together with other national legislation and international treaties, created mechanisms for the reestablishment of local forms of power and autonomy.[7] The recuperation and strengthening of indigenous customary law, taking into account Mayan *cosmovisión*, identity, and spirituality, became a linchpin of development and policy efforts relating to the construction of an inclusive legal system, one that recognized local indigenous authority. A central goal of this project was the rebuilding of local political and economic relations destroyed by the war and the recognition that many local institutions and structures of authority had been indelibly transformed by it, as well as by contemporary economic relations and migration.[8] But the mechanisms for achieving this were frequently what Handy has called "good governance as the new panacea" (2004: 560).

Within this evolving legal terrain, the Guatemalan state sought to decentralize power, placing more judicial responsibility at the level of towns. Handy (2004: 559–60) argues that rather than finding a way to comply with the Accord on Identity and Rights of the Indigenous Peoples and the systematic incorporation of local customs and institutions, a "good governance" vision ultimately came to mean the provision of "meaningful" government institutions to rural villages in the form of justices of the peace. These justices, he suggests, *might* have stood a chance at being effective local mediators if they spoke local languages, understood the bases of customary law, or had a grasp on local worldviews. Lacking these, and much else that might have equipped them to work in rural communities, "the medicine was worse than the disease" (Ferrigno quoted in Handy 2004: 560).[9] In her work on Santa Cruz Quiché, Sieder (2011c: 174) demonstrates that the relationship between local justice mechanisms and the state often coexists uneasily, placing indigenous authorities "in a state of permanent legal in-definition," never sure if their actions will be recognized as legitimate by the state or subject to criminal prosecution.[10]

Failed, weak, neoliberal, legally decentralized, or transitional, the state arrived in Todos Santos in the form of mandates, laws and legalities, investigators, and visions of democracy. And in the aftermath of the lynching, villagers did not necessarily turn away from the state, run from it, or seek to undermine it. Rather the state's presence was embraced by many for its potential to address unresolved local conflicts at the village level, some of which had lingered for decades. In the introduction to this volume, McAllister and Nelson ask, following Althusser, if the state remains a site and stake of struggle in postwar Guatemala. In the face of the anonymity granted by lynching and by widespread impunity, Todosanteros actively sought out the state's presence once it arrived and participated in state processes in the aftermath of the lynchings of Yamahiro and Castellanos. They did so because the state held emergent and yet-to-be-realized power—especially in this early moment of postwar promise—to exert forms of authority that Todosanteros envisioned as potentially beneficial. Although scholars of lynching generally view it as happening in the absence of the state, when the state was (eventually) present in Todos Santos, people sought it out and solicited its capacity to promote resolution. This draws our attention to the considerable ambiguity, the range of possibilities, promise, and disillusionment, the always in process yet never quite achievable relations between the state and those it governs. For some people in Todos Santos in particular and Guatemala more generally in 2000, the state-in-transition was a state of waiting, of promise, and of potential as citizens came to project on its imagination a realm of new possibility and hope. For others, it was a tool that could effectively be used in the attempt to address contemporary or historical conflicts and tensions. The state had immediate and tangible meanings, but these meanings were various and disparate.

War and the Ethnography of Aftermaths in Todos Santos

> In [the town of] Todos Santos sixty to eighty people were killed in 1981–1982. The army also burned an estimated 150 or more houses. Many of these houses remained destroyed and abandoned. We were told that the land of people who were killed is generally being used by relatives and not outsiders. Land does not appear to be available to buy, and this shortage may make it difficult for anyone returning from Mexico to buy land.
> **Beatriz Manz, *Refugees of a Hidden War***

Todos Santos is a picturesque and mountainous municipality of approximately twenty-five thousand people. Its historically chronic land shortages have been exacerbated by the steep terrain and the high-altitude plateau that compose much of its physical territory. Due to the subsistence pressures experienced by a growing population, wage-labor migration has been a long-term feature of life, and social divides among those who had land and those who did not dramatically worsened by the 1970s. War came to Todos Santos, as it did to many places throughout the highlands, in 1981. Early in that year, the first group of the Guerrilla Army of the Poor, both men and women, appeared during the Saturday market in Todos Santos. Approximately two thousand people came to listen to their message delivered in the *parque central* (Ikeda 1999: 8). In an act memorialized for generations of students of Guatemala in Olivia Carrescia's 1989 film on the violence in Todos Santos, *Todos Santos: The Survivors*, on March 16, 1982, the guerrillas forced community members to blockade the road with stones to impede the passage of army vehicles. Retribution immediately followed when the army captured six men, then tortured and executed them (CEH Case 5031). During this time the army also placed white-painted stones spelling *Todos Santos* on the mountain face directly across from the town center in order to more easily find it while patrolling the Cuchumatanes by helicopter (Perera 1995: 145).[11]

Thereafter two hundred to three hundred *kaibiles* (elite army operatives) moved in and conducted a swift and devastating campaign in which 150 houses were burned, the vast majority in the hamlet of El Rancho. The guerrilla had been active in this *aldea*, the largest and most heavily populated in Todos Santos. On the way from El Rancho to the town center, the soldiers raped anywhere from five to twenty-five women, some of whom later died from their wounds (Ikeda 1999). On March 23, 1982, the army gathered villagers in front of the church to announce that the entire village would be burned and Todos Santos would no longer be habitable. Adult males were locked inside the church and told that they would not live through the night. Threatened with immediate death if they tried to exit the building, the men waited out the long night; when the first rays of morning light filtered through the stained-glass windows, they realized there were no sounds outside and slowly opened the door. The army was gone. Turning on the radio, they heard that General Efraín Ríos Montt had toppled Lucas García in a coup the previous day and all army units had been called back to their bases.

By July 1982 a rural mayor was appointed, and civil patrols appeared in the town (see Kobrak this volume). The head of the patrol for the first decade was a charismatic community leader skilled at "singing the army's praises and denouncing the guerillas" to his bosses, while advising his patrollers to "look the other way if they encountered non-belligerent guerillas on their patrols" (Perera 1993: 152; Carrescia 1989). While the patrols of Todos Santos largely stayed out of the news, at the end of 1993 the news agency CERIGUA reported charges filed against them for the torture of an alleged former guerilla commander from the town who may have been responsible for the murder of eighty-three residents of the municipality (1993). The patrollers claimed that they had saved the man from near lynching when he returned to the town to survey land available for returning refugees as a member of the Un Permanent Commission on Refugee Status Land Committee.

Amidst a landscape marked by the physical remains of the violence — the rusting hulks of scorched buses and the charred remains of houses — long-standing personal tensions among villagers were politicized in new ways as the counterinsurgency state exerted its control. Warren (2002: 385) writes, "States use a variety of strategies to accomplish these forms of control, yet one commonality in the patterns is the demonization and dehumanization of the Other so that those captured in this category fell outside the routine discourse of moral claims" (2002: 385). Few Todosanteros commented on the war in those years, but those who did often expressed heightened emotions, threatening to boil water and throw it in the faces of their enemies (Perera 1995:146) or cut off body parts of those they felt to be responsible for the suffering of the community (Ikeda 1999). The quality of people's conflicts with one another and the ways they related them were notably more vehement in the mid- to late 1980s, as the longer-term effects of the war were realized. For example, in raising the conflict between Evangelicals and Catholics, an Evangelical man refers to Catholics as "devils with wings" (Carrescia 1989). Hatred for Todosanteros who went to the Ixcán to farm the rich land of that region was close to the surface; by accepting agricultural plots in a place that became a base of support for the guerrillas, these villagers had brought the wrath of the army down upon them all.

Rather than ascribing blame for the death of loved ones to the army or the guerrillas, as occurred in some places, Todosanteros focused on the neighbors or community members who might have been responsible for this fate, and their reasons were embedded in narratives of long-standing conflict, often stretching across generations. Quite frequently, as the epigraph to this section attests, these conflicts were about land and access to it.

It is precisely this knotty history of struggle with each other that emerged in lynching's aftermath as people attempted to account for their participation in the murders of Yamahiro and Castellanos. In one case, Doña Edna,[12] who was already under pressure to sell a prime piece of land, was forced to sell her coveted *milpa* (corn patch) cheaply to pay for a lawyer when she was accused of participating in the lynching by committing acts beyond her physical capability and condition. Wage-labor migrants to the United States, who were linked to the families agitating for the land, purchased it. In another case, Florencia's father was involved in a land dispute with the grandfather of Hernando. Florencia believes that Hernando reported her husband to the army as a subversive in order to get even with him and is therefore responsible for his death in 1982. As a result, some Todosanteros believe Florencia used this opportunity for vengeance by claiming that Hernando participated in the lynching. He was arrested, jailed, and lost his state job, for which he had trained for years. Hernando, in turn, vowed to take his revenge on Florencia, "even if it takes years." In yet another case, a young man was jailed for allegedly providing the gasoline that was used to burn Castellanos, the bus driver. Rumors circulated that someone who had a long-standing grudge against his father had accused him. Another version — corroborated by an independent Japanese tourist staying with the young man's family — attests to the contrary, that this man pulled Yamahiro's sister and father out of the mob and into the safety of his family's house. Undoubtedly the past shapes the forms and textures of violence in the present. But as these examples make clear, the insertion of places in particular neoliberal and postwar contexts shaped the form and framing of violence and of conflict in the present. In this case, the transitional moment was the year 2000, when the shiny promise of economic reform began to tarnish and rising numbers of young wage-labor migrants to the United States created new pressure for land.

In these narratives, years and generations of (not always physical) violence committed by Todosanteros against one another are linked to explain contemporary moments. "Even if it takes years" implies that these conflicts have a simmering life of their own that underlies everyday rhythms. Although some disputes span generations, they become newly consequential and significant in response to contemporary forces in the era after the peace accords and under neoliberal governance. Thus to understand lynching and other forms of violence, we should *also* be looking to the past and to the complexities and struggles of daily communal life, asking, What forces in the present make the past immediately relevant? In the encounter between Todosanteros and the transitional Guatemalan state in the aftermath of the lynching, histories of conflict with each other led people to name local names, which is important insofar as there were representatives of the state to listen and to punish.[13] While state intervention had not been typically sought or encouraged in local matters, individuals used the extraordinary presence of the state, as opposed to its everyday formations, for resolving historical conflicts and local antagonisms, a pattern established at least since the early 1980s.

But while a cascade of historical grievances animated actions within the municipality, Todosanteros venturing outside of it were subject to an increasingly tense environment, one informed by the highly emotional debates about lynching, location, and identity then swirling through the media. At the core of these debates was the dialectic between the country and the city described by Raymond Williams (1975), here overlaid by the ethnic divisions between the largely ladino inhabitants of the capital and the Maya of the highlands, demarcating the profundity of the production of difference undergirding national discourses of multiculturalism. Made visible wherever they went by their distinctive traje (worn by both men and women), Todosanteros were verbally and physically attacked for imperiling the economic well-being of the nation as a whole, for being so backward and uneducated that they lynched a tourist, and for drawing unwanted international attention to the slippages and vicissitudes of the peace process.[14] Authorities and other inmates treated jailed Todosanteros dreadfully. In fact when the first Todosanteros were taken into custody, the warden of the jail where they were held in the department capital of Huehuetenango called for backup, apparently fearing an unruly reaction to their presence in his facility.

One woman recounted suffering verbal abuse and being called a murderer while she waited for a bus in Huehuetenango. She and other Todosanteros, people told her, were responsible for a drop in the national economy. It was their fault that people were unemployed. As another woman remarked when I visited the village in July and August 2000, it may have appeared peaceful in the town, but in the aftermath of the lynching other Guatemalans continued to think terribly of them. She worried about the repercussions for Todosanteros who live outside the community, among them her children, who were studying in distant cities.

By the time I arrived in July, these tales were abundant, told by students traveling to their universities, mothers waiting in doctors' offices, and teachers attending national meetings. Indeed as I waited for a bus to Todos Santos on a street corner in Huehuetenango, I was asked why I wanted to go there, something that had never occurred in the many years I had been visiting and living there. "They are not *buena gente* [good people]," I was told. In addition to these local and national preoccupations, as international media outlets like Univision descended on the town, villagers began to worry about national and even international retaliation, the cessation of aid, and the rupture of relationships built over many decades. In order to gauge the international reactions to the lynching and its aftermath, old friends spent hours individually quizzing me, in my capacity as *tey xuj tkyol* (the Mam-speaking woman who laid her cards on the table by returning when many of the other foreigners were fleeing). What did I think when I heard about the lynching? How did my family, friends, and colleagues, many of whom had visited over the years, react? What did they think of Todos Santos now that tourists had been lynched there? Through these contacts and networks, Todosanteros assessed their social, political, and economic worlds, trying to plot a steadfast course for the future. Indeed in July 2000 I attended an evening meeting at which fifty people were present, an extraordinarily low turnout compared to the meetings I'd observed in the 1990s. The mayor canceled it on the spot, citing a lack of attendance unacceptable for the important planning at hand: setting a community-wide agenda for the coming year as well as a course for envisioning the future. By calling off the meeting, he signaled that he expected, and would insist upon, widespread participation, especially at a moment when community conflicts were once again circulating publicly.

Igniting a State of Panic: Rumors and Postwar Governance

Beware of those in whom the will to punish is strong.
Nietzsche

Panics have their own mechanics, as Roger Lancaster (2008: 45) has astutely observed.[15] At their core are acute states of fear fueled by the circulation of rumor and combined with heady amounts of morality. Indeed "panics" are often "moral panics," mixed as they are with the perception of often ill-defined threats to society, embodied in the scapegoat.[16] Multiple processes of moral panicking and scapegoating emerged around the lynching as villagers attempted to cope with swirling rumors and escalating fear, and the logic these produced. They themselves, in turn, were subsequently scapegoated, becoming the targets of moral and media panic. Todosanteros repeatedly cited the circulation of rumors as central to what happened in the market on the morning of April 29. In the period leading up to the lynching, schools had been closed for several days in Huehuetenango and streets were empty. People feared their children would be kidnapped for ritual use by satanic cults allegedly present in the area. Newspaper accounts accused teachers in Todos Santos of provoking fear and fueling the panic by closing the school; it was later explained that they were attending activities and meetings out of town, absences that had been scheduled for months in advance (Burrell 2000). Teachers are a key political group in Todos Santos, and several recent mayors have risen from their ranks. The accusations leveled against them for fomenting panic and fear also represented a way of challenging the local power they hold. The teachers' contribution to the climate that produced the lynchings was investigated at length, and they were exonerated in August 2000.

Rumors circulate frequently in Guatemala, as they do elsewhere. But only at certain times and in certain places do they escalate from stories of the potential for violence into violence itself. A glance into one of these moments provides us with a sense of the connection that rumors have to the workings of neoliberal power, politics, and governance. I borrow the Nietzsche quote from Lancaster's work, in which he traces out a user's guide to what he calls "the mechanics of panic." Panics, Lancaster shows, often arise in response to "false, exaggerated, or ill-defined moral threats" and the proposal to meet these threats via "punitive measures." When they occur, "moral entrepreneurs" cultivate an acute sense of fear to persuade others that action against a designated scapegoat will "set things right" (2008: 45–46). In what contexts did the stories of satanic cultists, bizarre rites, and child sacrifice resonate and begin to feel immediately threatening to Todosanteros? Rumors having to do with baby snatching, kidnapping, and organ harvesting have a long historical trajectory and circulate with some frequency in Guatemala. Often, foreign, middle-aged women are implicated in them, as was the case in 1994, when two women were attacked by angry mobs in the highlands and the coast (see Adams 1998). This was particularly true in the period leading up to and immediately after the war. Women of this demographic were often in positions of leadership and power in effecting the changes and the development and policy work of this period. Rumors served to undermine their authority by placing them under suspicion. Because of the immediate response that these kinds of rumor generate, they are often thought to be easily manipulated; each time they surface again there are corresponding and often credible calculations about why they gained credence. However, generalizing across all cycles misses how rumors are specifically constituted in particular places and how historical experience makes them threatening. Following the signing of the peace accords, the children of wealthy and not-so-wealthy Guatemalans actually *were* kidnapped for ransom; rates of international adoption increased even as the legitimacy of some adoption agencies was questioned; gangs claimed a distressing number of young people; and women and girls continue to be murdered in a devastating and largely unexamined feminicide. These methods of targeting children followed on the forcible abduction of boys into the army in the late 1970s into the 1980s and the earlier forced removal of children to work on large-scale plantations on the coast.

Rumor and gossip allow people "some measure of joint control over ambiguous stressful situations; they affect the solidarity of a group, creating a public that can then participate in collective action" (Samper 2002: 2). They are also creative endeavors that allow people to negotiate meanings from common histories and experiences (van Vleet 2003). Of the tension in the marketplace in the minutes leading up to the lynching of Yamahiro, Todosanteros told how—due to the rumors and gossip that had circulated in the previous days—some individuals were actively looking for satanists, wondering what they looked like and how they could be identified. They debated potential colors of clothing and styles of hats, but no one had ever seen a satanist before. They ultimately couldn't agree on what they were looking for. Others warned that this conversation itself was dangerous and pursuing it could potentially cause harm to the tourists, many of whom had come in by bus that morning for the market and were shopping, photographing, and wandering the streets. But rumors also snowball, taking on a life of their own and gaining power that, once launched, is difficult to stop. In the telling, people come to develop an understanding of themselves in relation to others and to forms of authority and governance. Often rumors develop in conjunction with confusion about vacuums of power, with uncertainty about who can and will act in relation to potentially explosive situations. If satanists did indeed arrive in the village and attempt to snatch children, Todosanteros understood that they were on their own. There would be no police assistance or intervention, a position that pointed to some stark realities and pitfalls of local "good governance" measures implemented to address the multiethnic, pluricultural, and multilingual promise of the peace accords. In many ways in 2000 Todos Santos represented a community that was attempting to synthesize promises, potential, and the past with complicated new legal contexts and realities. It was difficult, as this lynching and the many others that occurred throughout Guatemala (and Latin America) indicate, to resist the urge to punish when it became clear that neoliberal governance asked communities to undertake such a synthesis without providing the tools for facilitating such a process or clarity as to the manner in which it should be carried out. In this ambiguous terrain, panic, as Lancaster makes clear, was "ever more intricately woven into the basic structure of governance" (2008: 47) and in this place and time, rumor was its handmaiden.

Why, Todosanteros were asked, did this particular cycle of rumors have such an impact in the community when there were no previous incidents focused on tourists? One woman, referring to the wider impact of these rumors in the department of Huehuetenango, replied, "If those who are educated were mistaken, then so are those of us who aren't educated and who don't speak Spanish well. If they were mistaken, so too are we" (quoted in Gutiérrez and Kobrak 2001). Rumors circulated, but only some had traction, embedded as they were in a host of histories and contexts that led to this point. As White notes, "The very act of talking about oneself or others, disciplines" (quoted in Van Vleet 2003: 499). In this sense, as Todosanteros viewed themselves in relation to the state, the region, and local political and economic currents, the moral necessity of self-defense against the potentially advancing (but unknown and hence hidden) enemy was reinforced by circulating rumors and gossip. As events unfolded, it became increasingly difficult to pinpoint who was scapegoating and who was scapegoated. Analogous to how the anonymity of the mob allegedly protects actual perpetrators of lynching, the swirl of rumors unsettled responsibility and problematized accountability, adding additional complexity to the criminal investigation.

Legalities and an Imagining of the Future

In April 2001 the trial for the first three defendants in the Todos Santos case commenced. Their June 2001 acquittal reflected a host of tensions surrounding democracy, law, and citizenship in the post–peace accords era. In the face of pressure to convict, the court, presided over by Judge Josue Felipe Baquiax,[17] concluded that there wasn't sufficient proof or testimony to establish that the defendants incited the mob to commit the lynching. "The state of justice in Guatemala is being consolidated," Judge Baquiax told reporters after the verdict was read. "We simply couldn't condemn these people" (Reuters, June 26, 2001). Among the factors that the judge cited in his decision was the issue of parents' fear for their children, declaring that the frightened screams of Catarina Pablo, the mother of the crying child Yamahiro reached out to comfort, were a natural, suitable, and acceptable reaction for any mother who felt her child was in danger. This decision may have been couched in racial hierarchies about the presumed naturalness of the indigenous subject (see de la Cadena 1995).

At the time, I read Baquiax's verdict as placing the Todos Santos case firmly within the national "good governance" project of the postconflict Guatemalan state, pointing to the precarious nature of justice, citizenship, and the law at a critical moment. I viewed this as notable because of the particular characteristics of the state in transition and because of the dynamic nature of the notion of citizenship itself—a category with a social content that is contested and constantly subject to renegotiation and reinterpretation (see Sieder 2001: 203). But the perspective of hindsight also shows that the Todos Santos lynching case and its outcome were very much representative of what Sieder cites as popular expectations of justice versus recourse to courts: the former demands "immediate incarceration of the accused or public sanction and repentance," while the latter involves "the release of the accused for lack of evidence or on bail" (2008: 83). It is, however, significant, regardless of the outcome, that a verdict was reached in this case at all within the national context, where minute percentages of all cases across the board are actually tried. However, by its very nature, the postwar, postconflict state is defined by what came before it, that is, war or conflict, and this is used to ask citizens to exchange their immediate rights in return for rights in a theoretically democratic and hence better future. The combination of transition and the neoliberal outsourcing of legal responsibility and judicial administration has produced a peculiarly rights-less citizen asked to bear with the challenges and hardships of the present as an investment in a better national future.

By the time Baquiax's verdict was announced, few Todosanteros seemed to have kept up with the process or knew what actually happened to the three defendants and the original group of nine who were taken into custody. Indeed when I asked what was happening with these people just several months after the lynching, answers were vague. I was told that six of the defendants had been able to raise money to buy their way out of jail. When I asked whether they would be standing trial in the future, most people seemed to think that they had bought their way out of the situation once and for all, an understanding consistent with their experiences with the justice system. With enough money, I was told, anything could be resolved. The three who ultimately stood trial were supported throughout their incarceration by visits from family, who brought them food and other supplies. Todosanteros' disengagement with the law points to a profound sense of marginalization from legal processes of the state, one that by this point is felt by many if not most Guatemalans. However, marginalization, as Poole insists, is a powerful technique precisely because the margin "is *both* a real place . . . *and* a discursive and ideological position from which people learn how to speak about things like justice to the state and among themselves" (2004: 36). It is in this space that the alternatives that people draw upon flourish. Without a doubt, these include lynchings, reparamilitarization of villages (Burrell 2010), the increase in numbers of rural and urban gangs (Manz 2004; Burrell 2009, 2010; Levenson this volume), and debt migration. But also present is the fluorescence of Mayan community-strengthening efforts, including the revitalization and recuperation of various aspects of indigenous and customary law and, with them, the possibility for a future in which these are the primary methodologies by which people negotiate everyday life and legalities. As Sieder has demonstrated for the case of Santa Cruz Quiché, these forms operate in a complicated nexus with the state in that they seek to construct an indigenous authority as autonomous from the state, while also desiring "to transform the Guatemalan state, and to be part of it" (2011b: 178).

In conclusion, a harvest of violence forces people to contend with history, as this and many chapters in this volume show. But the headlong rush into the future often conceals the presently active engagements that people have with their past(s). This volume begins by asking "Where were you in 1992?" and "Where were you in 1999?" to pinpoint dates that have particular historical significance for the history of Guatemalans and of Guatemala. In Todos Santos we might ask, "Where were you on April 29, 2000?," the day that lynching shifted the social, economic, and political landscape in ways that are only now making themselves known. On that day, tourism, humble as it was, became less of a viable option.[18] Certainly, more people began to migrate, although many factors already emergent at the time of the lynching contributed to that outcome. Perhaps most significantly, as a complex relationship with the state and its limits was articulated through investigatory processes and prosecution and the effects that these did or did not produce, Todosanteros began to generate new local forms of power, governance, and justice.

Notes

1. This account of what happened is constructed from interviews conducted in July and August 2000.
2. See, for example, Mendoza and Torres-Rivas 2003; Kobrak 2003; Guttiérez and Kobrak 2001; Snodgrass Godoy 2002, 2004. The blog Linchamientos en Guatemala (http://linchamientos.blogspot.com) by Carlos Mendoza is an exhaustive compendium of debate and thought on lynchings in Guatemala and elsewhere.
3. One survived beating and burning and recounted the horror of watching as flames engulfed his body in the moments before he lost consciousness. He spent the next six weeks in agony before dying ("Anatomia de un linchamiento" 2009).
4. In a December 2009 report, Grupo de Apoyo Mutuo (GAM) provided statistics from the Guatemalan Supreme Court: by the beginning of December, there were forty-four deaths and 151 injured by lynching in 2009; in 2008, eight deaths were reported and 102 injured. Data compiled by Carlos Mendoza (http://linchamientos.blogspot .com, April 26, 2010, visited June 10, 2010) from the Ministerio de Gobernación, Unidad de la Información Pública from Policía Nacional Civil statistics indicate forty-nine deaths by lynching, 1 percent of a total of 6,498 violent deaths in Guatemala in 2009. The departments with the highest number of lynchings were Huehuetenango, with fourteen (six in the departmental capital) and Guatemala with eleven.
5. See http://cicig.org (visited Aug. 18, 2010).
6. Vilas (2003), Fuentes Diaz (2004), García (2004), and Goldstein (2003, 2004) are among those who have written about lynching in Mexico, Bolivia, and Ecuador.

While there may be hundreds of lynchings each year in Guatemala, none have been reported in its postwar neighbor, El Salvador, nor in Honduras, for example.

7. The Accord on the Identity and Rights of Indigenous People, signed in March 1995, contained the most important acknowledgments of the value of local knowledge and traditional judicial mechanisms relative to the national legal system. This Accord recognized a Maya worldview based on culture and land and acknowledged the presence of traditional juridical systems that were essential elements of social regulation and daily life in indigenous communities, part of the maintenance of their cohesion (IDIES 1999: x). On customary law, the Accord reads, "In applying national laws and regulations to the peoples concerned, due regard shall be paid to their customs or customary laws. These people shall have the right to retain their own customs and institutions, where these are not incompatible with fundamental rights defined by the national legal system and with internationally recognized human rights. . . . The methods customarily practiced by the peoples concerned for dealing with offenses committed by their members shall be respected" (Article 8).

8. In the attempt to implement and recuperate indigenous forms of law and authority, local indigenous leaders have been encouraged to experiment with new forms that can then be implemented locally. The vast bulk of this work is performed through linkages with international and national NGOs. See, for example, Sieder 2011b; Kalny 2010.

9. This, however, is not to imply a wholesale rejection at all levels of the legal-judiciary system: human rights training and democracy-building initiatives have had some influence on the local level, and indigenous groups increasingly turn to courts to defend collective and human rights. For different perspectives on this, see Sieder 2011a, 2011b; Ekern 2008.

10. Deborah Poole's (2004) work in Ayacucho refers to this conundrum as "between guarantee and threat," a liminal zone for indigenous authorities.

11. These stones were repainted in the mid-1990s, before the dissolution of the civil patrol, but in recent years they've become less readable. Occasionally well-meaning tourists attempt to organize projects to repaint them, clearly oblivious to their history and meaning.

12. All names have been changed.

13. I draw upon a literature that refers to the state as a domain that becomes knowable through everyday contact with state institutions and representatives. These include outposts like schools, health clinics, and post offices that impart nationally mandated order and discipline—particular ways of doing and knowing that constitute techniques of governing and complicate the conflicting pulls upon modern states between demands for good governance and increasing securitization. See, for examples, Abrams 1988; Joseph and Nugent 1994; Trouillot 2003.

14. Particularly as this peace process had been labeled such a success and one to emulate. Nelson quotes the attaché to the U.S. Embassy in Caracas, "Guatemala is our big success story" (2009b: xviii).

15. Nietzsche, *Thus Spake Zarathustra*, quoted in Lancaster 2008: 2. In the formulation of this section, I am heavily indebted to Lancaster's impressive work on contemporary sex panic and suburbia in the United States.

16. Lancaster draws attention to the deliberate attempt to reshape social relations often

at the center of moral panics, and in this sense their similarity to "social revitalization movements" that also seek to address "some real or perceived condition of moral decline and social disrepair" (2008: 45).

17. Baquiax went on to write an analysis (2003) and in 2009, in his capacity as the president of the Tribunal de Sentencia de Quetzaltenango, came under CICIG investigation with thirty other lawyers who, in 2007 and 2008, studied for master's degrees in *derecho penal* at the University of Seville. CICIG Commissioner Carlos Castresana accused the businessman and lawyer Roberto Lopez Villatoro of facilitating this in return for favors to be granted by the judges in their local capacities or in his reelection campaign (López Ovando 2009).

18. International press coverage and mention of the lynching in the *Lonely Planet* guidebook (the tourist's Bible) have severely reduced the number of visitors. Massive migration has somewhat made up for this loss but carries its own forms of sacrifice.

LABOR CONTRACTORS TO MILITARY SPECIALISTS TO DEVELOPMENT EXPERTS
Marginal Elites and Postwar State Formation

As I finish this chapter the impunity that has formed the foundation of contemporary state-society relations in Guatemala is becoming less sustainable as several generals are finally brought to trial. However, insecurity, generalized violence, and economic, social, and environmental vulnerability increasingly affect almost every Guatemalan, while forms of structural and political violence that have endured for centuries find new expression in economic crisis and the state's ineffectual and often repressive responses to citizen demands. The fieldwork on which this essay is based, however, took place at a moment when it seemed things might turn out otherwise. At the end of the 1990s many Guatemalans had staked their hopes on the "transition to democracy." The peace accords and new policies favoring decentralization and local development seemed to promise the end to long-standing patterns of violence.

This was also the moment of the foreign aid boom for development and peace, which saw more than a hundred new national and international NGOs established, offering services that, until then, had been the state's responsibility. In retrospect, it seems clear that the *poder local* (local power, the buzzword of the time) so enthusiastically implemented by the NGO-ization of the peace process was based on a perceived opposition between a violent, inefficient, wasteful, and corrupt state and the culturally relevant, politically responsive communitarian democracy of local structures. The surprising thing about this naïve notion of poder local was its willingness to ignore the deep local legacies of war, specifically the culture of violence, authoritarianism, and

impunity that permeated the apparently "untouched" Mayan highlands—
even as truth commissions, in a parallel peace process, busily documented the
acts of massive and extreme violence perpetrated not only by the army but
also by local military commissioners and civil defense patrols. The resulting
blindness to the deep tensions that structure "the local" means that millions
of dollars in aid have been invested in local development and empowerment
projects that often actively support the persistence of authoritarianism, political clientelism, corruption, nepotism, and a varied repertoire of destructive governance practices in indigenous communities.

In this essay I argue that the failures, deficiencies, and bad practices now
imputed to the personal failings of those placed in charge of the newly decentralized institutions of the state are in fact predictable responses to the
generalized application of state-building formulae that ignore histories of
violence and conflict, as well as the political culture of those identified as
leaders. The organizational structures of these "new" forms of government
in post-genocide Guatemala were established with little consideration of the
vast social, cultural, and economic differences across the national territory or
the need to develop the human, economic, technical, and administrative resources and capacities required to serve their intended purpose of responding to local populations. The introduction to this volume asks, "How could
all the labor (and money) put into processing peace, creating a culture of
dialogue rather than violence, empowering those most affected by the war—
indigenous people, women, and the poor—have produced so little of value?
Why does war persist in Guatemala's postwar?" In this chapter, I offer some
answers to those questions. I also show why the influence trafficking, illegal
commerce, summary violence, and impunity that imperil these "democratizing" political reforms are not external forces ("bad apples") but rather are
built into the structures themselves.

In San Bartolomé Jocotenango (San Bartolo hereafter), a poor and marginal K'iche' municipality in the Quiché, the violent matrix of the armed
conflict reworked social practices derived from the unjust and fraught
nineteenth-century project of modernization through export agriculture to
serve the project of counterinsurgent state formation (González 2002). Postwar development projects designed to redress Sanbartoleño wartime sufferings fail to address the origins of these practices and ultimately serve to consolidate the power and wealth of the same indigenous militarized merchant
elite responsible for wartime violence at the local level. The sobering case of
San Bartolo, I argue, exposes the deeply repressive foundations on which the
(re)design of the postwar Guatemalan state was established. It also suggests

that the formal divisions between the state, the economy, and society disintegrate under empirical scrutiny, demanding that we rethink what it means to re-form a state—one that has always served as an instrument of inequality, militarization, and violence—only through formal structures of governance.

From the *Finquero* to the Counterinsurgent State

During the second half of the nineteenth century, *finqueros* (large landholders) and the authorities directing the few state institutions present in a geography dominated by the plantations, collaborated to organize San Bartolo, like other municipalities on the periphery of the highlands, as a *finca de mozos* (worker farm) that would provide labor to the coffee, and eventually cotton and sugar, plantations of the Boca Costa and the Pacific coast. Sanbartoleño memories of the armed conflict are interwoven with this longer history of the dispossession and privatization of their communal lands at the hands of local ladino elites, as well as with their subsequent obligations to perform different kinds of precariously remunerated labor. Most of the men I interviewed remembered the inequities and illegalities implicit in the procedures for contracting (or "dragging," *jalando*) workers to the fincas in the hot and disease-ridden lowlands and the "forced" or "free" (*de puro gratis*) labors imposed on them at home by the authorities. San Bartoleños who participated in opposition movements in the 1960s and 1970s grounded their arguments for joining church, peasant, or guerrilla organizations in memories of an unjust and unequal finquero world. In their recollections, these injustices were intimately linked to the persecution, murder, and generalized destruction carried out by the army and the civil patrols in their communities after 1981. They also insisted that the magnitude and extension of the violence visited upon them by the state—in both the distant and more recent past—was terrifyingly difficult to understand because they were so out of proportion to their demands for justice.

K'iche' people made and continue to make moral claims through such oppositional organizing based on a past shaped by inequities, racism, and violence. Here, however, I examine those against whom these claims are directed: the local *indigenous* agents of the Guatemalan military, including military commissioners, specialists, and civil patrol commanders. I explore how they understand and legitimate their loyalties to finqueros and state authorities, especially the army, and the power and authority they gain thereby. First in relation to the plantations, then more directly in relation to the state, these men were charged with enforcing order and discipline in their municipalities. How did these actors articulate their long-standing economic and political interests through the responsibilities and tasks of counterinsurgency to create spaces in the post-genocide period for political and economic action in full enjoyment of impunity? Conscientious and meticulous ethnographic analysis of their strategies for performing this articulation reveals the different ways in which the state's disciplinary and regulatory policies molded local lives. It also provides a leverage point for critiquing the intimate connections between the older authorities and institutions of the finquero state and those empowered to configure the counterinsurgent, and now neoliberal, state from its margins. How do generalized political violence, authoritarian regimes, and emergent powers configure what people understand as community and community leadership? And given such leadership, what are the possibilities for the oppositional projects many Sanbartoleños have nurtured since the nineteenth century?

In the 1960s and 1970s in San Bartolo, as in many other highland communities, a significant group of young men reacted to the unbearable situation they faced as laborers forced to perform "free work." They joined prayer groups organized by Catholic Action, consumer and credit cooperatives, community improvement committees, local political groups affiliated with the Christian Democrats or peasant organizations, and eventually (in some cases) clandestine committees within the Guerrilla Army of the Poor (EGP). From these different, more or less leftist perspectives, some Sanbartoleños began to question the authority of a group of strongmen they identified as *los meros jefes del pueblo* (the *real* town bosses) or *los meros tenazudos* (the real tough guys) who had always decided who would be named to the posts of mayor and other municipal offices and otherwise openly exercised their influence in local political and judicial matters. This local elite was composed of K'iche' men with long histories working as *contratistas* (labor contractors) for the fincas, as well as merchants, bar owners, military commissioners, and mayors. The 1960s cotton boom further empowered these men to govern the municipality as a typical finca de mozos, existing principally to provide cotton plantations on the Pacific coast with seasonal migrant labor.

In the late 1970s the opposition groups converged in a movement against the unpaid duties entailed in serving as *alguaciles* and against obligatory labor on a road connecting San Bartolo with the departmental capital Santa Cruz del Quiché.[1] The leaders of this movement questioned the legitimacy and even legality of the authorities who forced them to labor without pay. They argued that these authorities had been designated arbitrarily by military commissioners rather than community consensus and that they exercised undue influence in municipal affairs in order to advance their own interests. In their first action, in 1977, they protested in front of the mayor's office and refused to work. In response the mayor arrested three of the leaders and made overt threats against other participants. But on this occasion imprisonment, which had been illegally applied since the end of the nineteenth century to intimidate nonconformists and repress protest movements, inspired further mobilization among Sanbartoleños, radicalizing their critique of the old system. The movement's leaders sought legal advice from the national institutions they had been working with and made contact with lawyers working for an NGO founded by Christian Democrat cooperativists, who brought legal charges against the mayor. This gambit worked, exposing the anomalies in municipal administration and forcing the departmental authorities to free the prisoners, abolish the position of alguacil, and end the demands for unpaid work on the highway.

This victory surprised the mayor and angered the men who, until then, had governed the municipality with little opposition. But it also had unintended consequences for the victorious opposition groups. Looking back, many participants now feel that their success in making legal demands provoked a critical shift to new and more intensified forms of illegality in municipal politics, because thereafter the meros jefes strengthened their ties to the army base in Santa Cruz del Quiché. In particular, the men serving as military commissioners received special training from the army, learning to write blacklists—the first headed by the names of the movement's leaders—and then carrying out their first overtly repressive actions.

Meanwhile those Sanbartoleños who sympathized with the EGP had radicalized their own position. Between August and November 1981 they carried out the first acts of guerrilla propaganda in the community, killing Angel Barrios, a member of one of the old ladino families that had benefited from the liberal expropriation of the municipality's communal lands and run a money-lending trade thereafter. Then EGP supporters attempted to assassinate the chief of the military commissioners and the mayor but only managed to kill the three men who accompanied them. Sanbartoleños identify this as the moment when persecution and massacres began to be generalized throughout the municipality. It was "the start of a time of darkness and death."[2]

These actions coincided with the launch of a major offensive by the army's Iximché Task Force, headed by General Benedicto Lucas García (brother of the military president) against the civilian population located in the area of operations of the Augusto César Sandino Front of the EGP, which covered northern Chimaltenango and southern Quiché. The area became a staging ground for months of massacres, pillage, and destruction. In San Bartolo the offensive began in October 1981 and ended in February 1982, leaving the hamlets of Sinchaj, Tacachat, Xoljuyup, and Las Canoas in ashes, their residents murdered or on the run. These massacres were carried out by uniformed troops joined by civil patrollers from the municipal town center and from the hamlets of Mulubá and Los Cimientos. The local operations of the campaign were delegated to the municipality's military commissioners. In a second offensive, between March and April 1982, these forces perpetrated more massacres, burning down houses and forests in the targeted hamlets, while the families who had previously taken refuge in the mountains were bombed and persecuted. The wives of men who had been killed or had fled were subsequently taken to the military base or to "women's houses," where they were systematically raped and obliged to work as servants to the soldiers. My understanding of what the subsequent decades of militarization of San Bartolo has meant for the daily lives of the majority of its residents is deeply informed by these women's memories.

Interests and Dividends of Counterinsurgency: The Merchants' Association

After 1981 the old military commissioners took over the local military base and the leadership of the recently formed Civil Defense Patrols. As part of the new counterinsurgency strategy implemented after the 1982 Ríos Montt coup, they received intensive training at the Santa Cruz military base and were promoted to specialist sergeant majors in the Civil Affairs (s-5) unit. Their task was to give concrete local form to the ideas, plans, and directives of the national counterinsurgent project. They were expected to draw on their intimate knowledge of the thoughts and visions of their neighbors to design the best means of persecuting them as the enemy. The promotion to specialist also meant a higher salary and prestige. For these men, therefore, fulfilling their military responsibilities almost always coincided with serving their personal interests: they were not only paid well but were officially sanctioned in stigmatizing, exiling, or even killing any and all opponents, which enabled them to consolidate their authority and power within the community.

Between 1981 and 1983 the military's strategy of scorched-earth destruction followed by sweeps through the countryside to recover and resettle the populations who had escaped focused on reordering local territories and everyday lives in the communities, an aim that also benefited the local militias who carried out these operations. In San Bartolo everyone I interviewed, including various former civil patrol leaders, made reference to the violent practices for self-enrichment carried out by men close to the army. Everyone could recall numerous cases of ordinary peasants who were "not involved in anything" but who were persecuted by local militia members in order to steal their property. For example, a woman whose family enjoyed a comfortable level of subsistence remembered, "The main head of the San Bartolo commissioners came personally to take the cows. He took eleven cows, seven chickens, six of those big turkeys, six *quintales* [six hundred pounds] of peanuts, ten *quintales* of beans, a truck full of corn. Since my father had planted quite a bit of corn, he came back with ten men and harvested everything my father had sown. Then he took it in a truck and sold it." Military commissioners and civil patrol leaders accumulated significant capital by appropriating and selling the harvests, animals, and material goods of the neighbors they murdered. Those they left alive had no recourse to being robbed, as these men and their army patrons were the only law. Years after the war, the inventories Sanbartoleños made of the belongings that had been stolen from them during military operations and the impoverishment this dispossession had caused made a dramatic contrast with the rapid enrichment the meros jefes achieved during those years. The pillaging that militarization enabled thus set in motion new dynamics of social and economic differentiation.

The meros jefes invested the capital they had accumulated in setting up grocery stores in the municipal center as San Bartolo, historically a town with little or no commercial activity, became a town of "well-stocked stores." Then they expanded, opening grocery and sundries stores in Guatemala City, Escuintla, and Amatitlán. The list of the municipality's principal merchants and those who managed to set themselves up in the capital coincides precisely with that of the former mayors, specialists, *contratistas*, military commissioners, and civil patrol leaders. One of these men explained, "The first man to get started in this business was Don . . . [a specialist sergeant major]. He began in 1982 or 1983, now he has eleven stores in the capital. My son-in-law also has a business and now he owns some vehicles as well. I also have my businesses in the capital. I have three stores."

According to a former civil patrol leader who is a member of the local Merchants' Association, to set up a store in the 1980s one needed start-up capital of between Q20,000 and Q30,000 (at a time when the quetzal was on par with the U.S. dollar). Making the business work also demanded understanding the networks of distribution and consumption in the poorer neighborhoods of the capital city or the southern coast and acquiring one or two bright young men (*patojos chispudos*) who could work in the store. These patojos had to be controlled with an iron fist to make sure they wouldn't steal or "laze around [*que no hueviaran*]." Every few months they would have to be rotated so that they wouldn't get any "bad habits" or "ask for silly things [*babosadas*]" like respect for workers' rights. This merchant had been a contratista in the 1970s, so the system of work he established in his store was based on the old concept of the foreman used on the fincas since the nineteenth century to mediate servile labor relations between the indebted worker and the boss or the lender who had "dragged" him in.

With the establishment of the civil patrol system, Sanbartoleños not only lost what they had gained in the 1977 struggles against forced labor but were also faced with newly stringent state demands on their time, increasing the risks they faced along with the number of tasks they had to perform and the time required to carry them out. In the municipal town center, local military agents organized patrollers into squadrons of eight, who patrolled both day and night. There was no space for arguing about the tremendous difficulties these demands entailed. When told, "Get to work!," all they could do was obey. In 1992 the civil patrol leaders transformed this obligation into a new means for extracting wealth from their victims by establishing fines for all men who missed a turn because they were sick or had left town to work on a finca or in a store in the capital. Each absent patroller had to pay Q2.50 for a missed day or night, or Q5 for missing both, although the frequency of assigned turns depended on the community. One man explained to me, "Now in San Bartolo [the municipal center] they are charging Q20 for a turn of two nights and three days. In other communities people pay Q2.50 for the night and in others Q5 for the night and day." Sanbartoleños who understood the "turn charge" as illegal and as a way for civil patrol leaders to openly extort other men in the community could no longer find external support for protesting such measures. The national-level allies they had counted on in the 1970s had been eradicated by the war.

In the 1990s those who had managed to enrich themselves through these forms of coercion organized the Merchants' Association, ostensibly to reactivate the traditional town fiesta but also to ensure that their chosen candidates would be appointed as mayors of the municipal government. To clean up their rather stained image and legitimate their control over the community, the army specialists and patrol leaders presented themselves as magnanimous philanthropists who could both finance festivities for the community and ensure the goodwill of the armed forces, transforming the town's anniversary into a space for representing and celebrating the military-backed power of the meros jefes. Conveniently it also served as a space for proselytizing the virtues of this group's mayoral candidates with the post-1986 return to "democratic" governance. The Association developed a strategy to wield power a bit more subtly by naming as mayor men who were not too burned by participation in the worst acts of wartime violence, on the condition that they remain loyal to the Association and to the armed forces. The choices offered for mayoral elections in San Bartolo thus depended on prior agreements among the leaders of the Association, the civil patrol leaders, and the army. One ex-mayor provided an example of the power the Association wielded over this process: "The decision was made exclusively by the Merchants' Association. Only they can say who will govern San Bartolo."

Establishing the Bases of the Postwar State: Security and "Development"

Militarization served to consolidate the wealth and power these men had accumulated through prewar mediations with the fincas. Distressingly, so did peace. The end of war brought a flow of outside wealth into the municipality in the form of development funds, a process that actually began in the mid-1980s. In April 1982 the army inaugurated its National Plan for Security and Development, also known as the Maximum Priority Action Plan, which proposed to "strengthen community organization and support to communities through local development programs, as a tactic for combating the guerrilla" (AVANCSO 1990: 94). The counterinsurgent strategists who elaborated the plan explained that the causes of "subversion" were heterogeneous but could be traced to social injustice, local political rivalries, uneven development, and the social dramas of hunger, unemployment, and poverty (Schirmer 1998: 87). But only *after* massacres and "softer" methods of pacification and psychological warfare conducted under the rubric of civil affairs had prepared the population for the state's interventions could these pressing human problems be addressed (Schirmer 1998: 110).

Comparing the tenets of this plan with the patterns of violence lived out in San Bartolo suggests the municipality served as a virtual model for its application, down to the last detail. During the period of destruction and death, the army and local allied forces killed or exiled the opposition and systematically prevented the formation of new leaders, organizations, or channels for community participation that would have opened spaces for even minimal autonomy. This successfully foreclosed the stirrings of demands for municipal revitalization and attempts to create new strategies for community development that had begun in the 1970s. Meanwhile the military put its local agents, the meros jefes, in charge of the new security and development strategy at the local level. In addition to leading the civil patrols and the municipal government, those with the strongest ties to the army administered all public and private business carried out in the municipality. When civilian governments began to implement projects through the Municipal Inter-Institutional Coordinator and new local Committees for Peace and Development, in San Bartolo the same local military agents controlled these new projects and activities. As a local state official told me, "It was the same *babosada* [trick] with a new name." What could change if the same people and the same paramilitary structures were in charge?

Training by army technicians and specialists gave the former military commissioners and civil patrol leaders the basic skills required to apply for and implement development projects, which they in turn used to present themselves to NGOs and foreign funders as representatives of their communities—including speaking for those community members who were victims of their own violent rule. Under the name of "improvement committees," which were accredited by the departmental government, they legitimated their leadership and thus their ability to administer development projects. For example, we see the direct intervention of the meros jefes in San Bartolo's UNICEF-financed Municipal Plan for Social Development, 1994–2000, whose first appendix lists the names of the ninety-one people involved in articulating the municipality's needs and establishing its future priorities. One hundred percent are men. Thirty-three represent security forces, including twenty-two patrol leaders, nine police officers, and two army specialists. The remaining fifty-eight are hamlet-level civil patrol leaders or military commissioners representing their local development committees. Nowhere is it explained why working groups on activities described as "strengthening internal community organization" or "gender inclusiveness" fail to include a single woman, nor why persons or groups in the community who are considered undesirable by the army are absent from the consultative process. No reference is made to the strict surveillance of all aspects of municipal life during that period nor the severe limits this placed on the participation of the supposed beneficiaries.

In their guise as leaders, local authorities presented themselves to NGOs, religious organizations, and civilian governmental agencies as those best able to "strengthen local power" and promote municipal development. When an official or technical advisor from one of the donors would ask to meet the beneficiaries of a given project to see what degree of "community participation" they entailed, these meros jefes would use their multiple connections (as employers, moneylenders, mayors, patrol leaders, fiesta organizers, etc.) to invite "their" people to assemblies, for example, asking the leaders of hamlet-level patrols to bring their patrollers—along with their wives and children—to create the image of a community that respected gender equality and worked collectively for development. In these assemblies the spokesmen or intermediaries between the officials and "the community" were normally men who were leaders of the civil patrols.

Development initiatives in the 1980s also centralized the decisions, management, actions, and resources of the committees for improving roads, building schools, installing electricity or water, and running the town fiesta under the Inter-Institutional Coordinator, presided over by the commander of the local military base, which also ran the more local rural development councils. According to one base commander, "Any plan, project, or initiative for community improvement needed the army's approval." Formally the mayor was in charge of seeking out and administering development projects, but he had to heed the orientation provided by the army's civil affairs unit and the military commissioners and patrol leaders. When I asked one mayor what his development work entailed, he made few bones about military influence over municipal affairs: "I have my advisors, and if I don't do something that comes from up there they'll say to me, 'Hey you, what happened? Why aren't you doing what we agreed? We made you mayor so you'd take care of our people!' . . . I'm basically the person who executes the project. I receive the money and carry out the project, but it's really all up to the Rural Development Council." These "orientations" came not only directly from "above" but also through and from the Merchants' Association, which helped shape the kind of projects "its people" needed. Within this logic, the important thing was to request the project and learn how to comply with the requisites imposed by the donors' bureaucracy, filling out the forms properly, and shuffling the necessary papers back and forth.

Development projects thus strengthened vertical tendencies in the local exercise of power and expanded the margins of arbitrariness and corruption in municipal administration and in the management of resources supposedly destined to alleviate the devastating effects of state violence. After the signing of the peace accords, these same men took control of the municipal councils for urban and rural development, administering the resources designated for "peace" and the 8 percent of the national budget delegated to the municipalities for implementing decentralized development projects. As a bonus, they also learned to manage projects implemented through the Social Funds of the World Bank.

"Development" as War by Other Means

The concept of "development" guiding the work of these newly minted local experts had its roots in the ideas about modernity and urbanism that the army had promoted in its infamous Development Pole villages. This framework privileged the construction of infrastructure and cement-block buildings, along with cosmetic projects aimed at mitigating the image of backwardness and exclusion of indigenous municipalities. These included reactivating the town fair, organizing and funding a military parade, establishing a new Baile del Convite (the Invitation Dance, which is not a traditional part of the festival and is associated with ladino celebrations), and other civic acts sponsored by the Military Zone that could be broadcast on television. Until 1996 most of these projects were carried out through the "forcivoluntary" labor of the civil patrollers. One of the mayors and patrol leaders of that period told me, "That's how I built eight schools! I'd come to the community and say, 'Gentlemen, that's it, you're going to have to work on our projects. So get to work!'" The concept of development and the working methods of this mayor also link his experience as a foreman on the fincas to the logic of the s-5's civil affairs strategies by making modernization and progress dependent on forced Indian labor. The millions of dollars, euros, or yen invested in local development during the peace process thus tended to serve developmental goals surprisingly similar to the army's priorities during the 1980s, using forms of discipline and punishment whose roots stretch still further back.

Within these development schemes there was no room to hear other voices, reestablish social relations broken by the war, or generate reflection and debate on the urgent needs of most Sanbartoleños. In other words, there was no space for participation by the people whose lives and livelihoods had been destroyed by scorched-earth military operations. Roads were built, but the mobility of the population was restricted by intensive surveillance. Outhouses were built, but no programs for environmental education or community health accompanied them. Schools were erected but so were obstacles to generalized participation in education. In the 1990s, for example, the patrol leaders prevented adults from participating in the classes offered by the state literacy program CONALFA by instituting a curfew that prohibited movement after 6 p.m., when the working day ended. People who had signed up for the program could not attend because they were afraid of what might happen, especially after rumors began to circulate that the patrol leaders were making a list of attendees.

A dramatic example of the persistence of military ideas and practices in peacetime development programs was the project "to aid the widows of the victims of the conflict." Given the vulnerability of most widows and their children in the Quiché, a number of different governmental and nongovernmental organisms implemented projects on their behalf. But in practice, the

FIG 10.1 Widows in San Bartolo. PHOTO BY MATILDE GONZÁLEZ-IZÁS.

coordination and administration of funds for this purpose were in the hands of the same military authorities responsible for the deaths of the widows' husbands. In addition to centralizing project management, these men used the projects to control the widows' movements and everyday lives, just as General Héctor Gramajo had suggested when he noted that the extermination of peasant leaders and the destruction of their hamlets ought to be accompanied by surveillance of their widows. In each hamlet, he argued, the number of widows should be recorded, along with "what and where they ate, who they fed, where their children were and who took care of them" (Schirmer 1999: 105). In San Bartolo the women I interviewed would tell me, "We are women, but they are always listening to us, they're always sending people to ask, 'What are they saying? What work are they doing? Who are they talking to? Where did that person they're walking with come from?' This happens every day. That's why we don't feel free to talk. All we can do is live with it."

This policy meant that the women were unable to meet on their own initiative or to establish a direct relationship with donors who sought to help them. Normally when a donor institution arrived in the municipality, the mayors and patrol leaders would make the first contact, and if they realized that the donor funded projects for widows, they would present themselves as the widows' benefactors. The women would be intimidated into showing up at an appointed place and time for an assembly to hear about the institution. During these meetings with people "from outside" the widows had to present themselves as worthy cases but never "open their trap [*abrir el pico*]" about the real conditions in which they lived. They also had to request aid from and accept the mediation of local military agents as their spokesmen and as the coordinators and managers of the funds granted on their behalf. To explain the strangeness of the widows' forced performance, the meros jefes would argue, "The women aren't participating because they don't speak Spanish, they don't know how to read and write, they never went to school, they don't know how to manage numbers. That's why we're here to help them." Following this routine, outside funders conducted meeting after meeting without ever learning how the women and their "coordinators" had arrived at this tutelary arrangement. A nun who observed this process explained, "The widows would meet because they were getting food from CARITAS, but the executive committee was composed of four men who were military commissioners. They acted as directors because they claimed that none of the women could read or write or speak Spanish. Plus they claimed that only men could safely travel to Santa Cruz del Quiché."

Sexual harassment and violence were used to intimidate the women. If they failed to attend a meeting or spoke "more than necessary," it was dangerous for them. Widows remember civil patrollers showing up at their house to bring them in if they missed a meeting; the same men would also return later at night and "knock on the door" (*tocarles la puerta en la noche*, a euphemism for rape). But attending meetings was also dangerous for the women because the men took it as a sign that they controlled not only the widows' projects but also their lives and their bodies. From the men's perspective, once their husbands were murdered, the women were left "loose" (*sueltas*); they "had no owner," and consequently could be "used" by the meros jefes for their own purposes. When women were returning home from meetings, their "project coordinators" would often pursue them and sexually abuse them on the road. They were obliged to keep silent about these experiences, even when talking with other women.

Toward the end of the 1990s the nuns at the local parish church began to accompany this group of women, and in this context the widows spoke for the first time about the sexual violence they had suffered at the hands of the meros jefes and started to demand that the institutions that were financing projects for widows stop allowing these men to coordinate their funds. From then on, women were able to meet alone, speaking in K'ichee', and a woman from the group was appointed as coordinator. Although this defiance of the absolute power exercised by their "coordinators" brought its own forms of intimidation and harassment, women at first experienced it as a liberation, and the accompaniment of the nuns limited the men's ability to act directly and with impunity against them. But soon the women began to face daily insults and harassment on the street, getting pushed and shoved around by patrollers, and to receive threats from families loyal to the patrols, causing some to withdraw from the group. One woman recounted, "Our own families began to say that we should leave the group to avoid problems with the authorities, because community work was not well regarded in the town. The patrollers always said that community work was not good. So women were afraid. Anything a commissioner or a patroller says is important to listen to."

Several years after this challenge and resulting setbacks, many of these women once again organized as a group to work in a project promoting horticulture, supported by the same nuns from the Quiché diocese. In addition to the women's growing vegetables to improve their family's diet, the project aimed to restore the women's self-esteem, their confidence in their group, and their right to speak about the rigid military structures that continued to shape their everyday routines. Although the economic impact of the project was negligible, participants valued the opportunity it gave them for mutual support and resistance to victimization. One woman said, "To get on with life we have to work in small groups. Small groups, but ones where we talk. We have to say what we feel. If we don't work like that we can't do it, because we can't just talk with anyone about our problems. Only with people who have suffered the same thing, only like that, not in front of everybody."

Local military agents spied on the group's movements and pestered them with inquiries into their activities. One woman remembers, "When we had a good harvest we would sell it in the market. They would come and ask, 'Why are you selling? Where are the seeds from?' They try to find everything out." Former patrollers would follow the women as they walked on the road, and while the women were working at home they would come and insult them: "They would laugh and say, 'Oh look, it's a man! She's using a hoe! Ay! How's your work? Are you doing piecework or are you assigned a *cuerda* [20 meters squared]? Or is it an inch?' That's how they would treat us, but we act like we don't hear. We let them go on and we keep working. We just want this to be over, to not have any more problems with these men." The army and its collaborators were able to use their influence over development to make people be quiet and obey, but they were not able to make people forget what had happened or to make their arrangements seem normal.

FIG 10.2 Former residents of San Bartolo, displaced during the war, return for a ritual of commemoration. PHOTO BY MATILDE GONZÁLEZ-IZÁS.

Theaters of Power

Establishing the developmentalist counterinsurgent state also demanded more symbolic strategies. Concerned to give the impression that everything was fine and just like before the war, which in turn afforded them a veneer of legitimacy, army civil affairs specialists performed an analysis of indigenous social systems, spatial organization, and traditional beliefs to decide what aspects of Mayan identity could be kept and what had to be changed to fulfill the military imperative of internal security (Ejército de Guatemala 1985: 16). Following this logic, the meros jefes of San Bartolo reactivated the yearly festival for the town's patron saint (August 22–24) with funds provided by the municipality and the Merchants' Association and gathered from charging delinquent patrollers.

Before the war this festival was primarily religious and commemorated the patron saints San Bartolomé of the church and San Bartolomé of the *cofradía* (Catholic brotherhood). In the 1970s the indigenous mayors, *principales* (traditional leaders), and members of the town's four cofradías organized the festival together with members of the local parish executive committee and Catholic Action catechists. After the genocide the festival was reorganized by the local military agents and the Merchants' Association, who sought to recast its cultural and religious significance in civic-military terms. It became instead a means of validating the new forms of patriotism and identity enacted in the civil defense patrols. These transformations complied with the notion of the "authorized Maya" articulated by Generals Gramajo and Juan Cifuentes, one whose radically new relationship to culture and religion would be defined by his estrangement from "politics" and his loyalty to the national symbols of the state, and by extension, the army.

Between 1992 and 1994, according to a local military commissioner I interviewed, the parade was thus "prettied up" by the inclusion of a "mascot," a six- or seven-year-old child wearing the uniform of the *kaibiles*, or Army Special Forces, with his face and body painted black and a miniature machine gun on his shoulder. This child represented the paradigm of the military warrior. Beginning in 1996 the town festival included a military parade, in which both uniformed soldiers and all local men who participated in the civil patrols marched. Most wore uniforms very similar to those used by the armed forces: olive-green fatigues, military boots, and T-shirts with insignias of the armed forces. Only the patrollers from the town center wore the municipality's traditional dress: a blue shirt, white pants, leather sandals, and a wide-brimmed straw hat. The first platoon of patrollers was headed by the representatives of the Santa Cruz del Quiché military base, the military commissioners, and the patrol leaders, along with some pastors from local evangelical churches. They were followed by the platoons of patrollers from each hamlet. At the end of the parade were the floats carrying the current and past years' queens, including Miss San Bartolo, a young ladina from the town center, and the Indigenous Queen and the Patroller Queen, along with various pickups adorned with political propaganda. The patrol leaders carried the national flag or placards with slogans like "The Civil Defense Patrol of Aldea X salutes the heroic Guatemalan Army" or "The Guatemalan Army and the Civil Defense Patrols defeated the enemies of the fatherland." With the introduction of such symbols, and the abundant use of nationalist emblems, marches, songs, and slogans, the army tried to reconfigure the local and ethnic identity of patrollers and the traditional festival into a nationalist and masculinist warrior identity shaped by military values, and thus to reframe the context in which Sanbartoleño daily and sacred life played out.

Not unlike the NGO-ization of grassroots politics, such displays were part of a carefully planned psychological campaign to "recuperate" indigenous Guatemala by making it more ladino, cultivating new sensations, attitudes, and behaviors to favor compliance with the army's institutional mission, even under ostensibly civilian governments. Inaugurated in 1995, a new dance per-

FIG 10.3 Convite dancers at the "new" traditional festival. PHOTO BY MATILDE GONZÁLEZ-IZÁS.

formance, the Baile del Convite, was created by the Merchants' Association to "beautify" the town festival. Unlike the Dance of the Conquest, traditionally performed during the festival to commemorate the town's history, this new dance mimicked the traditional performances of the ladino elites of Santa Cruz del Quiché.

At first it was only a pale imitation, lacking choreography, history, and meaning for ordinary Sanbartoleños. According to one organizer, the impact of this dance was entirely due to the magnificence of the costumes and the prestige and costliness of the marimbas hired to play music. But neither organizers nor dancers nor designers knew where the costumes came from or what they represented, beyond the display of wealth. One patrol leader and active organizer of the dance told me, "Some of the costumes cost fifteen hundred quetzals to rent just for one day. But many of the dancers rented costumes worth even more — two thousand, twenty-five hundred, even three thousand quetzals. I think those costumes represent warriors, Chinese, the princes of Spain and India. I don't really know where they're from, but they're from a lot of places, and that's why they're so expensive."

The function of this competitive dance as a manifestation of the power of the meros jefes becomes clear when it occupies virtually the entire space of the public plaza at exactly the moment when the procession and mass for the patron saints and the traditional Dance of the Conquest are taking place. The new dance pairs men wearing feathered headdresses, kings' crowns, brilliantly colored outfits, velvet and sequined capes, and patent leather boots, topped off by masks with ironic and warlike expressions in lines ordered by the group's internal hierarchies. At the head of the line are those wearing the most luxurious costumes — the executive committee of the Merchants' Association, the patrol commanders and subcommanders, and then the mayors and leaders of the development councils — followed by other local notables. At the end of the line are young Sanbartoleños who have served in the patrols or worked in the stores of older men in the capital. Their costumes are cheaper, from Q1,000 to Q1,500, but none of these youths actually has the money to pay for them, such that participating in the dance means they must indebt themselves to their employers for three or four months of work. They do so because participating confers prestige and reaffirms an arrogant and consumerist masculinity. "In that dance are all the big *cabronazos* (euphemistically, tough guys)," one young man told me. "That's where all the big men who run the town are, the real moneybags, who have cars and stores in the capital. They only speak in Spanish, they wear good watches, fourteen-karat gold chains, Rango boots, and Guess pants. Plus they have the money to pay for the best marimbas. That's why that dance is so cool."

The marimbas hired by the Convite organizers installed large speakers in all four corners of the central plaza. The deafening noise they produce is a serious obstacle to the smooth functioning of the concurrent church ceremonies and the Dance of the Conquest. But despite their success in displacing the others with their loud music and ostentatious dress, in the early years of the Convite the dancers moved timidly and stiffly through the space they had staked out as theirs, swirling around the plaza for an hour in slow, monotonous, and uncoordinated movements. Their Sanbartoleño spectators wore uncomfortable expressions, in part because they knew who was behind the masks and in part because of the visible expense of the costumes. One of the Convite dancers told me, "It's true, people who come to see the dance get freaked out. Because San Bartolo is actually a very backward town, but now we have a new dance, a really luxurious dance with really expensive costumes. The two marimbas they brought are pure luxury! They really make some noise. The whole town heard the noise, and that's why the Association collected fifty thousand quetzals to pay the marimbas, in addition to what the costumes cost."

As time went on, the Convite continued to occupy the central spot in the plaza next to the church and take place at the same time as the mass, and the speakers and horns of the hired marimbas continued to overshadow the preaching and singing from the church. The movements of the dancers have grown increasingly coordinated, sure, and violent. The rhythm of their performance articulates their real power with the powers represented in their disguises as princes, pirates, or warriors.

Through the Convite the meros jefes tried to reorient their community's collective imaginary and monopolize its public spaces of symbolic expression, marginalizing the cultural expressions of those linked to the Catholic Church and *costumbre* (tradition). The Catholic Church is one of the few institutions that managed to open spaces within which Sanbartoleños like the widows were able to speak about and remember what happened during the armed conflict, in the late 1990s particularly, through the work of the REHMI historic memory project and the Church's support for a group of displaced families resettling themselves in the community. The parish committee, the principales, and members of the local cofradías have also participated in initiatives to commemorate those who died in 1981 and to reunite the members of families who stayed in San Bartolo with those who fled to the capital or the coast. These forces were what the Convite organizers sought to trivialize and delegitimize. The dance is symbolic terrorism that performs the agency of men who consolidated their power by willingly carrying out the state's counterinsurgent project at the local level, while claiming affinity with cosmopolitan modernity and distance from their rural origins. The exercise of symbolic power in such contexts multiplies and reinforces a pattern of domination made effective in part by the appropriation of symbols and the reconfiguration of cultural relations of meaning and power.

The meros jefes were not entirely successful in their efforts to legitimate their actions in the town's historical memory by marginalizing the memory of the others whom they had violently excluded from power. Over time, the dancers of the Conquest not only remained in the plaza but hired a better marimba group, increased their numbers, and improved their costumes and dancing. Likewise the Catholic Church worked to strengthen community participation in the activities and rituals performed for the patron saints' commemoration. Increasingly the church fills up from August 21 to August 24. People from hamlets and the town center join together in ceremonies of baptism, marriage, first communion, and confirmation, at which new musical groups formed by young people from the hamlets perform. And August 24, when the Convite marimbas begin to transmit their deafening music, people are no longer intimidated. Instead they shut the church door and continue praying and singing while their own musical groups sing hymns and prayers. At the end of the mass they open the church doors, burn incense, and light firecrackers, while elders from the cofradías play the drums and the *chirimia*

FIG 10.4 The mayor surrounded by *los meros jefes* who approved his election, dressed in Convite costumes. PHOTO BY MATILDE GONZÁLEZ-IZÁS.

flute. Afterward the congregation leaves, singing and accompanying the procession of the church's San Bartolomé, unperturbed by what is happening in the central plaza.

Conclusion

The emphasis the Convite dancers place on hiring loud marimbas that can be heard in every corner of the town suggests that they need a deafening noise to drown out not only the voices but also the silence of all those who witnessed the acts of violence they perpetrated, to enable them to remain deaf to their own memories and conscience. The meros jefes need to demonstrate to themselves and their neighbors that San Bartolo is no longer the town of the 1980s, in which everyone remembered but kept quiet about what had happened. They need to impose their noise on the silence and the speech that breaks it to show that San Bartolo is no longer "a silent and silenced town."

The widows living under constant harassment, the former patrollers working for free to construct projects from which they receive no benefit, the young people indebting themselves to try to fit into the power hierarchy, the authorities getting rich off murder and violence as well as public administration and local development, all beg the question: How can we think about local empowerment and development in places where relations of power are founded on histories of violence and impunity? How can we overcome the breach between the reality people face on the ground and the discourses of decentralization, democracy, and poder local without a full accounting of the way local elites continue to coerce members of their communities and persecute those whom they understand as their enemies? How can local people actually improve their lives, made unimaginably worse by the destruction of the war and its aftermath, without addressing the impact of postwar strategies of security and development implemented *as* counterinsurgency that work not only on bodies and organizations but on worldviews and relationships in the very marginal locations that were most highly militarized during the armed conflict? Now that even the most enthusiastic theorists of neoliberalism have begun to recognize that current levels of violence in Guatemala and other postwar societies are intimately related to the state's reduced capacity and limited room for action under neoliberal policy, the time has come to rethink our impoverished discourses of state reform to include a more robust account of how structural, political, symbolic, and gendered formations of violence work together to produce and reproduce elite rule in particular places.

Note

1. Twenty-six men each year served as *alguaciles*, a community service post charged with "dragging" (*jalando*) workers from the hamlets to build or repair municipal infrastructure for free. They also had to sweep the streets, deliver messages and packages around the municipality, and attend to the requests and orders of municipal authorities. While based in historic forms of communal labor, in communities so twisted by finca logics they were rife with exploitation.
2. Unless otherwise noted, all quotations are from author interviews.

PART IV

WHITHER THE FUTURE?
Postwar Aspirations and Identifications

100 PERCENT OMNILIFE
Health, Economy, and the End/s of War

We in Civil Affairs don't give anything away free; *el pueblo* must earn everything [it receives]. There is no paternalism involved. But when they forge themselves, they do so by themselves, they are going to be free, they are going to have an education, they are going to have economic resources, but they will not be given anything free. Civil Affairs will induce them, will show them the way to forge themselves.

General Héctor Gramajo, quoted in Jennifer Schirmer, *The Guatemalan Military Project*

The End/s of War

Joyabaj and Zacualpa Quiché are close enough for the girls' basketball team in Joyabaj to train by running between them. Zacualpa, however, is one of the four genocide cases described in the United Nations truth commission report (CEH), and people there blame the Joyabaj civil patrols for much of the violence they suffered. "The army brought patrollers from Joyabaj. The people there are different. They are *fuerte, enojados, bravos* [strong, angry]. They came and killed the people of Zacualpa," the priest told me.

Patzulá is a hamlet of Joyabaj where, on a clear day, you can see all the way to the Pacific coast volcanoes that limn the vast sugarcane plantations where so many of Patzulá's boys break their hearts trying to cut seven tons of cane a day (Oglesby 2003, 2004). With no electricity in the hamlet, the stars are sharp and crisp at night. In Joyabaj Patzulá is known as a hamlet with get-up-and-go. People there were very active in the Catholic Action mobilizations in the 1960s and 1970s, and the hamlet owes its existence to their commitment to education. Originally just a neighborhood of Chorraxaj hamlet, parents organized to start their own school and then created a new village around it. Since 1999 (my first visit) they have *gestionado fondos*, raised money and organized human labor to quadruple the size of the school, adding a junior high and a computer lab run off a generator. They've also extended the road, and though it is still nearly impassible during the rains, people are very proud that they accomplished it *a puro pulmón*, by the sheer sweat of their brow.

While those in Zacualpa may view residents of Joyabaj and its hamlets as perpetrators, people in those villages also suffered terribly during the war. Is one a victim or a perpetrator if forced to participate in barbarous acts?[1] On July 10, 1980, Joyabaj's priest, Faustino Villanueva, was murdered. Army massacres began in the villages in early 1981. The anthropologist Simone Remijnse writes, "Tightly organized communities like Chorraxaj (including Patzulá and Nuevo Chorraxaj) . . . were the most prominent targets. The first recorded massacre . . . occurred in Chorraxaj on 14 January 1981. Nine of the 14 people killed were children who had fled into the forest when the military arrived" (2002: 117). People in Patzulá first gave shelter to others fleeing violence, leading the army to kill both hosts and refugees. Patzulá was abandoned for months as people fled, living "like animals" in the surrounding hills and ravines, eating what they could find, terrified the army would find and kill them. Men, women, and children were killed, bodies were mutilated and decapitated, and families were barred from burying the dead. "They were eaten by dogs . . . until they got fat. . . . If someone tried to [bury them] he would die just like the corpses," a survivor recalls (Remijnse 2002: 117).

Joyabaj was also one of the first places where the civil patrols were introduced as a control mechanism of and by the patrollers precisely because it was seen as subversive. Patzulá's patrol commander, José, was a catechist and remembers that period as a time of horror, when he had to live, as he said, with "two faces, one turned toward my people, the other to the army." Today he is widely acknowledged as a development leader, especially for his efforts on behalf of the road and the school.

The end or goal—the intended harvest of the crops people sowed in the ferment of the 1970s—was to improve life by assuring access to land, markets, and less exploitative work through roads, schools, labor and credit unions, production cooperatives, and accessible health care. At first this was perhaps less a revolutionary project than nonstate actors doing their own liberal modernization, what might be called biograssrootspolitics, as the post-1954 governments seemed content to *laisser mourir*, let (certain) people die.

The end or termination of many of those hopes in the destruction of the early 1980s and the ongoing, if less spectacular violences of the post-genocide has produced a necro-infused temporality and a risk-drenched terrain on which people continue to labor for improvement. In this chapter I explore these labors and the end/s of war through the experiences of a Mayan family whose men patrolled but were also part of the resistance inspired by liberation theology. The parents are Mayan cultural rights activists and struggle to get their children educated for success in the non-Mayan world. I am interested in the conditions of (im)possibility that both produce and limit what is imaginable in the postwar as well as what is enthusiasible. What allows people to once again feel something like eager interest or zeal?

Postwar Maya

When I first met Concepción she was teaching school in Patzulá, commuting weekly from her home in Joyabaj, and sleeping in a small room attached to the school with the three other teachers. By hooking into postwar NGO and development aid, individual sponsors, and indigenous-rights funding, Concepción and her husband, Miguel (a teacher in another hamlet), had scared up books for their schools, arranged for dozens of hamlet children to study when local educational resources were exhausted, and somehow managed, on their minimal salaries of about $250 a month, to have all seven of their children in school, one even studying medicine at the national university.

The importance of Mayan identity is essential to Concepción's educational philosophy, and she always and proudly wears her *traje* (traditional clothing). While many indigenous parents have incorporated the message that indigeneity equals backwardness and want their children to learn Spanish (and English) and nonindigenous lifeways as quickly as possible, she and Patzulá's parents are deeply committed to bilingual education and culturally sensitive curricula. They even ran a ladino teacher out of town for being insensitive to these values. Like Concepción, all of Patzulá's teachers are indigenous and deeply committed to what they now call "Mayan cultural survival," a phrase picked up from their classes in intercultural education on the weekends in the departmental capital of Santa Cruz. Patzulá, like most of Joyabaj's northern villages, is 100 percent Maya-K'iche', and the school proudly displays the banner of the Mayan Language Academy (ALMG).

As the CEH emphasizes, the centuries-long struggles of indigenous people for political representation, cultural rights, and economic survival, culminating in the mass mobilization of the 1970s, profoundly challenged Guatemala's racist hierarchies, which responded with genocide. But the current flowering of Mayan activism might also be seen as a harvest of that violence, as people cannily exploit the openings produced by the return to civilian rule, the global response to the Columbus Quincentennial, and the peace process to create institutional and legal infrastructures for ongoing struggle (Adams and Bastos 2003; Bastos and Camus 2003; Cojtí 2005; Nelson 1999). It might also be understood as a dialectical effect of the limits that ladino "racial ambivalence" (Hale 2006) imposed on political mobilization during the war. Achievements include the Accord on Identity and Rights of Indigenous Peoples and the state-backed but autonomous ALMG, which supports bilingual education in Patzulá with curricula, school materials, training for teachers, and the legitimacy that state backing carries. International fascination with indigeneity has also bankrolled a wide array of projects, from the mundane (potable water systems, latrines) to the esoteric (purchasing sacred areas from ladinos, reviving traditional dances, and creating a national organization of *aj q'ij* [traditional healers] and elders). Countering the great historic sweep of anthropological studies on the "decadence" of indigenous culture and "sad but unstoppable ladinization," in 2007 a five-volume collection on "Mayanization" appeared, chronicling not only the ongoing everydayness of indigenous identification but powerful "returns" of people who once identified as ladino (Bastos and Cumes 2007).

Jennifer Schirmer reads the conditions of possibility for these achievements in a more sinister sense. She chronicles how the military intellectuals General Héctor Gramajo and Colonel Juan Cifuentes mobilized the "sanctioned Maya" as an integral part of the army's hearts and minds campaigns after 1982. This apolitical and antisubversive Maya would be free to dress, worship, and entertain themselves as they pleased. (The army even provided traditional *temascal*, or sweat lodges, in refugee reception centers.) Schirmer says, "Such appropriations of Mayan custom and language do not serve to promote Mayan identity and culture: instead, they stand as a form of Sanctioned Maya prototype constructed and continually reconstituted through the military's optic, deprived of memory, and mute to the recent 'subversive' past" (1998: 115). Charles Hale has also questioned the postwar rise of the *indio permitido*, or authorized Indian (2006: 45, drawing on Silvia Rivera), as activists are allowed to work within postwar state institutions as long as they accept radical limits (i.e., market logics) on their claims for social and economic justice. Hale writes, "As long as cultural rights remain within these basic parameters [the ideology of capitalist productive relations], they contribute directly to the goal of neoliberal self-governance; they reinforce its ideological tenets while meeting deeply felt needs; they register dissent, while directing these collective political energies toward unthreatening ends" (75).

End/s, threatening and not, are a way to ponder Guatemala's multiple harvests of violence and wars by other means. Concepción and her community are experiencing the end of war—its apparent termination—and its ends, in the sense of its aims, purpose, or goals. Clearly one of the aims of the counterinsurgency was to destroy hope and enthusiasm, to suggest that resistance is futile, to constrict imaginaries. Improvement in the difficult lives led by so many highland Maya and poor ladinos was one of the ends, or intentions, of the war for the social and revolutionary movements. So how does one keep *this* end in sight? How do people hope, imagine, and remain willing to work for such a thing in the wake of genocide and forced collaboration? Are their best efforts always already Hale's "neoliberal self governance" or General Gramajo's counterinsurgency mandate that people "forge themselves"? How are we to differentiate between Hale's "unthreatening ends" and worthy ones?

Moving On Up

My friend, his first check was for two hundred fifty quetzals, then it went up to three-something, then it went up to four hundred and then half more again, eight hundred, then one thousand, every fifteen days, and I was earning a thousand a month and only with working a year at the store. So he beat me, because every fifteen days he had one thousand, that's two thousand a month, and I was only at one thousand a month and working all the time. One month, imagine! And that's how I realized

Silverio, from a hamlet of Joyabaj, seventeen years old

The aspiration to modernity has been an aspiration to rise in the world in economic and political terms, to improve one's way of life, one's standing, one's place in the world. Modernity has thus been a way of talking about global inequality and material needs and how they might be met. In particular it has indexed specific aspirations to such primary "modern" goods as improved housing, health care, and education (Ferguson 2006: 32).

By 2004 Concepción had left Patzulá to work with a bilingual education NGO so she could be at home, important because both Miguel and a daughter were suffering mysterious health crises unresponsive to medical treatment. When I visited in 2006, she told me a quite amazing tale of the past year. It began with a colleague at the NGO informing her about some medicine that might help her daughter, who had been incapacitated by her tenacious ailment. (Symptoms and failed medical interventions were described in great detail.) It would be a blow for a family so devoted to education if she dropped out of her prestigious boarding school. Miraculously the treatment had worked. Even better, without completely understanding how it happened, Concepción and her husband had won a free trip. With mounting excitement she revealed the exciting details: she, an indigenous woman from a tiny town in the back of beyond, who had rarely even ridden in a car, had been on an airplane! There she was in photos with Miguel, before takeoff, in flight, and arriving. In Spain! And from there onto a very large boat, a cruise ship! Nice, Monte Carlo, Florence, and Rome, where, as good Catholics, they went to the Vatican. Then, wonderfully, several days at sea where there was always food, day and night. Buffets that never stopped! You could eat whenever you wanted to! And everyone was so wonderful. The hours were filled not only with endless yummy delicacies but lots of fun, meetings, workshops, games, and treasure hunts. The days flew by, so many happy times, and then, more excitement, getting back on the plane!

This was all made possible by a product produced in Guadalajara, Mexico called Omnilife, an array of nutritional supplements in powder and liquid form that she believed had saved her daughter (see also Cahn 2011).

I was amazed and not quite sure what to make of my friend's exciting experiences. The products she had served me while we talked (powders mixed in bottled water) seemed to be mostly vitamins, aspartame, and caffeine. By my next year's visit Concepción and Miguel had won a car and been on another trip, to the Bahamas resort of Atlantis. And there were the photographs, Concepción and Miguel in the newspaper with their new automobile, Concepción and her (recovered) daughter, resolutely garbed in their Mayan traje, on the sparkling beach under the brilliant blue sky. Concepción and Miguel at a table loaded with food, sitting with large, nonindigenous people ("He's a doctor from Mexico!" she said proudly), posing in a lobby, arms linked with other non-Maya, smiling broadly in front of the pool.

When I had visited in 2006 Miguel told me that his illness had gotten worse. He had suffered nervous attacks, been hospitalized, and was being treated for severe depression, but nothing—including an exercise regime and antianxiety drugs—seemed to help. He no longer enjoyed anything: the teaching or even his children. He no longer worked in Mayan organizing, where he had been an important leader. "It's because of the war. We lived *entre miedo* [in fear], and it was so long! 1979 to 1985," and he began to count on his fingers. Twice through he counted, "Seventy-nine, eighty, eighty-one, eighty-two, eighty-three, eighty-four, eighty-five . . . seven years! All that time we were always afraid! Always! You just don't recover from this! I saw such horrible things, the army, the patrol. I saw people killed. I saw people tortured. And I couldn't do anything. I was afraid, so afraid! And I couldn't do any of the work I love. I couldn't support development. I couldn't help people. Because I didn't know," he paused. "You didn't know if what you were doing might get you killed. The army deceived me. I saw the terrible things they did."

Miguel had been very skeptical of Omnilife. "I don't know," he said. "I have seen a lot of people who are *engañadores* [con artists], and I thought this might be an *engaño* [trick] too. We have worked for many years to help our people, to develop our community. Many people trust us. I am afraid to lose that. What if it doesn't work? What if we lose their trust?" The allure of accompanying Concepción on the Mediterranean cruise, however, convinced him to sign on as her codistributor. While Concepción began distributing the product full time in 2006 ("I'm *cien por ciento* [one hundred percent] Omnilife"), Miguel continued to teach. He also began to study with an aj q'ij because one diagnosis was that his illness was a cosmic call to serve.

As I was leaving, Concepción said, "So, what do you think?" I said I was pleased she seemed so happy and had traveled to such exciting places. My own travel privileges, based in economic resources and my U.S. passport's easing of border crossings, are a constant topic of conversation in Joyabaj, where people are openly curious as to why their family members risk their lives and incur large debts to go to my country, but I come back every rainy season risk-free. "No, what do you think? Don't you want to be part of it too?" I was dumbfounded, as it had not crossed my mind. My family doesn't sell things, I wanted to stutter. The uglier aspect of the privilege divide was that I already had a house and a car and went on trips. "Okay, but maybe next time?" she said as I made my ungraceful farewell.

Next time was March 2008, and, along with a U.S. friend, we got the hard sell. Concepción had clearly developed a style for getting people into her network, and what we had intended as a social visit was formally organized. We were served Omni coffee and shown several DVDs, one showing the founder, Jorge Vergara, holding court at a Guadalajara "Extravaganza," a boisterous convention for distributors featuring testimonials about the positive effects of Omnilife on people's health and finances (with reminders that it is a supplement, not a medicine). Then Concepción urged us to focus on the testimonies of three indigenous people from Putla Oaxaca, as Don Nico (in efflorescent detail) told of life as a simple peasant barely speaking Spanish, then every symptom and doctor's trip, till Vergara jokingly asked him to hurry it up. In constant pain, at death's door, he discovered Omnilife through a local teacher and was cured. Not long after, miraculously, she gave him a piece of paper. "We didn't know what it was. We were going to throw it away. 'No! No!' the woman said. 'That's not paper! That's a check!' But we didn't know what a check was. 'It's money,' she told us. We had no idea!" he said, laughing. Here Concepción poked me and said, "That's just like me!" Later I would watch her show this part of the DVD to other Maya; their suture onto the Oaxacans always seemed very strong, with their familiar clothing and grammatical patterns of Spanish as a second language.

Then we watched a DVD of a youth conference held in Cancún that Concepción's youngest son, Pablo, had attended. He eagerly added firsthand accounts: "There were kids from all over Latin America, and even Russia. The best part was the spirit of the people. They had hope and energy. There! There! See the Venezuelan contingent? They were amazing! [They were definitely the rowdiest among a large and extremely peppy audience.] It's not like here. Here no one has energy, people don't seem to have any ideas, or even dreams, but there, it was different. I came back so ready to work, so eager to do more. In Guatemala young people are afraid. They are afraid to fail. They are ashamed and think that people look down on them." He was proud that by selling Omnilife he was financing his studies without taking any money from his parents. The final DVD was more explicitly about "economy," with Vergara, like any prosperity gospel proponent, repeatedly and proudly proclaiming he earned $700,000 a month.

Then Concepción, a bit nervously, launched into her spiel: "Like the Russian woman said in the video, there are no races, no countries in Omnilife. We're all together in this, people helping people [*gente que cuida a la gente*— the company motto]. You know lots of people, so this will be very easy for you. You can tell your compadres. You can share with your students. You must have some three hundred students, right? Maybe they have problems, you can advise them. The product is good for many things: gastrointestinal problems, constipation, liver issues, kidneys, diabetes, menstrual problems, even cancer!" She admitted that when she first started, it was all *nubes* (clouds), nothing was clear; she didn't understand the sales, the network, the points, the bronze, silver, and other levels, how the first check seemed to appear out of nowhere and the first trip just fell into her lap.[2] She described how she was recruited and how they enrolled her and a few other people. And this is when she enrolled me.

And she has enrolled many people, which is how she won the trips. The network of enrollees is the source of the mysterious checks and the points one collects to win prizes because Omnilife is a direct-sales pyramid scheme (like Herbalife and Amway) in which one accumulates points by selling the product and by recruiting more sellers. Concepción described this as educating friends and acquaintances about health and economic opportunities.

Network members are never supposed to exhibit the product or sell it in stores. It should only be "displaced" through person-to-person contact, and great emphasis is placed on following up with people, showing them you care.[3] Concepción said, "Jorge Vergara was thinking of people like us. If the man who owns the pharmacy on the main square were to sell Omnilife from such a centrally located place, what would happen to people like us, whose home is so far away from the market? Jorge gives everyone the same opportunities. You don't have to read or write, you don't have to speak Spanish well, you don't have to be rich already to benefit." Depending on how much they sell (each product has both a monetary and a point value), distributors can buy at gradually steeper discounts while still selling at retail prices (although many end up passing along the savings to their friends). In addition, as people in a network sell, a bit of their profit returns to the person who signed them up (for three "generations").

"Our family has changed." Concepción later told me. "We pay more attention to our health, to what we eat. In Patzulá I was explaining that unlike the soda and greasy food people eat now, Omnilife is healthy and natural. And a woman said to me, 'So this is just like our ancestors! This is the way we used to eat.' And that's when I realized that the product is very Maya, it is helping us get back to a more traditional diet, less Pollo Campero [the KFC of Guatemala]." She also emphasized that Vergara had shown sympathy to the Maya cosmovision and its respect for nature by going green,[4] devoting issues of the monthly magazine to global warming and switching from paper checks to direct deposit. (This means every distributor needs a bank account.)[5]

Another of Concepción's great satisfactions is that victims of the war are beginning to thrive on the opportunities created by Omnilife, like our mutual friend Esperanza of Patzulá, a woman whose husband was murdered by the army in 1981. "She can't read or write, she speaks no Spanish, but she can benefit too!" Esperanza had recently survived a frightening health emergency, when she was afflicted with terrible abdominal pain. Concepción and Miguel helped her get to the hospital. She needed an operation to unblock a duct in what I think was her gall bladder, but her daughter, also monolingual in K'iche', wouldn't give permission. Concepción whipped out her cell phone and frantically called Juan, Esperanza's son in Kansas, and got it worked out, then bundled her in their Omnilife-supplied car and drove to the department capital. Afterward Esperanza spent a month with Concepción recovering and taking a lot of Omnilife products. It was after this that she joined Concepción's network. When I saw Esperanza in July 2008, she was still in some pain but working again and thrilled that her son had been deported back to Guatemala. (Juan did not share her joy.) She asked if I were also in Concepción's network and then said, "It's very complicated, all the numbers! And the product is so expensive!!!"

Making Ends Meet: Postwar Economics

Here's the rub of Concepción's exciting and hopeful accounts. A single packet or dose of the product might run about Q8 (U.S.$1) retail, while a large (but more economical) bottle of vitamin powder was over Q200 ($30). In Joyabaj there are a lot of people who have almost no access to the cash economy. A mostly peasant-based subsistence economy made more difficult by land loss in the war combines with very few wage jobs to make Joyabaj a very poor place. Silverio, seventeen and quoted above, after a one-year "apprenticeship" working seven days a week from 5:30 a.m. to 10 p.m. in a sundries store, earned Q1,000 a month, or about $130. With little visible effort his friend earned twice as much selling Omnilife, which is why the product seemed like a miracle. Many migrate to the coast to work in the export-crop harvests; they often return sick, depleted, and with little money in their pockets (Oglesby this volume). A government teaching job, one that is "budgeted" (*presupuestado*), is highly coveted yet in a month pays only enough to buy about eight bottles of Omnilife product. Labor contractors, moneylenders, and store owners (often the same person) have done better, and as many ladinos fled during the violence more indigenous people began to fill these positions. Women are worse off: hours of shopping and food preparation may garner only two or three quetzales of profit per meal sold in a simple restaurant, and weeks of work and the extraordinary skill of weaving a *quipil* (traditional blouse) on a backstrap loom may net the weaver as little as Q40 ($7).

This is the survivalist grind of daily life for many, which exists alongside the massive economic and social transformations produced by transnational immigration and dollar remittances (Camus 2007; Falla 2008). Statistics are lacking for this gray economy, but multistory concrete-block buildings, satellite dishes, and stores selling luxury tiles and expensive motorcycles are increasingly visible, as are the banks. Lots and lots of banks. Almost every conversation turns to immigration, until it seems everyone one knows has gone or is planning to go. It costs between $3,000 and $4,000 to get to the United States, and most people go to *dueños de dinero* (moneylenders), where, if you are lucky, interest rates are 10 percent *a month*. Banks have more reasonable rates, but the collateral requirements are harder to meet. The debt grows quickly and can take several years to pay *if* you make it to the United States, *if* you find a job, *if* you aren't deported, and *if* you can keep sending remittances. I have heard of parents taking their children to aj q'ij to both bless their trip and curse them if they fail to send money home.

Families have lost their homes and land when the migration gamble failed, to the benefit of dueños del dinero, who acquire land as debt payment. The glitter of consumption and the allure of travel and adventure draw some to take these risks. For others it's a straight cost-benefit analysis: what one can earn increased by the exchange rate of 7.5 quetzals to the dollar. For others it has become a necessity: there just aren't many other ways to make money. José, the Patzulá community leader and former patrol commander, was almost killed several years ago in a car accident and still can barely walk. His family decided the only option was to take their son out of school (on a scholarship Concepción helped secure) and send him to the United States.

Grayer still, there is also a lot of narco-money sloshing around the Joyabaj-Zacualpa area. Whispers circulate: that workers in a restaurant sell cocaine, that a huge SUV belongs to the local dealer, of a mysterious gentleman nick-named El Millonario (the Millionaire), who, when asked to contribute to the Zacualpa festival, reached into his fanny pack and pulled out Q20,000 ($2,600) in cash (Nelson 2009a). But no one says much directly.

These emerging postwar structures of inequality layer on to the still un-settling effects on health and economy of the years of lost crops and missed education when people were displaced, and the loss of family members (and their earning power) murdered, starved, exiled, disappeared, or who are barely functioning because of war trauma. Throughout the highlands, being connected to the army made many people richer during the war through straight-up accumulation by dispossession: stealing land, livestock, and seed stores. Loss and gain, lack and abundance may be configured differently now than before the war—with some indigenous people sharing a bit more in the bounty—but they are densely intertwined through and across communities.

The Guatemalan government's National Reparations Program (PNR), be-ginning in 2004, is supposed to compensate war's losses. It was first imagined by activists as holistic, including material restitution, psychosocial rehabili-tation and therapy, memorials, communal health projects, scholarships, and government support for exhumations of clandestine cemeteries and for pun-ishing perpetrators. However, what is being offered is a payment of Q24,000 (about $3,200) per lost family member per household. However, it will only compensate for two people, regardless of how many were killed. As the PNR has acknowledged, it's a complicated, highly bureaucratic procedure to peti-tion for compensation, prove the family member is actually dead, and then actually get the money. The program concentrated its early efforts (and limited funds) on the CEH's genocide areas, including Zacualpa, and as of 2010 no checks had arrived in Joyabaj. Many people, like Esperanza, have given their emotionally taxing testimony and turned in the required paperwork and have been waiting several years for money to arrive. "¡Nada [Nothing]!" said Juan when I asked if they had received any support. "¡Nada, nada, nada!" While most agree that *la vida no tiene precio* (life has no price), many people also really need any money they can get their hands on (PNR 2007).

So there is simultaneously a lot of money circulating through Joyabaj and many people with no earthly means to access it. People are pushed to make hard "choices." Do you risk your *milpa* (cornfields) and possibly a child's life in hopes of remittances from the United States? Do you agree to move some cocaine in your truck? Do you tackle the numbers and try to sell an expensive product to your equally poor neighbors?

In turn, some of that circulating cash is being spent on Omnilife products. (You have to displace a lot to win a Mediterranean cruise!) Some buyers take them to counter the effects of migration: stress and anxiety about family members abroad or the physical effects of the journey, the rhythm and physicality of work in the United States (Juan was working twelve hours a day on a slaughterhouse line), and what it means to come back, physically and emotionally. Some are probably taking the products for similar lingering effects of the war, from which many, like Miguel, are finding it hard to come back.

What's Left?

Between Joyabaj and San Martín Jilotepeque there is a school with a colorful mural depicting the recent horrors of the civil war. It culminates in an image of healing and cultural revival: a mangled tree with new runners emerging from the ground, accompanied by the motto of the Campesino Unity Committee (CUC): "They cut our branches, they burned our trunk, but they cannot destroy our roots." Arriving in San Martín I spot a T-shirt with a similar tree and motto, "Strong Roots, Healthy Tree" and I'm cheered. San Martín should have counted as a paradigmatic case of genocide in the CEH report, but people were too afraid to sign their testimonies, so it could not be included (Bastos 2007). Given the strength of that reign of terror, it was gratifying to see someone publicly supporting the CUC. As he passed me, however, I saw that the back of the T-shirt told a different story. He was a distributor of Omnilife.

In many ways, the CUC was a harvest of earlier violence. In the 1970s it was a response to the difficulties of improving life within a raciological, militarized development paradigm with more emphasis on letting die than helping

FIG 11.1 An Omnilife distributor's "Strong roots, healthy tree" T-shirt. PHOTO BY DIANE NELSON.

live. The CUC crossed ethnic and geographical divides to demand land, better wages, safe work, and representation in local and national politics. These were the ends of their struggle, which were radicalized by the state's necropolitical response: making die. The CUC also grew out of the revolutionary movement's change in strategy after the state violence of the 1960s destroyed the hopes of a Cuba-like takeover based in small, focused armed groups. Instead they struggled for mass mobilization under the rubric of prolonged guerrilla war, of which the CUC became a central component (Brett 2007).

Francisca is a Maya-Kaqchiquel woman from a hamlet of San Martín, whose older sister was the first in their family to join the CUC. Their father was afraid, but their mother was enthusiastic as Francisca, though still just a girl, also began traveling around, talking about alternative futures. When government repression increased Francisca served as a guard to warn of army incursions. When soldiers massacred women and children returning from market, Francisca's family decided she should join the guerrilla to defend them. Her sister was already on the mountain. Only years after the fact did Francisca learn that her mother, brother, and a niece were killed by the army soon after she left. Her sister died in battle. After almost seventeen years in arms, in 1997 she and her husband were demobilized. It was not until the following decade that she was able to organize an exhumation of her mother's body and a proper burial in the cemetery. It was only then, she said, that she could finally sleep without the troubling dreams of her mother's unsettled spirit.

I met Francisca through Concepción, who told me, laughing, that she was my great-great-great-grandmother in Omnilife. We ended up making a family tree to show how I was connected to her through a network that passed through Concepción and a bevy of other people, with members all over Guatemala. We met in the bright and sparkling clean bathroom of the luxurious Camino Real Hotel in Guatemala City,[6] where several thousand Omnilife distributors were gathered for the inauguration of the Basic Course, which met one weekend a month for five months.

Concepción was there with eleven members of her network and clearly enjoying the national-level stature she was gaining. I found her spending a lot of time in that glittering bathroom as she was greeted by indigenous and ladina distributors alike and pinned down to explain her extraordinary success. "How do you do it?" "How did you win two cars?" "Tell us your secrets!" I watched her pride and growing ease at interacting with ladinos, her contentment at being recognized for her efforts and labor, her willingness—much commented upon by others—to help people out.

Concepción made it through primary and a few years of middle school. When she was fifteen her father took her to a coffee plantation, where she made tortillas starting at 11 p.m. and ending around 7 p.m., sleeping only about four hours. After one month she was ill from fever and exhaustion. While recovering she received a telegram about a job in Joyabaj for a woman who spoke Maya-K'iche'. She hurried back and found it was an international NGO called Alianza, the first to work in Joyabaj. She was hired and met Miguel, a coworker, and they began their family. Alianza arrived in Joyabaj after the 1976 earthquake that destroyed 95 percent of the buildings and killed over six hundred people. Simone Remijnse (2002) says their work, which joined progressive ladinos and indigenous people but focused on the indigenous villages, quickly angered the town's elites. The 1978 victory of Joyabaj's first indigenous mayor, of the left-leaning Christian Democrat Party, increased the anxieties of some ladinos of a long-feared retribution by their indigenous neighbors. The excruciating pain that Miguel expresses, that he was not allowed to "do any of the work [he] love[s] . . . support[ing] development . . . help[ing] people," arises from the counterinsurgency's response to these fears. Remijnse says words like "'social promotion,' 'community organization,' and 'awareness raising' were branded as subversive activities by many authorities at municipal, departmental, and national levels. . . . These words were central to Alianza's work. An indigenous woman remembers that 'when the Violence came, they [military] said they [Alianza] were bad people. They said that the help of Alianza was bad help . . . and that the houses Alianza had built were no good. . . . They said that Alianza had planted the guerrilla'" (104). After the 1980 murder of the priest, several family members and friends of Alianza employees were tortured and killed, and the program shut down. In late 1981, when it tried to return—with the express permission of the army—the local contact, a well-respected ladino, was disappeared (104–6). I have talked to Miguel several times about this period as we ponder the stubbornness of his depression, but Concepción rarely mentions it. It was from the stage in the bright convention hall at the luxury hotel, surrounded by hundreds of Maya and ladina women, all Omnilife distributors, that I heard more.

The Omnilife Basic Course consists of five modules, addressing gender identity (what it means to be a woman and what it means to be a man), creencias (beliefs), perdón (forgiveness), and carencia y abundancia (lack and abundance). Men and women meet separately, and the modules feature short lectures; small group discussions; frequent breaks to stretch, dance, sing, or simply meditate to music; film viewings and discussion; and public testimonial work with the leaders, who are clinical psychologists. The dynamic is Oprah Winfrey–esque, with a tough love feel and strong engagement from the audience.

To my surprise the workshop leaders made no mention of the Omnilife company or the products. They never talked about selling or commerce of any kind. They (and Concepción) reiterated that the course was for personal development, nothing more. Having self-righteously pictured a hall of unsophisticated folks being bludgeoned with slick sales talk and low-rent motivational speaking (it cost Q150 to attend), I was rather taken aback to hear the same analysis of gender as a power relation, not biology, that I teach in my women's studies classes.

After the first day we reunited with the men of the Joyabaj contingent, who seemed enthused and confused. Discussing our day we were joined in the gilded lobby by a ladina woman from the ancestor side of Concepción's network who laughed at their befuddled expressions. "You've seen the film, haven't you?" she asked. "Don't worry! It's taken me four or five times to understand it." The men seemed grateful to have their feelings echoed by a native Spanish speaker. I was intrigued and itchy the whole next day to see this enigmatic cinematic event that took five viewings to get. The opening credits finally rolled, and I realized it was *Fried Green Tomatoes*, an arty U.S. film with an explicit antiracist message and not so implicit lesbian heroines, as well as cannibalism and a woman who breaks through walls. Afterward the facilitator led us through several hours of dissecting its message and discussing who the women identified with in the film. Surprisingly, several women felt most kinship with the abusive husband who ends up on the grill.

Several months later, on the first day of the Lack and Abundance workshop, I sat beside Sebastiana, a member of Concepción's network from Zacualpa who worked at the Maya Legal Defense Office in Santa Cruz Quiché. She told me she had been enrolled in Omni for four months but hadn't been able to sell anything. She didn't have the nerve. She also wanted to recount her testimony on the stage but always felt too afraid. The next morning the therapist told a story about a wedding in Cancún being rained out, but how some guests, rather than let it be ruined, transformed the rain into abundance and kept on dancing, despite see-through clothes and bedraggled hairdos. "That is abundance: when you find joy in what others see as loss." Sebastiana raised her hand, and when the therapist didn't notice (Sebastiana is quite small), she stood up. The therapist was welcoming when Sebastiana said she needed to tell her story and congratulated her on insisting on being heard. I felt a bit aghast at the distance between what we had just heard about the bourgeois beachside wedding and what I knew Sebastiana was about to recount. For most everyone else, however, it all seemed to fit together.

Sebastiana took the microphone and said that when she was eight years old the army had tortured and killed her father. Then they burned her home, and she, her mother, and her younger siblings fled into the mountains, living on what they could find, starving, trying to keep the little ones alive, afraid, afraid all the time. She had grown up without the love of her father, without his support, trying to help her mother when she was still a child herself. By this time most people in the room were crying. The therapist encouraged others with similar experiences to come up, and to my surprise Concepción went. They all put their hands on Sebastiana, and the therapist began to work on her: "If your father were here today, what would he want?" Sebastiana couldn't speak at first because she was crying. "He would want the best for me." "So," said the therapist gently, "how can you attain what your father wants? He is dead. You are alive. The past is past. We can remember it, but we can't let it hurt us."

After pushing Sebastiana pretty rigorously on these points for what seemed like a long time, the therapist asked for the other women's stories. Concepción said that, during the war, she and Miguel were working to help people. But then they heard that their good work was dangerous. The army had a list of names, and Miguel's was on it. They had nowhere to go, so Miguel hid in the house, hiding away, so afraid! They had a little store, and with Miguel in hiding, a cousin who was a bit mentally retarded looked after it, but the army took him away. So Concepción put her baby on her back and went to the convent, where the army was stationed. She was afraid, but she had to get him out, he didn't understand, he was just trying to help. It was horrible inside, she could hear people screaming, it smelled bad, and the soldiers made fun of her. "Do you want to spend some time here? We'd be happy to have you and your baby stay!" Here she had to stop her story and collect herself. The other women supported her. "I got too afraid then. I had to leave him there. What could we do? Thank God about fifteen days later they let him go. He was starved, tortured, but he was alive."

The emotional intensity of these testimonials was then channeled into a small-group exercise that included shared massages and meditation and culminated with each member telling her companions a set of positive phrases — "You are wonderful," "You deserve to be happy" — that were repeated back as we circled her for several minutes. We finished by laying our hands on her as we fell silent. Most people in our group cried and one collapsed. Finally, we spread out on the floor with scissors, glue, and old magazines to create a "dream map," a set of images to help visualize our futures (an Oprah technique; Grose 2008). All of the women around me, Maya and ladina, pasted images of cars, exotic locales they hoped to visit, and buildings (including New York's Metropolitan Museum). Some had images of children in school or wearing graduation mortarboards. (So, while her 100 percent engagement with the market project of Omnilife has displaced education for Concepción, many of the women seem to see it as a means to that end.) Concepción had all of these and a picture of a sexy white guy striding down the street. I teased her about shopping for a boyfriend, and she said, very seriously, "No, I want my husband to be this happy and this confident again."

Making Ends Meet

"Social promotion," "community organization," and "awareness raising" were branded as subversive activities.

Former Alianza activist, quoted in Simone Remijnse, *Memories of Violence*

In the winter of 2000 there was a landslide in the ravine behind the Joyabaj convent—the convent Concepción had visited with her baby on her back. The jumble of human bones that surfaced forced official recognition of the army's "public secret" of using the ravine as a body dump. While the 1990s brought numerous exhumations throughout the highlands, no one had dared organize one in Joyabaj. This, however, couldn't be ignored. A friend told me, "They found some bodies and then more and more. More than twenty-five. The forensic anthropologists came, working so hard, sweating, in the heat. Many people came down from the villages to see, to see if they were their family. But it was very hard to tell."

For some the war ended in 1983 as the scorched-earth massacres were scaled back. For others it was the end of armed hostilities on December 29, 1996, and for others when the UN peacekeepers left in 2005 (along with many international donors). Of course, for people like Miguel and Sebastiana, the war is still going on. And that is a lesson of this book as well, that the present must be understood through this past that unexpectedly surfaces in ravines and luxury ballrooms. I am also suggesting that Concepción's (and her network's) participation in Omnilife is another harvest of violence.

General Gramajo, the mastermind of Guatemala's "transition to democracy," described the army's ends, or goals, as training *el pueblo* to "earn everything (it receives)" (quoted in Schirmer 1998: 114). The self-forging market effects of Omnilife in Joyabaj are unfolding within spaces shaped by the massive violence that programmatically destroyed many efforts to reach the goal of a better life, one that would include "health and economy": safe work conditions, education, and maybe a car, or even a trip somewhere. The shock of this violence, as Naomi Klein (2007) reminds us, was brutal and specific in Guatemala but also unfolded within a globalizing doctrine. Foreclosing all options but the market, people are left to do it themselves, without support from the state (unless you're a military contractor or Wall Street risk taker). The ends, or goals, of the Guatemalan Army and of global financial structures seem to meet in that mythic benumbed hyphenated moment of "forced-voluntary (*forzovoluntario*), coercive-consensus" "choice" to "forge themselves" (Schirmer 1998: 114, 117).

I've told this story by accompanying Concepción on her glittery rise through the Omnilife pyramid (she has since won cruises through the Greek islands and a trip to the Holy Land with a stop in Istanbul) while seeking to temper it with Esperanza's worries about the numbers and the expense. Readers more experienced with pyramid schemes already know that, like capitalist democracy, they promise that anyone can rise but are structured to benefit the few, no matter how hard anyone else works. The more cynical among you will have already noted how closely selling the products, and the entrepreneur self-making it entails, conforms to General Gramajo's civil affairs prescription. And that Jorge Vergara makes $700,000 a month by astutely combining the "unique local knowledge and morality . . . and relations of mutual trust and reciprocity with fellow community members . . . with enterprising community-based self-development efforts, growing technical and market-based expertise, and . . . propensity for risk taking" of my friends as they so closely hew to Monica DeHart's description of the "ethnic entrepreneur" (2010: 2). To take seriously these counterinsurgent underpinnings and new-fangled yet classic forms of accumulating surplus out of subprime spaces like Zacualpa and Joyabaj makes me feel that saying anything positive about Concepción's experience with the products just buys in to the empty allure of freedom and individualized "progress" that Gramajo and his fellow apologists for violent neoliberalism promise citizens of all "postwar" nations, from Guatemala to Iraq.

Once social promotion, community organization, and awareness raising are branded subversive, is the only recourse a different "brand," in this case Omnilife? Can we say only that the bad guys won, the "economic hitmen" (Perkins 2004) are in charge, and human attempts to meet our basic material needs must abide by their rules? Is there no alternative to, as Schirmer says, living "deprived of memory, and mute to the recent 'subversive' past"? Well, to some extent, no. Critics are right to raise the alarm and remind us of the structures of power that undergird our attempts at agency, foreshorten our imagined horizons, drain our enthusiasms, legitimate market solutions to structural violence, and are more than willing to murder us if we resist. Pablo's frustrations that his schoolmates "are afraid to fail" is a harvest of violence. It is the world in which his family is trying to survive, and maybe aspire to improvement, while being *gente que cuida a la gente*, people who care for and about other people. We may mourn the lost conditions of possibility for radical social change that existed in the 1970s, when people were willing to sacrifice for a greater good than a "free" trip to the Bahamas. But that was a different moment than the present. How do we make those ends meet the current conditions of possibility, make the aspirations of the late

1970s meet the "unthreatening ends" that Hale says (somewhat cavalierly) are "permitted" today?

I am uncomfortable reading Concepción, Miguel, Francisca, and Sebastiana as simply dupes of what Hale calls neoliberal multiculturalism. While apparently falling prey to Omnilife's sophisticated manipulation of indigeneity, consumer sparkle, and self-help affirmation, they don't seem any more conned by it than the rest of us caught in late capital's meshes of commodified subjectivization, military optics, and the boom in affective labor. They say they participate in Omnilife because they deeply enjoy helping people. They understand themselves to be supporting their communities, rebuilding networks torn brutally apart by the war, and finding a way to survive and to give their children a home, food, and education in a scary globalized economy, although perhaps not in a form they would have chosen under other circumstances. When I asked Francisca, the former combatant, about the connections between her years in the guerrilla and her work with Omnilife, she sighed. "Jorge Vergara is a businessman. We know that. But who else will give me a job? I don't speak Spanish well. I never went to school. I have no résumé. After the war, what could I do?" They are educating their friends and neighbors and improving their health, maybe less by taking nutritional supplements than by paying attention to diet and exercise, and rebuilding social ties. They are subverting the "rule of experts" because, unlike most medical doctors, they attend to people in their own languages, with no set schedule or time limit, and, similar to "traditional" healers, often have quite detailed knowledge of a person's family, economics, community standing, and role during the war that helps them diagnose causes and prescribe cures (not to mention cell phone access to relatives in the United States). Pragmatically health is a function of household economy, and Omnilife offers a way for some to earn money without the risks of migration or narcotrafficking. They are not living so *entre miedo*, constantly in fear, that their deeply felt desire to "support development . . . to help people" will get them killed. And, as the Mayan anthropologist Irmalicia Velásquez Nimatuj wisely pointed out when I first shared my astonishment at the effects of Omnilife, they don't have to kill anyone.

Carlota McAllister movingly evokes the conditions of im/possibility the war imposed on people in Chupol, a strongly proguerrilla village not far from Joyabaj. The human ability to differentiate good from bad and to act on that understanding is called *conciencia* and is seen as a basic feature of a good person. State counterinsurgency and revolutionary defeat cut knowing from doing, introducing a gap at the core of the human. It created an ongoing state of anguish, an imbalance that knocks everything else out of whack. The struggles of the past fifteen years have been to get back to a very minimal status quo from which to begin working, to fulfill Concepción's dream map that Miguel be happy and confident again. Francisca's achieving something as banal and everyday as knowing where her deceased loved ones are so she can visit them on All Saints Day took years of painful effort. (One friend participated in twenty-one exhumations before they found his father, horrifyingly, under the very field where he played *futból* as a teen.) Yet that knowing and doing are essential to the human sturdiness (*salud*) necessary to do anything else in life—which is why disappearance and clandestine cemeteries were widespread counterinsurgency strategies.

Discussing the 1970s, Domingo Hernández Ixcoy, one of the founders of the CUC, said, "There was always activism, people fighting and seeking ways to develop. There were the cooperatives and trying to get fertilizer, but each offered only part of a solution. People would be blocked for a little while and then they would become more active." All the efforts to make the National Reparations Program a holistic response to the war have been reduced to a monetarization of suffering (1 death = $3,200), while Omnilife seems to offer both economic promise and ongoing, interethnic, communal therapeutics. I certainly wish it weren't market benevolence providing what state biopolitics and left modernization are not: recognition of indigenous people, spaces where ladinos and Mayas interact, class mobility, therapy, pleasure, body work, a sense of luxury, support for aspirations, or a bit of security (for some) within a massively insecure world. I am also not suggesting that "displacing" Omnilife products is resistance in the guise of neoliberalism. It is a capital formation complexly linked to prosperity gospel forms, but also to Mayan heritage and postrevolutionary dreams of improvement. But I also do not see a frictionless imposition of Gramajo's "dream map." The networks that Concepción and her community are forming through the product and its various articulations are complex machines that link pre- and postwar forms of organizing, self-making, and folk medicalization of a transnational product.

Looking at the hopeful examples of peoples throughout Latin America refusing the "freedom" promised by corporate globalization, it behooves us to remember that few of them have suffered as Guatemalans have. Perhaps Omnilife, its networks, and the hope (even if it's an engaño) it is planting in some young people will, dialectically and in ways difficult to foresee, lead to other harvests. Perhaps it will make other ends meet.

Notes

Heartfelt thanks to the *gente que cuida a mi*, especially Concepción and her family (pseudonyms), and the many Xoy who have supported this work over more than a decade, especially Anastasia Mejia and Doña Cae. Liz Oglesby, Simone Remijnse, Carlota McAllister, Matt Creelman, Gladis Pappa, Santiago Bastos, Manuela Camus, Irmalicia Velásquez Nimatuj, Carlos Fredy Ochoa, Emily Adams, Mark Driscoll, and Oxidate members have made this possible.

1. In Joyabaj in 1982 the army called together all the men of the town and various outlying villages and made them walk through the night to the hamlet of Xeabaj, where they were forced to kill the residents with their machetes. Estimates of those murdered range from fifty to two hundred. "A river of blood ran down the mountain," a witness told Simone Remijnse (2001: 463).

2. Sugarcane plantations similarly quantify men's labor and distribute points in attempts to motivate and enthuse them to increase productivity, although the gender mode is distinct from Omnilife's (Oglesby 2003: 661).

3. Omnilife testimonies focus on general frustrations with biomedical health care — emotions not limited to distributors. I often hear similar tales of health crises, cavalier and even abusive treatment by medical staff, and the limited efficacy of expensive medicines. This is often understood as racism and classism. "They treated me badly because they think I'm poor and I won't pay, just because I wear *corte* [Mayan clothing]," said a woman in Joyabaj.

4. Corporate social responsibility, sometimes called "greenwashing," occurs when business expresses concern for the environment or human needs. It is a central plank in neoliberal development policies, as Oglesby (2004, this volume) critically addresses for the World Bank–award-winning Guatemalan sugar producers' humanitarian foundation.

5. While many people, especially those with family in the United States, have bank accounts, in Joyabaj many do not. When Juan, described below, was in Kansas, Esperanza received his remittances through a friend.

6. The same hotel where sugar elites hold their seminars (Oglesby this volume).

THE *SHUMO* CHALLENGE

White Class Privilege and the Post-Race, Post-Genocide
Alliances of Cosmopolitanism from Below

Within the living memory of many Guatemalans acts of genocide were committed against indigenous people, and arguably against the collectivity of the
Mayan people as a whole.[1] In such a context, understanding the workings of
racism is critical, as is elaborating an antiracist politics that will not only pre
vent genocide from recurring but also transform the conditions that made
it possible in the first place. These conditions are always also discursive and,
I argue, include the anthropology of Guatemala produced within the North
American academy, especially its accounts of relations between indigenous
and nonindigenous Guatemalans. As I detail below, anthropology—like
so much of U.S. hegemonic "culture," from foreign policy to commodity
styles and the way its images of modernity are tied to racialized identities—
participates in the processes of nation and state formation in Guatemala to
an unusual extent. This leads, I argue, to a responsibility to revisit anthropology's understandings of how "race" and "racism" work in Guatemala and
to retheorize these concepts in terms that can further an antiracist politics.

Perhaps the most prominent concept within this anthropological tradition
is that of "cultural change," first elaborated in village studies by Robert Redfield, Sol Tax, and others. Extrapolated from accounts of highland communities where Indians were dominated by a small class of ladinos recently empowered by the national-level liberal reforms, it posits "change" as progress
toward the consolidation of a harmonious Guatemalan nation. Obstructing
this change is the cultural dichotomy between Indians and ladinos. A tendency to map this dichotomy onto the troubled history of race relations in the

United States, in turn, makes ladinos effectively appear as whites in anthropological accounts of their relationship to indigenous people, reducing Guatemalan racism to anti-indigenous sentiment and making ladino racism against Indians the sole axis on which Guatemala's deep historical and social contradictions—and thus its inability to achieve social harmony—turn.

A significant corollary to this paradigm posits North American anthropologists as the saviors of indigenous people, defending them from the ladino demons who torment them (to paraphrase Gayatri Spivak, as white people saving brown people from tan people). Such a position, however, requires ignoring both the geographies of imperial whiteness that situate Guatemala as a banana republic and the internal complexities of pigmentocratic hierarchies *within* Guatemala. Most ladinos are considered inferior to both the descendants of the Spanish occupiers (the *criollos*) and to the post-nineteenth-century elites descended from northern European immigrants (see Solano this volume). The criollos in turn wish to be considered as white as their gringo neighbors and conspicuously perform Euro-American–identified styles—including speaking English and showing familiarity with U.S. academic discourse—as signs of a cosmopolitanism that also "whitens."[2] But while many ladinos may share the anthropological imaginary in which they appear as white, their claim to that status is not recognized by those who dominate the transnational social-racial hierarchy in which both Guatemalans and foreign anthropologists participate. The difficulties ladinos face in claiming whiteness before both national and global audiences point to a critical gap in anthropological analyses of Guatemala's troubles. Beginning in the Liberal era, elite immigration from northern Europe and the United States in pursuit of profit from plantation agriculture, and the fluid and intimate exchanges among such white expatriates, missionaries, bureaucrats, *finqueros*, and anthropologists that shaped this phenomenon, are rarely considered. Consequently the small but extremely powerful minority of Euro-American Guatemalans—who are the primary beneficiaries of the regressive agrarian and fiscal structures that still govern the country—becomes anthropologically invisible. Meanwhile this minority enforces a dichotomy perhaps more fundamental to Guatemalan life than that between Indians and ladinos: that between *gente decente*, "people we know, decent people" to *gente corriente*, "everyone else." The latter category includes not only all indigenous people but most common, or what I'm calling *plebeian* ladinos,[3] who are stigmatized as *shumos, mucos,* or *choleros. Gente decente* is a term that biologizes class distinction, but it is not, any more than *ladino* or *shumo*, reducible to race, especially in the U.S. sense of the one-drop rule.[4]

This chapter intervenes in this ideological space by showing how imperial whiteness deploys antishumo racism to confront threats to its hegemony over Guatemala. Adapting Kurasawa's (2004) and Calhoun's (2002) discussions of cosmopolitanism and global politics, I argue that contemporary Guatemala is undergoing a symbolic war between a cosmopolitanism from below, which is influenced by the immigrant Mayan and ladino diaspora throughout North America, and a cosmopolitanism from above, which sustains the oligarchic values attached to the plantation economy and export agriculture, and the privilege of moving freely at the global scale that these values confer only on certain Guatemalans. In fact since it has primarily been white northerners who move easily (legally), the elite's ability to do so becomes somewhat racialized. When their hold on this symbolic capital is threatened by lower class migrants who speak English and sport U.S. fashion, such upstarts are also racialized, I argue, through the term *shumo*. Early participants in this cosmopolitanism from below were lower level guerrilla cadres and popular movement representatives, often very poor indigenous people like Rigoberta Menchú Tum, and ladinos who began to travel for training, medical care, and political campaigns and as exiles. Since the late 1970s Guatemalan labor migrants and refugees have also come to participate, often as low-wage workers in factories or farms, in extensive networks that range from their homeland through Mexico and the border states of the United States, and more recently into the U.S. Northeast and Midwest and Canada, becoming a quotidian presence in many major North American metropolises (Hagan 1994; Hamilton and Stoltz 2001; Menjívar 2002; Loucky and Moors 2000; Popkin 2005). Unlike elite Guatemalan travelers who shopped and vacationed in the North, this diaspora is composed largely of Mayan and other impoverished survivors of both political violence and the neoliberal policies the violence ushered in, who have managed to become North American despite the best efforts of the elite to contain them at home (Arias 2003; Chinchilla et al. 1993; Millard and Chapa 2004; Wilson 2004). These Guatemalan North Americans are the other face of Guatemalan cosmopolitanism, whose traditional representatives fend off challenges to their privilege through the racist discourses I address below. Paying attention to differentiations within white/ladino identities *and* connections between the apparently dichotomous positions of ladino and Indian enshrined in much anthropology is important for understanding actual "cultural changes" in war's aftermath. Focusing on power differentials that are *not* distributed through such a dichotomy helps us see other reasons why Guatemala has not achieved a "harmonious nation."

Here I argue that antishumo, antimuco, and anticholero sentiments are vital weapons in the war between these two cosmopolitanisms, which is being waged in part through the production and circulation of class and ethnic prejudices among young Guatemalans. By analyzing racist humor that circulates on the Internet in emails and websites and data from interviews and informal conversations conducted between 2001 and 2003 with first-year university students and high school seniors in lower-class public schools and middle- and upper-class private schools in Guatemala City,[5] I suggest that anti-shumo sentiment is a reaction to the encroachment on the sovereign territory of the middle and upper classes by newly mobile working-class Indian, quasi-Indian, ladino, or Afro-Guatemalans. These jokes and narratives ridicule social climbing and "new money" and denigrate those who attempt to leave their assigned slot in local and global hierarchies. Shumos dare to mimic the values, manners, and consumption patterns of gente decente, and in doing so they challenge the legitimacy of imperial whiteness as the primordial determinant of social location in Guatemala. I also ask how anthropology can contribute to an antiracist politics that encourages alliances between plebeian ladinos and Maya rather than setting them against one another.

Indians, Ladinos, and Anthropologists

Guatemala's failure to become a homogeneous and progressive nation after the liberal reforms in the nineteenth century has been blamed on those stigmatized as *Indians* (Grandin this volume). Nation-building discourse offered Indians a solution to this problem: cease to be Indians by incorporating themselves into "modernity" through education in both the scholarly and cultural senses. The falsity of this already racist promise has been amply documented, but its premises structured generations of anthropological research into Guatemalan "ethnic" categories. Douglas E. Brintnall (1979) shows how Robert Redfield and Sol Tax saw ladinos as *indios revestidos*, or dressed-up Indians, and describes this as an ethnographic generalization that Indians and ladinos are not racial groups but cultural or ethnic ones, differentiated by language, dress, and participation in indigenous civic and religious hierarchies (*costumbre*). Tax was uncomfortable characterizing Indians and ladinos as races because doing so risked imputing racial problems to Guatemala that he felt didn't actually exist. Morris Siegel (1941), noting the slow pace of cultural change in San Miguel Acatán, disagreed with Tax's assertion that racism was not a problem in Guatemala, describing the ladinos there as whites who believed in the racial superiority of whiteness and considered Indians to be their racial inferiors. For Siegel, this ideology was necessary, however, because he thought that if indigenous people adopted the dress and language of their white bosses they would be indistinguishable from them and thus present a grave danger to white superiority. Brintnall likewise recognized the existence of Guatemalan racism, but by treating ladinos as synonymous with white people, he suppressed the existence of white/r Guatemalans, those who claim Mediterranean, Anglo-Saxon, or Nordic ancestry and thus differentiate themselves *racially* from ladinos.

None of these anthropologists questions why ladinos, whom they consider to be "truly" Indians, want to be recognized as whites, even though they frequently failed to have the phenotypical and social attributes necessary to gain this recognition. Essentially they took for granted the desirability of pure whiteness for all nonwhite people. Denouncing the absurdity of ladino racism toward indigenous people thus became a means of denigrating the racially impure and the *mestizo*, while repudiating the possibility that nonwhites might ever aspire to be the equals of whites. The effect of this, Carol A. Smith argues, was a failure in anthropology to adequately conceptualize the relations between race and culture and race and racism, contributing, ironically, to the "Guatemalan and Latin American supposition that racism doesn't exist in Latin America" (1999: 93). This was because Guatemalans "fail" to discriminate in the same terms against all those who have a drop of indigenous blood, as would happen in the United States if citizens there had an ancestor of "black blood." In the process, the complexities of an imperial racism that denigrates ladinos for being mongrels, and the contradictory identifications of nonwhite plebeians who discriminate against Indians and desire to be white, disappear.

Refusing to examine the convergence of anti-indigenous and anti-ladino/"mongrel" sentiment in reproducing an ideology of the moral superiority of whiteness has significantly narrowed the scope of anthropological analysis in Guatemala. While many anthropologists have devoted themselves to the study of "penny capitalism" (Tax 1953), the tasks of addressing the *junker* capitalism of transnational corporations and the *finquero* elite in Guatemala or making critical judgments about the 1954 restoration of Guatemala to the status of a banana republic ruled by these forces are rare.[6] With certain notable exceptions, even the bravest denunciations of the genocidal consequences of the 1954 coup have failed to examine the relationship between ideologies of imperial whiteness and cold war anticommunism in the processes of nation building and nation destroying that U.S.-backed counterinsurgency has inflicted on Guatemala. Anthropological understanding of the Guatemalan Left is also profoundly shaped by this anticommunist antiracism. If racism is only about ladino oppression of Mayas, a decolonizing, anti-imperial antiracism that includes both indigenous people and ladinos becomes impossible. The insurgency and other popular struggles that have sought to inhabit this impossibility are written out of anthropological accounts of Guatemalan history. This leaves capitalism triumphant as the passage that must be negotiated in the inevitable transition of all peoples toward liberal democracy rather than an impediment to liberation that must be entirely dismantled.

Antiracist activism that defends Mayas from ladinos without criticizing the imperial power of the United States and its allies in the upper echelons of Guatemala's elites, therefore, does not escape reproducing the tutelary structures that favor the planetary minority to which most anthropologists belong. To imagine an antiracism that does address these structures requires anthropology to develop a new postimperial and transnational account of how racism works—not only in Guatemala but in relations between Guatemala and the United States—by investigating the cult of racial purity and racial and cultural authenticity that operates in both countries and the resulting stigmatization of the hybrid or mixed. This new antiracism should revisit prejudices and narratives that continue to exercise hegemonic force both locally and globally—the myth of the lazy native, the criminalization of poverty, and ideas about the dirtiness, drunkenness, feminization, and hypersexualization of those perceived as racial and social inferiors—thus exposing the disdain for the hybrid as the powerful instrument of political demobilization that it is. Attempting to begin this process, here I take up the figure of the shumo (and its cousins, the muco and cholero)—the déclassé, marginal, lower-class, stigmatized plebeian mongrel—as both an existing identity position and the self-constituting other for hierarchized senses of self.

Shumos, Mucos, and Choleros

Eating Pollo Campero on the airplane . . . Ahhhh, the shumo.
"Shumometer, version 1.0," April 2001

In the post-genocide years, indictments of those responsible for the irremediable backwardness of society and its institutions have increasingly been directed at those called shumos, mucos, and choleros rather than indios. While many Guatemalans believe that *indio* has a phenotypic existence—that they can always "tell" when someone is indigenous even if he has changed his name or speaks Spanish—the term is extremely slippery. Anyone who says something vulgar, makes a bad play in soccer, or just acts stupid can be called indio, and nonindigenous parents sometimes admonish their children with the warning "No seas indio" (Don't be an Indian). (With the rise of the Mayan movement one sometimes hears "No seas Maya" to mean the same thing.) *Shumo* is similarly racially coded yet not at all fixed. Many of the shumo's disturbing characteristics are the same as those historically associated with ladinos. In the late 1990s, newspapers, Internet documents, theater performances, and radio programs began to feature narratives ridiculing and denigrating those who attempted to leave their assigned slot in the local and global hierarchies of whiteness. Shumos, mucos, and choleros represent agents of disturbance for these hierarchies, for they are *igualados* (equalizers), a common elite Guatemalan term of condemnation for those who act as the equals of those they should recognize as their social superiors. With the insurgency defeated, these igualados represented the new enemy.

In "La shumada," an article that appeared in the right-of-center newspaper *Siglo XXI*, Alfred Kaltschmitt, on October 11, 1999 (the eve of Columbus Day, a date closely connected to Mayan resistance, and the same year the peace accords were rejected in the Consulta Popular), clearly articulates the danger shumos present to the symbolic order of imperial whiteness. His piece both links antishumo discourse to earlier racist discourses on Indians and reveals its differences. He writes that shumos are "dirty, abusive, impertinent, thieving, vulgar, lazy and rude," but he takes pains to clarify that "shumo-ness . . . has nothing to do with racial differences . . . because there are white, yellow and black shumos" and that "shumo-ness does not originate in poverty, because there are poor people who are decent and respectful." Instead, "shumoness" is a phenomenon of "bad taste." Shumos "fill the airplane with the smell of fried chicken and stuff the luggage compartments with tight shapeless bundles." Rap is shumo, but marimba, if not played correctly, "can become shumo too." Extravagant fashions and body piercing "are totally shumo." Speaking to an audience implicitly composed of gente decente ("people we know"), he warns, "Shumos are invading us. . . . They are choking us with their dirt and vulgarity." The problem with this invasion is that "shumos don't hesitate to take what doesn't belong to them, because they have no respect for other people's property, just their own." Indeed shumos exhibit "an incorrigible rebelliousness against the rule of law" and an "anti-systemic attitude" that he finds all too familiar in the immediate postwar years: "Left wing people are responsible for kindling the fire of the shumos. For years the Left has been providing them with cheap dialectics and perverse theories that justify shumos' attitude and rebelliousness. The reason for that is that Left wing politics is full of shumos. Shumos agitate for social rebellion with absurd justifications, as if you could have rights with no responsibilities and a place and post without work and dedication." The shumo's crude imitation of the patterns of consumption of la gente decente is frightening and repellent because it recalls other challenges to the political and cultural hierarchies that organize relations of servitude in Guatemala.

La Jacky is a character created by the progressive Guatemalan comedian Mónica Recino. She appears on a popular radio show and is frequently quoted by her listeners. Somewhat in the mode of Steven Colbert in the United States, she pushes "decent people's" reactions to an extreme and makes the assumptions implicit in Kaltschmitt's "La shumada" a source of humor. In an interview with the journalist Juan Luis Font (2001), La Jacky — whose name, short for "Ya Quisieras" (You Wish), mocks the aspirations of social climbers — says she feels less threatened than "offended" by the new rich showing off their money:

> It's *disgusting* [originally in English] to see mucos disguised as decent people. To see people who should be bodyguards walking around with bodyguards. People should know their place in society. A muco's energy and my energy just don't mix, no matter how much money they have. You know, people think I care only about money, but that is not so, it's a question of having refinement, elegance. . . . The *new rich* are those who think they can buy anything with money. And really *my place* can't be bought. That is, what nature didn't give you, the Instituto Central para Varones won't supply.

The exchange, which took place in the wake of the defeat of the neoliberal finquero Oscar Berger by the populist thug Alfonso Portillo in the 1999 presidential elections, also reinforces the link between antishumo sentiment and the naturalizing of white sovereignty over the Guatemalan nation:

Juan Luis Font: Was it painful to see people like you out of government?
La Jacky: Who do you mean?
JLF: I mean people of high breeding, of good stock, like you.
LJ: Ah, you are talking about the *canche*. [This term applies to people with blond hair or a light complexion and here refers to the notably fair-skinned and blond ex-president Alvaro Arzú, nicknamed "the Golden Monkey," then a member of Berger's political party.] . . . I used to ask

him, "*Canche,* how can you govern a country so full of *choleros*?" and he'd reply: "Because I love my country." He really dedicated his whole self to it. He was a martyr.

Arzú's "martyrdom" in the service of unworthy choleros links antishumo sentiment to older nation-building discourses.

One of the few Guatemalan columnists who openly denounces antishumo sentiment is Carolina Escobar Sarti (2000). For Escobar, it serves as an index of an imaginary in which Guatemala is properly "a nation of bowed heads, such as those of the obedient servants who know their place in society—and in the master's house," whose defense requires symbolic and sometimes material violence: "In such a nation of castes, the fact that shumos appropriate spaces that had previously been reserved for the so-called nice or decent people is repudiated, and shumos are excluded from national life. . . . Shumos exist to confirm that discrimination is a fact, to solve some people's identity problem and to validate a system that establishes a convenient order." These hegemonic representations racialize inequality and legitimize dictatorship as the only means of pacifying those who are considered inferior.

The naturalizing of the hierarchy that subordinates shumos to gente decente is also reproduced in documents forwarded widely on the Internet, such as the apparently jokey "Shumometer, version 1.0." Using the form of U.S. online sites like You Might Be a Redneck If . . . , but distinguished from them by its rejection of any identification with the category being defined, the Shumometer lists attributes and activities that may seem normal but actually reveal one's shumo-ness while, less humorously, condemning *igualamiento* and rehearsing a series of violently racist prejudices about the dark plebeian. It ends by calling for, in an echo of the genocide, a "Guatemala free of shumos."

Paying homage to European classical tradition, the Shumometer begins by claiming the term originates in the Latin *shumo vulgaris.* In the same mocking tone, the anonymous authors assert that, "while the origin of the word is uncertain, it is generally considered that it came into use to describe the emergence of a primitive group of hominids who refused to evolve either culturally or socially, and preferred instead to keep their little backward caveman customs alive." The primitiveness of shumos is evident in their grotesque speech and deportment. Thus you are a shumo if, when greeting someone, you say, "¡Gusto *en* verte!" rather than the grammatically correct "gusto *de* verte" or "Buendía," "Buena tarde," or "Buena noche" when these expressions should all be pluralized. (These usages are often signs of Spanish being someone's second language.) Vulgar shumos spit on the street to clear their throat or blow their nose into their hands and fling the snot to the ground. The disciplined bourgeois body desired by the authors of the Shumometer likewise feels threatened by the premodern shumo habits of grabbing "the forearm of a person when shaking hands," calling someone's attention with sounds such as "ChstChstChstChst," having inappropriate body hair—in the case of a woman, failing to shave the legs or armpits, and in the case of a man, growing a thin and wispy moustache or beard (also often a sign of indigenous heritage)—or, for women, "if your nail polish looks flaky (how much time and/or money does it really take to take good care of your nails, to avoid the 'ceviche-maker manicure'?)."[7] And it is shumo to "whistle at women in the street (and pretend to look elsewhere when they turn to look at you)," or throw "your plastic bag of mango with *pepitoria* [the remains of a popular street snack] or any other garbage out the window and onto the street." "The SHUMO," the document concludes, in an echo of Kaltschmitt, "is a social (or antisocial), cultural (even though they have no culture, by their own choice), existential condition rather than a racial trait. He has a characteristic way of walking, tricky ways, and form of expression. . . . SHUMOS are lazy, whining, treacherous, cheap drunks, idiosyncratic, macho, cowardly, ignorant, and generally, but not always, criminal."

The Shumometer makes the stakes of these grotesque behaviors clear by taking aim at those transnational networks that symbolically revolve around Los Angeles or Chicago rather than Miami, which is where rich Guatemalans go for shopping and entertainment. Los Angeles has the second largest population of Guatemalans in the world, after Guatemala City, and is denounced as the "Mecca of the shumos," with Chicago not far behind. LA is also marked by a large Mexican American and African American presence, adding a differently racialized ("ghetto") tint to the shumo. Thus a person is a shumo if he adopts "Mexican" musical tastes or, more explicitly, if "he listens to *norteño* music (at a very loud volume)" or "pretends to be a black rapper." You are a shumo if, as part of your daily attire, you like to dress in "a white T-shirt with a Los Angeles or Chicago sports team logo under a white button-down shirt," if "your favorite basketball or baseball team is from L.A. or Chicago," or "if you never take off your hat all day, no matter what (or if you wear it backwards); wear a tie to an important reception, but with a *chumpa* [jacket rather than suit coat]; or use black shoes with white socks—as if dark socks were more expensive . . . (this is a definitive feature)." Other instances of the cultural war between decent and regular people in Guatemala can be found at the website Some Signs That You Are a Loser (with *Loser* in English in the original), where one sign is "Your favorite basketball team is the Lakers or a Chicago team . . . because you have a friend who went over 'there' to work!," and at cerotes.com and shumos.com, which list the various attributes of the shumo: "My car, my dress style, my appearance, my accent, my name." The number of such sites and the devotion of time and energy by their authors to delineate these figures of horror and fascination in such exquisite detail give a sense of the psychic stakes in these relationships.

As a transnational subject, a member of a migrant or translocal community that lacks "education" and "high culture," the shumo, muco, or cholero is also stigmatized as a *cholo latino* or a Mexican *naco* (a Mexican insult that uses the name of an indigenous nation to ridicule the poor and tacky). Some Signs That You Are a Loser also crosses Mexican and U.S. borders, repeating several themes addressed in the Shumometer but with the fundamental criterion that being a loser means enjoying excessive familiarity with Mexican TV culture "because you speak like Adal Ramones [host of the Mexican show *Otro Rollo*]" and "you followed the full two series of the Mexican show *La Academia*, choosing as your favorite performer Miriam or Yahir." There is also the Loser Wannabe, the International Loser, the Innocent Loser, and the Loser Snob, who doesn't know what SUV stands for "and who doesn't have even one." Loser Hypershumo is the person who has a "car with one or more NO FEAR, NITTO, RACING TEAM stickers, or any other such sticker like .COM, BAD BOYS or a little boy urinating." A Poor Loser is the person who has "more than four pirate CDs bought on Sixth Avenue or at a traffic light" and finally, a Loser is a person who uses the word *loser*, while himself being a Loser.[8]

In a context in which using English terms or demonstrating fluency in "the white man's tongue" is still a marker of social superiority, it matters *where* one learned this language. Thus a sign of being a loser is if you "sing songs in English and didn't even pass course 1 of the IGA," or worse still, "you didn't go to the IGA, but the CIAV."[9] Within the diaspora there are now large numbers of working-class indigenous and ladinos who have been exposed to English and who can thus threaten the symbolic heritage of the social elite, which includes giving English first names to their children. Thus the documents insist that while it is proper to have a name such as Wilmer if your surname is Plotcharsky, if your surname is Chonay (a clearly Mayan surname), such a first name makes you a Loser. Indians and shumos don't have the right to those names, much less to reinvent them by modifying their spelling or adapting them to their own symbolic representations. A person is a shumo if he or she has a name such as "Gerson, Guilian (William), Jonatan, Yorch

(George), Cristofer, Yulissa, Yesenia, Yadira, etc." And if that is the case "you should definitely have it changed."

Some of the most anxious expressions of antishumo sentiment arise around that most powerful symbol of technological modernity (and manhood): the automobile. The fact that indigenous or ladino immigrants often return from the United States with secondhand cars to use or sell has modified that symbol by democratizing the prestige associated with car ownership and the ability to pollute the air with car noises and fumes. Since the Guatemalan elite cannot limit plebeian access to cars, shumo-ness is assigned according to the brand and color of the car a person drives, the music played in it, the size of the speakers, and the decoration. Shumo cars are decorated with stickers in English and flashing or fluorescent lights, fitted with polarized "bodyguard" windows, alarms that sound at every stoplight, and large speakers for loud music. In the United States a similar class or race site of distinction would divide those who admire low-riders and other cars decorated by their Californian, Texan, Chicano, *pocho*, African American, or white-trash owners who "custom fit" their cars to make them more flashy and aurally inescapable, and those who shudder at their approach. The Internet quiz "Measure Your SQ" (Shumential Quotient) also links these characteristics to the inappropriate mobility of the shumo by arguing that a shumo is someone who "has at least four relatives living in the United States and travels there at least three times a year to bring back a couple of wrecked cars." Shumos think that "having a Honda is a status symbol," and a shumo "has more cars than fit in the family's garage, and therefore parks several of them on the street, even though putting them all together you don't get one whole decent car."

The links between the hatreds voiced on these antishumo sites and other forms of social violence emerge in the presentation of the shumo as a person who is discursively subject to sexualized violence by his social superiors. For example, "Measure Your SQ" has a final section recommending actions that should be taken to vaccinate people who are showing one or two symptoms of *shumitis*, a chronic and highly contagious disease, "which has acquired epidemic proportions in Guatemala," and that "should be treated as any medical condition." Therapy for these borderline cases consists of administering "eight daily extra-strength doses of CLASS," which come in "three-inch-wide suppositories, to guarantee better absorption." Likewise the insults and jokes used by fans of the Cremas de Comunicaciones, a Guatemala City soccer team associated with *caqueros* (the rich), when attacking their rivals, the lower-class–identified Rojos del Municipal, stigmatize the Rojos not only as servants or choleros but also as homosexuals and bastards. A particularly cruel sample of this humor describes their mothers as raped women whose cholero sons are *hijos de puta* (sons of whores), sexually impotent, cuckolded, criminals, animals, shit, or garbage, and rejected by all women except prostitutes. In anti-shumo discourse, shumos are subject to violent suppression because they are profoundly impure.

In the Zona Viva, the Liveliest Place Is Where the Mucos Are

Nowhere are the consequences of antishumo discourse more evident than in the criminalization of Guatemala's nonwhite and plebeian youth. Guatemalan nation building understands a particular urban way of life, lived out by those few residents of the capital who are educated, Europeanized, white, or mestizo, (i.e., nonindigenous), as the only one conducive to achieving the purportedly universal positive values of civilization, capitalism, Christianity, cultural modernity, and the free market (Foley 1990; Willis 1981). Radical antishumo morality therefore becomes a duty of Guatemalan citizenship. As an example of this increasingly naturalized attitude, in the final section of the Shumometer the authors assert:

> The preceding is NOT about "good" kids or "upper class Daddy's boys." It's a reality. If the "experts" in *chapina* [slang for Guatemalan] sociology are offended, it's because one of these shoes fits them. If you suffer at least ONE of the above characteristics or symptoms, you are a SHUMO. Period. If you find any of these characteristics in someone, tell them without fear that he or she is a SHUMO. The shumo is the reason why we are how we are. . . . It has nothing to do with the dollar, the government (which is full of shumos, by the way), nor with the church, nor the gringos, nor ANY of that. It's the shumos. Period.

Within this discourse, hopes for the nation's future rest on youth who attend private schools and have access to the right cars, brand-name clothing, air travel, international hotels, health care, labor rights, paid vacations, computers, cell phones, correctly acquired foreign languages, and other material and symbolic goods. Youth who cannot claim these attributes are subject to the full force of the violence necessary to keep a nation of bowed heads submissive (see Levenson this volume).

Unsurprisingly, therefore, some of the most elaborated discourse on la shumada comes from within the culture of the elite and would-be elite youth who are called upon to police the boundary separating them from their undesirable shumo shadows. In the stratified local geography that delineates class, culture, and race hierarchies among the youth of Guatemala City, where you live and which school you attend are critical factors. The city, whose metropolitan area had a population of 3.1 million in 2010, is divided into twenty-two zones. The traditional zones where the rich used to live are Zones 9 and 10, now known as the "Zona Viva," where the embassies, hotels, bars, restaurants, and discotheques are concentrated, and Zones 13, 14, and 15. More recently the wealthiest families have moved to the outskirts of the city, on the highway to El Salvador, bringing their private schools, bodyguards, exclusive clubs, hospitals, and shopping centers with them. As a result of this segregated pattern of urban residence, many youth have never been to their city's downtown and are more familiar with Miami or Houston. The poorest areas, with the highest levels of poverty and criminality, are on the periphery of the old downtown: Zones 5, 6, 7, 8, 19, 21 and the dreaded Zone 18 (see also Way 2012). Living in the old downtown itself, in Zones 1 to 4, which the rich abandoned in the 1940s and 1950s, does not guarantee any social status. This strict mapping of class or race onto urban space also means that if you do not have a car or use only public transportation, you belong to the lowest sector of society and probably are one of the many people of Maya descent who were pushed to the city by wartime displacement or extreme rural poverty.

If you are young, moreover, a key social indicator besides your place of residence, phenotype, money, dress, and the car that you (may) drive is whether or not you attend a private school, especially those that used to be exclusively for "old money," like the Liceo Guatemala, Liceo Javier, Colegio Belga, or Colegio Monte María. Since the middle class has now invaded these institutions, it is more prestigious if you attend still more exclusive schools, like the Colegio Maya or the Colegio Americano. If you go to a public school, even if it is one of the old ones founded during the Liberal Reform, you clearly belong to the lower echelons of society. Elaborating on the configuration of inequality by zones, the school system provides a further spatial fix for a rigidly hierarchized urban youth culture.

Elite high school students deploy antishumo discourse to forge identities as good bourgeois citizens. Ursula Herrera, a senior math and physics student at one of the most exclusive schools in Guatemala City, discussed shumo dress, specifically its exaggerated and imitative character, as an example of what she considers "bad taste," lack of "class," and the characteristic shumo overornamentation: "Sometimes a person isn't a complete shumo, but uses shumo things and you can say, 'Hey, you really are shumo with those shoes,' or, you know, the stickers on their car or some other detail." Shumos, according to Ursula, are people who dress with no "class." "I don't really know how to define 'class.' It's like they want to imitate . . . maybe like ladinos who want to imitate gringos, and the Indians who want to imitate ladinos. It's like an ugly way of being, no class whatsoever.... Again that word [class], you know, they want to wear designer jeans and all. . . . how can I explain? I could tell you what a shumo looks like: loose pants, with big labels."

Shumo style is tasteless, as Nancy Fernández of the Liceo Benjamin Franklin (in Zone 15 and for children of elites) elaborates, because it is a poor imitation, one that is out of place. "If you go to Panajachel and you wear a *camisa típica*, a *morral*, and a little hat you fit perfectly in the environment. But if you go to Jutiapa in the Oriente, you look all wrong if you dress like that.[10] You look like a muco." "You call someone muco," Eduardo Ramirez, who just graduated from one of the most expensive high schools in Zone 15, echoes, "because he doesn't dress like he is supposed to, like people our age dress." In her own take on cars and shumos, Ursula says, "Their cars are always full of stickers and have a big exhaust pipe that goes bbbbbfffffffffffff. That is so classic of someone you'd call shumo. Not all shumos have cars. But if a person sees something like that, they'd say, 'Ah, what a shumo car.' And the music, typical, top volume. They need speakers this size [huge]." Josefina is a student in her last year of bachillerato at Liceo Hispano Americano, a private school in Zone 1, favored for the impoverished middle class of Guatemala City. She explains, "There are those who like rock music, then there are mucos, and *normal* people who listen, let's suppose, to Roberto Carlos [a very popular mainstream Brazilian singer] and stuff like that." Shumo exaggeration and noisiness reflect subnormal powers of judgment.

This poor judgment is not only distasteful but is also threatening. Eduardo links shumo dress to rebelliousness through the image of Che Guevara:

> Young people who wear clothes with [Che Guevara's] image are shumos to some extent, and they shouldn't dress like that. Why? Because he was against his nation's policies. So now that is like having a T-shirt with the picture of . . . I'm sure there are T-shirts of Osama bin Laden, and why? Because he was against the United States, he rebelled against them. So this muco or shumo or whatever you call this person of little culture always likes to go against everything. "Look, come at seven," you say. So he arrives at six-thirty. Why? Because he was told to come at seven. They are rebels, but not the good kind who want to make things better, but rebels who are against everything and who aren't happy with anything.

Although this link between shumos and insurgents might appear to politicize the challenge they present to decency, antishumo discourse insists that their rebellion is congenital rather than political. Carmen Salazar, a student at the lower-middle-class Instituto de Señoritas Belén, thinks that shumos are "people who are stubborn. A shumo is someone who, when you ask them to do something, they won't do it, or you'll say 'Do such and such,' and they will do the opposite." Such character flaws also link shumos to older racist discourses about Indian stubbornness and stupidity. When I mentioned to Albertina Rodriguez, who studies at the School of Commerce (a public school in down-scale Zone 1), that a student of the Colegio Irlandés had told me that only shumos wear Che Guevara T-shirts, she responded, "He probably says that because he thinks a lot of himself. He thinks he's the best. A shumo is an indigenous person, and that is the word most often used to discriminate against them . . . but you can use it with nonindigenous people as well. Supposing you are wearing a Che T-shirt and they say, 'Look, he wears that shirt. Ah, well, it's so shumo.' So it means you are imitating them [indigenous people]." In general, the boundaries between shumos and Indians are fluid. "Shumos," says Albertina, "can be distinguished from the rest by the way they talk, the way they walk. You can tell they are indigenous, also because of their physical features — that's why people say, 'Ah, that's a *shumito* [adding the diminutive -ito can show endearment but also denigration].'" However, even though it is synonymous with "Indian," she adds, "the word *shumo* is used when a person has attitudes that are not accepted by the group, so that you tell someone, 'Ach, you are being so shumo, you are pure shumo,' that is, you are saying they are Indians, although maybe their attitude had nothing to do with indigenous peoples, but it is still a way of insulting someone." Perhaps the most pungent description of the relationship between these two forms of racialization is offered by Nancy Guzmán, a senior high school student at the private but lower-class Zone 1 Liceo Escocés: the word *shumo*, she says, "refers to an Indian, but is much worse than Indian."

As creatures who are worse than Indians, shumos are not only racialized by their attitude but criminalized for it. Ernesto Santizo, a senior student at a lower-middle-class private school in Zone 1, argues, "A muco and a shumo are the same shit, although a shumo might just fuck around and a muco is most surely a *marero* [gang member] or thief. Mucos are all thieves. Most mucos are indigenous. Both are *mara* [gang-members] that don't give a fuck about anything, they don't carry a cell phone or designer clothes. They just like to fuck around. These mucos don't go to school, or if they do it's just to give everyone a pain in the ass." Nancy Fernández likewise adds criminalizing elements to her description of shumo dress, incorporating mucos and choleros as well in a hierarchical definition: "Being muco is worse than being cholero. A muco is lowest on the ladder. Most are also choleros and are involved in maras, they use, you know, loose shirts, loose pants that reach to the knees, baseball caps put on backwards, and many bracelets. They even look dirty."

But as the concern with elaborating these definitions suggests, the fluidity with which objects and trends circulate within a highly commodified youth culture, even in rigidly hierarchical Guatemala City, makes it difficult to keep a firm distance from la shumada. Eduardo Ramírez, for example, develops a complex social taxonomy for the Zona Viva of Guatemala City, the nightclub district in Zone 10 that serves as a microcosm for the social, racial, and cultural divisions of the country:

> At the Zona Viva, I could define for you the places where each kind of people goes and why the music they play there attracts them. The liveliest place is the mucos'. . . . Well, it's supposed to be lively. I don't think that's where you can have the best time, but it is the noisiest place. Like it or not, that music is just noise, it's noisy, and it seems people like to hear noise. That is the Saboy and the Khalúa, further down. Then there's Scream, where everyone dances only *trance* because the lights and all are for that type of thing, and that is not for caquero or shumo people, but for *intermediate* people. Then there is Level, which is not muco but close enough, and at the top there's Salambú, where I've never been but it's much like the Saboy and the Khalúa. At the top of the list you could put Sambuca, which is where nice people go. There are also places for people who like heavy metal, others for people who like *fresa* music, they call them *fresas* [literally, strawberry, here referring to upper class, snobs].

Eduardo's affirmation that the liveliest place is where the mucos are reflects Ursula's sense that "people accuse others of being shumos, but sometimes they enjoy those shumo things too."

Students are sometimes able to recognize the function of the shumo in reproducing all too evident race and class hierarchies. For example, Ernesto Alvarado, who is studying to be an accountant at a lower-class private high school, said, "Anyone with no dough is shumo." Daniel Sanchez, who is a senior student at the male-only Instituto Nacional Central para Varones says that being shumo "is being *natural* [indigenous], and *muco* means poor. They are discriminatory terms, like *indio* or *cholero*." He sees a gender divide in the discourse: "These are words that people use a lot at school, but girls use them most. . . . They relate to a guy because of the car he drives or because of his money. . . . They see other guys who have less and they begin to rub it in their faces. Maybe that's why." *Cholero* in Nancy's definition "is a word to identify poor people, people who haven't had the opportunities we had."

In my interviews, however, moments like this, in which someone might feel tempted to sympathize with the shumo, quickly segued into a reaffirmation of normalcy, defined as acceptance of the status quo. For example, Eduardo continues his account of the city's musical tastes thus:

> I like all kinds of music, all except that vulgar muco music that brings nothing good. On Sixth Avenue you see lots of mucos listening to their kind of music. Why? Because they are against something and maybe they don't even know against what. . . . They aren't doing so well in business or anything else, they are against that. The thing is to be against. I think mucos are disoriented, confused. Maybe that is why everyone is against them.

Likewise working-class Ernesto recovers from his moment of possible sympathy by asserting that "shumos want everything, but they are nothing." A cholero, Carmen adds, "is when you ask someone, 'Look, do this thing,' and maybe you say please, but they reply 'Who do you think you are, I am not your servant!' That happens most when someone asks a favor and the other person replies, 'Ah, no, they think I am the errand boy, the cholero.'" For her, a cholero "is like an extremist, too funny, but not nice funny but, you know, heavy [*pesado*]."

Disrespecting the Canche

Antishumo sentiment suggests both an inchoate sense of Guatemala's structural inadequacies and anxiety about the unsettled class, geographic, race, and status borders between country and city and within the city's zones. These unsettlings are linked to transnational border crossings and their uncanny hometown effects: how the Maya and lower-class ladino diaspora in North America is changing the meanings of being poor, Indian, quasi-Indian, and young in post-genocide Guatemala. Historically, based in U.S. anthropologically inflected ideas of "development" and nation building—or what I would call anticommunist modernization—indigenous people were targeted for "culture change," that is, ladinization and *mozo*-ization (becoming wage laborers rather than independent peasants). I think we now see a shift to targeting the young, unemployed, and poor dark-skinned plebeians who may be either indigenous or ladino and are stigmatized as shumos, mucos, and choleros. This population, however, is the target of criminalization rather than improvement and, in classic neoliberal style, is enjoined to take all the risk of "development" on themselves, assuming the debt and physical danger of getting to the United States so they can send back the remittances the national economy depends upon.

Yet the symbolic war between gente decente and gente corriente or shuma that I have described here also opens space to question the legitimacy of fair-skinned canches as adequate representatives of the Guatemalan nation in the post-genocide era. For example, Antonio Echeverría, of the Liceo Benjamin Franklin, deflates the pretensions of Guatemalan whiteness when describing his classmates:

> These aloof "Europeans" were born right here, and are ladinos anyway. They are too proud to say they are ladinos. One says ladinos are the offspring of a taxi driver and a whore. He says, "Taxi drivers are ladinos, and so are whores." And what do you think most of the people in the school are? Most are ladinos! Only two or three of these idiots who have their heads in the clouds say they are German, European! The worst of it is that these were people from Cobán, where they used to marry Indian women so that their land would not be taken away from them. The uncle of one who says he has German ancestry slept with one of the Indian women at the plantation, and the girl was red-haired, just like the jerk [*cerote*] himself.

Antonio responds to the implied denigration of his own (ladino) forebears by those "too proud to say they are ladinos" by pointing out that, red-haired as they might be, they too could be the product of a forced sexual relation with an Indian woman, and thus just as ladino as those they despise.

Standoffs between the 1999 presidential candidates—Alfonso Portillo, from Ríos Montt's authoritarian populist Guatemalan Republican Front and supported primarily by indigenous people, and Oscar Berger, the white finquero running for the neoliberal pro-business National Advancement Party (PAN; see Solano this volume)—revealed similar challenges. Berger's vice-presidential candidate, Arabella Castro, campaigned by praising PAN's president Alvaro Arzú (La Jacky's "martyr" for the nation), in terms that genuflected to shumo anticanche sentiment: "All those that said that a canche was not going to work for poor people are sorry for not being *panistas*" (*Prensa Libre*, June 28, 1999). A month later, Portillo, in consummate *shumo* style, inverted the hierarchies of whiteness in his own favor, defiantly declaring, in reference to Berger, "I am not afraid of that *canchito*" (*Prensa Libre*, July 18, 1999). (Portillo won, but Berger came back to win in 2004.) The immense energetic motor animating antishumo sentiment reflects the deep anxieties generated by the growing strength of this defiance.

Portillo's regime deployed the violence and corruption stereotypically associated with la shumada to intimidate the canches, not unlike how Antonio replaced the prestige associated with white European blood with the humiliating possibility of a violently illegitimate and thus indigenous origin. However, these political and symbolic defiances do little to shift the paradigm of imperial whiteness itself, and such relational identifications may continue to validate local hierarchies associating civilization with racial and cultural purity—of both canches and Maya.

So, what form of antiracist politics can help demolish these hierarchies without naturalizing the ladino privilege of violent dominion over indigenous Guatemalans? And what politics might take up the possible hybrid alliances germinating in the emerging, rebellious, simultaneously plebeian and cosmopolitan, postracial identification of the shumo? Perhaps we need to define this as a struggle for representation and justice rather than defending the biologization of politics or the phenotypical racialization of community.

An Antiracist Politics?

In *"Más que un indio": Racial Ambivalence and Neoliberal Multiculturalism in Guatemala*, Charles R. Hale (2006) compares racism in the United States and Guatemala to suggest that what he calls "racial privilege" cannot be voluntarily abolished by acts of the conscience or solidarity. For Hale, racial privilege is a complex of material and symbolic advantages that do not depend on the individual will of those who enjoy them but rather on structural social inequalities between whites or ladinos and those who are their dark-skinned subalterns. Like U.S. whites, born to advantage, ladinos learn that they are "more than an Indian" and will tend to defend that position, even if they are willing to accept in principle that "we are all equal." In Guatemala, Hale argues, a gradual and still incomplete transition is taking place, from a classical racism that insisted on the inferiority of indigenous people to a "new cultural racism" that reproduces ladino-indigenous hierarchies with the argument that indigenous culture prevents its bearers from acquiring what they need to participate in modernity. He is pessimistic about the possibility of ladino-indigenous alliances in a context in which, he claims, ladinos have never felt the boots of the oppressor.

Yet to make this argument Hale must erase both the distinction between the "European" or "really white" Guatemalan elites and most ladinos—the very frontier between gente decente and the shumo that I have been mapping here—and the fact that ladinos in Guatemala constitute a large sector of the rural and urban proletariat and precariat as well as the transnational diaspora. Poor ladinos, along with indigenous migrant workers, were instrumental in the strike by the Campesino Unity Committee of 1980, and, with indigenous *compañeros*, made up the rank and file of the guerrilla struggle and the popular movement. It would be naïve to say these relations of "difficult complementarity" (Bastos and Camus this volume) were idyllic, but it seems equally problematic to reduce decades of complex resistance practices to the same racial divide fetishized by Tax and Redfield (only now laying the blame for Guatemala's lack of progress on recalcitrant ladinos who can't appreciate the Maya as gringos do). In fact the ambiguously raced, lower-class but striving, Che Guevara–T-shirt–wearing, fluent in English, Spanish, and Maya shumo who so (rightly) worries the gente decente seems to be the *product* of these very alliances.

And, despite Hale's pessimism, a survey of world-changing struggles against slavery, colonialism, civil rights violations, apartheid, and imperial oppression reveals that white "progressivism" has played an important role in antiracism—even a decisive one. Anthropology as a discipline has often been at the forefront of such struggles, articulating trenchant critiques of its own racist origins that have helped to decolonize the metropolitan academy and sciences. Indeed few organized subaltern movements can afford to do away with all alliances with more privileged sectors if they wish to succeed. The cross-class and cross-race relationships forged over the past forty years, and new ones being made in the diaspora by working-class Mayas and ladinos who have become Central American Americans, are examples of just such alliances. Drawing on revolutionary experiences in Guatemala, migrants have animated labor struggles in the United States (Fink 2004; Wellmeier 2001) and been at the forefront of struggles against deportation and for other immigrant rights. The consumer behaviors that mock upper-class "rights" to cars and other goods are also accompanied by revitalizing forms, like women investing in traditional Maya garments they were unable to afford before and migrant remittances buying housing, farmland, and material for traditional artisanal crafts, as well as paying for elaborate housewarming, *quinceañera*, and wedding celebrations and children's education. The new or revitalized political, economic, and cultural capacities of migrants do not escape either local or transnational racial hierarchies, but they do challenge those hierarchies with their incorporation of ladinos working alongside Maya under the same challenging conditions, just as they did on the south coast plantations and in guerrilla columns and refugee camps during the war.

At all levels of practice and discursive production, such co-laboring can be productive. Carol A. Smith (1999) says that her conversations with "academics of color" have been indispensable for expanding her theoretical and political sensitivity to racism. The inverse is also true: many Guatemalans — ladinos, Mayas, Afro- and Asian-Guatemalans, and even members of the criollo elite — can say that we have broken through the methodological restrictions imposed by the indigenous-ladino dichotomy and undertaken our studies of global racist hierarchies thanks to our conversations with so-called white academics. However, these alliances are by their very nature political ones, to which the application of labels like "racial," "interethnic," or "national" is itself a political act.

I would connect this to the politics of the shumo diaspora in North America, which challenges us to understand its radical modification of the conditions of access to markers of superiority that were once considered the symbolic patrimony of the Guatemalan elite. Their *cosmopolitanism from below* is transforming the cartographies of transnational power by quietly defying the racist moral leadership that still dominates everyday interactions in this new transnational Central and North American society. Their stigmatized hybridity overflows the limited space of antiracism as tutelary solidarity and philanthropy from above.

I have explored the simultaneous challenges to and policing of race and class boundaries in North American anthropology and Guatemalan history, revolution, popular culture, and diaspora to illuminate interconnections, continuities, and transformations. The privileges at stake are immense and demand continuing labor to create a different kind of "cultural change," one that ensures transnational citizens' rights for all members of this grand diaspora — regardless of when, how, and where they left or now reside — so that everyone enjoys the mobility of the anthropologist.

Notes

1. Some of the identity terms in this essay may be offensive, but I repeat them in order to indicate their use by my interlocutors. *Indian* or *indio* remains a symptom par excellence of the continuing power of historic forms of racism. *Indigenous* is used more often by the mainstream, influenced by national and international parlance and legislation, and *Maya* alludes to the wide-ranging counterhegemony being articulated through ancestral knowledges, the *buen vivir*, or living well as collective well-being, and other politicized identificatory practices.

2. It would take another essay to outline the hierarchies *within* Euro-American whiteness (Mediterranean, German Nordic, Anglo-Saxon) as perceived by those aspiring to whiteness in Guatemala. The held-over colonial attitudes of the nineteenth cen-

tury, with the overt francophilia of the Liberal Reforms and the sense that the Old Country is whiter than the United States "color" Guatemalan elites' ideal others. Carlos Navarrete Cáceres describes how once, in the presence of General Ramón Ydígoras Fuentes (1958–62) and an educated foreigner, he questioned the latter's opinion, for which the president scolded him, "And you think you know more than the Frenchman?" This is a system where it is always essential to be "more than an Indian" (Hale 2006), yet one is always "less than" a French person.

3. With similar imperial origins as the word *ladino* (originally meaning a non-Roman who spoke Latin), *plebeian* signifies a member of the ancient Roman lower classes — as opposed to patrician — and has come to mean vulgar, coarse, or common, an identity I explore in more detail in González Ponciano (2005).

4. Based in market relations of human bodies, it meant that even a great-great-great-grandchild of an enslaved African (who might look no darker than her white father) would "count" as black. (This "rule" makes Barack Obama, son of a Caucasian mother, the first "black" U.S. president.)

5. In response to the fears expressed by the students I interviewed, I identify some of the private schools with fictitious names. For instance, Colegio Irlandés and Liceo Benjamin Franklin are for the children of the elites who live in Zones 15, 14, 13, 10, or 9, or Carretera a El Salvador and visit the Zona Viva or the shopping mall La Pradera. Despite the racial and cultural pride attached to its name, the Liceo Escocés, another fictitious name, is a lower-class, private high school in Zone 1. At the other extreme, public schools, often meant for boys and girls studying to be educators or shopkeepers, are the Instituto Normal para Señoritas Belén, the Instituto Normal para Señoritas Centro America, the Escuela de Comercio, the Instituto Técnico Vocacional, and the Instituto Nacional Central para Varones and are situated mostly in the capital city's downtown.

6. The Prussian term *junker* seems particularly apropos of Guatemala in the sense of a member of a class of aristocratic landholders, strongly devoted to militarism and authoritarianism, from among whom the German military forces recruited a large number of its officers.

7. This refers to the toll it takes on one's hands to handle the oysters and other seafood used in the popular dish ceviche.

8. This echoes an earlier common saying: "No hay indio más indio que él que le dice indio a otro indio" (There is no indio more indio than the one who calls another indio indio).

9. The IGA is the Instituto Guatemalteco Americano, established in 1945 and a leading institution in cultural relations between the United States and Guatemala. The CIAV, the Centro de Inglés Audiovisual, is a private school that offers English courses for low-income students.

10. Panajachel is a tourist town, also known as Gringotenango, on Lake Atitlan in the indigenous highlands. She is describing Mayan fashion, a woven shirt and bag, which is also associated with hippies. Jutiapa is a province in the semiarid eastern part of the country inhabited primarily by self-identified ladinos, known for its "frontier" fashion of cowboy boots, Stetson hats, and pistol holsters.

A GENERATION AFTER THE REFUGEES' RETURN
Are We There Yet?

A Clash of Expectations

It is September 27, 1996. A high-level delegation from the Guatemalan government is in Mexico paying a visit to fellow Guatemalans who have spent fourteen years in refugee camps. The refugees, however, are distrustful of such efforts to woo them home. One of the visitors, a prominent presidential advisor and chief negotiator in the peace accords about to be concluded, speaks eagerly to his audience. Himself a former insurgent, he believes they will respond to his heartfelt description of how the current government is willing to transform Guatemalan society in meaningful ways through the peace accords. "This is not just a negotiation, this is a political dialogue, in order to achieve a better Guatemala," he tells them.

As an example, he cites the provision in the accords projecting that within four years every single Guatemalan child will be offered schooling through third grade. Given illiteracy rates and the lack of any school at all in countless villages, he understands this is a significant government commitment and announces it with pride. Around me, the refugees listen quietly, some taping the presentation for future analysis and as proof of promises made. In this model refugee settlement in Campeche, virtually all children are in primary school and many reach secondary school as well. In front of me, a man with all the attributes of a typical *campesino* (peasant) writes in a belabored way in his tattered notebook. I look over his shoulder as he writes, "Education only to the third grade. . . ."

Between 1981 and 1984 the United Nations High Commissioner for Refugees (UNHCR) extended refugee status to more than forty-five thousand rural (and mostly Mayan) Guatemalans in southern Mexico, people who were fleeing direct repression or the rumor of war as it drew near. Most went to Mexico with the idea of staying a few weeks until "things calmed down," but in the end most spent between one and two decades in the camps. In 1987 a group of male political activists with broad backing in the camps formed the Permanent Commissions of Guatemalan Refugee Representatives (CCPP) in Mexico to negotiate the terms of return with the Guatemalan government. While guerrilla cadres from the Guatemalan National Revolutionary Unity (URNG) were actively involved with the Permanent Commissions, the CCPP's broad appeal among most refugees stemmed mostly from the inherent logic of strength in numbers. Regardless of their individual politics or war experiences, the movement gave refugees the hope that a safe and dignified return to Guatemala was possible if people collectively pressured the government for guaranteed conditions for all. By 1992 the Permanent Commissions' leaders had successfully negotiated minimal conditions for an "organized and collective" return. Known as the October 8 Accords, these agreements stressed the government's commitment to human rights and access to land and prompted the collective return of approximately twenty-three thousand people between 1993 and 1999. Altogether some 43,500 refugees came home between 1984 and 2000, including children born in the camps as well as returnees not affiliated with the organized returns. About twenty-two thousand—half of them children born in Mexico—opted to stay.

In the 1990s Guatemalan refugees were the vanguard of Guatemala's future. Having overcome some of the worst of the violence, they projected hope for Guatemala's path to peace. As a movement they were making demands for access to land and a just, nonmilitarized society that were still barely being voiced inside Guatemala, and they had proved adept at leveraging international pressure to make the Guatemalan government pay attention. By 1997 there were resettled or newly formed rural communities located in Huehuetenango (nine), Alta Verapaz (eight), Petén (nine), the Ixcán region of Quiché (ten), and in the south coast region (twelve). The negotiation process and attendant international attention created a propitious scenario as returnees had access to land, development projects, and strong international support. But as the disappointment the campesino refugee expressed about the diminished educational opportunities "back home" illustrates, the gap between refugee aspirations and the reality that awaited them was often vast.

Rather than the new, just, and prosperous Guatemala that the revolutionary years had promised, they have had to settle for a positive spin on the ongoing hardships they share with other rural Guatemalans.

Here I delve into this gap by recalling the vision and promise refugees brought back to Guatemala. I also explore the fate of their hopes and dreams as the triumphant return was followed by more mundane struggles for re-incorporation. In the process, many communities, especially in the Ixcán region, found themselves wrenched by profound internal divisions as the intense unities forged around common experiences in wartime and shared short-term goals unraveled in the face of new conflicts. Donor fatigue, the disbanding of governmental commissions established by the peace accords, and renewed militarization in many returnee areas affected by the grow-ing drug trade also meant setbacks for the minimal early gains in safety and psychological security, economic viability, and prospects for the next genera-tion. These troubling reversals of what had seemed like an irresistible move-ment forward beg the following questions: What can refugee "reintegration" mean in a society where so few rural Guatemalans have access to the eco-nomic, social, political, and psychological components of the minimum well-being that would constitute "integration" in the first place? Working toward concrete future projects is also made more difficult by the unstable founda-tions of their collective identity. To be a "returned refugee" is always to hark back to a receding past of common hardship and oppression (that can be as divisive as it is unifying) rather than a clear and necessarily shared vision of the future. How long must one be "back home" before one stops being a returnee? What might then hold people together to face the challenges of surviving in postwar neoliberal Guatemala, especially in attempts to create projects that are not about return?

I first visited the Chiapas, Mexico refugee camps and Guatemalan high-lands in 1985 and then returned in 1988 as a researcher with the Guatema-lan social science institute AVANCSO, traveling through rural communities marked indelibly by war displacement, just as the first trickle of repatriates began arriving from Mexico (AVANCSO 1990, 1992). Later, as a staff mem-ber of the UNHCR's Guatemala office and part of the team mediating the government-to-refugee dialogue to operationalize the refugees' return from 1992 to 2000, I was a direct participant in the ups and downs of the often tumultuous process. Collaborating with the United Nations Commission for Historical Clarification (CEH) in 1998 allowed me to review the testimonies submitted by returnees at that juncture, and I participated in different UN and interinstitutional fora that evaluated the return process and its prospects (Instancia Mediadora and GRICAR 1999; UNHCR 1999; Worby 2000; UNHCR and ASIES 2000; Cabarrús et al. 2000). After opting for my own repatriation to the United States, I continued to follow the return's aftermath through frequent travel to Guatemala. This was supplemented by bumping into returnees who had subsequently migrated to my new home in the San Francisco Bay Area, including receiving phone calls about those detained by Immigration and Customs Enforcement (ICE) and following still others via Facebook. The experience of exile creates irrevocable change, as evoked by the Guatemalan refugee return story. But exile is also familiar to all those who have negotiated transnational identities and confronted the difficult choices wrought by crossing borders.

Daze of the Jungle: Returnee Unity Put to the Test in Ixcán

It is difficult to overstate the great promise returned refugee communities seemed to offer to Guatemalan society. Compared to other rural Guatemalan actors, the refugees had highly effective organizations and visionary goals. Observers and refugees alike remarked repeatedly on the unexpected silver linings that had emerged from the violence of war and harsh reality of exile: the suffering of the displaced had evolved into gains with potential to spill over more broadly within the communities they had left behind. In Mexico refugees had gained advantageous skills and knowledge and become familiar with Mexican education, health, and transportation systems that worked relatively well compared to those in the isolated and neglected Guatemalan villages they had left behind. Many had acquired public speaking experience, and monolingual Maya-speakers typically had added Spanish to their toolkit.

While still in Mexico, many expressed their determination to bring their new organizational models, outspoken voices, and broad vision of the world and its possibilities home to neighbors in ways that would lead to future progress. As one returnee leader stated in a forum evaluating the 1992–99 period:

> There is a multiplier effect of everything we learned while in refuge. We transmit our organizational methods and experiences to our neighboring communities, which often have had no access to the benefits of getting community projects [funded] or government-sponsored public works because they are not organized and often because they don't even know that they have rights that they should be demanding. (Instancia Mediadora 1999: 24)

In some ways the returnees fulfilled a vanguard role simply by demanding one. Before any comprehensive peace accords were signed they successfully brought the government to the negotiating table. They focused national and international attention on the militarization and impoverishment of rural communities, thereby helping support other grassroots movements. Their powerful demonstration effect was clear in the triumphant first "return" in January 1993. Contravening the government's request to quietly cross directly from Chiapas into the Ixcán region, a caravan of some 2,500 returnees, escorted by international observers and luminaries like Rigoberta Menchú, wound its way for several days overland, cheered on by crowds that lined the highway and greeted with a series of celebrations in Guatemala City. Such inspiring events helped pull attention and funding toward returnee and neighboring communities, just as the refugees had planned.

Not planned, however, was the almost immediate foundering of refugee unity once the movement touched Guatemalan soil. The refugees outwardly projected a united front based on the bonds of a shared Maya culture and similar experiences of exile, an image often accepted uncritically by outside observers. However, return communities consistently experienced internal debate and conflict in the resettlement process and were often fractured by return rather than being reunited by it. In fact most returnee communities were actually new, either situated in regions previously unfamiliar to the occupants or made up of inhabitants from many different refugee camps who did not initially know each other. Even when people returned to their original homes, they soon lost the illusion that they could simply reconstitute their old communities.

The most serious conflicts erupted in Ixcán, the lowland jungle region bordering Mexico, where several communities were part of the collective return movement. In the 1960s and 1970s Ixcán was part of the agricultural frontier and epitomized the social experiments of the day, including kibbutz-type settlements, commercial cooperatives, and ethnically mixed communities. In 1972 a small band of mostly 1960s guerrilla veterans launched what would become the Guerrilla Army of the Poor (EGP) in Ixcán, a process described in Mario Payeras's *Days of the Jungle* (1983). By the 1980s Ixcán was best known for the utter destruction wrought there by the army counterinsurgency and for the open conflict between the army and the guerrillas that endured there into the early 1990s, long after other areas were pacified. Then Ixcán came to symbolize a test case to see if violent history could be turned around by the peace accords implementation (FGT and Fundación Arias 1998). As the region of greatest refugee exodus (CEH 1999), Ixcán received more returning refugees than any other.

Ixcán returnees anticipated a number of conflicts as they prepared to go home. The war years were marked, as many essays in this volume show, by an onslaught of army and government red-baiting: anyone who became a refugee was branded a subversive, a characterization eagerly embraced by those who had occupied refugee lands in the refugees' absence (AVANCSO 1990; DIDE 1994). Returnees were prepared ideologically for the aftereffects of military hearts-and-minds campaigns and knew that the army held full sway, that the guerrilla was still present, and that new settlers were on their lands. Other external obstacles, including land mines, also shaped where returnees could resettle and their (not always successful) efforts to regain their lands (Worby 2002b). Through it all, the returned refugees presented themselves as a group united by their common suffering, common enemies, and common goals vis-à-vis the new settlers who branded them subversives, and against the army and government placing roadblocks in the way of their returning under their own terms.

But even as the January 1993 caravan wound triumphantly through the highlands, the growing differences among EGP-affiliated activists debating the future of the war effort, which eventually affected many campesino and grassroots groups, were already at work (Bastos and Camus 2003: 108–13 and this volume; Velásquez Nimatuj this volume). I was in a UNHCR vehicle when the caravan suddenly stopped on the Pan-American Highway for an extended delay. The radio chatter was about the unexpected decision of the returnees to deviate from the planned itinerary. But after a wait, the demand was inexplicably reversed and the caravan continued. I learned only years later that two rival "advisors" were battling over control of the movement in the name of their respective sides of the growing split between EGP factions. Although Bastos and Camus comment that in the early 1990s many conflicts within EGP-connected organizations "were resolved without ruptures" (2003: 110), in the case of the returnees the trickle-down effects of these battles were just beginning.

Just as returnee groups were debating their autonomy from the URNG, the latter was trying to present a united front while negotiating with the government and working to establish a legitimate political party that anyone could affiliate with openly. Within the URNG an ongoing debate in wartime about the role of civilian populations in the armed struggle was spilling over to the postconflict transition period. For refugees, vital issues were at stake, such as when and where to return, whether the returnee demands would be independent of the URNG's strategy in conducting and ending the war, and the extent to which funds given to refugee groups were or should be siphoned off to the guerrilla for the war effort (a process known as skimming, *descreme*, later acknowledged by URNG commanders; see Fuentes Mijangos 2008: 74).

As none of this could be discussed openly, disputes quickly degenerated into highly emotional "You were a guerrilla" and "You were an army sympathizer" shouting matches. Some critics of the URNG were former cadres themselves, disillusioned—sometimes vehemently—with the guerrilla's war strategy, including treatment of the indigenous and the civilian population more generally, and with its failure to fulfill so many hopes. But some of the leaders rejecting any alliance with the URNG were also opportunists, involved in land grabs and other abuses of power, which undermined their credibility. The alliances this group of returnees initiated with the army appeared to go far beyond the stated goal of establishing autonomy from the URNG. At this time the guerrilla organizations were still a clandestine movement and the military aspect of the war remained quite hot in Ixcán, so denouncing someone as a guerrilla still put them at considerable risk.

In 1997, when the war was supposed to be over, conflicts among returnees had become explosive, especially in the five communities affiliated through the Ixcán Grande cooperative. Two opposite bands, one quietly sympathetic to the guerrilla cause and one against anything associated with it, were by now firmly established, and virulent public discussions about each individual's history and current attitude toward the guerrilla left very little neutral ground. The peace accords and resulting guerrilla combatant demobilization process set off six months of violence in Pueblo Nuevo (part of the cooperative). In January 1997, in a contentious assembly election, the anti-URNG contingent took control of the Ixcán Grande cooperative executive committee, turning subsequent meetings into shouting matches. MINUGUA, the UN peace accord verification mission, documented threats of physical attack against those dissenting from this contingent, including warnings that such dissidents could lose their family land rights. "Extra" lands (often belonging to refugees still in Mexico) were supposedly being distributed to friends and allies of the new leadership. This was occurring just as Ixcán lands, out of circulation during the war years, were increasing in value in the postwar economy, a process I discuss in more detail below (see also Solano this volume). Lands were now eyed as a potential source of oil (as petroleum companies began to explore the area) and for their proximity to the Mexican border, of interest for both legal and illicit trade ("De la guerra militar a la guerra política" 1997).

Responding to the URNG's call to fill out the ranks and thus increase its political impact, some returnees went off to the guerrilla demobilization camp established temporarily on Ixcán Grande cooperative-owned lands. Some of those appearing in the camp had been combatants, often secretly, while others were simply unarmed political supporters. Both irked those who wanted not only to sever any present political ties to the URNG but also to reject the appearance of any historical connection. This anti-URNG group began to work to prevent those who went to the demobilization camp from being able to return home.

In May 1997 a group of demobilized combatants returning home to Pueblo Nuevo was refused entry, and some inhabitants threatened to burn accompanying UN and government vehicles. The next morning a village mob destroyed the meetinghouse of the women's organization Mamá Maquín, accusing its members of being guerrilla sympathizers. This followed an unsigned letter faxed in April to international agencies in the name of "Ixcán communities" promising that "organizations like Mamá Maquín and [human rights promoters] OPODEDHEGUA will be eliminated in our communities because they are grassroots groups of the URNG." The fact that accusations of being guerrilla sympathizers became a legitimate way to intimidate and disarticulate women who had been outspoken and organized around asserting their rights was not lost on the women involved (Worby 2002a; Falla 2006).

Returnees said the situation was a terrifying revival of the insecurity they felt as the 1970s repression began, when a personal dispute with another neighbor or a flimsy rumor could lead to blacklisting and even death. A letter from members of the cooperative addressed to the Guatemalan president and the URNG commanders said:

> The [current] situation of aggression, confrontation and lack of respect among us has been developing over the last two years. With the signing of the Peace Accords, we felt hopeful. . . . But now we are fearful and even feel terrorized because in our very communities we are attacking one another. Peace has not come to Ixcán Grande. Here there are no winners or losers. . . . Rather we are all losers with this fratricidal conflict. (Asociados . . . Ixcán Grande 1997)

This conflictive situation was "resolved" when the government, via its National Fund for Peace (FONAPAZ), placated the anti-URNG leadership by promising to finance the legalization process leading to individual landholdings in exchange for allowing community members to return from the demobilization exercise. Thus, indirectly, the struggle over participation in the guerrilla demobilization led to the dismantling of the Ixcán Grande cooperative itself. Once the land was no longer held jointly, the whole purpose of the transcommunity cooperative structure was lost.

In other communities, divisions developed along similar lines, and new alliances were formed that would have previously been considered impossible. In nearby Cuarto Pueblo an estimated 350 people were killed in a February 1982 army massacre, yet in 1998 a "friendship committee" was formed between some returnee leaders and the local military base. At the time, survivors explained that this was simply a decision that could prove useful "if the war starts up again" (Davis 1998; see also Iznardo 2002). The army promised to contribute to road construction and provide other aid to Cuarto Pueblo in exchange for community willingness to reexamine historic prejudices against the army and accept an army outpost within community boundaries. The Catholic Church's Ixcán parish newsletter commented on the dilemma faced by Cuarto Pueblo inhabitants, who needed a road but were resentful that the army was in charge: "The [army] friendship committees and [new] co-op leadership manipulate the population. The army denies any connection with the friendship committees but we all know that they were created with army support and that many of their members go regularly to the army to inform on the population, and that they intimidate and trick the community" (Atz'am 2000). These same community leaders also actively opposed community members' legal case against the military for the 1982 massacre there (author interview 2009).

Rather than experiencing these incidents as a normal expression of democratic debate in a postconflict scenario, those involved found them disturbingly reminiscent of the war. The military asked its former victims to give it and the new postwar nation a chance but undermined its overtures by engaging in insidious (and achingly familiar) attempts to buy or coerce followers. The UN documented secret payments by the army to community members-turned-informers, and the offers of road-building and development projects seemed more than implicitly to be in exchange for not prosecuting the army for its crimes. Internal divisions in turn stymied returnee goals of development and were a disincentive for outside support and funding. Rather than the old neighbors / new settlers challenges that the returnees had anticipated, many seemed dazed by their return to the jungle and the unexpected enmities encountered there.

As time went on, many returnees expressed regret and shame about the internal problems that derailed common community goals and hindered external support. Eventually these tensions dissipated, and they no longer dominate public life in these communities, but they prompted lasting consequences: decreased public participation and little incentive to assume leadership roles. Some returnee families left, a few forced out of the very communities they had worked so hard to regain, while others sold their lands, taking advantage of escalating prices once cooperative landholding was dissolved. A church bulletin described the aftermath in Pueblo Nuevo: "Our cooperatives are sad and of low morale because of so much disorder and division of these past years. . . . It seems as if the co-op members are no longer interested in any co-op business, they just want to get their [individual] land titles and no longer be bothered with the [co-op] payments and dues" (Correo de la Selva 1999). The force that sustained collective hopes and dreams throughout displacement and exile was no match for the conditions of return.

Economic Reintegration and the Promise of Land

Refugee experts call meaningful economic reintegration key to a successful repatriation. For returning Guatemalans, would this mean maintaining the subsistence levels experienced in Mexico? Returning to the same (deficient) level as other Guatemalan rural neighbors—which had led so many of them to organize cooperatives, jungle colonization, and peasant leagues or to join the armed struggle in the first place? Or could they aspire to more? In 1996 a forum of returnee representatives, government officials, and international and national advocates attempted to define successful reintegration via the idea of a family's "dignified standard of living" (*vida familiar digna*). The terminology was used in the October 8, 1992, accords in reference to government land allocations per family. Since operationalizing the concept had become a source of conflict, the meeting was called to formally debate and define the term. The forum recommended including food security, housing, access to education, health care, recreation, clothing, credit, basic services such as electricity and potable water, and basic infrastructure such as roads as necessary for a *vida digna*. In addition, a family should be able to produce enough to allow savings for future development, and land allocations should be sufficient to avoid excessive out-migration or division of land into increasingly smaller plots with each passing generation (Instancia Mediador 1996).

In practice, however, returnees' economic situation seems far from dignified. Of course, the development potential of each community depends on how much external aid they received to begin with and how much they receive now, the functionality of their organizational structures, land quality, extent of established production previous to settlement, and proximity or ease of access to markets and infrastructure. The majority of communities opted for production of staples (corn and beans) combined with commercial crops (coffee, cardamom, natural rubber, sugarcane, fruit, heart of palm) and cattle to propel them beyond poverty. With the exception of a handful of communities with good-quality land and favorable locations, however, prospects never really looked good, even to begin with, and opportunities for commercial credit and technical assistance remain limited. Furthermore there were no safeguards built in to protect against market fluctuation, environmental degradation, or natural disasters.

The UNHCR's preliminary analysis of forty-seven returnee communities (Worby 2002b) found that only five (12 percent) had the potential to go beyond subsistence agriculture and attain economic growth over the medium term. At the other extreme, thirty-two (74 percent) could only aspire to subsistence agriculture. Of these, by 2001 eighteen had failed to generate even small surpluses, putting them at risk of not meeting basic needs under normal conditions, let alone in case of natural disaster or other difficulties. Notably this analysis preceded the sudden twin devastations in 2005 of sharply declining coffee prices and Hurricane Stan.

Attempts at alternative development have included production of natural shampoos, sustainable harvesting of rainforest products, a processing plant to pack hearts of palm for the national market, and ecotourism based on the combined draw of the natural wonders in their remote communities and the intrigue of their war-time experiences. For example, the large caves in Santa Maria Tzejá, Ixcán, fit both categories, as the community's tour guide will tell you: spectacular on their own, they also provided refuge when townspeople fled the very army rampage in February 1982 that caused so many to go into exile, dividing the community between Guatemala and Mexico for twelve years.

Alongside the challenges of determining what to produce and how to sell it is the question of how to organize social relations and land tenure in ways that correspond to ideals formed in pre- and postwar struggles but that are also viable for production and marketing in the new Guatemalan economy. Cooperatives that collectively market their members' goods and offer needed community services (stores or transportation) persevere in many communities. While often not enjoying the 100 percent membership that defined the colonization efforts of the 1970s, they remain important ways villagers buy and sell collectively while allowing for different levels of production and consumption by individual member families.

As a concrete result of refugee women's organizing in the Mexican camps, new organizations, especially the group known as Mamá Maquín, took on land tenure issues as they specifically affected women. Women's land access became a banner cause, based in analyses of private and public sphere inequalities. These showed that women's household labor was not recognized by spouses or by state entities when it came to titling or controlling the land acquired and maintained through the sweat equity of both men and women. Refugee women worked to take advantage of the transition moment of the return and land acquisition process to reaffirm their rights as co-owners of family and communal lands and to work toward having such rights recognized and implemented (Organización . . . "Mamá Maquín" 1999; García Hernández 1998).

Despite refugee women's vibrant movement to gain equal right to lands upon return, cooperative regulations and the limited imaginations (or blatant discrimination) of those implementing them have meant that women are mostly excluded from formal membership unless they are widows or represent an absent partner. And, no matter the form of tenure, women have tended to lose these hard-fought rights when forms of land tenure changed after the return (Worby 2002a, 2002b). Specifically, where the land was purchased in the name of a group of refugee co-owners, women's struggles got them included on the initial ownership documents. But once the land was transferred to a cooperative (with the ultimate goal of creating family-level ownership), women were once again left out—even as they argued strenuously for two heads of the same household to have a "voice and vote" in the cooperatives without doubling family co-op dues or other obligations. In a few communities, women's land rights are universal, especially where changes to titling procedures of national lands dictated the inclusion of men and women equally or where the organizational capability of the women was particularly strong. There are also communities in which both men and women are cooperative members and in which some couples have chosen the female head of household as representative, but these are exceptions.

Whether based in traumas of wartime betrayal or the commonsense acknowledgment that concentrated resources attract greed, people have become wary of risking too much in a structure where their investment could be lost to corrupt leaders or paid employees. Feeling they've been fooled once, many have chosen to withdraw from group economic ventures to avoid being fooled again. In La Lupita in Suchitepéquez a corrupt and inept group of young cooperative leaders were removed from their posts in 2000 for gross negligence, although they were never prosecuted (Fuentes Mijangos 2008). The community eventually overcame this blow, but in the words of a community leader, "This [situation] made for a difficult moment and affected how interested people remained in continuing to work collectively. . . . These acts of corruption of the previous co-op leadership were one of the reasons that the people later approved the dividing up of the land that led to disbanding the [collective] cattle project" (quoted in Fuentes Mijangos 2008: 128).

As a mechanism to manage communal lands, cooperatives turned out to be an intermediate step in some cases where the real goal was to divide land so that each individual family held a title. The so-called dismemberment (*desmembramiento*) of communally titled lands in favor of families (or male heads of households) obtaining individual title to specific plots has marked returnee communities throughout the country (see also Velásquez Nimatuj this volume). There are pros and cons to each of the three most common forms of land tenure: individual title, collective title for named individuals, or collective title with fluid membership through a legal entity such as an association or cooperative (Worby 2002a). Collective control via associations or cooperatives was mostly promoted by government programs and NGOs, while most families advocated for individual titles as a way to assure control, including being able to leave an inheritance to their children and guarantee land rights even for those with minority viewpoints, who otherwise could be expelled from the community with little recourse. They recognize, however, that with individual titles the community as a whole loses any say over who can buy their way in or accumulate land in ways that replicate the economic stratification and unequal privilege that were part of the roots of the conflict (Worby 2002a; Hurtado Paz y Paz 2008b: 195–97).

One unexpected result of refugee demands for land and the government decision to satisfy them through purchases on the private market was that some wealthy landowners were able to make a tidy profit selling poor-quality, isolated, and often overpriced lands (Worby 2002a). In turn, once families gain individual land titles they may be tempted to sell if faced with a medical emergency or to launch a family member's migration venture, and there are entrepreneurs and companies ready to buy (most recently in returnee areas to consolidate plantations that produce African palm for biofuel). This may leave people once again dependent on renting others' lands or selling their labor on Guatemalan plantations (Hurtado Paz y Paz 2008b; Solano 2010b).

The apparent failures of so many initiatives based in careful planning from exile, grueling hard work to remake community life, and institutional initiatives that were, at least at first, amply supported by national and international organizations raise serious questions about a working economic model for rural Guatemala more generally (see Gonzalez-Izás this volume). Most models and plans dreamed up before the return were agriculturally based and involved competing more successfully in the marketplace; few have proved feasible. In some cases this is because the numbers for projected timelines, costs, and production were too optimistic even in good times and because plans did not take into account real-life community idiosyncrasies, the changing world economy, or the possibility of natural disasters. As a consequence, to stay afloat the returnees have resorted to a variety of strategies, including dividing up communal lands for family-based use, diversifying skill sets within the family, and migrating in search of work.

The Remilitarization of Returnee Communities

Seventy-eight percent of Guatemalan refugees returned before the peace accords were finalized, meaning their initial reintegration was to a country still formally at war. At first the return was framed by refugee fears of army repression alongside desires to flex their political muscle by demonstrating what kind of new Guatemala they wished to shape, one in which the army would be subservient to civilian rule and restricted to defending national borders instead of implementing internal repression. These played out in acts of what was basically political theater between returnee communities and the army. In 1994 and 1995, when patrolling army units were sighted within the boundaries of Ixcán returnee communities, residents invoked the rights of private property owners and accused the army of trespassing and intimidation. They denounced these violations and on several occasions even surrounded and "detained" the soldiers while international observers and national authorities were called to mediate, drawing up agreements between the local army commander and community leaders as to where and when the army could be present. Elsewhere in the country returnees successfully pulled off similar moves, for example in early 1995, when inhabitants of Nueva Esperanza (Nentón, Huehuetenango), feeling protected by the presence of nonprofit organization representatives as witnesses, detained a group of soldiers until the governmental human rights ombudsman office could appear on the scene to mediate the soldiers' departure (Chanquin Miranda 2007: 121).

This sense of returnees' command of the "peaceful and civilian" nature of the return was shattered when a trespassing army patrol gunned down eleven people in the returnee community of Xamán, Alta Verapaz, in October 1995. Similar to other cases, Xamán inhabitants had escorted the soldiers to the middle of town, where they were surrounded by a circle of men, women, and children. The returnees then held forth on the perceived violation to their rights and demanded that the soldiers wait for the arrival of outside observers. However, neither the soldiers nor their commander was prepared to play their role in the pageant of a new demilitarizing Guatemala, framing the incident instead by their standard storyline of displaced people being guerrillas or guerrilla sympathizers (CEH 1999, illustrative case 3). Panic ensued among the soldiers, and the tragedy unfolded with a hail of bullets striking unarmed villagers.

What this meant for returnees was not only that soldiers could fire on them in broad daylight with impunity but also that the nonviolent forms of struggle that had been used successfully to prompt mediation by outside (usually international) arbiters, leading to tangible or political victories, were no longer guaranteed. The fact that it took almost a decade for justice to be done was devastating to those who witnessed the crime (as they could not conceive of a process where this had to be further proved) and augured poorly for other legal processes aimed at punishing both material and intellectual authorship of crimes committed in the early 1980s.

Such instances of military power getting the upper hand contribute to the sense that more recent militarization, even when supposedly directed at recognized threats such as drug traffickers, is really a tactic for controlling political activism. In one example, dozens of camouflaged soldiers overran the Ixcán returnee community of Ixtahuacán Chiquito in August 2006 while seven helicopters circled overhead. Government and army officials stumbled over different explanations: that they were stalking a known drug lord or, alternatively, seeking an arms cache of the guerrilla (officially disarmed for a decade). Organizations that had been fighting for control over local natural resources, however, were quick to see antidrug rhetoric as a pretext to "intimidate the population and inhibit the . . . struggle firmly opposing the hydroelectric project known as Xalalá and the oil company projects" (communiqué, quoted in Solano 2006). The immediate effect was a nightmarish return to soldiers in camouflage rounding up villagers at gunpoint while others gathered their children and ran for the cover of the jungle. Although the army, to much applause, had abandoned its infamous military operations base in the Ixcán in 2004 and turned over its installations, associated with mass repression, to the national university and local maternity hospital, it reopened the base in 2009. This occurred just as local activism against international investments in extractive industries was growing. Ironically, when the nominally socialist president Alvaro Colom welcomed the soldiers back in February 2010, he justified their return as part of efforts to deliver on the security offered in the 1996 peace accords (see the president's website Comunicacioncolom 2009).

Inhabitants do face real problems of criminal gangs, drugs, contraband, and related lawlessness. Many, however, see the military as less a solution than part of the problem, as army officials and even the institution as a whole are seen as directly linked to these lucrative trades. A long list of organizations rejected the army's 2009 return to the Ixcán in no uncertain terms:

> Government spokespersons have stated that the military base has been reestablished with the intention of guarding the borders and combating common and organized crime, as well as more generally stabilizing the region. We the people of the Ixcán are clearly tired of violence, insecurity, assassinations, robberies and assaults. But militarization is NOT the solution. The priorities should be eradicating impunity and strengthening and refining our justice system and the National Civil Police, so that these institutions can actually fulfill their prescribed functions. As long as 98% of criminal offenses remain in impunity, criminals will continue to operate freely in the country. (Organizaciones Sociales 2009)

The communiqué also pointed out that crime could increase from brothels and taverns related to the soldiers' presence, and rumors persist to this effect. In 2010 one Ixcán man assured me that twenty homicides had occurred nearby, following the army's return. He commented, "Instead of bringing peace, they are disrupting it further."

The growing economic force of illicit business (drugs, arms, migrant smuggling) in the midst of impoverished communities also potentially drives another wedge into communities already divided by the political differences from the war years. In communities where some inhabitants are actively involved in drug running and related activities, people do not dare speak out for fear of reprisals. Children of the organized women and men who returned to Guatemala to speak truth to power, willing to confront even the dreaded army when it encroached on their communities, now "choose" silence. Such choices follow recent histories of purges from the community for speaking out against corrupt leaders now that guns and guns-for-hire are in plentiful circulation. Another persistent and divisive fear is that young people will be drawn to illegal economic activities because these are lucrative and need workers in a place where there are few other options. Ricardo Falla (2006) describes young people in Ixcán coming of age in an environment of drug trafficking, contraband, lynching of petty thieves, domestic violence, and rape—all going unreported and unpunished. What are the possibilities that this generation will carry on their parents' dreams that a new Guatemala will be built from within?

Migration: Still on the Move

Given the many limitations they face in their communities of return, many residents are instead "choosing" the new exile of migration. The United States beckons to young men and women willing to try their luck, as well as to older men and women with families hoping to save for capital improvements at home or to pay for children's schooling or other basic needs. Mexico also remains an option for seasonal employment, especially for communities near the border and for returnees born in Mexico who can exercise their Mexican citizenship. In some cases whole families have moved back to the Mexican refugee camps they once left so hopefully, while others have opted for immigration within Guatemala, selling their land claims in returnee communities in search of greener pastures. The historical strategy of having a stake in more than one place continues to broaden economic opportunity while also giving families a safety valve should violence, natural disaster, or economic catastrophe make one place less viable.

Before it became a given that returnee communities would join the swell of rural communities sending their members *al norte*, the hope was still that the lands and other hard-won gains of the return movement would allow stability and permanence for the returnees. But even in one of the best-case scenarios, like La Trinidad in Escuintla, a well-organized and united community founded on the south coast in 1998 by refugees with common roots in Huehuetenango, such hopes fell short. Although they were not starting from scratch, like so many returnees, because they settled lands already in coffee production, this good fortune was reversed as coffee prices fell sharply following the return. Margarita Hurtado Paz y Paz (2002) documented the outflow of workers—first men seeking work on neighboring coffee farms, then single men and women seeking service jobs in nearby towns, the capital, and Mexico, and finally larger numbers leaving their families for the United States. By early 2002, 20 percent of the community's men were in the United States, and those left behind expressed both envy of and resentment toward these potentially privileged few. Women and children temporarily deprived of their family members, at risk of hardship and worse in the United States, faced a series of emotional and practical difficulties (Hurtado Paz y Paz 2002). In contrast, because of profitable cattle and mango projects as well as more options for paid work locally, by 2007 only a handful of people from La Lupita in lowland Santo Domingo, Suchitepéquez, had gone to the United States (Fuentes Mijangos 2008: 108). In La Lupita and many other returnee communities, members are encouraged not to abandon collective endeavors for migration, in part by rules that they must compensate for an absence with fines or work shifts carried out by family members left behind (Hurtado Paz y Paz 2001; Camus 2008).

In the Barillas, Huehuetenango, returnee community of Nueva Generación Maya, also a "made in Mexico" group, migration to the United States began in 1996, at first with one or two people leaving per year, later reaching a total of twenty-five people in 2005. The results of a household study showed that 11 percent of the community's population was in the United States, affecting 43 percent of the 109 households surveyed; 77 percent of the migrants were men. Because of migration, 38 percent of the households were headed by women with a male partner absent. (Two single mothers also migrated.) About half migrated as single men or women, and the rest left partners or children (Camus 2008).

As in Guatemala more generally, migration for returnee communities is a double-edged sword. Even when economically successful it results in family separation and community dispersion. On the one hand, when plentiful, migration-generated remittances allow individual families to build homes and send their children to high school and even to college, fulfilling some of the transformational goals set in the return. On the other hand, migration earnings can contribute to economic stratification, fomenting envy and inviting the further concentration of capital. Furthermore, as individuals increasingly focus on their own economic gains, time put into collective endeavors diminishes, changing the entire tone of community life when compared to what the returnees initially envisioned. One of Laura Hurtado Paz y Paz's interviewees among Ixcán migrants said, "We expected more from the Peace Accords. When there wasn't much, the people said: let's each do it on our own, there's no use waiting for [results] from our community-level efforts as these are going very slowly" (2001: 35). Along the same lines, returnees told me they hoped the requirement of their donated labor to community economic projects would diminish over time, thus "setting them free" to work hard (individually) to earn money needed to pay off the collective debt on the land (author interview 2001).

At the dawn of the new millennium returnee communities still hoped that a migrant spending two or three years away was a tolerable sacrifice to resolve a short-term crisis or permit a long-term investment. A decade later, however, the U.S. recession coupled with the skyrocketing cost and increasing danger of crossing Mexico and successfully evading stronger U.S. border security simply means that those who do migrate are deeper in debt and find less work. And they can no longer engage in the circular migration patterns that used to allow for periodic family reunification. Fear of leaving the United States before becoming successful economically (an increasingly elusive possibility) leads to becoming "trapped in *el norte*" as the three- or four-year plan stretches into uncertainty. Despite increasingly ubiquitous cell phones in the Guatemala countryside and growing access to the Internet, accessible at least in municipal town centers, it is still common for families to have little information about and scant contact with relatives in the United States. While not unique to returnee communities, the emotional effects and the resulting estrangement between couples and increasing numbers of youth growing up without one or both parents are phenomena with long-term effects that will continue to resonate in families with long experience of fragmentation.

As migration becomes a rite of passage for youth, it erodes the hope that a successful return will create an environment and provide a livelihood back home that will attract and sustain the next generation. Binational status, easing access to Mexico, and the already tenuous bonds returning adolescents had for Guatemala made some travel back and forth inevitable for that first generation of young returnees. That the newest generation, with little direct memory of Mexico, is joining the outflow defies returnee hopes but also places their communities on an equal footing with their neighbors. The stigma of migration, initially seen as abandoning the collective cause, has worn away as the numbers of those leaving the community continue to grow.

The Fruits Yet to Harvest

Despite all the limitations and disillusionment, simply setting foot in a return community can make evident differences with nonreturnee neighbors. The inhabitants have organized and demanded support for improved housing, basic services, and access to roads and potable water. They have set new standards for free expression, as former refugees readily articulate their version of historical events with little trepidation, and they were often the first to offer their testimonies in the "historical memory" projects of both the Catholic Church's historic memory project and the CEH. Monuments listing victims' names now stand in many communities as reminders of war-time atrocities, and anniversaries of massacres are commemorated, helping to break the unwritten rule that this history should remain hidden. Local theater groups even reenact histories of army violence in both returnee and nonreturnee communities (Taylor 1998; Falla 2006; Manz 2004). Children learn about the 1980s and the time in Mexico as part of history classes in some communities in ways yet to penetrate the mainstream curriculum (Shea 2005; Oglesby 2007a).

Promised "education only to the third grade" from the beginning, returnees aspired to even more than sixth grade for their children. While in Mexico many refugees became education promoters, a sort of "barefoot teachers" of grades one to six. Nearly all returnee children, both boys and girls, enrolled in elementary school, and they invited children from neighboring villages to join them. As their children studied elbow-to-elbow, neighboring villages began to overcome their fears and suspicions of returnee communities and saw them as a regional asset. The promoters undertook additional training in order to qualify for salaries as government teachers, and many became involved in revamping the curriculum. Some communities sought to change the rigid traditional Guatemalan education by incorporating elements of Maya culture and their own history as refugees in the curriculum and by using more participatory techniques.

Several returnee communities have founded middle schools, a rarity in rural Guatemala, which act as magnets, drawing students from around the region. Where such schools are most visionary, young people study history by interviewing their elders and science by running their own tree nurseries or conducting local biodiversity studies and, in student theater, have taken on subjects such as women's rights, war-time traumas, and controversial regional infrastructure projects like hydroelectric dams. These middle schools have created a pipeline allowing rural youth to aspire to high school education and beyond. But despite impressive gains, returnees face many obstacles in education. Schools have limited supplies and textbooks, and the teachers are still not adequately trained, making it tempting to fall back on traditional methods and materials ill adapted to the needs students face.

Some observers also worry that access to higher education will result in a brain drain from the rural communities, as the best and the brightest seek professional employment in the urban areas. For that reason, the community of Santa Maria Tzejá in Ixcán requires that scholarship recipients complete a year of community service and contribute a portion of their future salary to a community scholarship fund. In hopes of creating a pool of visionary community leaders rather than benefiting a few individual families, the Santa Maria Tzejá students formed an association to promote group activism and seek economic opportunities so they can work in their home region (Taylor n.d.). Many have worked in municipal government, in agricultural or veterinary extension services, in forest resource management, and even as lawyers, while others are teachers in the Ixcán's other villages. A journalism student from this community has gone on to be a TV reporter for Guatevision; his on-the-ground coverage of issues affecting the Ixcán is now posted on YouTube. While some graduates are making their mark in their home regions, others must seek work elsewhere in the country or outside their field of training, while still others are in the United States as factory, field, or domestic workers. Another long-term issue is whether education will irrevocably divide a generation used to the classroom from their parents who work the fields, haul the water, and tend the animals, especially in communities where connecting new educational opportunities to an honoring of community history has not been emphasized.

Returned refugees (and their organizations) have undergone an inevitable transition not only in focus but also in identity. Financial incentives, mainly from international funders, pushed them to claim membership as war victims (*damnificados de la guerra*) alongside others who experienced displacement and repression. Moving beyond the returnee label might seem a natural step and simply a matter of time for the new generations. But for the refugees in Mexico who anticipated a vida familiar digna back in Guatemala, working to continue their movement indefinitely is a political strategy, a way of demonstrating how exile changed them. They are different from both the Guatemala that was and the Guatemala that had changed in their absence. Returnees often refer to the importance of maintaining that difference, or their perception that the difference exists, even as it is no longer tangible in daily life. The 1996 peace accords did not discuss when the special condition of "displaced" or "resettled displaced" should or could end. In retrospect, a URNG leader active in the peace negotiations acknowledged that the "resettlement" accord, like the plan to quickly disburse reparations, was meant as a short-term goal to level the ground among Guatemalans and produce the conditions for addressing the country's more profound and structural problems, not as a way to perpetuate "the displaced" as an identity (author interview 2000). Needless to say, no aspect of peace accord implementation was simple, adequately financed, or completed in a timely manner, adding to the temptation to identify as a victim, which might at least bring psychological as well as economic advantages.

In another illustration of the ill-defined transition to becoming no longer displaced, many of the organizations that served the refugees well in exile did not necessarily correspond to their needs as returnees. Some continued to unify returnee communities for a time before fading away, and some evolved to focus on regional issues together with nonreturnee communities. The Permanent Commissions, already divided into three suborganizations by 1993, fractured further, experienced internal purges, and gradually lost credibility among their grassroots base. By 2001 they had all but faded from view as a national-level organization, with some former leaders settling into community life, some seeking roles in local politics, and some living outside return communities altogether. A few of these refugee leaders created the Union Campesina de Guatemala (Peasants' Union of Guatemala) as an intermediary to help communities obtain projects from government agencies. The latter joined forces with the UNE Party on the eve of President Alvaro Colom's 2007 election in the hopes of guaranteeing direct lines to community project funding in return for turning out the vote (author interview 2007) and (unsuccessfully) ran a candidate who had been a prominent refugee and returnee leader for a congressional seat in the 2011 elections.

The women's organization Mamá Maquín was suppressed in some return communities (Mateo and Camus 2007; Manz 2004; Fuentes Mijangos 2008: 111). In others it is a fixed and active presence, managing economic or social projects and working as a network with a strong voice in regional and national debates, taking positions on international trade agreements, and highlighting rural and indigenous communities' complaints around the presence and policies of mining and energy companies. Madre Tierra, the refugee women's organization in three south coast return communities, also had problems that led to its disbanding in one, Nuevo Mexico, which has had a conflictive internal history, stymieing prospects more generally. In the case of La Lupita, Madre Tierra became known for successful economic project management and regional networking, as two-thirds of the association members come from four neighboring nonreturnee communities (Fuentes Mijangos 2008).

Depending on the community, other organizations that grew out of the refugee camp sectors (youth, religious groups, and health, educational, and human rights promoters) continue formally or informally. Some functions, particularly in education, have been absorbed into state-supported salaried positions. Debate continues about which contributions to the community should be remunerated (often education and health work are) and which are volunteer (manual labor for infrastructure, cooking for community activities, carrying out rotating leadership positions). Where there has been enough foreign or government funding, communities have tried to pay for community or cooperative labor so members can earn a wage without leaving the community. Where funds are available, paying expenses (*viáticos*) for traveling on community business or attending trainings has become standard practice but also dampens initiative to take on work entailing time or travel that is not compensated.

Returned refugees face the same problems as all rural Guatemalans: lingering fears of violence even when the source of the violence has changed; insufficient land for future generations; lack of rural economic opportunity;

pressure to migrate; government neglect of basic social services; and environmental degradation. If their social change agenda has not advanced as quickly as many hoped, returnees have nevertheless made important social contributions and impressive strides in rebuilding their communities and influencing policy and politics regionally and nationally. Just as the organizing experiences of the 1970s and 1980s would not be forgotten or reversed by a decade of harsh repression, the ongoing positive effects brought by those who overcame displacement and loss to triumphantly reclaim their right to return and prosper are still playing out.

WORKS CITED

Abrams, Philip. 1988. "Notes on the Difficulty of Studying the State." *Journal of Historical Sociology* 1 (1): 1–18.

Adams, Richard. 1970. *Crucifixion by Power: Essays on Guatemalan National Social Structure, 1944–1966*. Austin: University of Texas Press.

Adams, Abigail E. 1998. "Gringas, Ghouls, and Guatemala: The 1994 Attacks on North American Women Accused of Body Organ Trafficking." *Journal of Latin American Anthropology* 4 (1): 112–33.

———. 2001. "'Making One Our Word': Evangelical Q'eqchi' Mayans in Highland Guatemala." In *Holy Saints and Fiery Preachers: The Anthropology of Protestantism in Mexico and Central America*, edited by James W. Dow and Alan R. Sandstrom. Westport, Conn.: Praeger.

Adams, Abigail E., and Timothy J. Smith. 2011. *After the Coup: An Ethnographic Reframing of Guatemala 1954*. Urbana: University of Illinois Press.

Adams, Richard, and Santiago Bastos. 2003. *Las relaciones étnicas en Guatemala, 1944–2000*. Antigua, Guatemala: CIRMA.

Ajxup, Virginia, Oliver Rogers, and Juan José Hurtado. 2010. "El movimiento maya al fin del Oxlajuj B'aqtun: Retos y desafíos." In *El movimiento maya en la década después de la paz, 1997–2007*, edited by Santiago Bastos and Roddy Brett. Guatemala City: FyG Editores.

Albizúres, Miguel Angel. 1987. *Tiempo de sudor y lucha*. Mexico City: Editorial Praxis.

Alonso, Conrado. 2000. "Contrastes: Por todos los diablos." *Prensa Libre*, May 3.

Álvarez Aragón, Virgilio, and Ricardo Sáenz de Tejada, eds. 2008. *Izquierdas y construcción de orden democrático en Guatemala: Una aproximación a las elecciones de 2007*. Guatemala City: Fundación Friedrich Ebert.

Americas Watch. 1982. *Human Rights in Guatemala: No Neutrals Allowed*. New York: Americas Watch.

———. 1989. *Persecuting Human Rights Monitors: The CERJ in Guatemala*. New York: Americas Watch.

Amnesty International. 2002. *El legado mortal en Guatemala: El pasado impune y las nuevas violaciones de derechos humanos*. New York: Amnesty International.

"Anatomia de un linchamiento." 2009. *elPeriódico*, December 26.

Arce, Alberto. 2012. "Trabajo infantil y explotación laboral en el azúcar de Guatemala." *Plaza pública*, January 12. http://plazapublica.com.gt/content/trabajo-infantil-y -explotacion-laboral-en-el-azucar-de-guatemala. Accessed June 4, 2012.

Arendt, Hannah. 1951. *The Origins of Totalitarianism*. New York: Harcourt Brace Jovanovich.

Arias, Arturo. 1985. "El movimiento indígena en Guatemala: 1970–1983." In *Movimientos populares en Centroamérica*, edited by Daniel Camacho and Rafael Menjívar. San José, Costa Rica: Editorial Universitaria Centroamericana.

———. 1990. "Changing Indian Identity: Guatemala's Violent Transition to Modernity." In *Guatemalan Indians and the State: 1540–1988*, edited by Carol Smith. Austin: University of Texas Press.

———. 2003. "Central American-Americans: Invisibility, Power and Representation in the US Latino World." *Latino Studies* 1: 168–87.

Arias, Arturo, ed. 2001. *The Rigoberta Menchú Controversy*. Minneapolis: University of Minnesota Press.

Asad, Talal. 1997. "On Torture, or Cruel, Inhuman, and Degrading Treatment." In *Social Suffering*, edited by Veena Das, Arthur Kleinman, and Margaret Lock. Berkeley: University of California Press.

Asociados de la Cooperativa Ixcán Grande. 1997. "Afectados y preocupados por la difícil situación." Letter to Señor Presidente Constitucional de la Republica de Guatemala y Señores Comandantes de la URNG. Ixcán Grande, April 7.

At'zam. 2000. "Guatemala: Región pastoral del Ixcán." No. 5. Newsletter. Guatemala City: Catholic Church.

AVANCSO 1988. *Por si mismos: Un estudio preliminar de las maras en la Ciudad de Guatemala*. Guatemala City: AVANCSO.

———. 1990. *Política institucional hacia el desplazado en Guatemala*. Guatemala City: AVANCSO.

———. 1992. *¿Dónde está el futuro? Procesos de reintegración en comunidades de retornados*. Guatemala City: AVANCSO.

———. 1993. *Aqui corre la bola*. Guatemala City: AVANCSO.

———. 1999. *Por los caminos de la sobrevivencia campesina*. Guatemala City: AVANCSO.

———. 2000. *"Heridas en la sombra": Percepciones sobre la violencia en áreas pobres urbanos y periurbanos de la Ciudad de Guatemala*. Guatemala City: AVANCSO.

———. 2008. *Las políticas de reconocimiento: Una mirada al quehacer sobre racismo y discriminación en Guatemala*. Guatemala City: AVANCSO.

Azpuru, Dinorah. 1999. "La consulta popular: Un voto dividido." Working Paper No. 243. In *La consulta popular y el futuro de Guatemala*, edited by Cynthia J. Arnson. Washington, D.C.: Woodrow Wilson International Center for Scholars.

Babb, Florence E. 2001. *After Revolution: Mapping Gender and Cultural Politics in Neoliberal Nicaragua*. Austin: University of Texas Press.

Bancroft, Hubert Howe. 1887. *The History of Central America*. 8 vols. Vol. 3, *The Works of Hubert Howe Bancroft*. San Francisco: History Company.

Baquiax, Josué Felipe. 2003. *Los Juzgados de Paz comunitarios y su incidencia en el acceso a la justicia de los Pueblos Indígenas*. Quetzaltenango, Guatemala: Universidad Rafael Landívar.

Bastos, Santiago. 2006a. "Construcción de la identidad maya como un proceso político." In *Mayanización y vida cotidiana: La ideología multicultural en la sociedad guatemalteca*, vol. 1, edited by Santiago Bastos and Aura Cumes. Guatemala City: Cholsamaj.

———. 2006b. "Prólogo: Los actores sociales en una década olvidada." In *Movimiento social, etnicidad y democratización en Guatemala, 1985–1996*, edited by Roddy Brett. Guatemala City: FyG Editores.

———. 2007. "Violencia, memoria e identidad: El caso de Choatalúm (San Martín Jilotepeque, Chimaltenango)." In *Mayanización y vida cotidiana: La ideología multicultural en la sociedad guatemalteca, los estudios de caso*, edited by Santiago Bastos and Aura Cumes. Guatemala City: Cholsamaj.

———. 2010. "La política maya en la Guatemala posconflicto." In *El movimiento Maya en la década después de la paz, 1997–2007*, edited by Santiago Bastos and Roddy Brett. Guatemala City: FyG Editores.

Bastos, Santiago, and Roddy Brett, eds. 2010. *El movimiento maya en la década después de la paz (1997–2007)*. Guatemala City: FyG Editores.

Bastos, Santiago, and Manuela Camus. 1993. *Quebrando el silencio: Organizaciones del Pueblo Maya y sus demandas (1986–1992)*. Guatemala City: FLACSO.

———. 1994. *Sombras de una batalla: Los desplazados por la violencia en la Ciudad de Guatemala*. Guatemala City: FLACSO.

———. 1995. *Abriendo caminos: Las organizaciones mayas desde el Nobel hasta el Acuerdo de Derechos Indígenas*. Guatemala City: FLACSO.

———. 2003. *Entre el mecapal y el cielo: Desarrollo del movimiento maya en Guatemala*. Guatemala City: FLACSO, Cholsamaj.

Bastos, Santiago, and Aura Cumes, eds. 2007. *Mayanización y vida cotidiana. La ideología multicultural en la sociedad guatemalteca*. 4 vols. Guatemala City: Cholsamaj.

Bello, Walden. 2008. "Manufacturing a Food Crisis: How 'Free Trade' Is Destroying Third World Agriculture—and Who's Fighting Back." *Nation*, June 2, pp. 16–21.

Beverley, John. 1999. *Subalternity and Representation: Arguments in Cultural Theory*. Durham: Duke University Press.

———. 2004. *Testimonio: On the Politics of Truth*. Minneapolis: University of Minnesota Press.

Binford, Leigh. 1996. *The El Mozote Massacre: Anthropology and Human Rights*. Tucson: The University of Arizona Press.

Binford, Leigh, and Aldo Lauria-Santiago. 2004. *Landscapes of Struggle: Politics, Community, and the Nation-State in Twentieth Century El Salvador*. Pittsburgh, Penn.: University of Pittsburgh Press.

Boff, Clodovis, and Leonardo Boff. 1987. *Introducing Liberation Theology*. Tunbridge Wells, U.K.: Burns and Oates.

Bogdan, Rebecca. 1982. "Bank of America in Guatemala: Bankrolling the Right-Wing." *Multinational Monitor* 10 (3).

Bossen, Laurel. 1982. "Plantations and Labor Force Discrimination in Guatemala." *Current Anthropology* 23 (3): 263–68.

Boteach, Melissa. 2002. *La crisis gestando en Guatemala: Oportunidades y consideraciones con relación a la reforma agraria y crisis de café*. Washington, D.C.: ActionAid USA.

Brenner, Neil, Jamie Peck, and Nik Theodore. 2010. "Variegated Neoliberalization: Geographies, Modalities, Pathways." *Global Networks* 10 (1): 182–222.

Brett, Roddy. 2006. *Movimiento social, etnicidad y democratización en Guatemala, 1985–1996*. Guatemala City: FyG Editores.

———. 2007. *Una guerra sin batallas: Del odio, la violencia y el miedo en el Ixcán y el Ixil, 1972–1983*. Guatemala City: FyG Editores.

———. 2010. "De movimiento indígena a complejidad política: La evolución de las políticas indígenas, 1996–2007." In *El movimiento maya en la década después de la paz, 1997–2007*, edited by Santiago Bastos and Roddy Brett. Guatemala City: FyG Editores.

Brintnall, Douglas. 1979. *Revolt against the Dead: The Modernization of a Mayan Community in the Highlands of Guatemala*. New York: Gordon and Breach.

Brown, Richard, and Richard Wilson. 2009. *Humanitarianism and Suffering: The Mobilization of Empathy*. Cambridge: Cambridge University Press.

Burchell, Graham, Colin Gordon, and Peter Miller. 1991. *The Foucault Effect: Studies in Governmentality*. Chicago: University of Chicago Press.

Burgos-Debray, Elisabeth 1984. *I, Rigoberta Menchú: An Indian Woman in Guatemala*. Translated by Ann Wright. New York: Verso.

Burguete, Araceli. 2010. "Autonomía: La emergencia de un nuevo paradigma en las luchas por la descolonización en América Latina." In *La autonomía a debate: Autogobierno indígena y estado plurinacional en América Latina*, edited by Araceli Burguete Cal y Mayor, Miguel González, and Pablo Ortiz. Quito, Ecuador: FLACSO, GTZ, IWGIA, CIESAS, UNICH.

Burrell, Jennifer L. 2000. "The Aftermath of Lynching in Todos Santos." *Report on Guatemala* 21 (4): 12–15.

———. 2009. "Intergenerational Conflict After War." In *Mayas in Postwar Guatemala: Harvest of Violence Revisited*, edited by Walter Little and Timothy J. Smith. Tuscaloosa: University of Alabama Press.

———. 2010. "In and Out of Rights: Security, Migration and Human Rights Talk in Postwar Guatemala." *Journal of Latin American and Caribbean Anthropology* 15 (1): 90–115.

Cabarrús, Carlos Rafael. 1975. "En la conquista del ser: Un estudio de identidad étnica." Master's thesis, Universidad Iberoamericana, Mexico City.

———. 1978. La estratificación, pista para la intelección de los grupos étnicos. *Estudios centroamericanos*: 27–46.

Cabarrús, Carolina, Dorotea Gómez Grijalva, and Ligia González Martínez. 2000. *Las mujeres refugiadas y retornadas en Guatemala: Desafios y enseñanzas del refugio y la reintegración*. Guatemala City: Consejería en Proyectos.

Cahn, Peter. 2011. *Direct Sales and Direct Faith in Latin America*. New York: Palgrave.

Calhoun, Craig. 2002. "Imagining Solidarity: Cosmopolitanism, Constitutional Patriotism, and the Public Sphere." *Public Culture* 14 (1): 147–71.

Cambranes, Julio C. 1985. *Café y campesinos en Guatemala, 1853–1897*. Guatemala City: Editorial Universitaria.

Camus, Manuela. 2005. *La Colonia Primero de Julio y la "clase media emergente."* Guatemala City: FLACSO.

———, ed. 2007. *Comunidades en movimiento: La migración internacional en el norte de Huehuetenango*. Guatemala City: INCEDES, CEDFOG, Consejería en Proyectos.

―――. 2008. *La sorpresita del norte: Migración internacional y comunidad en Huehuetenango*. Guatemala City: INCEDES, CEDFOG.

―――. 2010. "El movimiento indígena en Huehuetenango." In *El movimiento maya en la década después de la paz, 1997–2007*, edited by Santiago Bastos and Roddy Brett. Guatemala City: FyG Editores.

Carmack, Robert. 1983. "Spanish-Indian Relations in Highland Guatemala, 1800–1944." In *Spaniards and Indians in Southeastern Mesoamerica: Essays on the History of Ethnic Relations*, edited by Murdo J. MacLeod and Robert Wasserstrom. Lincoln: University of Nebraska Press.

Carmack, Robert, ed. 1988. *Harvest of Violence: The Mayan Indians and the Guatemalan Crisis*. Norman: University of Oklahoma Press.

Carrescia, Olivia. 1989. *Todos Santos: The Survivors*. New York: First Run, Icarus Films.

Casaús Arzú, Marta. 1992. *Guatemala: Linaje y Racismo*. San José, Costa Rica: FLACSO.

Castillo, Iván. 2010. "En Torno a Especificidades Observables en Movimientos Indígenas de Lucha contra la Acumulación Global en el Altiplano Occidental Guatemalteco." In *El Movimiento Maya en la Década después de la Paz, 1997–2007*, edited by Santiago Bastos and Roddy Brett. Guatemala City: FyG Editores.

CEH (Commission for Historical Clarification). 1999. *Guatemala: Memoria del silencio, Tz'inil na'tab'al*. 12 vols. Guatemala City: United Nations Office of Project Services.

Central American Business Network. 2010. "Sugar Mill Invests $93 million in Guatemala." May 18.

CERIGUA, Centro de Reportes Informativos de Guatemala. 1993. "Refugees Plan Return to Occupied Site." *Weekly Brief*.

Chanquin, Miranda, V. 2007. "La re-composicion de las formas sociales de convivencia en grupos de población desarraigada por la violencia política en Guatemala: Los casos de CPR-Sierra y refugiados-retornados." Ph.D. dissertation, FLACSO-Mexico.

Chase, Jacquelyn. 1999. "Trapped Workers, Urban Freedoms and Labor Control in Brazilian Agriculture: Evidence from Southwest Goias." *Journal of Rural Studies* 15 (2): 201–20.

Chatterjee, Partha. 1993. *The Nation and Its Fragments: Colonial and Postcolonial Histories*. Princeton: Princeton University Press.

Chavkin, Sasha, and Ronnie Greene. 2011. "Thousands of Sugarcane Workers Die as Wealthy Nations Stall on Solutions." *International Consortium of Investigative Journalists*, December 12.

Chinchilla, Norma, Nora Hamilton, and James Loucky. 1993. "Central Americans in Los Angeles: An Immigrant Community in Transition," In *In the Barrios: Latinos and the Underclass Debate*, edited by Joan Moore and Raquel Pinderhughes, 51–78. New York: Russell Sage Foundation.

Cojtí Cuxil, Demetrio. 1997. *Ri maya' moloj pa Iximulew: El movimiento maya (en Guatemala)*. Guatemala City: IWGIA, Cholsamaj.

―――. 2005. *Ri k'ak'a saqamaq' pa Iximulew. La difícil transición al estado multinacional: El caso del estado monoétnico de Guatemala, 2004*. Guatemala City: Cholsamaj.

Cojti Cuxil, Demetrio, and Waqi' Q'anil. 1994. *Politicas para la reivindicación de los mayas de hoy (Fundamento de los derechos específicos del Pueblo Maya)*. Vol. 1. Guatemala City: Cholsamaj.

————. *Ub'anik ri una'ooj uchomab'aal ri maya' tinamit: Configuracion del Pensamiento Politico del Pueblo Maya*. Vol. 2. Guatemala City: Cholsamaj.

Colby, Benjamin, and Pierre L. van den Berghe. 1969. *Ixil Country: A Plural Society in Highland Guatemala*. Berkeley: University of California Press.

Colvin, Christopher J. 2004. "Ambivalent Narrations: Pursuing the Political through Traumatic Storytelling." *PoLAR: Political and Legal Anthropology Review* 27 (1): 72–89.

COMG. 1991. *Rujunamil ri mayab' amaq': Derechos específicos del Pueblo Maya*. Guatemala City: Rajpopi' ri Mayab' Amaq', Consejo de Organizaciones Mayas de Guatemala.

Comité Pro-Paz y Justicia. 1982. *Situación de los derechos humanos en Guatemala*. Mexico City: Comité Pro Justicia y Paz de Guatemala.

Comunicacioncolom. 2009. *Inauguración brigada militar de Ixcán*. Internet video. December 3. http://www.youtube.com/user/comunicacioncolom. Accessed January 15, 2013.

Contreras Reynoso, José Daniel. 1951. *Una rebelión indígena en el partido de Totonicapán en 1820: El indio y la independencia*. Guatemala City: Imprenta Universitaria.

Cook, Garrett. 2000. *Renewing the Maya World: Expressive Culture in a Highland Town*. Austin: University of Texas Press.

Copeland, Nicholas. 2007. "Bitter Earth: Counterinsurgency Strategy and the Roots of Mayan Neo-Authoritarianism in Guatemala." Ph.D. dissertation, University of Texas at Austin.

Correo de la Selva. 1999. *Noticias de las comunidades: Pueblo Nuevo*. Ixcán, Quiché: Candelaría de los Mártires.

Crush, Jonathan. 1992. "Power and Surveillance on the South African Gold Mines." *Journal of Southern African Studies* 18 (4): 825–44.

Cumes, Aura. 2007. "Unidad nacional y unidad del Pueblo Maya." In *Mayanización y Vida Cotidiana: La ideología multicultural en la sociedad guatemalteca*, vol. 1, edited by Santiago Bastos and Aura Cumes. Guatemala City: Cholsamaj.

Das, Veena. 2007. *Life and Words: Violence and the Descent into the Ordinary*. Berkeley: University of California Press.

Das, Veena, and Deborah Poole, eds. 2004. *Anthropology in the Margins of the State: Comparative Ethnographies of the State in Latin America, Africa, and South Asia*. Santa Fe, N.M.: School of American Research Press.

Davis, A. 1998. "Homegrown Insurgency in Ixcán Grande." *NCOORD Newsletter* 7 (3): 4–8.

Debray, Régis, and Ricardo Ramírez. 1975. "Guatemala." In *Las pruebas de fuego: La crítica de las armas*, edited by Régis Debray. Mexico City: Siglo XXI.

DeHart, Monica. 2010. *Ethnic Entrepreneurs: Identity and Development Politics in Latin America*. Stanford, Calif.: Stanford University Press.

de la Cadena, Marisol. 1995. "Women Are More Indian: Ethnicity and Gender in a Community Near Cuzco." In *Ethnicity, Markets and Migration in the Andes: At the Crossroads of History and Anthropology*, edited by Olivia Harris and Brooke Larson. Durham: Duke University Press.

"De la guerra militar a la guerra política." 1997. *Inforpress Centroamericana*, May 2.

Delgado, Guillermo. 1996. "Entre lo popular y lo étnico." In *Pueblos indios, soberanía y globalismo*. Quito: Abya-Yala.

Delhaye, Philippe. 1968. *The Christian Conscience*. New York: Desclee.

Demoscopía. 2007. *Maras y pandillas, comunidad y policía en Centramérica: Hallezgos de un studio integral*. San José, Costa Rica: Demoscopía S.A.

Dickens de Girón, Avery. 2011. "The Security Guard Industry in Guatemala: Rural Communities and Urban Violence." In *Securing the City: Neoliberalism, Space, and Insecurity in Postwar Guatemala,* edited by Kevin Lewis O'Neill and Kedron Thomas. Durham: Duke University Press.

"DIDE: Dirigentes de refugiados son voceros de la insurgencia." 1994. *Siglo XXI,* May 13.

Doyle, Kate. 2007. "The Atrocity Files: Deciphering the Archives of Guatemala's Dirty War." *Harpers Magazine* (Dec. 2007): 52–64.

Ebal, Richard. 1972. "Political Modernization in Three Guatemalan Indian Communities." In *Community, Culture, and National Change: Political Changes in Guatemalan Indians Communities,* edited by Richard N. Adams. New Orleans: Middle American Research Institute.

Ejército de Guatemala. 1985. *Manual de acción cívico militar.* Guatemala City: Ejército de Guatemala.

Ekern, Stener. 2008. "Are Human Rights Destroying the Natural Balance of Things? The Difficult Encounter between International Law in Mayan Guatemala." In *Human Rights in the Maya Region,* edited by Pedro Pitarch, Shannon Speed, and Xochitl Leyva-Solano. Durham: Duke University Press.

Elich, Christina. 2007. "El enfoque de derechos humanos sobre resarcimiento en Guatemala y la cooperación del Programa Nacional de Naciones Unidas para el Desarrollo (PNUD) con el PNR." In *La vida no tiene precio: Acciones y omisiones del Resarcimiento en Guatemala.* Guatemala City: PNR.

Elton, Catherine. 2000. "Guatemala's Lynch-Mob Justice." *Christian Science Monitor,* December 1.

Equipo de Reflexión, Investigación, y Comunicación (ERIC). 2005. *Maras y pandillas en Honduras.* Tegucigalpa: Editorial Guaymuras.

Escobar, Lucía. 2009. "Tarde de caos en Panajachel." *elPeriódico.* December 7.

Escobar Sarti, Carolina. 2000. "Shumos en un pais de castas." *Prensa Libre,* January 27.

Falla, Ricardo. 1980. *Quiché rebelde: Estudio de un movimiento de conversion religiosa, rebelde a las creencias tradicionales, en San Antonio Ilotenango, Quiché (1948–1970).* Guatemala City: Editorial Universitaria de Guatemala.

———. 1992. *Masacres de la selva: Ixcán, Guatemala, 1975–1982.* Guatemala City: Editorial Universitaria.

———. 2000. "Research and Social Action." *Latin American Perspectives* 27 (1): 45–55.

———. 2006. *Juventud de una Comunidad Maya: Ixcán, Guatemala.* Guatemala City: AVANCSO.

———. 2008. *Migración transnacional retornada: Juventud indígena de Zacualpa, Guatemala.* Guatemala City: AVANCSO.

———. 2011. *Negreaba de zopilotes: Masacre y sobrevivencia finca San Francisco, Nentón, 1871–2010.* Guatemala City: AVANCSO.

Fassin, Didier. 2008. "The Humanitarian Politics of Testimony: Subjectification through Trauma in the Israeli-Palestinian Conflict." *Cultural Anthropology* 23(3): 531–58.

Ferguson, James. 1994. *The Anti-Politics Machine: "Development," Depoliticization and Bureaucratic Power in Lesotho.* Cambridge: Cambridge University Press.

———. 2006. *Global Shadows: Africa in the Neoliberal World Order.* Durham: Duke University Press.

Fernández Fernández, José Manuel. 1988. *El Comité de Unidad Campesina: Origen y desarrollo*. Mexico City: Centro de Estudios Rurales Centroamericanos.

FGT and Fundación Arias. 1998. *La gobernabilidad democrática a partir de los Acuerdos de Paz: El caso de Ixcán*. Guatemala City: Fundación Guillermo Toriello, Fundación Arias.

Figueroa Ibarra, Carlos. 2000. "Revolución y violencia en Guatemala: 1954–1972." Ph.D. dissertation, Universidad Nacional Autónoma de Mexico.

Fink, Leon. 2004. *The Maya of Morganton: Work and Community in the Nuevo New South*. Chapel Hill: University of North Carolina Press.

Fischer, Edward F. and Peter Benson. 2006. *Broccoli and Desire: Global Connections and Maya Struggles in Postwar Guatemala*. Stanford, Calif.: Stanford University Press.

Foley, Douglas. 1990. *Learning Capitalist Culture Deep in the Heart of Tejas*. Philadelphia: University of Pennsylvania Press.

Font, Juan Luis. 2001. "La gente es rematerialista y retacaña." *elPeriódico*, May 20.

Forster, Cindy. 2001. *The Time of Freedom: Campesino Workers in Guatemala's October Revolution*. Pittsburgh: University of Pittsburgh Press.

Foucault, Michel. 1977. *Discipline and Punish: The Birth of the Prison*. New York: Vintage Books.

————. 1980. *History of Sexuality, Vol. 1, An Introduction*. Translated by R. Hurley. New York: Vintage Books.

Foxen, Patricia. 2008. *In Search of Providence: Transnational Mayan Identities*. Nashville, Tenn.: Vanderbilt University Press.

Freire, Paolo. 2000. *Pedagogy of the Oppressed*. 30th anniversary ed. New York: Continuum.

Fuentes Díaz, Antonio. 2004. "Linchamiento en Mexico." In *Ecuador Debate*. Quito: Centro Andino de Acción Popular.

Fuentes Mijangos, Camlin. 2008. *La Lupita y su lucha contra la pobreza: La construcción compartida de un proyecto de vida*. Guatemala City: FLACSO.

FUNDAZUCAR. 1992. *Costa Sur 2* (2). Newsletter.

————. 1999. *De la caña se hace el desarrollo: Informe de actividades, 1995–1998*. Guatemala City: FUNDAZUCAR.

GAM (Grupo de Apoyo Mutuo). 2009. *Informe sobre la situación de derechos humanos y hechos de violencia, primer semestre 2009*. July. Guatemala City: GAM.

García, Eduardo. 2004a. "Cooperación internacional, ¿medicina o droga?" Part 1. *Inforpress*, June 4, 8–9.

————. 2004b. "Cooperación internacional, ¿medicina o droga?" Part 2. *Inforpress*, June 11, 5–6.

————. 2004c. "Cooperación internacional, ¿medicina o droga?" Part 3. *Inforpress*, July 2, 6–7.

García, Fernando. 2004. "Linchamiento: Justicia por mano propia o justicia indígena?" *Ecuador Debate* 61: 259–70.

García Hernández, María. 1998. "The Implementation of the Guatemalan Peace Accord with Special Reference to Women Returnees from Mexico." In *Women's Land and Property Rights in Situations of Conflict and Reconstruction: A Reader Based on the February 1998 Inter-regional Consultation in Kigali, Rwanda*, edited by Alfred Buregeya. New York: United Nations Development Fund for Women.

Garrard-Burnett, Virginia. 2010. *Terror in the Land of the Holy Spirit: Guatemala under General Efraín Rios Montt, 1982–1983*. Oxford: Oxford University Press.

Gellert, Gisela. 1999. "Migration and the Displaced in Guatemala City in the Context of a Flawed National Transformation." In *Journeys of Fear: Refugee Return and National Transformation in Guatemala*, edited by Liisa L. North and Alan B. Simmons. Montreal: McGill-Queens University Press.

Gellert, Gisela, and Silvia Irene Palma Calderón. 1999. *Precaridad urbana, desarrollo comunitario y mujeres en el área metropolitana de Guatemala*. Debate 46. Guatemala City: FLACSO.

Gidwani, Vinay K. 2008. *Capital, Interrupted: Agrarian Development and the Politics of Work in India*. Minneapolis: University of Minnesota Press.

Gill, Leslie. 2004. *The School of the Americas: Military Training and Political Violence in the Americas*. Durham: Duke University Press.

Gleijeses, Piero. 1992. *Shattered Hope: The Guatemalan Revolution and the United States, 1944–1954*. Princeton: Princeton University Press.

———. 2002. *Conflicting Missions: Havana, Washington, and Africa, 1959–1976*. Chapel Hill: University of North Carolina Press.

Goldin, Liliana R. 2009. *Global Maya: Work and Ideology in Rural Guatemala*. Tucson: University of Arizona Press.

———. 2011. "Labor Turnover among Maquila Workers of Highland Guatemala: Resistance and Semiproletarianization in Global Capitalism." *Latin American Research Review* 46 (Fall 3): 133–56.

Goldman, Francisco. 2007. *The Art of Political Murder: Who Killed the Bishop?* New York: Grove Press.

Goldstein, Daniel. 2003. "In Our Own Hands: Lynching, Justice and the Law in Bolivia." *American Ethnologist* 30 (1): 22–43.

———. 2004. *The Spectacular City*. Durham: Duke University Press.

González, Matilde. 2002. *Se cambió el tiempo: Conflicto y poder en territorio k'iche' 1880–1996*. Guatemala City: AVANCSO.

González Ponciano, Jorge Ramón. 2005. "De la patria del criollo a la patria del shumo: Whiteness and the Criminalization of the Dark Plebeian in Modern Guatemala." Ph.D. dissertation, University of Texas, Austin.

Gramajo Morales, Héctor Alejandro. 1995. *De la guerra ... a la guerra: La difícil transición política en Guatemala*. Guatemala City: Fondo de Cultura Editorial.

Grandin, Greg. 1997a. "The Strange Case of la Mancha Negra: Mayan-State Relations in Nineteenth Century Guatemala." *Hispanic American Historical Review* 77 (2): 211–43.

———.1997b. "To End with All These Evils: Ethnic Transformation and Community Mobilization in Guatemala's Western Highlands, 1954–1980." *Latin American Perspectives* 24 (2): 7–34.

———. 2000a. *The Blood of Guatemala: A History of Race and Nation*. Durham: Duke University Press.

———. 2000b. "Chronicles of a Guatemalan Genocide Foretold: Violence, Trauma, and the Limits of Historical Inquiry." *Nepantla: Views from the South* 1 (2): 398–412.

———. 2004. *The Last Colonial Massacre: Latin America in the Cold War*. Chicago: University of Chicago Press.

———. 2006. *Empire's Workshop: Latin America, the United States, and the Rise of the New Imperialism.* New York: Metropolitan Books.

Grandin, Greg, Deborah Levenson-Estrada, and Elizabeth Oglesby, eds. 2011. *The Guatemala Reader: History, Culture, Politics.* Durham: Duke University Press.

Grose, Jessiva. 2008. "Life in the Time of Oprah." *New York Times,* August 17.

Gudmunson, Lowell, and Hector Lindo-Fuentes. 1995. *Central America, 1821–1871: Liberalism before Liberal Reform.* Tuscaloosa: University of Alabama Press.

Guha, Ranajit. 1988. "The Prose of Counter-Insurgency." In *Selected Subaltern Studies,* edited by Ranajit Guha and Gayatri Chakravorty Spivak. New York: Oxford University Press.

Gupta, Akhil. 1998. *Postcolonial Developments: Agriculture in the Making of Modern India.* Durham: Duke University Press.

Gurriarán, Javier. 1989. *La resistencia en Guatemala: Nunca tuvo la montaña tantos caminos en Guatemala.* Mexico City: Editorial Nuestro Tiempo.

Gutiérrez, Gustavo. 1988. *A Theology of Liberation: History, Politics, and Salvation.* Maryknoll, N.Y.: Orbis Books.

Gutiérrez, Maria Estela, and Paul Kobrak. 2001. *Los linchamientos: Posconflicto y violencia colectiva en Huehuetenango, Guatemala.* Huehuetenango, Guatemala: CEDFOG.

Hagan, Jacqueline Maria. 1994. *Deciding to Be Legal: A Maya Community in Houston.* Philadelphia: Temple University Press.

Hale, Charles R. 1998. "La nueva política del Banco Mundial sobre los pueblos indígenas: Experiencias latinoamericanas, implicaciones para Guatemala." Paper presented at Las VIII Jornadas Lascasianas conference, Guatemala City.

———. 2004. "Rethinking Indigenous Politics in the Era of the 'Indio Permitido.'" NACLA 38 (1): 16–20.

———. 2005. "Neoliberal Multiculturalism: The Remaking of Cultural Rights and Racial Dominance in Central America." POLAR 28 (1): 10–28.

———. 2006. *"Más que un Indio": Racial Ambivalence and Neoliberal Multiculturalism in Guatemala.* Santa Fe, N.M.: SAR.

Hale, Charles, Mark Anderson, and Edmund T. Gordon. 2001. "Indigenous and Black Organizations of Central America: Struggle for Recognition and Resources." Unpublished manuscript, Ford Foundation.

Hamilton, Nora, and Norma Stoltz Chinchilla. 2001. *Seeking Community: Guatemalans and Salvadorans in Los Angeles.* Philadelphia: Temple University Press.

Handy, Jim. 1984. *Gift of the Devil: A History of Guatemala.* Toronto: Between the Lines Press.

———. 1994. *Revolution in the Countryside: Rural Conflict and Agrarian Reform in Guatemala, 1944–1954.* Chapel Hill: University of North Carolina Press.

———. 2004. "Chicken Thieves, Witches, and Judges: Vigilante Justice and Customary Law in Guatemala." *Journal of Latin American Studies* 36: 533–61.

Harding, Susan. 2001. *The Book of Jerry Falwell: Fundamentalist Language and Politics.* Princeton: Princeton University Press.

Harnecker, Marta. 1999. *Haciendo posible lo imposible: La izquierda en el umbral del siglo XXI.* Mexico City: Siglo XXI.

Harvey, David. 2003. *The New Imperialism.* Oxford: Oxford University Press.

———. 2005. *A Brief History of Neoliberalism.* Oxford: Oxford University Press.

Hayden, Tom. 2004. *Street Wars*. New York: New Press.

Hollander, Nancy Caro. 1997. *Love in the Time of Hate: Liberation Psychology in Latin America*. New Brunswick, N.J.: Rutgers University Press.

Hooks, Margaret. 1991. *Guatemalan Women Speak*. London: Ciir.

Hoyos de Asig, Maria del Pilar. 1997. *¿Dónde estás? Fernando Hoyos*. Guatemala City: Fondo de Cultura Editorial.

Huggins, Martha Knisely. 1991. *Vigilantism and the State in Modern Latin America: Essays on Extralegal Violence*. New York: Praeger Publishing.

Hunt, Nancy Rose. 2008. "An Acoustic Register, Tenacious Images, and Congolese Scenes of Rape and Repetition." *Cultural Anthropology* 23(2): 220–53.

Hurtado Paz y Paz, Laura. 2001. "Factores determinantes de migraciones emergentes en comunidades reasentadas en Ixcán (1997–2001)." Master´s thesis, Universidad del Valle de Guatemala.

———. 2008a. *Dinámicas agrarias y reproducción campesina en la globalización: El caso de Alta Verapaz, 1970–2007*. Guatemala City: FyG Editores.

———. 2008b. *Las plantaciones para agrocombustibles y la pérdida de tierras para la producción de alimentos en Guatemala*. ActionAid Guatemala.

Hurtado Paz y Paz, Margarita. 2002. "'Aquí estamos esperándolos': Vivencias de mujeres retornadas esposas de trabajadores migrantes en los Estados Unidos, el caso de la Colonia 15 de Octubre, La Trinidad, Escuintla." Master's thesis, Universidad de las Regiones Autónomas de la Costa Caribe Nicaragüense URACCAN/ESIDIR.

IDIES. 1999. *El Sistema Jurídico Mam*. Guatemala City: Universidad Rafael Landívar.

Ikeda, Mitsuho. 1999. *The Cultural Involution of Violence: A Guatemalan Highland Community and Global Economy*. Osaka: Osaka University Center for Studies of Communication Design.

ILEURL (Instituto de Lingüística y Educacion de la Universidad Rafael Landívar). 2007. *El encantamiento de la realidad: Conocimientos Mayas en prácticas sociales de la vida cotidiana*. Guatemala City: ILEURL.

INCITE! Women of Color against Violence, ed. 2007. *The Revolution Will Not Be Funded: Beyond the Non-Profit Industrial Complex*. Cambridge, Mass.: South End Press.

Inforpress. 1997. "De la guerra militar a la guerra política." Inforpress Centroamericana, May 2.

Instancia Mediadora. 1996. *Resumen de taller de la Instancia Mediadora y GRICAR sobre el soporte poblacional*. Guatemala City: Instancia Mediadora.

Instancia Mediadora and GRICAR. 1999. *El proceso de retorno de los refugiados guatemaltecos: Una visión desde la mesa de negociación*. Guatemala City: Editorial Serviprensa.

Inter-American Commission on Human Rights. 1993. *Fourth Report on the Situation of Human Rights in Guatemala*. Washington, D.C.: Organization of American States (OAS).

———. 1994. *Annual Report of the Inter-American Commission on Human Rights*. San José, Costa Rica: Organization of American States (OAS).

———. 2005. *Annual Report of the Inter-American Commission on Human Rights*. Washington, D.C.: Organization of American States (OAS).

International Finance Corporation. 2007. *Pantaleón Sugar*. Project No. 25449. Washington, D.C.: World Bank Group.

Iznardo, Francisco. 2002. "Guatemala, Militarization in Ixcán: Thin Red Lines." *Revista Envío* 248, March.

Jonas, Susanne. 1994. *La batalla por Guatemala: Rebeldes, escuadrones de la muerte y poder estadounidense.* Caracas, Venezuela: FLACSO/Nueva Sociedad.

———. 2000. *Of Centaurs and Doves: Guatemala's Peace Process.* Boulder, Colo.: Westview Press.

Jones, Grant. 1998. *The Conquest of the Last Maya Kingdom.* Stanford, Calif.: Stanford University Press.

Joseph, G. Gilbert, and Daniel Nugent, eds. 1994. *Everyday Forms of State Formation.* Durham: Duke University Press.

Kalny, Eva. 2010. "They Even Use Us as a Factory for Their Children": Perspectives on Free Trade Agreements in Guatemala. *Social Analysis* 54 (1): 71–91.

Katz, Friedrich. 1988. "Rural Uprisings in Preconquest and Colonial Mexico." In *Riot, Rebellion, and Revolution,* edited by Friedrich Katz. Princeton: Princeton University Press.

Kermode, Frank. 1979. *The Genesis of Secrecy: On the Interpretation of Narrative.* Vol. 1977–1978. Cambridge: Harvard University Press.

Klein, Naomi. 2007. *The Shock Doctrine: The Rise of Disaster Capitalism.* New York: Metropolitan Books.

Klemm, David E. 2008. "Philosophy and Kerygma: Ricoeur as Reader of the Bible." In *Reading Ricoeur,* edited by David M. Kaplan. Albany: State University of New York Press.

Knight, Alan. 1994. "Racism, Revolution and Indigenismo: Mexico, 1910–1940." In *The Idea of Race in Latin America, 1870–1940,* edited by Richard Graham. Austin: University of Texas Press.

Kobrak, Paul Hans. 1997. "Village Troubles: The Civil Patrols in Aguacatán, Guatemala." Ph.D. dissertation, University of Michigan.

———. 1999. *Organizing and Repression in the University of San Carlos, Guatemala, 1944–1996.* Washington D.C.: American Association for the Advancement of Science.

———. 2010. *Huehuetenango: Historia de una guerra.* Huehuetenango, Guatemala: CEDFOG.

Konefal, Betsy. 2010. *For Every Indio Who Falls: A History of Maya Activism in Guatemala, 1960–1990.* Albuquerque: University of New Mexico Press.

Koselleck, Reinhardt. 1985. *Futures Past: On the Semantics of Historical Time.* Cambridge: MIT Press.

Kurasawa, Fuyuki. 2004. "A Cosmopolitanism from Below: Alternative Globalization and the Creation of a Solidarity without Bounds." *European Journal of Sociology* 45 (2): 233–55.

Lancaster, Roger. 1988. *Thanks to God and the Revolution: Popular Religion and Class Consciousness in the New Nicaragua.* New York: Columbia University Press.

———. 1992. *Life Is Hard: Machismo, Danger, and the Intimacy of Power in Nicaragua.* Berkeley: University of California Press.

———. 2008. "State of Panic." In *New Landscapes of Inequality: Neoliberalism and the Erosion of Democracy in America,* edited by Jane Collins, Micaela di Leonardo, and Brett Williams. Santa Fe, N.M.: SAR Press.

"La semilla de las maras: Testimonio de un niño marero." 2005. *Revista Domingo, Prensa Libre,* April 3.

Latin America Political Report. 1979. "Colom Argueta's Last Interview" 13 (14).

Le Bot, Yvon. 1995. *La guerra en Tierras Mayas: Comunidad, Violencia y Modernidad en Guatemala, 1970–1992.* Mexico City: Fondo de Cultura Económica.

Legge, Karen. 1995. *Human Resource Management: Rhetorics and Realities.* Basingstoke, U.K.: Macmillan.

Levenson-Estrada, Deborah. 1988. *Por si mismos: Un estudio preliminar de las maras en la Ciudad de Guatemala.* Guatemala City: AVANCSO.

———. 1994. *Trade Unionists against Terror.* Chapel Hill: University of North Carolina Press.

Leys, Ruth. 2000. *Trauma: A Genealogy.* Chicago: University of Chicago Press.

Li, Tania. 2007. *The Will to Improve: Governmentality, Development, and the Practice of Politics.* Durham: Duke University Press.

"Linchamiento del sastre." 2009. *elPeriódico,* May 10.

"Linchamiento de un sastre." 2010. *elPeriódico,* March 10.

Lipietz, Alain. 1982. "Towards Global Fordism?" *New Left Review* 132: 33–47.

Little, Walter E., and Timothy J. Smith. 2009. *Mayas in Postwar Guatemala: Harvest of Violence Revisited.* Tuscaloosa: University of Alabama Press.

López García, Julian. 2010. *Kumix: La lluvia en la mitología y el ritual Maya-Ch'orti'.* Guatemala City: Cholsamaj.

López García, Julian, Santiago Bastos, and Manuela Camus. 2009. *Guatemala: Violencias desbordadas.* Córdoba, Spain: University of Córdoba Press.

López Ovando, Olga. 2009. "FRG habría pagado viaje de 12 magistrados a España." *Prensa Libre,* May 7.

Loucky, James and Marilyn M. Moors. 2000. *The Maya Diaspora: Guatemalan Roots, New American Lives.* Philadelphia: Temple University Press.

Lovell, W. George. 2005. *Conquest and Survival in Colonial Guatemala: A Historical Geography of the Cuchumatán Highlands, 1500–1821.* Montreal: McGill-Queen's University Press.

Lovell, W. George, and Christopher H. Lutz. 2009. *Historia sin máscara: Vida y obra de Severo Martínez Peláez.* Guatemala City: Centro de Estudios Urbanos y Regionales de la Universidad de San Carlos and FLACSO.

Maass, Peter. 2005. "The Salvadorization of Iraq." *New York Times Magazine,* May 1.

Macías, Julio César. 1997. *La guerrilla fue mi camino.* Guatemala City: Editorial Piedra Santa.

MacLeod, Morna. 2008. "Luchas político-culturales y auto-representación maya en Guatemala." Ph.D. disseration, Universidad Nacional Autónoma de México.

Mahoney, John. 1989. *The Making of Moral Theology: A Study of the Roman Catholic Tradition.* New York: Clarendon Press.

Manz, Beatriz. 1988. *Refugees of a Hidden War: The Aftermath of the Counterinsurgency in Guatemala.* Albany: State University of New York Press.

———. 2004. *Paradise in Ashes: A Guatemalan Journey of Courage, Terror, and Hope.* Berkeley: University of California Press.

Martínez Peláez, Severo. 1977. "La sublevación de los zendales." *Criterio universitario,* vol. 8 Chiapas: Universidad Autónoma de Chiapas.

———. 1991. *Motines de indios: La violencia colonial en Centroamérica y Chiapas.* Guatemala City: FyG Editores.

————. 2009. *La patria del criollo: An Interpretation of Colonial Guatemala*. Translated by W. George Lovell and Susan M. Neve. Edited by Christopher Lutz. Durham: Duke University Press.

Masquieira, Manuel. 2003. "Juventud marginal, necesitada de jubileo." *Promotio Iustitiae* 77: 18–22.

Mateo, Maria and Manuela Camus. 2007. "Una mujer q'anjob'al de Mamá Maquín." In *Comunidades en movimiento: La migración internacional en el norte de Huehuetenango* (Konob'laq yin ek'jab'b'ahilal: b'eytzejtoqb'ahil b'ay juntzanoqxa konob'laq yuj heb' kajan ajelb'a ajtoq Chinab'jul), edited by Manuela Camus. Guatemala City: INCEDES, CEDFOG.

Matthew, Laura E., and Michel R. Oudijk, eds. 2007. *Indian Conquistadores: Indigenous Allies in the Conquest of Mesoamerica*. Norman: University of Oklahoma Press.

MAYAS. 1990. "Guatemala: De la república burguesa centralista a la república popular federal." In *Guatemala: Seminario Sobre la Realidad Étnica*. Mexico City: Centro de Estudios Integrados de Desarrollo Comunal, Editorial Praxis.

McAllister, Carlota. 2002. "Good People: Revolution, Community, and Conciencia in a Maya-K'iche' Village in Guatemala." Ph.D. dissertation, Johns Hopkins University.

————. 2008. "Rural Markets, Revolutionary Souls, and Rebellious Women in Cold War Guatemala." In *In from the Cold: Latin America's New Encounter with the Cold War*, edited by G. Joseph and D. Spenser, 350–77. Durham: Duke University Press.

————. 2010. "A Headlong Rush into the Future: Violence and Revolution in a Guatemalan Indigenous Village." In *A Century of Revolution: Insurgent and Counterinsurgent Violence during Latin America's Long Cold War*, edited by Greg Grandin and Gilbert Joseph. Durham: Duke University Press.

McCleary, Rachel M. 1999. *Dictating Democracy: Guatemala and the End of Violent Revolution*. Gainesville: University of Florida Press.

McCreery, David. 1994. *Rural Guatemala 1760–1940*. Stanford, Calif.: Stanford University Press.

————. 1995. "Wage Labor, Free Labor and Vagrancy Laws: The Transition to Capitalism in Guatemala, 1920–1945." In *Coffee, Society and Power in Latin America*, edited by Lowell Gudmundson, William Roseberry, and Mario Samper Kutschbach. Baltimore: Johns Hopkins University Press.

Mendizábal, Sergio. 2006. *Interculturalidad democrática: La discusión sobre estado, nación, sujetos sociales, etnicidad y praxis*. Guatemala City: Instituto de Lingüística y Educación, Universidad Rafael Landívar.

Mendoza, Carlos. 2012. "Linchamientos en Guatemala: Registro y análisis de episodios sobre esta forma de violencia colectiva, desde una perspectiva comparada." http://linchamientos.blogspot.com. Accessed January 15, 2013.

Mendoza, Carlos, and Edelberto Torres-Rivas, eds. 2003. *Los linchamientos: ¿Barbarie o justicia popular?* Guatemala City: Colección Cultura de Paz.

Menjívar, Cecilia 2002. "The Ties That Heal: Guatemalan Immigrant Women's Networks and Medical Treatment." *The International Migration Review* 36 (2): 437–66.

Mérida, Cecilia, and Wolfang Krenmayer. 2008. *Sistematización de experiencias de la asamblea departamental por la defensa de los recursos naturales renovables y no renovables de Huehuetenango, 2006–2007*. Guatemala City: CEDFOG.

Mersky, Marcie, and Naomi Roht-Arriaza. 2007. "Guatemala." In *Victims Unsilenced: The*

Inter-American Human Rights System and Transitional Justice in Latin America. Washington, D.C.: Due Process of Law Foundation.

Millard, Ann V. and Jorge Chapa. 2004: *Apple Pie and Enchiladas: Latino Newcomers in the Rural Midwest.* Austin: University of Texas Press.

MINUGUA (Misión de Verificación de las Naciones Unidas en Guatemala). 1999. "Resultados de la verificación de la fuga de presos ocurrida en Huehuetenango." Press Release, May 11. Guatemala City: MINUGUA.

———. 2003. *Fourteenth Report on Human Rights of the United Nations Verification Mission in Guatemala.* Vol. A 58/566. Guatemala City: MINUGUA.

———. 2004. *Ninth Report of the United Nations Verification Mission in Guatemala.* New York: United Nations.

Miranda, Ernesto. 2005. World News, National Public Radio, March 17.

Montejo, Victor. 2005. *Maya Intellectual Renaissance: Identity, Representation, and Leadership.* Austin: University of Texas Press.

Moodie, Ellen. 2010. *El Salvador in the Aftermath of Peace: Crime, Uncertainty, and the Transition to Democracy.* Philadelphia: University of Pennsylvania Press.

Najarro, Edgar Ruano. 2005. "La rueda del tiempo y la violencia en el agro." *Prensa Libre,* February 20.

Nelson, Diane M. 1999. *A Finger in the Wound: Body Politics in Quincentennial Guatemala.* Berkeley: University of California Press.

———. 2009a. "Mayan Ponzi: A Contagion of Hope, a Made-off with Your Money." *e-misférica* 6 (1). http://hemisphericinstitute.org/hemi/en/e-misferica-61. Accessed January 18, 2013.

———. 2009b. *Reckoning: The Ends of War in Guatemala.* Durham: Duke University Press.

"New Law Eases Terms in Guatemala." 1983. *Platt's Oilgram News* 61 (182).

Nordstrom, Carolyn. 2007. *Global Outlaws: Crime, Money, and Power in the Contemporary World.* Berkeley: University of California Press.

Nuñez, Juan Carlos. 1996. *De la ciudad al barrio: Redes y tejidos urbanos, Guatemala, El Salvador and Nicaragua.* Guatemala City: Universidad Rafael Landivar.

ODHAG (Oficina de Derechos Humanos del Arzobispado de Guatemala). 1990. *Informe Anual.* Guatemala City: Office of the Archbishop.

———. 1991. *Informe Anual.* Guatemala City: Office of the Archbishop.

———. 1992. *Informe Anual.* Guatemala City: Office of the Archbishop.

———. 1993. *Informe Anual.* Guatemala City: Office of the Archbishop.

Offit, Thomas A. 2008. *Conquistadores de la calle: Child Street Labor in Guatemala City.* Austin: University of Texas Press.

Oglesby, Elizabeth. 2001. "Machos and Machetes in Guatemala's Cane Fields." NACLA *Report on the Americas* 34 (5): 16–17.

———. 2002. "Politics at Work: Elites, Labor and Agrarian Modernization in Guatemala, 1980–2000." Ph.D. dissertation, University of California, Berkeley.

———. 2003. "Machos, machetes y migrantes: Masculinidades y dialécticas del control laboral en Guatemala." *Estudios migratorios latinoamericanos* 17 (52): 651–80.

———. 2004. "Corporate Citizenship? Elites, Labor and the Geographies of Work in Guatemala." *Environment and Planning D: Society and Space* 22 (4): 553–73.

———. 2007a. "Educating Citizens in Postwar Guatemala: Historical Memory, Genocide, and the Culture of Peace." *Radical History Review* 97: 77–98.

———. 2007b. "Trabajo y gobernabilidad en la Costa Sur." In *En el umbral: Explorando
Guatemala en el inicio del Siglo Veintiuno*, edited by Clara Arenas Bianchi and Matilde
González. Guatemala City: AVANCSO.

Oglesby, Elizabeth, and Amy Ross. 2009. "Guatemala's Genocide Determination and
the Spatial Politics of Justice." *Space and Polity* 13 (1): 21–39.

O'Neill, Kevin Lewis. 2010. *City of God: Christian Citizenship in Postwar Guatemala.*
Berkeley: University of California Press.

O'Neill, Kevin Lewis, and Kedron Thomas, eds. 2011. *Securing the City: Neoliberalism,
Space, and Insecurity in Postwar Guatemala*. Durham: Duke University Press.

"Operators in Guatemala Propose Changes in Hydrocarbon's Rules." 1983. *Platt's Oilgram News* 61 (214).

Organización de Mujeres Guatemaltecas Refugiadas en México "Mama Maquín." 1999.
*Nuestra experiencia ante los retos del futuro: Sistematización del trabajo de las mujeres de
Mamá Maquín durante el refugio en México y su retorno a Guatemala*. Chiapas: Organi-
zación de Mujeres Guatemaltecas Refugiadas en México "Mamá Maquín."

Organizaciones Sociales. 2009. "Declaración con motivo del foro del pueblo y organizaciones del Ixcán por la defensa del territorio del derecho a alimentarse, el respeto a la
autodeterminación de los pueblos y el medio ambiente." October 23. http://coindeguate
.blogspot.com/2009/10/declaracion-de-las-organizaciones-de.html.

Pansini, Joseph J. 1977. "El Pilar: A Plantation Microcosm of Guatemalan Ethnicity."
Ph.D. dissertation. University of Rochester.

Pandey, Gyanendra. 1988. "Peasant Revolt and Indian Nationalism: The Peasant Movement in Awadh, 1919–22." In *Selected Subaltern Studies*, edited by Ranajit Guha and
Gayatri Chakravorty Spivak. New York: Oxford University Press.

Pastor, Rodolfo. 1987. *Campesinos y reformas: La Mixteca, 1700–1856*. Mexico City: Colegio de México.

Paul IV. 1965. "Pastoral Constitution on the Church in the Modern World (Gaudium et
Spes)." In *The Second Vatican Council*. Vatican City: Holy See.

Payeras, Mario. 1983. *Days of the Jungle: The Testimony of a Guatemalan Guerrillero, 1972–
1976*. New York: Monthly Review Press.

Peacock, Susan C., and Adriana Beltrán. 2003. *Hidden Powers in Post-Conflict Guatemala:
Illegal Armed Groups and the Forces Behind Them*. Washington, D.C.: WOLA.

Perera, Victor. 1995. *Unfinished Conquest: The Guatemalan Tragedy*. Berkeley: University
of California Press.

Perkins, John. 2004. *Confessions of an Economic Hit Man*. San Francisco: Berrett-Koehler.

Petras, James, and Henry Veltmeyer. 2003a. *La globalización desenmascarada: El imperia-
lismo en el siglo XXI*. Mexico City: Universidad Autónoma de Zacatecas, Miguel Porrúa.

Petras, James, and Henry Veltmeyer. 2004. *Un sistema en crisis: La dinámica del capita-
lismo de libre mercado*. Mexico City: Lumen.

Piel, Jean. 1995. *El departamento del Quiché bajo la dictadura Liberal (1880–1920)*. Guatemala City: FLACSO.

PNR (Programa Nacional de Resarcimiento). 2007. *La vida no tiene precio: Acciones y
omisiones del resarcimiento en Guatemala*. First Thematic Report 2006–7. Guatemala
City: PNR.

Pollack, Aaron. 2005. "K'iche' Uprising in Totonicapán: The Places of Subaltern Politics." Ph.D. dissertation, Clark University.

Poole, Deborah. 2004. "Between Threat and Guarantee: Natural and Legal Jurisdictions on the Margins of the Peruvian State." In *Anthropology in the Margins of the State*, edited by Veena Das and Deborah Poole. Santa Fe, N.M.: School of American Research Press.

Popkin, Eric. 2005. "The Emergence of Pan-Mayan Ethnicity in the Guatemalan Transnational Community Linking Santa Eulalia and Los Angeles." *Current Sociology* 53 (4): 675–706.

Poraiser, Andrés. 2010. "Seguimos atrapados en la finca: Entrevista con Gustavo Palma y Juan Pablo Gómez." *Inforpress Centroamericana*, March 19–26.

Porras Castejón, Gustavo. 2007. "Introducción: El programa nacional de resarcimiento: Cómo se quiso, cómo es, y cómo debe ser." In *La vida no tiene precio: Acciones y omisiones del resarcimiento en Guatemala*. First Thematic Report 2006–7. Guatemala City: PNR.

Posner, Mark. 1990. *The Mode of Information*. Chicago: University of Chicago Press.

Rabinow, Paul, ed. 1984. *The Foucault Reader*. New York: Pantheon.

Rama, Angel. 1996. *The Lettered City*. Edited by John Charles Chasteen. Durham: Duke University Press.

REMHI (Recuperación de la Memoria Histórica). 1998. *Guatemala: Nunca más*. 4 vols. Guatemala City: Oficina de Derechos Humanos del Arzobispado de Guatemala.

Remijnse, Simone. 2001. "Remembering Civil Patrols in Joyabaj, Guatemala," *Bulletin of Latin American Research*. 20 (4): 454–69.

———. 2002. *Memories of Violence: Civil Patrols and the Legacy of Conflict in Joyabaj, Guatemala*. Amsterdam: Rozenberg

Restall, Matthew, and Florine Asselbergs. 2007. *Invading Guatemala: Spanish, Nahua, and Maya Accounts of the Conquest Wars*. University Park: Pennsylvania State University Press.

"Revista Domingo." 2005. *Prensa Libre*. April 24.

Reyes, Virgilio. 1998. "Poder local y bosques comunales." In *Cuadernos Debate No. 43*. Guatemala City: FLACSO.

Ricoeur, Paul. 1980. *Essays on Biblical Interpretation*. Philadelphia: Fortress Press.

Robert F. Kennedy Memorial Center for Human Rights. 1993. *Persecution by Proxy: The Civil Patrols in Guatemala*. New York: The Robert F. Kennedy Memorial Center for Human Rights.

Robinson, William. 2003. *Transnational Conflicts: Central America, Social Change and Globalization*. London: Verso.

Rodríguez, Martín P. 2004. "EEUU molesto por genérico." *Prensa Libre*, December 27.

Roldán Andrade, Úrsula. 1994. "Alcances y limitaciones del movimiento indígena-campesino protierra, de los vecinos de Cajolá frente a la demanda de acceso a la tierra (Municipio de Quetzaltenango)." Technical thesis, Centro Universitario de Occidente, Universidad de San Carlos de Guatemala.

———. 1998. "Estrategias ocupacionales de la juventud rural y su impacto en la economía campesina. (Realizado en los municipios de Concepción Chiquirichapa y San Juan Ostuncalco, del Departamento de Quetzaltenango)." Master's thesis, Centro Universitario de Occidente, Universidad de San Carlos de Guatemala.

Rose, Nikolas. 1998. *Inventing Our Selves: Psychology, Power, and Personhood*. Cambridge: Cambridge University Press.

——.1999. *Powers of Freedom: Reframing Political Thought*. Cambridge: Cambridge University Press.

Roseberry, William. 1993a. "Beyond the Agrarian Question in Latin America." In *Confronting Historical Paradigms: Peasants, Labor and the Capitalist World System in Africa and Latin America*, edited by Fred Cooper, Allen Isaacman, and Florencia E. Mallon. Madison: University of Wisconsin Press.

——. 1993b. "Hegemony and the Language of Contention." In *Everyday Forms of State Formation*, edited by Gilbert Joseph and Daniel Nugent. Durham: Duke University Press.

Ross, Fiona C. 2003. *Bearing Witness: Women and the Truth and Reconciliation Commission in South Africa*. London: Pluto Press.

Rudenberg, Cheryl A. 1986. "Israel and Guatemala: Arms, Advice, and Counterinsurgency." *Middle East Report* 140: 16–22, 43–44.

Rus, Jan. 1999. "If Truth Be Told: A Forum on David Stoll's Rigoberta Menchú and the Story of All Poor Guatemalans." *Latin American Perspectives* 26 (6): 5–88.

Saad-Filho, Alfredo, and Deborah Johnston, eds. 2005. *Neoliberalism: A Critical Reader*. London: Pluto Press.

Sáenz de Tejada, Ricardo. 2003. *El pueblo maya en Guatemala: El surgimiento de un sujeto político (1950–2000)* Master's thesis. CIESAS-DF, Ciudad de México.

Saldaña-Portillo, María Josefina. 2003. *The Revolutionary Imagination in the Americas and the Age of Development*. Durham: Duke University Press.

Salomon, Leticia. 1993. *La violencia en Honduras 1980–1993*. Tegucigalpa: CEDOH-CONADEH.

Samper, David. 2002. "Cannibalizing Kids: Rumor and Resistance in Latin America." *Journal of Folklore Research* 39 (1): 1–32.

Sanford, Victoria. 2006. "Excavations of the Heart: Reflections on Truth, Memory and Structures of Understanding." In *Engaged Observer: Anthropology, Advocacy, and Activism*, edited by Victoria Sanford and Asale Angel-Ajani. New Brunswick, N.J.: Rutgers University Press.

Saul, Stephanie. 2005. "Drug Lobby Got a Victory in Trade Pact Vote." *New York Times*, July 2.

Savenije, Wim, and Chris van der Borgh. 2002. "Youth Gangs, Social Exclusion and the Transformation of Violence in El Salvador." In *Armed Actors: Organized Violence and State Failure in Latin America*, edited by Kees Koonings and Dirk Kruijt. London: Zed Books.

Schirmer, Jennifer. 1998. *The Guatemalan Military Project: A Violence Called Democracy*. Philadelphia: University of Pennsylvania Press.

Schmölz-Häberlein, Michaela. 1996. "Continuity and Change in a Guatemalan Indian Community: San Cristóbal-Verapaz, 1870–1940." *Hispanic American Historical Review* 76 (2): 226–48.

Scott, David. 2004. *Conscripts of Modernity: The Tragedy of Colonial Enlightenment*. Durham: Duke University Press.

Scott, James. 1998. *Seeing Like a State: How Certain Schemes to Improve the Human Condition Have Failed*. New Haven: Yale University Press.

SEGEPLAN. 2009. *Plan de desarrollo de la* FTN. Government of Guatemala.

———. 2011a. *Diagnóstico territorial. Franja Transversal del Norte (*FTN*). Un corredor de desarrollo.* Vol. 1. Government of Guatemala.

———. 2011b. *Plan de desarrollo integral. Franja Transversal del Norte (*FTN*). Un corredor de desarrollo.* Vol. 2. Government of Guatemala.

Segovia, Alexander. 2002. *Transformación estructural y reforma económica en El Salvador: El funcionamiento económico de los noventa y sus efectos sobre el crecimiento, la pobreza y la distribución del ingreso.* Guatemala City: FyG Editores.

Shea, Randall. 2005. "What Role for the Memories of War in Our Teaching?" June 2. http://www.sancarlosfoundation.org.

Sheehy, Kate. 2011. "Mysterious Kidney Disease in Central America." Public Radio International, December 12.

"Shumometro 2001" http://espanol.groups.yahoo.com/group/mosaicochapin/message /5329.

Sieder, Rachel. 2001. "Rethinking Citizenship: Reforming the Law in Postwar Guatemala." In *States of Imagination: Ethnographic Explorations of the Postcolonial State,* edited by Thomas Hansen and Finn Stepputat. Durham: Duke University Press.

———. 2007. "The Judiciary and Indigenous Rights in Guatemala." *International Journal of Constitutional Law* 5: 211–41.

———. 2008. "Legal Globalization and Human Rights: Constructing the Rule of Law in Postconflict Guatemala?" *Human Rights in the Maya Region: Global Politics, Cultural Contentions and Moral Engagements,* edited by Pedro Pitarch, Shannon Speed, and Xochitl Leyva Solano. Durham: Duke University Press.

———. 2011a. "Building Mayan Authority and Autonomy: The 'Recovery' of Indige nous Law in Post-Peace Guatemala." *Studies in Law, Politics, and Society* 55: 25–57.

———. 2011b. "'Emancipation' or 'Regulation'? Law, Globalization and Indigenous Peoples' Rights in Post-War Guatemala." *Economy and Society* 40 (2): 239–65.

———. 2011c. "Contested Sovereignties: Indigenous Law, Violence and State Effects in Postwar Guatemala." *Critique of Anthropology* 31 (3): 161–84.

Siegel, Morris. 1941. "Religion in Western Guatemala: A Product of Acculturation." *American Anthropologist* 43: 62–76.

Silver, Sara. 2003. "Guatemalan 'Peace Bond' Causes Alarm." *Financial Times,* January 8.

Similox Salazar, Vitalino. 2006. *Una Approximacion al Fenomeno de las Maras y Pandillas en Centroamerica, Punto de Partido para la Reflexion y Accion de la Comunidad Cristiana Mesoamericana.* Tegucigalpa: Comunidad Cristiana Mesoamericana.

Smith, Carol, ed. 1990. *Guatemalan Indians and the State: 1540–1988.* Austin: University of Texas Press.

———. 1999. "Interpretaciones norteamericanas sobre la raza y el racismo en Guatemala." In *Racismo en Guatemala. Abriendo el debate sobre un tema tabú,* edited by Clara Arenas Bianchi, Charles R. Hale y Gustavo Palma Murga. Guatemala City: AVANCSO.

Smith, Waldemar R. 1977. *The Fiesta System and Economic Change.* New York: Columbia University Press.

Smith-Ayala, Emilie. 1991. *The Granddaughters of Ixmucane: Guatemalan Women Speak.* Toronto: Women's Press.

Snodgrass Godoy, Angelina. 2002. "Lynching and the Democratization of Terror in

Postwar Guatemala: Implications for Human Rights." *Human Rights Quarterly* 24 (3): 640–61.

———. 2004. "When 'Justice' Is Criminal: Lynchings in Contemporary Latin America." *Theory and Society* 33: 621–51.

Solano, Luis. 2005. *Guatemala: Petróleo y minería en las entrañas del poder.* Guatemala City: Inforpress Centroamericana.

———. 2006. *Error político en operación antidrogas resucita fantasma del terror.* Inforpress Centroamericano, August 25.

———. 2008. "Los círculos de poder en el gobierno de Álvaro Colom y de la Unidad Nacional de la Esperanza (UNE)." *El Observador* Nos. 11 y 12. Febrero-abril.

———. 2010a. *El mercado de los agrocombustibles: Destino de la producción de caña de azúcar y palma africana de Guatemala.* Guatemala City: ActionAid.

———. 2010b. *Palma africana: Agronegocio que se expande.* Guatemala City: ActionAid.

———. 2011. "Valle del Polochic: El poder de dos familias." *Enfoque* 16, May 9.

Solares, Jorge. 1993. "Guatemala: etnicidad en tierra arrasada." In *Los problemas de la democracia.* Guatemala City: FLACSO.

Sommer, Doris. 1991. "Rigoberta's Secrets." *Latin American Perspectives* 18 (3): 32–50.

Spivak, Gayatri. 1988. "Can the Subaltern Speak?" In *Marxism and the Interpretation of Culture,* edited by Cary Nelson and Larry Grossberg. Urbana: University of Illinois Press.

Stoll, David. 1999. *Rigoberta Menchú and the Story of All Poor Guatemalans.* Boulder, Colo.: Westview Press.

Storey, John. 2007. *Human Resource Management: A Critical Text.* Florence, Ky.: Cengage Learning.

Strathern, Marilyn, ed. 2000. *Audit Cultures: Anthropological Studies in Accountability, Ethics, and the Academy.* London: Routledge.

Taibbi, Matt. 2010. "The Great American Bubble Machine." *Rolling Stone,* April 5.

Taracena Arriola, Arturo. 1997. *Invención criolla, sueño ladino, pesadilla indígena. Los Altos de Guatemala: De región a estado, 1750–1850.* Antigua, Guatemala: CIRMA.

Taracena Arriola, Arturo, Enrique Gordillo, and Tania Sagastume. 2004. *Etnicidad, estado y nación en Guatemala, 1808–1944.* Vol. 2, *¿Por qué estamos como estamos?* Guatemala City: Centro de Investigaciones Regionales de Mesoamérica.

Tax, Sol. 1963. *Penny Capitalism: A Guatemalan Indian Economy.* Chicago: University of Chicago Press.

Taylor, Clark. 1998. *Return of Guatemala's Refugees, Reweaving the Torn.* Philadelphia: Temple University Press.

———. 2013. *"Seeds of Freedom": Liberating Education in Guatemala.* St. Paul: Paradigm Publishing.

Theidon, Kimberly. 2010. "Histories of Innocence: Postwar Stories in Peru." In *Localizing Transitional Justice: Interventions and Priorities after Mass Violence,* edited by Rosalind Shaw and Lars Waldorf. Stanford, Calif.: Stanford University Press.

Tobar Estrada, Anneliza. 2007. *Entre mundos ajenos: encuentro de percepciones de jóvenes pandilleros, ex-pandilleros y acompañantes sobre la sociedad guatemalteca.* Guatemala City: FLACSO.

Toj, María Rosario. 2007. "Mujeres mayas vinculadas al movimiento popular y revolucionario: vinculación, participación y rupturas." In *Programa de formación pueblos indígenas, género y participación política*. Guatemala City: Instituto de Estudios Inter-étnicos de la Universidad de San Carlos.

Torres-Rivas, Edelberto. 2007. "Las izquierdas, Rigoberta Menchú, la historia." *Cuadernos del presente imperfecto*, No. 1. Guatemala City: FyG Editores.

Trouillot, Michel-Rolph. 2003. *Global Transformations: Anthropology and the Modern World*. New York: Palgrave Macmillan.

Tsing, Anna. 2004. *Friction: An Ethnography of Global Connection*. Princeton: Princeton University Press.

Uk'u'x B'e. 2005. *El movimiento maya: Sus tendencias y transformaciones, 1980–2005*. Guatemala City: Asociación Maya Uk'u'x B'e.

UNDP. 2010. *Guatemala: hacia un Estado para el desarrollo humano*. Guatemala City: UNDP.

UNHCR (United Nations High Commissioner for Refugees). 1999. *El retorno de los refugiados guatemaltecos: Experiencias de vida en el refugio, traslado y reasentamiento*. Guatemala City: UNHCR/ACNUR, CEAR, IM-GRICAR, CCPP, PDHG.

UNHCR (United Nations High Commissioner for Refugees) and ASIES. 2000. *Informe de investigación: La seguridad jurídica de la tierra de la población desarraigada*. Guatemala City: UNHCR/ACNUR.

URNG. n.d. Comentarios sobre el texto "Guatemala: De la republica burguesa centralista a la republica popular federal." Unpublished document.

USAID. 2010. Country Profile: Guatemala. *Land Tenure and Property Rights Portal*. http://usaidlandtenure.net/sites/default/files/country-profiles/full-reports/USAID_Land_Tenure_Guatemala_Profile.pdf. Accessed January 7, 2012.

U.S. Army, and U.S. Marine Corps. 2007. *Counterinsurgency Field Manual*. Chicago: University of Chicago Press.

van Oss, Adriaan C. 1986. *Catholic Colonialism: A Parish History of Guatemala, 1524–1821*. Cambridge: Cambridge University Press.

van Vleet, Krista. 2003. "Partial Theories: On Gossip, Envy and Ethnography in the Andes." *Ethnography* 4: 491–519.

Vela, Manolo. 2009. "Los pelotones de la muerte: La construcción de los perpetradores del genocidio guatemalteco." Ph.D. dissertation, Colegio de México.

———, ed. 2011. *Guatemala: la infinita historia de las resistencias*. Guatemala City: Magna Terra Editores.

Velásquez Nimatuj, Irma Alicia. 2002. *La pequeña burguesía indígena comercial de Guatemala: Desigualdades de clase, raza y género*. Guatemala City: Cholsamaj/AVANCSO.

———. 2008. *Pueblos indígenas, estado y lucha por la tierra en Guatemala: Estrategias de sobrevivencia y negociación ante la desigualdad globalizada*. Guatemala City: AVANCSO.

Vilas, Carlos. 2003. "(In)justicia por mano propia: Linchamientos en México Contemporáneo." In *Linchamientos: ¿Barbarie o "justicia popular"?* edited by Carlos Mendoza and Edelberto Torres-Rivas. Guatemala City: Colección Cultura de Paz.

Warren, Kay. 1978. *The Symbolism of Subordination: Indian Identity in a Guatemalan Town*. Austin: University of Texas Press.

———. 1998. *Indigenous Movements and Their Critics: Pan-Maya Activism in Guatemala*. Princeton, N.J.: Princeton University Press.

———. 2002. "Toward an Anthropology of Fragments, Instabilities, and Incomplete Transitions." In *Ethnography in Unstable Places: Everyday Lives in Contexts of Dramatic*

Political Change, edited by Carol J. Greenhouse, Elizabeth Mertz, and Kay B. Warren. Durham: Duke University Press.

———. 2003. "Voting against Indigenous Rights in Guatemala: Lessons from the 1999 Referendum." In *Indigenous Movements, Self-Representation, and the State in Latin America*, edited by Kay Warren and Jean Jackson. Austin: University of Texas Press.

Watanabe, John. 2000. "Culturing Identities, the State, and National Consciousness in Late Nineteenth-Century Western Guatemala." *Bulletin of Latin America Research* 19: 321–40.

Way, J. T. 2012. *The Mayan in the Mall: Globalization, Development, and the Making of Modern Guatemala*. Durham: Duke University Press.

Weld, Kirsten. Forthcoming. *Paper Cadavers: The Archives of Dictatorship in Guatemala*. Durham: Duke University Press.

Wellmeier, Nancy J. 2001. "West Palm Beach, Florida and Phoenix, Arizona: A Continuum of Response to the Maya Presence." In *Manifest Destinies: Americanizing Immigrants and Internationalizing Americans*, edited by David W. Haines and Carol A. Mortland. Westport, Conn.: Praeger Publishers.

Williams, Raymond. 1975. *The Country and the City*. Oxford: Oxford University Press.

Willis, Paul. 1981. *Learning to Labor: How Working Class Kids Get Working Class Jobs*. New York: Teachers College Press.

Wilson, Ruth. 2004. *Immigration: A Look at the Way the World Is Today*. Mankatu, Minn.: Black Rabbit Books.

Wilson, Richard. 1995. *Maya Resurgence in Guatemala: Q'eqchi' Experiences*. Norman: University of Oklahoma Press.

———. 2001. *The Politics of Truth and Reconciliation in South Africa: Legitimizing the Post-Apartheid State*. Cambridge: Cambridge University Press.

Worby, Paula. 2000. *Lessons Learned from UNHCR's Involvement in the Guatemala Refugee Repatriation and Reintegration Programme (1987–1999)*. Geneva: UNHCR.

———. 2002a. "Changes and Opportunities Wrought by Exile and Repatriation: New Identities among Guatemalan Refugee Women." In *Ethnic Conflict: Religion, Identity, and Politics*, edited by Symeon Giannakos. Athens: Ohio University Press.

———. 2002b. *Los refugiados retornados guatemaltecos y el acceso a la tierra: Resultados, lecciones y perspectivas*. Guatemala City: AVANCSO.

———. 2006. "Phoning Home: Family Separation among Mexican and Central American Day Laborers and Strategies to Maintain Mental Well Being." Paper presented at the Latin American Studies Association meetings, May, San Juan, Puerto Rico.

World Bank. 2007. *World Development Report 2008: Agriculture for Development*. Washington, D.C.: World Bank Publishing.

Yoldi, Pilar. 1996. *Don Juan Coc: Príncipe q'eqchí, 1945–1995*. Guatemala City: Piedra Santa, Fundación Rigoberta Menchú.

Yudice, George. 1991. "Testimonio and Postmodernism." *Latin American Perspectives* 18 (3): 15–31.

Zimmerman, Marc. 1991. "Testimonio in Guatemala: Payeras, Rigoberta, and Beyond." *Latin American Perspectives* 18 (4): 22–47.

CONTRIBUTORS

Jennifer Burrell is the author of *Maya after War: Conflict, Power and Politics in Guatemala* (2013) and the coeditor of *Central America in the New Millennium: Living Transition and Reimagining Democracy* (2012). She first went to Todos Santos in 1993 and lived there for thirty-six months between 1996 and 2000, during the end of the armed conflict and in the first years following the signing of the peace accords. More recently Burrell has worked with Mexican and Central American migrants to New York on issues of health care access. She is currently researching ideas and practices of *seguridad* and human rights in Guatemala and among the Todosanteiro diaspora. From 2001 to 2005 she worked as a consultant to the Argentine Forensic Anthropology Team.

Manuela Camus and **Santiago Bastos** are Spaniards and anthropologists who came to Guatemala together in 1987. They first worked at FLACSO-Guatemala researching the survival strategies of the urban poor, including "urbanized" indigenous people and those recently displaced from the highlands, and began their long-term work on the emerging Mayan movement. This shared work resulted in three volumes fundamental to understanding indigenous politics in postwar Guatemala: *Quebrando el silencio: Organizaciones del Pueblo Maya y sus demandas (1986–1992)* (1993), *Abriendo Caminos: Las organizaciones mayas desde el Nobel hasta el Acuerdo de derechos indígenas* (1995), and *Entre el mecapal y el cielo: Desarrollo del movimiento maya en Guatemala* (2003), among other titles. Camus has since specialized in urban anthropology and international migration, publishing *Ser indígena en la capital* (2002), *La colonia Primero de Julio y la "clase media emergente"* (2005), and *La sorpresita del Norte: Comunidad y migración internacional en Huehuetenango* (2008). Bastos continues to analyze the ethnic dimensions of Guatemalan society, indigenous mobilization, and the effects of multicultural policies in works such as *Las relaciones étnicas en Guatemala, 1944–2000* (2003, with Richard Adams), *Etnicidad y fuerzas armadas* (2004), and the three-volume *Mayanización y vida cotidiana* (2007, coedited with Aura Cumes). Since 2008 they have lived in Guadalajara, Mexico, where Camus is a researcher at the University of Guadalajara and Bastos teaches at CIESAS.

Matilde González-Izás is a Guatemalan historian and sociologist who, as a community activist and academic, has been involved in the struggles for social change since the early 1980s. Her work focuses on contemporary problems of social inequality, racism, and violence associated with capitalist modernization, and state formation in historical perspective. She has worked as a researcher at AVANCSO and FLACSO and is currently at the Rafael Landivar University. She is the author of *Conflicto y Poder en Territorio K'iche 1880–1996*; *Se cambió el tiempo, memorias indígenas sobre la guerra*; *Las accidentadas trayectorias de la modernización capitalista en Guatemala 1810–1860*; *Estado, Territorio, ¿Gobernabilidad o gobernanza? La contienda conceptual en América Latina*; and "*Modernización, racismo y violencia en Guatemala 1880–1930.*"

Jorge Ramón González Ponciano is a Guatemalan anthropologist and researcher at the Center for Mayan Studies of the National Autonomous University of Mexico. He left Guatemala to go into exile in Mexico in 1980, and at the turn of the millennium spent several years in the United States, where he received his PhD from the University of Texas in 2005. In Chiapas, where he has lived on and off for several decades, he has worked as a journalist for ENFOPRENSA, a development consultant in the Lancandon forest, and a faculty member at the Autonomous University of Chiapas in San Cristóbal de las Casas. In his different locations, his work has been guided by a concern to understand racism as a key concept for analyzing Guatemalan political and social reality, focusing specifically on the role played by ideologies of whiteness and white identity in the workings of Guatemalan racism. He also explores the rich and creative *malas palabras* and grotesqueness in Guatemalan popular culture that both contest these ideologies and maintain their violent effects, while conjuring forms of cosmic fear. His publications include "Esas sangres no están limpias" (1999), *De la Patria del Criollo a la Patria del Shumo: Whiteness and the Criminalization of the Dark Plebeian in Modern Guatemala* (2005), and "*No somos iguales*": *La "cultura finquera" y el lugar de cada quien en sociedad en Guatemala* (2007). Currently he is conducting transnational fieldwork with Central American migrants as they move among their homelands, Mexico, and the United States and on the construction of the exotic and tourism development in Chiapas and Guatemala.

Greg Grandin, a professor of history at New York University and a member of the American Academy of Arts and Sciences, worked with the United Nations' Commission for Historical Clarification, the Guatemalan truth commission. He is the author of a number of books, including *Blood of Guatemala: A History of Race and Nation* (2000), which won the Latin American Studies Association's Bryce Wood Award; and *The Last Colonial Massacre: Latin America in the Cold War* (2004), which examines decades of political mobilization and repression in Guatemala's Polochic Valley leading to the 1978 Panzós massacre. He is also the author of *Empire's Workshop* (2005) and *Fordlandia* (2009), which was a finalist for the Pulitzer Prize, the National Book Award, and the National Book Critics Circle Award. Most recently he has been the Gilder Lehrman fellow at the New York Public Library's Cullman Center for Scholars and Writers.

Paul Kobrak moved to Aguacatán, Huehuetenango in 1991 to teach middle school. He lived in Guatemala's western highlands during the end of the armed conflict and the years following the peace accords. In addition to his chapter here, he wrote a social history of the Aguacatán civil patrol system. After receiving his doctorate in sociology at the University of Michigan, he consulted for various international organizations, authoring reports on state violence in Guatemala, the postwar lynching phenomenon, migrants and deportees stranded on the Mexico-Guatemala border, Aguacatán's history of ethnic relations, and government repression of students and faculty at the University of San Carlos. He also submitted an amicus curiae brief to the Public Prosecutor's Office on cases of genocide committed by the army under Efraín Ríos Montt. He combined his research on guerrilla organizing and state repression into a history of the armed conflict presented to rural communities in Huehuetenango. He now lives in Brooklyn and is the director of risk reduction in the HIV-prevention program at the New York City Department of Health and Mental Hygiene.

Deborah T. Levenson is the author of *Por Sí Mismos, un estudio preliminar de las "maras" en la Ciudad de Guatemala* (1987), *Trade Unionists against Terror, Guatemala City, 1954–1985* (1994), *Hacer la juventud: Jóvenes de tres generaciones de una familia trabajadora en la Ciudad De Guatemala* (2004), and *Adiós Niño: Death, Politics and the Mara Gangs of Guatemala City* (2013), and is a coeditor of *Guatemala in Rebellion: Unfinished History* (1983) and *The Guatemala Reader: History, Culture, Politics* (2011). An associate professor of history at Boston College who first went to Guatemala in 1978, she is also part of the epistemic community formed by the Association for the Advancement of Social Sciences in Guatemala (AVANCSO). She is grateful to many thoughtful Guatemalan activists, whether in the streets, urban workplaces, the countryside, or research centers, universities and secondary schools, who so intensely care about the fate of humanity.

Carlota McAllister is a U.S. Guatemalan Canadian associate professor of anthropology at York University in Toronto. At the turn of the millennium, she worked as a volunteer with the Foundation for Forensic Anthropology in Guatemala on the four exhumations they performed for the CEH before doing fourteen months of fieldwork in Chupol, where she developed a great affinity for rebellious people. Her monograph on Chupol, *The Good Road: Conscience and Consciousness in a Postrevolutionary Guatemalan Village*, is forthcoming. Currently she is working on a book project about a dam conflict in southern Chile, which pits the bearers of different traditions for claiming private property rights and territorial sovereignty against one another in a struggle over the relationship between capitalism and nature in legendary Patagonia.

Diane M. Nelson is a cultural anthropologist and has worked in Guatemala since 1985, first researching refugee issues, human rights, and the Guatemalan army's "model village" programs. She then focused on the state's responses to the emerging Mayan rights movement in the context of peace treaty negotiations and the Columbus Quincentennial, and later on how people throughout the country were addressing the ends of war. Interested in subject formation, political economy, gender and sexuality, popular culture, and science and technology studies, she seeks in her work to engage with violence and great human suffering while not falling victim to shock and awe. Her books include *Guatemala: Los polos de desarrollo: El caso de la desestructuración de las comunidades indígenas, A Finger in the Wound: Body Politics in Quincentennial Guatemala, Reckoning: The Ends of War in Guatemala*, and is working on a manuscript provisionally titled *Who Counts? Quantities' Qualifications in Guatemala's After/math*. She is thankful to the students at Duke University for paying her salary.

Elizabeth Oglesby has worked in Guatemala since the 1980s, where she was the editor of *Central America Report* (*Inforpress Centroamerica*) and a researcher with the Association for the Advancement of the Social Sciences in Guatemala on a project coordinated by the Guatemalan anthropologist Myrna Mack, studying Guatemalan refugee and displaced populations and the aftermath of counterinsurgency. In the early 1990s she was the associate editor of *Report on the Americas* (North American Congress on Latin America, New York City). In the late 1990s she was a member of the research and writing team of the Guatemalan Commission for Historical Clarification. The research presented here was funded by the National Science Foundation, the Social Science Research Council, the Inter-American Foundation, and the Woodrow Wilson National Fellowship Foundation. In 2003–4, Oglesby was a Carnegie Council fellow studying historical memory in Guatemala, and she is currently researching the impact of mass deportation in the United States and rural Guatemala (funded by a Wenner Gren International Collaborative Research Grant). She is a coeditor, with Greg Grandin and Deborah T. Levenson, of *The Guatemala Reader: History, Culture, Politics* (2011). She is an associate professor of geography and Latin American studies at the University of Arizona, Tucson.

Luis Solano is an economist and investigative journalist. He attended the Guatemalan National University in the early 1980s, graduating with a prize-winning thesis that evolved into *Guatemala: Petróleo y minería. En las entrañas del poder* (2000). From 1988 until its closure in 2010, he was a writer and editor for *Inforpress Centroamericana*, an influential Guatemala-based weekly print publication documenting Central America's politics and economy. From 2002 to the present he has worked with *El Observador* in Guatemala, where he is also a founder and part of the editorial staff, an initiative producing printed and electronic-based media and accompanying Guatemalan rural communities and organizations in gathering, systematizing, and analyzing information. His journalistic work in the past twenty-five years has produced hundreds of articles, providing fact-finding and analysis on Guatemala not found elsewhere on topics such as the country's business and power elite, petroleum and mining, biofuel production, historical genesis of land conflicts, government and international development initiatives, and military and war-time history. He has undertaken consultancies for ActionAid and Oilwatch Mesoamerica, among others, and his work has been reproduced in European and U.S. publications.

Irmalicia Velásquez Nimatuj is the executive director of the Mecanismo de Apoyo a Pueblos Indígenas Oxlajuj Tz'ikin (Support Mechanism for Indigenous Peoples). As a journalist, anthropologist, and international spokeswoman she has been at the forefront of struggles for respect for indigenous cultures. She is the first Maya-K'iche' woman to earn a doctorate in social anthropology, and she initiated the court case that made racial discrimination illegal in Guatemala. She has won numerous academic fellowships and awards for her journalism, She is a member of the Latin American Consulting Group of Indigenous Leaders for UNICEF and participates in the UN through the Permanent Forum on Indigenous Issues. She is the author of *Pueblos Indígenas, Estado y Lucha por Tierra en Guatemala: Estrategias de sobrevivencia y negociación ante la desigualdad globalizada* (2008) and *La pequeña burguesía indígena comercial de Guatemala: Desigualdades de clase, raza y género* (2002). She writes a weekly newspaper column in *elPeriódico de*

Guatemala and through both her political and academic efforts seeks to create viable and realistic ways to create equality for indigenous people and a truly democratic and participatory Guatemala.

Paula Worby began working in Guatemala in 1985. From 1988 to 1992 she was a member of the research team at the Association for the Advancement of Social Sciences in Guatemala, undertaking groundbreaking consecutive studies on the situation of Guatemala's internally displaced and returning refugees. In 1992 she began working for the United Nations High Commissioner for Refugees' Guatemalan office, where, until 2000, she was immersed in the mediation process between the organized Guatemalan refugees and the government shaping the refugees' collective return. At UNHCR she also specialized in land tenure issues, women's formal access to land, and community conflict resolution and has published numerous articles and monographs on these topics. In 1998 she was posted by UNHCR to work with the Commission for Historical Clarification as an expert on Guatemalan's war-time displaced. Worby received a United States Institute of Peace grant to systematize "lessons learned" in the Guatemalan refugee resettlement process and was a fellow at the Yale Agrarian Studies Center. She currently works in California with Mexican and Guatemalan immigrant day laborers as associate director of the nonprofit Multicultural Institute. She holds a doctorate in Public Health from UC Berkeley and is collaborating on a UC Berkeley grant project from the National Institutes of Health focused on the structural determinants of immigrant worker health.

INDEX

310, 320–22; upper-, 310, 319, 323, 327; working-, 39, 157, 159, 198, 200–201, 310, 317, 324, 327

CODISRA (Commission against Discrimination and Racism), 1, 88

coffee, 12, 34, 55, 57, 59–62, 64–65, 134–35, 144, 159, 174–75, 182, 189, 198, 219, 225, 227, 263, 291, 298, 340, 346; boom, 121, 147; crisis, 28; economy, 14, 25, 29, 49, 173, 189

cofradía, 50, 67, 276, 280

cold war, 13–14, 40, 189, 311

Colom, Alvaro, 130–31, 134, 136, 344, 351

colonialism, 50, 51, 190, 234, 327; neo-, 124

Colotenango, xii, 60, 218–20, 222–26, 228–31, 233–40

Columbus Quincentennial, 2, 77, 80, 170, 176, 191, 288, 367, 379

COMG (Council of Mayan Organizations), 77–79

Commission Against Discrimination and Racism (CODISRA), 1, 88

Commission for Historical Clarification. See CEH

Committee for Peasant Unity (Comité de Unidad Campesina, CUC), 15, 99, 143, 218, 223

Communist Party (PGT), 65. See also Guatemalan Workers Party

Communities of the Population in Resistance, 35, 96

CONAVIGUA (National Coordination of Guatemalan Widows), 17, 91n4, 228, 230, 236–37

conciencia (conscience), 96, 101, 108–9, 112–14, 304

confession, 42, 95

conflict, 5, 16, 51, 55, 58–61, 63, 67, 76, 94, 96, 133, 140, 148–49, 159, 221, 236, 242–43, 248, 251, 253, 262, 272, 332–37, 339, 342, 351; agrarian, 123, 138, 180, 189; armed, 6, 17, 33, 83, 98, 114, 174, 177, 218, 222, 224, 233, 235–37, 263, 280, 282; post-, 90, 256–57, 335, 338

CONIC (National Indigenous and Campesino Coordinating Council), 18, 29, 172, 177, 181, 185–88

Conquest, 36, 52–53, 156, 280; Dance of the, 278–79

conservative, 50, 55, 56, 58

Consulta Popular, 6, 82, 83, 86, 313

convite (invitation dance), 272, 278–81

cooperation, 33, 201, 242. See also development

cooperative, 15, 34, 63, 65, 67, 148, 184, 264, 286, 305, 334, 336–42, 351

Coordination of the Mayan People's Organizations of Guatemala (COPMAGUA), 23, 71–72, 79–85

corporate social responsibility, 144, 146, 153, 160, 165, 306n4

Corral, Enrique, 35, 109, 113

corruption. See auditing

cosmopolitanism, 40, 44, 308–10, 328

costumbre (traditional practices), 98, 280, 310

counterinsurgency, 3, 5, 8, 15, 19, 23–25, 35, 39, 42, 66, 69, 75, 84, 113–14, 120, 123, 128, 133, 174, 233, 237, 239n6, 250, 264, 266, 282, 289, 299, 304–5, 335; massacre, 3, 15, 17, 51, 53, 65, 68, 73, 75, 93, 120, 123, 141n7, 183, 202, 204, 207, 217n16, 219–25, 239n4, 265–66, 269, 286, 298, 302, 338, 348; psychological warfare, 5; scorched-earth, 3, 25, 44, 51, 60, 73, 86, 104, 123, 220, 266, 272, 302; tactics: executions, 14, 53, 60, 65

court cases, 20. See also trials

coyuntura, 19, 44

criollo, 12, 51, 53–55, 74, 91n1, 308, 328

Cuarto Pueblo, 338

De León Carpio, Ramiro, 126–27, 182–83, 230

democracy, 24, 35, 39, 81, 243–44, 247, 256, 259n9, 261, 282, 303, 312; neoliberal, 246; transition to, 24, 302, 261

development, 4, 13–14, 25, 27–28, 34, 37–39, 42, 62, 64, 76, 83, 86–87, 91nn5–6, 97, 119, 120, 122–27, 131–33, 136–39, 144–46, 148, 153–55, 160–62, 165, 167n12, 216n7, 217n18, 218, 222, 213, 235–36, 246–74, 254, 261–62, 269, 270–72, 275–76, 279, 281–82, 286–87, 290, 296, 299, 303–4, 306n4, 324–25, 331, 338–40; community, 136, 269; funding, 21, 24–25, 33–35, 37, 45n3, 75, 80, 201, 205, 231, 246, 272, 287, 334, 338, 351; international, 33, 145; war by other means, 35, 271; will to improve, 4, 24. See also NGO; solidarity displacement, 21, 101, 120, 132, 136, 320, 332, 339, 350, 352

dispossession, 8, 13, 59, 119, 120, 138, 263, 267; accumulation by, 12, 28, 30, 295, 134, 165

Domingo Morales, Efraín, 227, 230

Dominicans. *See* Catholic church

drugs: gangs and, 11, 39, 208, 209, 211, 344; illegal, 32, 39, 163, 345; legal, 26, 290; narcotrafficking, 7, 39, 121, 189, 304

economy, 6, 12, 24, 25, 28, 29, 31–32, 49, 52, 57, 67, 95, 120, 124, 126, 128, 131–32, 145, 158, 199, 252, 263, 292, 294–95, 302, 304, 325, 340; coffee, 14, 29, 173, 189; global, 25, 31, 49, 66, 87, 125, 190–91, 304, 343; illegal, 199; informal, 8, 32, 157, 198; neoliberal, 7; plantation, 8, 309; shadow, 32

EGP. *See* URNG: member organizations

Ejidos, 54, 61

Elites, 5, 8, 32, 54–56, 120, 124, 131, 142n10, 142n12, 153, 162, 175, 189, 190, 261, 263, 278, 298, 308, 321, 329n5; business, 120, 132–33, 144; Guatemalan, 13, 56, 137, 312, 326, 239n2; local, 60, 282; national, 66, 120, 124–25; oligarchy, 6, 70, 72, 129, 138, 145, 174; sugar, 28, 146, 306n6

El Quiché, xii, 119, 122, 163, 191n3

engañados (fooled or duped), 2, 4, 6, 17, 40, 42, 291

Escuintla, xii, 267, 346

Estrada Cabrera, Manuel (president), 61, 63, 122, 173, 184

exhumation, 34, 231, 295, 298, 302, 305

exile, 3, 11, 34, 42, 44, 51, 79, 191n3, 206, 269, 295, 309, 333–34, 339–40, 342, 346, 350

Evangelical, 4, 16, 44, 65, 88, 107, 201–2, 205, 210, 277

eviction, 7, 122, 131–32, 135, 165, 170, 178, 181, 183, 186

extractive industry, 119, 125, 127–29, 138, 344. *See also* resource extraction

Falla, Ricardo, 29, 67, 109, 345

FAMDEGUA (Families of the Disappeared), 17

FAR. *See* URNG: member organizations

fear, 5, 16, 21, 28, 31, 32, 39, 53, 55–56, 78, 82, 170, 180, 197, 203–4, 208, 214–15, 228–29, 234–35, 252–54, 256, 290, 298–99, 304, 319, 329n5, 337, 343, 345, 348–49, 351

feminicidio (also feminicide), 7, 203, 254

festival (fiesta), 39, 72, 272, 276–78, 295

finca, 65, 133–34, 151, 239n4; *finquero*, 263

Foucault, Michel, 5, 15, 166n7. *See also* biopolitic

Francisco Marroquin University, 126, 128

Franja, The, 122–27, 130–33, 136–41

Franja Transversal del Norte (FTN), xii, 28, 32, 119–21, 131

FRG (Guatemalan Republican Front), 42–43, 82, 238, 325. *See also* Portillo, Alfonso; Ríos Montt, Gen. Efraín

FUNDAZUCAR (National Sugar Foundation), 146, 153–57, 160–62, 165, 167nn19–20, 168n28, 168n33

G2 military intelligence. *See* army

GANA (Grand National Alliance party), 130

gangs, 3, 7, 11, 31, 37, 39, 100, 195–96, 201–16, 217n14, 217n17, 254, 257, 344; members, 196–98, 200–202, 206–12, 217n14, 217n21, 322. *See also* maras

García Granados family, 126

gender, 3, 17–18, 31, 34, 39–41, 149, 170, 172, 270, 282, 299, 306n2, 323. *See also* masculinity; women

genocide, 6–7, 9, 11–12, 19, 22–23, 29, 41, 43–44, 52, 68–69, 86, 120, 203, 216n6, 276, 285, 287, 289, 296, 307, 315; post-, 10, 22, 29, 40–41, 43, 125, 262, 264, 307, 312, 324–25. *See also* Commission for Historical Clarification (CEH); counterinsurgency

Gerardi, Juan (Bishop), 129. *See also* CEH (Commission for Historical Clarification)

Godínez, Alberto, 227, 236

"good governance", 247, 255–56

Gramajo, Héctor (general), 15, 69, 70, 273, 277, 285, 288–89, 302–3, 305

Grand National Alliance party (GANA), 130

Guatemalan Republican Front (FRG), 42–43, 82, 238, 325. *See also* Portillo, Alfonso; Ríos Montt, Gen. Efraín

Guatemalan Workers Party (PGT), 14. *See also* Communist Party guerrilla, 17, 23, 33, 42–44, 56, 65, 69, 73–78, 82, 88, 96, 100, 103–4, 123, 128, 134–35, 218–38, 239n6, 249–50, 265, 269, 297–98, 304, 309, 327, 331, 334–37, 244; groups, 15, 35, 45n3, 174; movement, 15, 39, 97; organizations, 15, 144, 179, 180, 263; warfare, 1, 59, 60, 336. *See also* Guatemalan National Revolutionary Unity (URNG): Guerrilla Army of the Poor (EGP); rebels

Gutiérrez, Dionisio, 129

Hale, Charles, 85, 171, 245, 288–89, 304, 236–37
hegemony, 75, 147, 309, 370; counter-, 328
Hernández Ixcoy, Domingo, 305
Herrera family, 70n3, 126, 128, 132, 147, 153; Julio, 148, 154; historic, 28, 61, 82–83, 87, 124, 161, 188, 280, 282n1, 288, 328, 338, 348; history, 3, 6, 9, 11–12, 17–18, 21, 26, 40, 49–51, 63, 65–66, 69, 77, 79, 81–82, 91, 99–100, 104, 109, 114, 121, 126–27, 141, 147–48, 155, 158, 165–66, 167n24, 181, 190, 196, 205, 213, 218, 237, 242, 250, 258, 263, 278, 307, 312, 334, 349, 351
Hoyos, Fernando, 109, 113, 224
Huehuetenango, xii, 52, 60, 88, 119, 122, 134, 141n7, 147, 176, 218–38, 239nn6–7, 241, 244, 252–53, 255, 258n4, 331, 343, 346–47
human rights, 20, 22, 34, 37, 63, 69, 79, 82, 84, 93–94, 98–100, 129, 133, 150, 177, 188, 218, 223–24, 227–33, 236–37, 242, 244, 259n7, 259n9, 331, 337, 351; activists, 5, 7, 23, 229; groups, 63, 133; ombudsman, 183, 229–30, 343; violations, 5, 17, 45n2, 76
humanitarian, 23, 33, 95–102, 114, 306n4; humanitarianism, 95, 98, 100, 102
hydroelectricity, 8, 120–21, 124, 128, 130–31, 139, 344; dams, 18, 89, 349

Identity Accord, 80, 85, 247, 288
ILO Convention 169, 80, 88–89
impunity, 17, 19, 23, 32, 91, 203, 218, 230–31, 245, 248, 261–62, 264, 275, 281, 344–45
indigenous: mayor (*cabildo*), 50, 54, 56; people, 2, 6, 9, 12–13, 15, 18, 33, 39, 53, 56, 72, 74–75, 80, 84–85, 87, 90, 91n2, 97, 101, 106, 120, 122, 171–73, 177, 182, 191n4, 233,

247, 259n7, 262, 287–88, 291, 294–95, 298, 305–12, 322, 324–26; organizations, 71, 74, 181; women, 1, 10, 17, 40, 87, 91n6. *See also* Maya
insecurity, 7, 30, 261, 337
insurgency, 61, 67, 69, 222, 224, 312
INTA (National Institute for Agrarian Transformation), 122, 127, 174–76, 183–85
International Commission against Impunity (CICIG), 44, 245, 258n5, 260n17
International Monetary Fund (IMF), 25–26
Ixcán, xii, 14, 37–38, 41, 65–67, 89, 120, 127, 130, 133, 136–37, 141nn6–7, 250, 331–49

Japan, 34, 156, 242; Japanese, 39, 241–42, 251
Jesuit. *See* Catholic church
Joyabaj, xii, 30, 65, 163–64, 169n37, 240n13, 285–91, 294–304, 306n1, 306n3, 306n5
justice, 7, 10, 17, 20, 23, 35, 37, 44, 62, 87, 168n28, 172, 188, 190, 201, 230–31, 233–34, 242, 243–45, 247, 256, 258, 263, 288, 326, 244; injustice, 35, 108, 114, 179, 269; social, 201–12, 210; system, 232, 240n12, 257, 345

kaibiles (army special forces), 32, 204, 239n16, 249, 277
K'iche'. *See* indigenous
kidnapping, 8, 14, 203, 244, 254

labor, 8–9, 12–13, 21–30, 37, 39, 50, 58–60, 62–63, 67, 82, 97, 113, 125, 139–40, 143–58, 160–65, 166n7, 167nn11–13, 176, 179–80, 184–85, 190, 197, 199, 239n5, 261–64, 282n1, 286–87, 298, 304, 306n2, 319, 327–28, 341–42, 347, 351; "flexibilization" of, 153, 160; forced, 13, 50–52, 57, 62–63, 166n5, 263, 268, 272; market, 28, 152–53, 159; migrant (workers), 40, 148–49, 159–60, 166n5, 167n15, 250–51, 264, 309, 327; plantation, 57, 60, 62, 145–46, 149, 152, 157, 164; relations, 62, 145, 164, 268; vagrancy laws and, 50, 57, 62; wage, 25, 57, 66, 165, 248, 250–51, 324. *See also* union
La Barranca, 222, 228–39, 240n11, 240n13
ladino, 1–3, 11–14, 42, 56–68, 77, 84
Land reform, 24–25, 65, 122, 131, 135, 172, 219. *See also* agrarian: reform

La Perla, 133, 141n7

law, 6, 7, 10, 23, 26, 56, 61–62, 88–89, 126, 129, 159, 165, 170–72, 183, 188, 207, 233, 247, 256–57, 259n8, 269, 344; customary, 34, 36, 247, 259n7; rule of, 39, 190, 231, 234, 243–46, 313; vagrancy, 13, 50, 57

Left, the, 6, 21, 41, 67–68, 78, 83, 91, 97, 167n15, 203, 235, 312

left-wing, 4, 205, 313–14

legal system, 39, 91n3, 245, 247, 259nn7–9

liberalism, 50, 62, 96

Liberal Reform, 12, 307, 310, 320, 329

liberation theology. See Catholic church

local power (*poder local*), 34, 261, 282. See also development

Los Naranjales, 229–30

Lucas García, Benedicto (general), 265

Lucas Garcia, Fernando Romeo (general), 125–56, 128, 133–34, 141n3, 220, 249

Lux de Cotí, Otilia, 6, 20

lynching, 39, 203, 241–58, 259n6, 260n18, 345

machismo, 11, 164

Madre Tierra, 351

mala gente, 103–4

Mam. See indigenous

Mamá Maquín, 20, 337, 340, 351

Mano Blanca, 125–26, 134

maquila, 26, 144, 166n8, 168n29

maquiladora, 28, 157, 159

maras, 7, 37, 39, 195–216, 322–23. See also gangs

markets, 5, 13, 17, 25, 27, 31, 32, 36, 37, 41, 57, 66, 99, 124, 131–32, 136, 141nn5–6; free, 24–26, 319; global, 13, 124, 144, 147, 157, 172, 189, 190, 198, 201, 220, 228, 238, 241, 246, 249, 253, 255, 275, 288, 293, 301–3, 305, 329n4, 339–40, 342; labor, 28, 152–53, 159; national (Guatemalan), 29, 125, 340

Martínez Peláez, Severo, 13, 51, 53–54, 57

Maryknoll. See Catholic church

masculinity, 149, 164, 213, 279

Maya: Achi', 14, 121; -K'iche', 41, 98, 109, 174, 191n1, 287, 298; Mam-, 170, 191n1, 241; movement, 75, 83, 86; organization, 71, 74, 77, 79–81, 83, 86; *Pueblo*, 71, 74, 76–77, 80, 88; -Q'eqchi', 119; women, 34, 44, 187

MAYAS (Movement of Support and Mutual Aid), 74, 76

Menchú Tum, Rigoberta, 309; Nobel Peace Prize and, 1, 2, 78

Mendez Ortiz, Arturo, 238

Merchants' Association, 266–68, 271, 276, 278–79

meros jefes, 264–70, 274–81

Mesoamerican Project. See Plan Puebla-Panamá

mestizo, 3, 156, 311, 319

Mexican Revolution, 49–51

Mexico, 30–33, 35, 38, 45n3, 49–52, 54, 55, 60, 120, 123, 130, 132, 141n5, 159, 202, 207, 220, 240n11, 245, 248, 258n6, 290, 309, 330–34, 336, 339, 340, 346–51

migration, 28–33, 54, 58, 88, 122, 159, 164, 187, 189, 204, 238, 246–48, 295–96, 304, 339, 342, 346–48

military, 5, 7, 13–17, 30–33, 35, 42, 56, 57, 62, 64–70, 76, 78, 82–84, 103, 105–6, 120–35, 141nn3–4, 141n7, 144, 166n9, 173, 174, 180, 188, 195–96, 201–3, 213, 216n1, 218, 221–25, 229–35, 239n5, 239nn6–7, 261–77, 285–88, 299, 302, 304, 329n6, 335–36, 338, 344–5. See also army

minifundio/a, 12, 160

mining. See resource extraction

MINUGUA (The United Nations Verification Mission in Guatemala), 233–34, 243, 336

MLN (National Liberation Movement), 66–67, 125–26, 134–35

modernity, 242, 246, 271, 280, 289, 307, 310, 318–19, 326

Momostenango, 54, 59–61

Monocrop, 8, 130, 136, 139; monocropping, 137

Morales, Sebastián, 99, 111, 178

movements, 25, 56, 62, 97, 150, 152, 190, 196, 201, 238n1, 245, 265, 273, 275, 279, 327, 334; clandestine, 15, 44; indigenous, 75, 190, 191n3; opposition, 63, 65, 263; revolutionary, 71–72, 83, 97, 201, 289; social, 12, 18, 28, 43, 260n16, 289

Movimiento Indio Tojil. See MAYAS (Movement of Support and Mutual Aid)

mozo (worker), 12–13, 28, 121, 324; finca de (worker farm), 59, 70n3, 263–64
muco, 308–24

narcotrafficking, 39, 121, 189
narrative, 12, 93, 96, 101–4, 107, 110, 113, 202, 211, 217n16, 243, 250–51, 310, 312–13; heroic, 102, 104, 106; historical, 101–3, 114; traumatic, 100–102, 106
National Advancement Party (PAN), 125–27, 130, 325
National Civil Police, 233, 245, 345
National Coordination of Guatemalan Widows. *See* CONAVIGUA
National Indigenous and Campesino Coordinating Council. *See* CONIC
National Institute for Agrarian Transformation (INTA), 122, 127, 174–76, 183–85
National Police, 194, 210, 217n19, 230, 233–34; Archives, 21
National Reparations Program (NPR), 17, 295, 305
National Sugar Foundation. *See* FUNDAZUCAR
neoliberalism, 25–26, 39, 41, 128, 246, 303, 305
NGO, 11, 34–40, 119, 146, 168n32, 204–5, 217n19–10, 259n8, 261, 265, 270, 287, 289, 298, 342; evangelical, 201; NGO-ization, 37, 261, 277; ONG-ización, 33, 43. *See also* nongovernmental organization
nickel. *See* resource extraction
Nobel Peace Prize. *See* Menchú Tum, Rigoberta
nongovernmental organization, 33, 76, 119, 161, 175, 201, 245
Novella family, 126–28, 130, 135

October Revolution, 13, 63–66; Arbenz, Jacobo (colonel), 13, 64, 66, 125; Arévalo, Juan José, 13; government, 122; reforms, 134–35
oil, 8, 119, 123–38, 141n2, 142n10, 142n12, 336, 344
oligarchy. *See* elites
Omnilife, 40, 44, 290–94, 296–305, 306nn2–3
ONG. *See* NGO

Opus Dei. *See* Catholic church
Ordóñez Colop, David, 65
Ordoñéz Porta, Edgardo, 129
ORPA. *See* URNG: member organizations

PACS. *See* civil (defense) patrols
Pampas del Horizonte, 173
PAN (National Advancement Party), 125–27, 130, 325
Pantaleón, 145–54, 162, 166n8, 169n38
Panzós Massacre, 51, 93, 120
paramilitary, 3, 8, 66, 121, 128, 135, 233, 270
Patzulá, 285–89, 293, 295
peace, 9, 11, 17, 19, 23–24, 26, 33–35, 78–88, 150, 154, 162, 176, 179, 181, 188, 200, 230–36, 244, 247, 252, 259n14, 261, 262, 269–72, 288, 331, 337, 345; accords, 5, 7, 10, 71, 80–86, 123, 125–26, 154, 156, 162, 165, 166n9, 196, 203, 207, 228, 232, 247, 251, 254–56, 261, 271, 313, 330, 332–37, 344, 347, 350; -keepers, 10, 39, 302; post-, 72, 88; treaty, 1, 17, 27, 34, 87, 181
peasant, 13, 27–28, 49–51, 57, 59, 60, 63–64, 66, 70n3, 72–74, 82, 109, 112, 120–23, 131–33, 136–37, 140, 144, 167n15, 171, 174, 179–81,188, 190, 219–20, 223, 225, 234, 237, 239n5, 263–64, 267, 273, 219, 293–94, 324, 330, 339; indigenous, 16, 50, 61, 120, 138, 170–72, 177, 180, 188, 238; peasant union, 13, 63–67, 351. *See also* campesino/a; Peasant Unity Committee (CUC)
pentecostal, 15–17
Pérez Molina, Otto (general), 41–42, 231
Permanent Commissions of Guatemalan Refugee Representatives (CCPP), 91n4, 331
petroleum. *See* resource extraction
PGT, 14, 65
Plan Puebla-Panamá, 130, 133, 141n5
plantation, 12, 15, 28, 31, 34, 51, 57, 59, 62–65, 68, 121, 124, 130, 132, 134–35, 138, 141n7, 143–47, 152–65, 167n13, 167n15, 169n39, 174, 177, 184, 189, 219–21, 223, 227, 238, 254, 263–64, 285, 298, 306n2, 308, 325, 327, 342; economy, 6, 8, 309; finca, 65, 133, 134, 151, 239n4; labor, 60, 62, 145–46, 149, 152, 157, 164; latifundia, 12

Plataforma Agraria. *See* agrarian: platform

union (*continued*)
labor, 144, 155; peasant, 13, 64–66. *See also* activist
United Fruit Company (UFC), 13, 64, 122, 126, 135
United Nations (UN), 183, 233–34; Children's Fund (UNICEF), 185, 201, 270; Commission for Historical Clarification. *See* CEH; Convention 169, 80, 88–89; High Commission for Refugees (UNHCR), 331–32, 335, 340; Development Program (UNDP), 144, 162, 216n7; human development report, 162; Peacekeeping Mission, 10, 34, 39, 162, 302; Verification Mission in Uruguay (MINUGUA), 233–34, 243, 336
uprising, 4, 13, 28, 50, 53–60, 70n1; Tzeltal, 53. *See also* protest
United States, 11, 14, 26, 33–34, 49, 74, 142n10, 148, 185, 189, 206, 216n7, 246, 250, 251, 259n15, 304, 306n5, 308–14, 318, 321, 325–27, 329, 333, 350; CIA, 13; Cold War and, 13, 33; migration, 28–32, 88, 159, 238, 246, 294–96, 346–48
URNG (Guatemalan National Revolutionary Unity), 1, 17, 34, 42–43, 49, 72–90, 125, 154, 178, 181, 218, 224, 228, 238, 331, 335–37, 350; member organizations: Guerrilla Army of the Poor (EGP), 15, 35, 45n3, 66, 74, 79, 91n4, 99, 109, 111–14, 123, 133, 177, 179–81, 202, 218–26, 230, 235–37, 239nn5–6, 239n8, 249, 264–65, 334–35; Organization of the People in Arms (ORPA), 15, 65, 91n2, 91n4, 174; Rebel Armed Forces (FAR), 13–15, 65–66, 123
USAID (United States Agency for International Development), 122, 154, 156

Vatican II. *See* Catholic church
victimization, 100, 275

victims, 3,6, 7, 17, 19, 21, 36–37, 69, 75, 93–94, 97–102, 124, 200, 204, 239n6, 239n8, 242–45, 268, 270, 272, 293, 338, 348, 350
violence: army, 219, 222, 224, 238, 348; political, 157, 218, 236, 261, 264, 301; rural, 51, 61, 63, 67, 70; sexual, 95, 274; state, 75, 124, 195, 203, 205, 217n9, 223, 233, 271, 297; structural, 172, 203, 303. *See also* repression
vitamins, 163, 290, 294

war: civil, 9, 10, 12–13, 26–27, 51, 65, 70, 120, 123, 145, 243, 296; cold, 13–14, 40, 189, 311; guerilla, 3–4, 14, 59–60, 297, low-intensity, 110
Widmann family, 119, 134–5; Berger, 131–33, 135; Lagarde, 119, 135; Luna, 134–35
witness, 19–20, 65, 94–96, 100–108, 113–14, 183, 209, 216n1, 229–31, 239n10, 244, 281, 306n1, 343–44. *See also* testigo
women, 3, 4, 7, 9, 18, 31, 36, 39, 54, 75, 79, 88, 95, 97, 100–104, 155, 158, 171, 173, 175–76, 181–86, 188, 197, 206, 213, 219, 244, 246, 249, 252, 254, 262, 26, 273–75, 286, 294, 298, 300–301, 316, 327, 337, 340–47; indigenous (*also* Indian; Mayan), 1, 17, 40, 44, 91n6, 170, 172, 187, 299, 325; ladina, 299; organizations, 34, 82, 337, 351; oppression of, 190; refugee, 340–41, 351; rights, 10, 34, 349; violence against, 66, 319
Women's Commission, 177, 186
World Bank, 25–27, 155–56, 164–65, 172, 189–90, 271, 306n4

Xalalá, 139, 344
Xemal, 222, 225, 227–28, 230, 236–37, 239

Yamahiro, Saison Tetsuo, 241–43, 248, 250–51, 255–56